RESEARCH METHODS AND STATISTICS FOR PSYCHOLOGY

RESEARCH METHODS AND STATISTICS FOR PSYCHOLOGY

Wendy A. Schweigert

BRADLEY UNIVERSITY

Brooks/Cole Publishing Company
Pacific Grove, California

I (**T**) **P** ™ The trademark ITP is used under license.

Brooks/Cole Publishing Company
A Division of Wadsworth, Inc.

Printed in the United States of America
10   9   8   7   6   5   4   3

Library of Congress Cataloging-in-Publication Data

Schweigert, Wendy A.
    Research methods and statistics for psychology / Wendy A.
Schweigert.
        p.   cm.
    Includes bibliographical references and index.
    ISBN 0-534-21756-7
    1. Psychology—Research—Methodology.
    2. Psychology—Statistical methods.   I. Title.
BF76.5.S337   1994
150′ . 72—dc20   93-24216
                                                                    CIP

Sponsoring Editor: *Jim Brace-Thompson*
Marketing Representative: *Danny Murphy*
Editorial Associate: *Cathleen S. Collins*
Production Coordinator: *Penelope Sky*
Production: *Cecile Joyner, The Cooper Company*
Production Assistant: *Micky Lawler*
Manuscript Editor: *Steven Gray*
Permissions Editor: *Carline Haga*
Interior Design: *Jeanne Calabrese*
Cover Design: *Katherine Minerva*
Interior Illustration: *Carl Brown*
Typesetting: *Asco Trade Typesetting Ltd.*
Cover Printing: *Color Dot*
Printing and Binding: *Arcata Graphics/Fairfield*

THIS BOOK IS PRINTED ON ACID-FREE RECYCLED PAPER

This book is dedicated to Virginia Brabender and Danny Moates. She was my introductory psychology and experimental psychology instructor, and he was my graduate adviser. She sparked the fire, and he fanned the flames.

Contents

CHAPTER 3

Observational Studies and Descriptive Statistics   42

CHAPTER 4

Mail Surveys, Telephone Surveys, and Personal Interviews   98

CHAPTER 5

Hypothesis Testing and the Single-Group Design 144

CHAPTER 6

Introduction to Experimentation 172

CHAPTER 7

*Between-Subjects Design with One Independent Variable
Containing Three or More Groups*   206

CHAPTER 8

Within-Subjects Design   234

CHAPTER 9

Factorial Designs   268

CHAPTER 10

Quasi-Experimental Designs   302

Preface

I have yet to meet an instructor of research methods and statistics courses in psychology who does not believe that students in courses that integrate these two topics learn and understand the material much more thoroughly than do students who are taught the two topics separately. But the lack of appropriate textbooks has been a significant drawback in the development of these integrated research methods and statistics courses. This book has been written to meet this need.

This book offers an integrated presentation of both research methods and statistical topics for introductory-level students. The chapters, for the most part, are organized so that a methodological approach is considered in the first half of the chapter, and appropriate statistical techniques are considered in the second half. For example, Chapter 3 covers observational designs. In the first half of the chapter, different types of observational designs are discussed (naturalistic, disguised participant, structured observation, and so on); in the second half of the chapter, descriptive statistics are introduced. Similarly, in Chapter 6, experimentation and the two-group design are introduced, followed by a presentation of the independent-samples *t*-test and the Wilcoxon's rank-sum test.

The material covered in this book is comparable to that covered in both an introductory-level research methods text and an introductory-level statistics text. Both correlational and experimental designs are discussed, as well as quasi-experimental designs, single-subject designs, and physical trace and archival data studies.

The statistics covered include descriptive statistics, z-tests and t-tests, and one-way and two-way ANOVAs. Nonparametric tests discussed include the χ^2 goodness-of-fit test, test of independence, and test of homogeneity of proportions, as well as the Wilcoxon's rank-sum test, the Wilcoxon's matched-pairs summed-ranks test, and the Kruskal-Wallis nonparametric analysis of variance. Unlike in most texts, nonparametric techniques are presented alongside their parametric counterparts so that students will more clearly understand when to use each.

The statistics are presented at a level appropriate for students with little or no background in mathematics beyond high school algebra. In addition, the presentation describes how to calculate these analyses by hand. One reason for this approach is that not all students on all campuses have access to computers and appropriate software. The more important reason, however, is that I firmly believe that students—especially those who are not mathematically sophisticated—gain a better understanding of what a technique does when they calculate it by hand.

Every effort has been made to make the writing engaging and easy to understand. Important terms and concepts are presented in bold print and defined within the text. These terms also appear in summary lists at the end of each chapter, as a guide for review, and in the Glossary at the back of the book. The examples are simple and straightforward and require little explanation, so each one readily achieves its goal of illustrating a point or demonstrating a technique. Too often, when examples from published research are presented, the reader becomes bogged down in the fundamental theory underlying the example and loses track of the reason the example was introduced. Published examples are scattered throughout this text, but they have been chosen specifically because they are both good and easy to understand. I want students to realize that research is not difficult, that it does not have to involve fancy equipment, and that a person can undertake a project without having years and years of training in an area.

This book was designed for use in courses that combine the presentation of research methods and statistics. The methodology information is presented in sufficient detail, however, that it could also be used in a standard research methods course. The statistical material in Chapters 3 through 9 increases in difficulty and sophistication and probably should be presented in that order. The material in Chapters 2, 10, 11, and 12, however, could be moved around without confusing the reader. Because the material of two texts has been combined into one, it may be difficult to cover the entire book in one semester. Portions of chapters not typically covered in your course, or the last three chapters on quasi-experimental, single-subject, and physical trace and archival data studies, could be omitted if necessary.

If this book meets my goals for it, students who use it will find that statistics constitutes a useful set of tools to help researchers answer important questions, and that research is an exciting and stimulating endeavor.

I would like to express my sincere gratitude to Matt Roworth for his helpful comments on earlier drafts of these chapters, and to David Tudor, who convinced me to begin this project. I am also grateful to the following reviewers for their comments and suggestions for improving the manuscript: Clint Anderson of Provident College, Cole Barton of Davidson College, Clarke Burnham of the University of Texas at Austin, Shirlee Fenwick of Augustana College, Katherine Klein of North Carolina State University, John Mavromatis of St. John Fisher College, Donald Pannen of the University of Puget Sound, John Sparrow of the State University of New York at Geneseo, Diane Winn of Colby College, and Larry Wood of Brigham Young University. I would most especially like to thank my husband, Jim Sullivan, for his patience and support during the entire process. A more tolerant man has yet to be born.

Wendy A. Schweigert

RESEARCH METHODS AND STATISTICS FOR PSYCHOLOGY

I

Introduction to the Scientific Method

I was in my introductory psychology class when I was bitten by the research bug. I suddenly realized the power of research—that, by simply planning ahead and making observations carefully and objectively, I could *know* something that no one else had ever known before. And the process of learning this information involves no more than some problem-solving skills, creativity, and curiosity.

I have been addicted to research ever since, both conducting my own and teaching others how to conduct theirs. One of my greatest thrills as a teacher is to watch students discover for themselves that scientific research is not the dull, dry, uninteresting process they somehow thought it was, but that instead it's downright fun.

Students are most familiar with conducting research by scouring the library for information relevant to a topic. Scientific research, however, is considerably different. Although scientific research requires library work, the bulk of the information learned from scientific research is gained in the laboratory or in the field by collecting data. **Data**, which are observations, are then organized and summarized so that the researcher can answer the question behind the study.

Scientific research is conducted by using a process called the **scientific method**, which is the general set of procedures used to gain information in the sciences. It is the process of making *systematic* observations in an *objective* manner. The observations are made in this manner so that the results of the research will be meaningful and unambiguous, uncontaminated by biases of either the participants or the researcher.

Psychology is the scientific study of behavior. Thus, research psychologists are scientists and use the scientific method in their endeavors to learn more about the behavior of animals and humans.

The research psychologist's job is to identify and explore phenomena by collecting and analyzing data. The data are interpreted with the help of mathematical techniques called statistical procedures.

Researchers vary considerably in their knowledge of statistical procedures. This is not surprising, since the study of statistics (which are used in disciplines as diverse as marketing and theoretical mathematics) has developed into a scholarly discipline of its own. Relatively few research psychologists are expert in both their area of psychology and the mathematical bases of statistics (although such people do exist). Luckily for the rest of us, competent use of statistical techniques does not require a thorough understanding of the theory and mathematics underlying them. One can use statistics without being a statistician, just as one can drive a car without being a mechanic.

To conduct sound and informative research, a research psychologist must have solid knowledge of research methods and of the appropriate use of statistical procedures. Perhaps less obviously, the knowledgeable clinical psychologist must also understand research methods and statistics. Only by understanding how research is done correctly and what statistical techniques are appropriate can a clinician adequately comprehend and critique the articles published in professional journals. Research criticism involves identifying not only the flaws of a particular study but also the contributions that it may make. Only by understanding research methods and statistics, for example, can a clinician determine whether the results of a study describing a new therapeutic technique reflect the benefits of the therapy or the poor research skills of the investigator.

Knowledge of research methods and statistical techniques is not only important for professional psychologists; it can also be of great value to any educated consumer. Research and statistical knowledge can help guide people in making all types of decisions—a shop owner who wonders if staying open on Sunday would be profitable, a business person who wants to determine whether an advertising campaign has been effective, or a reader who wishes to interpret a graph in the newspaper or to determine whether a 5% increase in the President's approval rating reflects a meaningful increase or merely a chance fluctuation in survey results.

Some unscrupulous individuals will toss about manipulated and meaningless statistics to further their own ends. They will suggest that their information is "scientific" and thus should be taken as factual when it is really misleading or downright fallacious. Knowledge of research methods and basic statistical techniques is often the best defense against this type of deception.

Although the practical value of knowledge about scientific research and statistical methods makes gaining this knowledge worthwhile, the motivations of most researchers are less pragmatic. While the research process at its best is wholly systematic and objective, the drive to do research is very subjective. Scientific research allows one to fulfill one's curiosity in a most satisfying manner. Being able to contribute to the body of knowledge bit by bit is enticing. Meeting the challenge of designing a way to answer a previously unanswered (and perhaps even unasked) question is exciting. Even though it may be momentarily discouraging when a research project does not provide the expected results, this feeling is soon replaced by more curiosity, more questioning, more research, and more answers.

The satisfaction of having met the challenge of answering questions about behavior only makes research more addictive to the research psychologist. Behaviors are not always easy to study. Behaviors, in psychology, comprise not only overt physical movements, but also more subtle physiological and psychological responses. Behaviors studied by psychologists include mental behaviors, such as reading, listening, comprehending, storing information, and recalling information. Behaviors may be emotions such as happiness, depression, boredom, anger, and fear. Not all behaviors can be measured directly, and often the challenge for a researcher is to develop a way to make indirect measurements.

A researcher who wishes to study hunger, for example, must decide how hunger will be measured. Should the participants be asked to rate their hunger? What if the subjects are small children or animals? If the participants can answer, does one person's report that he or she is very hungry mean the same as another person's report? Perhaps hunger could be measured in terms of blood sugar levels or by number of calories ingested during the preceding 24 hours. There is more than one right way to measure behaviors, so a researcher must be prepared to choose among many alternatives—or even to develop a new measure when necessary.

Behaviors are not always consistent, and the process of studying a behavior can change the behavior itself, a problem called **reactivity**. For example, a supervisor may enter a classroom to observe the interactions between the students and a teacher. The students (and the teacher) immediately put on their best behavior. The supervisor's presence has affected the very behaviors that he or she was trying to observe.

Often behaviors are affected by subtle, unrecognized factors. A person's mood, for example, may be affected by the time of day, the color of the room, the weather, or even a tight pair of shoes. Obviously a researcher cannot control everything that might affect the behaviors being studied, but part of the challenge of psychological research consists of designing projects in which the researcher can identify the factors that are causing the behavior and at the same time take special precautions to prevent other factors from also having an effect.

The special challenges of psychological research will be made clear in this book, along with techniques that can be used to avoid the problems these challenges may cause. This information will allow you to evaluate the research of others thoroughly and critically, and it will provide you with the skills to conduct high-quality research of your own.

KNOWLEDGE IN THE SCIENCES

The scientific method is the method of inquiry used by scientists to acquire knowledge. Scientists feel reasonably confident in results of research that have followed the scientific method. What is *known* in the sciences has been learned by using this method. To place what this means in context, let's consider other ways of acquiring knowledge.

Many things are "known" to you. Volumes could be filled with your specific knowledge of your hometown, your family, your religion, your coursework, and the world political situation. But relatively little of what you know was acquired through use of the scientific method. A person who says that he or she *knows* something may have learned that information in any of a number of ways. No single way of acquiring knowledge is necessarily better than another, but some questions are better answered (or can only be answered) by one or another approach.

INTUITION AND SUPERSTITION

My grandmother firmly believed—in her mind, she *knew*—that the number 13 was unlucky. She held a **superstition**, a belief or fear based on faith in chance, magic, or irrational feelings that ignores the laws of nature (*Funk & Wagnalls* 1983; *American Heritage Dictionary* 1985). Superstitions are based on personal *subjective* feelings, as opposed to *objective*, verifiable experience. Many otherwise rational people believe in one or more superstitions. They often realize that their beliefs are irrational, but they continue to wear lucky shirts, knock on wood, and steer clear of black cats.

Intuition is direct knowledge or awareness of something without conscious attention or reasoning (*Funk & Wagnalls* 1983). Intuition, like superstition, is a wholly subjective experience; it is based entirely on personal feelings. Intuition, however, has a better reputation than superstition, perhaps because knowledge gained without reason is not always contrary to reason. While few decisions should be made based on a belief in superstitions, an argument can be made that the answers to some questions might best be based on intuition. Perhaps you've been advised at some point to "go with your gut feeling"—in other words, to use your intuition.

AUTHORITY

A more universally accepted approach to knowing is by the method of **authority**. In this method, information is learned from the reports of a trustworthy source. People tend to believe and to feel that they "know" information that has been reported to them by someone in a position of authority. Students listen to lectures by college professors, read textbooks written by other college professors, and rarely question the material presented because college professors are assumed to be authorities on the topic of focus. Television news anchors are rarely swamped with calls questioning the veracity of their news stories, because people believe the anchors have valid sources. This is not to say that people blindly accept all they are told. Educated consumers do not believe everything they see on television or read on the cover of the grocery store tabloids. How likely you are to believe the information transmitted to you depends on the respect you have for the veracity and reliability of the information source.

The method of authority is a more rational approach to knowing than belief in superstition or dependence on intuition, but it is not without its flaws. A person's perception of an authority figure is often tainted by personal feelings; I may tend to believe what one person tells me simply because I like that person. Moreover, in most cases, the learner knows very little about how the information was acquired by the authority. Did the authority learn it from another authority? How was it learned originally—through direct observation or through someone else's intuition? Urban myths, such as stories of people attempting to dry their dogs in the microwave, are spread and believed because people do not question the source: a friend of a friend of mine.

RATIONAL-INDUCTIVE ARGUMENT

One of the most highly respected methods of acquiring knowledge is by **rational-inductive argument**. This is the primary method of knowledge acquisition in nonscientific academic disciplines, such as history, philosophy, and literature. Based on the text of an author's works and the historical events of the times, a scholar draws some general conclusions about that author. Or one may become familiar with what others have said about a topic and then form rational arguments to defend a specific idea or thesis. Of course, this approach to acquiring knowledge is not limited to academicians. And not all use of rational-inductive argument is based on extensive research on an area. We use this approach every day when trying to explain why we voted for a certain politician, why we didn't like a movie, or why our friends should go to the restaurant we prefer.

A rational-inductive argument may be well-conceived and based on verifiable facts. Indeed, rational-inductive arguments can be objective. The process of arguing, however, is susceptible to subjectivity and bias. Biased arguments can be based on a selective use of the available facts. Thus a white supremacist who refuses to acknowledge the valuable contributions of other races to human progress is using rational-inductive argument in a biased manner.

The contributions of rational-inductive argument to the world's body of knowledge should not be undervalued. Although the process of using this approach is susceptible to subjectivity, users of rational-inductive argument often avoid subjectivity and bias, thereby producing important, useful, and meaningful commentaries and theories. It is impossible to imagine what the state of our intellectual development would be without rational-inductive argument.

THE SCIENTIFIC METHOD

The scientific method consists of the collecting of observations in a *systematic* and *objective* manner to test predictions, called **hypotheses**. When the data are consistent with a hypothesis, the hypothesis is supported. It is by conducting research and testing hypotheses that scientific knowledge is acquired.

Research in science, however, is not totally objective. Decisions about what topic to research and, to some extent, how the results of the research should be interpreted are vulnerable to subjectivity. Science differs from the other ways of knowing, though, in that the data are collected and the hypotheses are tested objectively.

CONCEPT QUESTIONS I.I

Identify the different ways of knowing (superstition, intuition, authority, rational-inductive argument, or the scientific method) used in each of the following scenarios.

a. A child believes that Santa Claus is real because Mom and Dad say he is.

b. Dr. Jones argues that the causes of World War I were nationalistic feelings within the different European countries; he backs his arguments with evidence about the economic, social, and international environments of the time.

c. The Tastey Company knows that its cola tastes better than the competitor's because people who did not know which cola they were drinking chose Tastey Cola more often than the other brand.

d. I know the brakes are wearing out on my car because my mechanic looked at them and told me so.

e. The electrician checked each of the circuit breakers independently before concluding that the problem was a short in the third breaker.

f. The athlete knew he would have a good game because he wore his lucky socks.

g. I think that people should go and see my favorite movie because the plot is enthralling, the acting is well done, the photography is excellent, and the script is fantastic.

h. I knew that my house was going to be broken into because I've been very paranoid about the neighborhood ever since I came back from vacation.

The essential task in conducting scientific research is to collect the data in a manner that permits only one explanation for the obtained results. The researcher attempts to design a study without **confounds**. Confounds are flaws in the design of a study that permit competing explanations of the results. For example, imagine a study in which participants (usually referred to in research as **subjects**) are randomly assigned to one of two groups. One group is simply told to study a list of 20 words for 5 minutes, and the second group is given instructions for a special mnemonic (a memory technique) that may help them remember the words. If the only difference between Group 1 and Group 2 is the mnemonic instructions, then any difference in performance between the groups is probably attributable to those instructions. But what if the room is noisy for the first group and quiet for the second? Then differences in performance could be a result of the mnemonic instructions or of the noise level in the room or even of a combination of the two. Now the results of the experiment are ambiguous; there is more than one possible explanation for the results.

One important way to avoid confounds and ambiguity in research is by carefully defining all of the important concepts. Perhaps a researcher is interested in the effect of stress on work efficiency, and the researcher plans to study this effect by inducing stress in half of the subjects and then measuring all of the subjects' performance on some task. The researcher's first job is to define the terms *stress* and *work efficiency*. Dictionary definitions are not precise enough for a researcher's needs. What is required is a definition that tells the reader exactly what was done to induce or measure the things referred to by the terms. In this example, the researcher must explain how stress was induced and exactly how performance was measured. Thus the researcher must provide **operational definitions** that define the exact procedures used to produce a phenomenon or to measure some variable. In our example, the researcher may induce stress in one group of subjects by telling them that the experiment involves a harmless yet somewhat painful shock (later, of course, the researcher should explain to the subjects why this deception was deemed necessary). This information about the shock is the operational definition for stress in this experiment; it describes the precise procedures used to induce stress. The operational definition of work efficiency must be equally precise. Perhaps our researcher will measure work efficiency by the number of anagrams from a list of 10 that are solved during a 3-minute interval. This operational definition of work efficiency tells the reader what task was performed, for how long it was performed, and what measurement of it was made. Together, these operational definitions of what was induced and what was measured supply considerable information about the research project. Clear operational definitions are important for clear communication; weak operational definitions leave room for confusion and ambiguity. We will examine operational definitions more closely in a later chapter.

CONCEPT QUESTIONS I.2

1. An acquaintance mentions that the arthritis in her hands has been bothering her, but says that she has been rubbing herbal cremes into her knuckles and has found this to be beneficial. What explanations other than the efficacy of the herbal cremes might account for the improvement she feels?

2. In a taste test between Tastey Cola and Quencher Cola, tasters are always presented with Quencher Cola first; then they are given a salted cracker, and then presented with Tastey Cola. Although the tasters do not know which cola is which, they report that Tastey Cola tastes better than Quencher. Several confounds in this study suggest alternative explanations for the results. Which ones can you identify? What improvements in the design of the study would you suggest?

3. Which of the following is the most complete operational definition?
   a. Learning is defined as the amount of information retained after a period of time.
   b. Learning is defined as the number of correct responses on a 25-question multiple-choice test that covers material presented in a lecture.
   c. Learning is defined as studying for an exam for 30 minutes.
   d. Learning is defined as a relatively permanent change in behavior that occurs because of experience.

4. A researcher wishes to investigate the effect of the temperature in a room on the mood of those in it. The terms *temperature* and *mood* must be operationally defined. What are some possible operational definitions this researcher could use?

When conducting research by the scientific method, a researcher is typically interested in knowing how one thing (such as mnemonic instructions) affects something else (such as memory performance). Consider the study described earlier, where one group receives no instructions and the other group receives mnemonic instructions. The researcher will try to hold everything constant between the two groups of subjects. The groups will be tested on the same day, in the same room, by the same experimenter. The two groups will have the same amount of time to study the same list of 20 words, and they will be given the same amount of time to recall the 20 words. The only difference between these two groups is that one group will receive the mnemonic instructions and the other will not.

What the researcher changes or *manipulates* in an experiment is called the **independent variable**. The different ways in which the independent variable is measured are referred to as the **levels** of the independent variable. In this case, the two levels of the independent variable, memory instructions, are whether or not the subject receives the mnemonic instructions. The group of subjects that receives the treatment being tested is often referred to as the **experimental group**. The group that does not receive the treatment being tested—in this case, the group that does not receive the mnemonic instructions—is called the **control group**. The control group is treated in exactly the same manner as the experimental group except for the manipulation of the independent variable. The control group is used to demonstrate that any difference between the performance of the control group and the performance of the experimental group is attributable to the independent variable and not to some other aspect of the experiment.

The effect of the mnemonic instruction in this experiment is measurable by comparing how well the experimental group remembers the 20 words and how well the control group does so. What the experimenter *measures* in *both* the experimental and control groups is called the **dependent variable**. Here, the dependent variable is the number of words recalled.

In some types of research, it may not be possible to *manipulate* the independent variable; instead, the levels of the independent variable are *selected*. For example, suppose a researcher is interested in the effects of gender on mathematical ability. A variable can be manipulated only when the researcher can decide who does and who does not receive different levels of the independent variable. Because the researcher cannot decide whether a subject will be a male or a female, gender cannot be manipulated. Gender is a **subject variable**—a characteristic of the subject that can be measured. When the independent variable is a subject variable, its levels can be selected but not manipulated. This distinction is important when one attempts to draw conclusions from the results of research. If the independent variable is manipulated, and the results warrant such a conclusion, one can claim that the independent variable had a *causal* effect on the dependent variable. If the independent variable is selected but not manipulated, one can only conclude that levels of the independent variable and measures of performance on the dependent variable are *related*. A causal relationship, however, cannot be established. If a researcher found a difference between genders on mathematical ability then the researcher could conclude that these two variables are related. The evidence does *not* suggest, however, that gender causes a difference in mathematical ability, any more than it suggests that mathematical ability causes a difference in gender. There is no way of ruling out any number of alternative explanations, such as that one gender receives more background or more encouragement in mathematics than the other. This distinction between causal evidence and evidence of relationships will be discussed more thoroughly in other chapters. For now, the more important distinction is between independent variables (including subject variables) and dependent variables. As a general rule, researchers using the scientific method attempt to identify the effect of the independent variable on the dependent variable.

CONCEPT QUESTIONS 1.3

1. In an experiment comparing the effect of study materials on test scores, one group of subjects is instructed to take their own notes on a videotaped lecture, and the other group of subjects is instructed to take notes on an outline of the lecture. Three days following the lecture, all of the subjects take a short test on the material, and their test scores are recorded.
   a. What is the dependent variable in this study?
   b. What is the independent variable in this study?
   c. How many levels of the independent variable are there in this study?
   d. Is the independent variable a subject variable?

2. Volunteers over the age of 21 participate in a study that is designed to investigate the effects of alcohol on visual acuity. The subjects all have 20/20 vision. One-third of the subjects drink 2 ounces of alcohol, one-third of the subjects drink 1 ounce of alcohol, and one-third of the subjects consume a drink containing no alcohol. After consuming the drink, each subject undergoes a test for visual acuity.
   a. What is the dependent variable in this study?
   b. What is the independent variable in this study?
   c. How many levels of the independent variable are there in this study?
   d. Is the independent variable a subject variable?

3. In a study of the effect of gender on color preference, males and females were asked to choose their favorite shade of blue from among seven possible choices. Their choices were then compared.
   a. What is the dependent variable in this study?
   b. What is the independent variable in this study?
   c. How many levels of the independent variable are there in this study?
   d. Is the independent variable a subject variable?

A researcher is able to make systematic and objective observations by developing clear operational definitions and by controlling for all possible confounds when designing and carrying out a research project. However, the mere fact that one researcher was able to identify an effect of an independent variable upon a dependent variable does not, by itself, mean that the effect actually exists. The strongest support comes when different researchers using different subjects and different types of research designs are able to replicate the results and also find the effect. It is also important that the effect be consistently replicable. If an effect is sometimes replicated and sometimes not, other (unknown and uncontrolled) variables may be affecting the results. Studies that are unable to replicate an effect should not be considered a failure. The information these studies provide is useful and important for guiding additional research.

THE OBJECTIVES OF SCIENCE AND THE SCIENTIFIC METHOD

Research based on the scientific method can provide information about how one variable affects another variable, or about how two or more variables are related. This information can be used to achieve a number of goals: description, explanation, prediction, and control.

The results of scientific research can be used to identify and **describe** phenomena. For example, I may believe that taking and studying one's own notes leads to better test performance than studying someone else's. I can determine whether this phenomenon exists by conducting an experiment in which a colleague (who does not know the purpose of the study) presents a lecture to a class. Half of the class members have been randomly chosen to take their own notes, and the others have been asked to listen attentively to the lecture but not to take notes. The notes are taken from the notetakers after the lecture, to prevent them from studying them, but these are returned during the study session prior to a test on the lecture material. The subjects who only listened to the lecture are provided with a lecture summary to study during the study session. Next, all of the subjects take a test on the lecture material. The test scores are then compared. This experiment will provide descriptive information about the notetaking phenomenon. It will demonstrate whether the anticipated notetaking effect occurred in this situation and, if it did, how large or small the difference is between notetakers and summary-studiers. Further research might address whether this phenomenon occurs in all classes or whether it occurs with all instructors. Descriptive research plays an important role in science by identifying and describing phenomena so that later explanations of these phenomena may be proposed.

Explanations of research attempt to offer reasons why a phenomenon occurs that will account for previous observations and descriptions of the phenomenon. For example, suppose that the notetakers scored higher on a test of the lecture material than did those who studied a lecture summary. A researcher might propose that this phenomenon occurs because the process of notetaking helps a student learn the material better during the lecture than does simply listening. From this explanation, specific predictions or hypotheses can be derived and tested.

Based on the explanation proposed above, one might **predict** that notetakers will perform better on a test than listeners when neither group is allowed to study before the test. An experiment can then be designed to test this hypothesis. If the results of the experiment are consistent with the hypothesis, this supports the explanation that the process of notetaking is important. Predictive ability adds value to an explanation, since an explanation that can predict future results is worth more to a researcher than an explanation that can only account for past research findings.

With an understanding of the causes of a phenomenon and the ability to predict results based on that explanation can also come the ability to **control** the phenomenon. If we know that excessive stress can cause psychophysiological ailments such as headaches and ulcers, we also know that we can reduce the chance of suffering from these ailments by reducing the amount of stress in our lifestyle. Not all research in psychology leads so directly from description to control, but control is one of the major goals of applied psychological research.

As in other fields, **applied research** in psychology is research whose results are immediately relevant in a practical setting. Research that attempts to identify new and effective therapy techniques is applied research, as is research that tests the worth of different teaching methods or the most efficient layout for a keyboard. The results of research on these and other topics can often be applied directly to a problem in order to control behavior—an aspect of applied research that many find particularly satisfying.

Not all research results are immediately applicable to a specific problem, nor were they ever intended to be. The results of **basic research** may have no immediate practical use; explanation, rather than application, is typically the goal of basic research. The basic researcher's motivation often comes from an insatiable curiosity and a desire to gain knowledge for knowledge's sake. Basic and applied research are related, however. The results of previous basic research often lay the groundwork for applied research, and investigations into practical questions can also suggest research questions to the basic researcher.

A WORD ABOUT THEORIES

A psychological theory is a set of related statements that explain and predict phenomena. The statements used in a theory can be laws, principles, or beliefs. **Laws** are very specific statements that are generally expressed in the form of a mathematical equation involving only a few variables. Laws have so much empirical support that their accuracy is beyond reasonable doubt. The law of gravity is an example of such a theoretical statement. My mental health would be questioned if I began publicly to doubt the accuracy of the law of gravity. While several laws exist within the "hard" sciences such as physics and chemistry, most psychological laws have been discovered in the area of psychophysics. Weber's law is an example. It states that, for any particular sensory modality, such as vision, the size of the difference threshold for a particular type of stimulus is constant; this law is written as $\frac{\Delta I}{I} = K$, where I is the magnitude of the stimulus, ΔI is the difference threshold, and K is constancy.

Principles are more tentative than laws. They are statements that predict a phenomenon with a certain level of probability. A description of positive reinforcement can be stated as a principle: Positive reinforcement increases the probability that a contingent behavior will occur again. The principle of positive reinforcement can be used to predict how likely an event is to occur, but not with total accuracy. Psychology is replete with principles.

The third type of statement found in psychological theories is **beliefs**—statements based on personal feelings and subjective knowledge about things that cannot be tested scientifically. Freud's theory of the id, the ego, and the superego contains a number of belief statements about the existence and function of these three entities.

The theory is useful to psychoanalysts as a way to conceptualize the workings of the mind, but it is of less value to the scientific researcher because the belief statements cannot be tested. No one has been able to demonstrate the existence of the id, the ego, or the superego. Beliefs are avoided within scientific psychology theories because they are untestable.

Theories often explain a set of related observations or phenomena; for example, the behavioral theory of learning attempts to explain the effects on behavior of positive reinforcement, negative reinforcement, punishment, and schedules of reinforcement. From this theory, as from any scientific theory, a researcher can derive specific testable hypotheses that serve as the bases for scientific investigations. Thus, from the behavioral learning theory in general, and from the principle of positive reinforcement in particular, a researcher may predict that people will be more apt to stick with a weight loss program if they receive positive comments about their progress than will people who receive no feedback about their progress. This is a specific, testable hypothesis derived from a more complex theory. Support for the theory comes, of course, from support for the hypothesis. Should the hypothesis fail to be supported, the theory may require some modification or, in the most extreme case, may have to be discarded.

Theories are evaluated by a number of criteria. Once such criterion is called **parsimony**, which suggests that, of two equally accurate explanations, the one based on the simpler assumptions is preferable. For example, a theory of extrasensory perception (ESP) attempts to explain and predict what appear to be occurrences beyond the explanatory capacity of present-day physical theory, such as sending messages telepathically or moving objects psychokinetically. But accepting the ESP theory's explanation for these events requires abandoning assumptions of contemporary physical theory. For instance, psychokinesis suggests that physical objects can be influenced without transmitting or transferring any physical energy, an assumption that runs counter to present-day knowledge of physics. Until scientific research presents considerable solid, replicable evidence that supports ESP theory and refutes present-day theory, it is more parsimonious to explain apparent occurrences of psychokinesis, telepathy, and so on in terms of coincidence and magician's tricks. It is simpler to maintain the assumptions of present-day theories in dealing with these events than it is to discard them in exchange for assumptions that are as yet unsupported (Kalat 1990). In general, if two competing theories are equally good at explaining behavior, the theory with the fewer assumptions or the better supported assumptions is deemed superior.

Another criterion by which to evaluate theories is **precision**. A good theory is precisely stated. This might mean that it consists of mathematical statements or a computer program. Or it might be stated in standard English, but with carefully defined terms. A precise theory, regardless of the language used to state it, is written to avoid ambiguity and misinterpretation.

Related to precision is a third criterion by which to judge theories, **testability**. A sound scientific theory is testable. To be testable, a theory must be expressed in a form that holds out the possibility of its being proved wrong. If one predicts from Freudian personality theory that fixation at the oral stage of psychosexual development will lead to some type of overuse or underuse of the mouth, then oral fixation could predict either overeating or anorexia; or it might predict loquaciousness or taciturnity. A theory that is capable of explaining all results is untestable and judged a poorer scientific theory than a testable one.

A fourth criterion for judging scientific theories is apparent **accuracy**. A parsimonious, precisely stated theory yielding testable hypotheses has little value if all of its hypotheses are left unsupported. A good scientific theory should both fit the known facts and predict new ones. This, however, leads to what might appear to be a paradox: A theory can never be proved true.

Results consistent with predictions derived from a given theory may be found over and over, but this does not prove that the theory is true; it simply supports the theory. The results *may* have been found because the theory is true, but they may have occurred because another theory, making the same predictions, is true. It could be that the theory is true thus far, but is incomplete and can not explain phenomena in as yet unstudied areas. The research results may actually be an artifact (a by-product) of the research method, and would not be found if another method were employed. Or the results may simply have occurred by chance. If I predict that when I let go of a pencil in the air it will fall to the floor, and instead the pencil floats, this evidence refutes the theory of gravity as it stands today. But if the pencil hits the floor, that does not prove the theory of gravity, although it does add additional support to it.

Just because a theory can never be proved does not mean that research is a waste of time. As support for a theory accumulates, confidence in the veracity of the theory increases. Therefore, even though a theory may never be proved correct, it can accumulate enough support to be assumed correct. In science, the only way to accumulate this support is through research.

HOW TO DO SCIENCE

Conducting scientific research involves a series of steps. The steps are, in general, the same for any scientific research project; only the specifics differ from project to project. These steps are outlined in Figure 1.1.

FIGURE I.I   *Steps involved in conducting scientific research.*

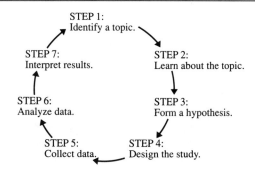

The first step is to identify the topic to be studied. At first this can be somewhat difficult—not because there are so few topics to choose from, but because there are so many.

A way to begin is to think about courses you have had in psychology and related fields. What courses were your favorites? Thumb through your old introductory psychology textbook. Which chapters did you find most fascinating? Choose a topic to research that you find particularly interesting; research is a time-consuming task and can become tedious if you aren't especially curious about the questions you have asked.

Once you have identified the topic, the second step is to learn about what has already been done in the area. The library is your primary source for this information. The results of previous research on your topic may be found in whole books or in book chapters. Research journals publish descriptions of individual research projects, as well as review articles describing the results of many projects. (For more information about journal articles and literature searches, see Appendix C.) Courses and textbooks can also serve as sources of information about an area. Less frequently considered, but often very worthwhile, is actual correspondence with the experts and researchers in a field. These individuals can provide valuable information about details and nuances of their work that would be unavailable elsewhere. The impetus for specific research projects may appear during your review of the area. Perhaps you find the results of a study dubious and wish to replicate it. Maybe you'd like to try to detect a particular phenomenon under a different set of circumstances. You might decide to combine ideas from two different studies or to conduct the next in a series of projects. The only way to learn from others' experiences, to discover what has been done, and to identify the questions that remain to be answered is by becoming familiar with the literature in the area.

Following your review of the previous literature, the third step is to form a hypothesis. This entails narrowing your focus from a general area of research to a specific question that you want your study to answer. Your predicted answer to your research question is the hypothesis. Hypotheses can be derived from theory or from previous research, or they may simply reflect curiosity about a topic.

Perhaps you learned about research conducted on eating disorders at about the same time you learned about operant conditioning in one of your psychology classes. You might wonder if operant conditioning can be used to modify eating behaviors, by using positive reinforcement to increase eating. A hypothesis needs to be precisely stated in a testable manner; therefore, this hypothesis needs to be honed somewhat. Perhaps it develops into something such as this: Subjects who receive positive reinforcement contingent upon eating will consume more food than subjects who do not recieve positive reinforcement.

The fourth step involves designing your study so that the results either support or refute your hypothesis. This is when you decide *exactly* how you will make your observations. Here you must operationally define your terms and design your investigation. Continuing with our eating behaviors example, the phrases "positive reinforcement contingent upon eating" and "consumption of food" need to be defined operationally. Maybe *positive reinforcement* will be defined as complimentary statements about the subject's hair and clothing made within 1 second after the subject eats a potato chip. The food has been defined as potato chips. The consumption of potato chips might be measured in grams. The research design that is implied in this hypothesis involves an experimental group (which receives the positive reinforcement) and a control group. Many other types of research designs can be used to test hypotheses, each with its own advantages and disadvantages. The choice of research design is often a function of a balance between the benefits and pitfalls of the design, the practical concerns of the particular situation, and personal preference.

Many other specific decisions about your study must also be made at this stage. Who will be the subjects in your study? How many will you need? Will they be tested altogether, in small groups, or individually? How will the potato chips be presented? Will the same experimenter interact with all of the subjects? Where and when will this experiment take place? How long will it take? Should the subjects be asked to refrain from eating for some amount of time prior to the study? When will the subjects be told the true purpose of the study? As the questions are answered and the experiment begins to take shape, it is important to keep a wary eye out for potential confounds. The challenge is to design your study so that the results either clearly support or fail to support your hypothesis.

The fifth step in conducting scientific research is to make your observations and collect your data according to the procedures prescribed in your research design.

Courtesy of Sidney Harris

Here is where attention to detail during the design stage pays off. It is often unwise to change procedures after a study is underway, since this complicates the task of interpreting the results. However, even the most experienced researchers are occasionally surprised by problems that arise while the data are being collected, and sometimes this forces them to scrap the project and redesign the study. Surprises are not necessarily bad, though: with every surprise comes a bit of new information and perhaps the seed of new research efforts.

In the sixth step, the data that have been collected are summarized and analyzed to determine whether the results support the hypothesis. The process of summarizing and analyzing the data is called **statistical analysis**. By using statistical analysis, you can determine the likelihood that your results are due to chance and the degree of confidence with which you can state that your results reflect reality.

Finally, the seventh step involves interpreting the results of the statistical analyses and drawing conclusions about your hypotheses. Here you determine the implications of your results in relation to the topic you focused on in step 1. Often interpretation raises new unanswered questions that can serve as the focus of another research project, and so the cycle begins again.

SCIENCE AND STATISTICS

Statistics are the tools researchers use to organize and summarize their data. If you collect memory test scores from 100 subjects, you have 100 numbers. Little useful information can be gleaned from 100 individual numbers; they need to be organized. In this regard, it might be useful to know what the highest and lowest scores are (the range), or what the most common score is (the mode), or what the middle score is (the median). Certain statistical tests can help you determine whether one group of subjects scored *significantly* better on a test than another. The term "significantly" means that the difference is of such a magnitude that it is unlikely to have occurred by chance alone.

A **population** is all of the individuals about whom a research project is meant to generalize. A population can be as broadly defined as all of the people in the world, or even all living organisms. Or the population can be more narrowly defined, such as all 18- to 22-year-olds, or all psychology majors at a particular school. Typically, a researcher cannot test all members of a target population. Instead, only a small percentage of that population can be tested—a **sample** of the members. Based on findings from that sample, the researcher wants to make valid generalizations about the population.

Let's assume that a researcher has conducted a mnemonic instructions experiment, and the mnemonic group has performed better than the control group. Perhaps the subjects in the mnemonic group recalled an average of 18 out of 20 words, whereas members of the control group recalled an average of 16 out of 20 words. At this point the researcher has not yet supported the hypothesis that mnemonic instructions lead to better memory performance, even though 18 is a bigger number than 16. The researcher knows that the *sample* of subjects in the mnemonic group outperformed the *sample* of subjects in the control group, but the researcher does not know at this point how likely the same difference is to exist in the *population*.

RESEARCH CRITICISM

In the process of learning how to conduct well-designed research, you will also gain critical thinking skills and the ability to critique other research. Do not believe that just because a study has been published it must be good. Often errors in design slip past the editors and reviewers of the research journals, or what was not seen as a problem at first becomes a problem as new research is conducted. As you read the research literature, you must evaluate each study to determine whether it provides useful information and whether the researchers made errors that weaken their conclusions.

As you read a description of a research project, pay attention to whether the arguments made are logical. Are terms clearly defined? Are operational definitions provided? Consider how the subjects were chosen. Are they representative of the population? Was the manner in which the investigation was conducted clearly stated so that another person could repeat it? Were any potential confounds included in the design? Were the conclusions consistent with the results of the study? Are there any alternative explanations that the researchers may have missed?

Psychology is the scientific study of behavior. Everything that research psychologists "know" about human behavior has been learned through research conducted in accordance with the scientific method. Learning about the scientific method in psychology will enable you to become a better evaluator of all research, and perhaps you will be motivated to add to the body of knowledge with research of your own.

IMPORTANT TERMS AND CONCEPTS

data	operational definition	basic research
research	experimental group	laws
hypothesis/hypotheses	control group	principles
scientific method	independent variable	beliefs
subjective/objective	dependent variable	theory
superstition	subject variable	parsimony
intuition	description	precision
method of authority	explanation	testability
rational-inductive argument	prediction	accuracy
confounds	control	statistical analysis/analyses
subjects	applied research	sample/population

QUESTIONS AND EXERCISES

1. A researcher is investigating the effect of mood on eating. Subjects in a sample of undergraduate females (ages 18–22) are randomly assigned to one of two conditions: the depressed condition or the neutral condition. Subjects assigned to the depressed condition are hypnotized and a depressed mood is induced. Subjects in the neutral condition are hypnotized and a neutral mood is induced. Following hypnosis, subjects are offered a plate of cookies as they watch a travel film about Paris. The number of cookies eaten by each subject is recorded.
   a. What are the operational definitions for *eating*, *depressed mood*, and *neutral mood* in this study?
   b. Identify the experimental and control groups.
   c. What is the independent variable? How many levels of the independent variable are there?
   d. Is the independent variable manipulated or selected?
   e. What is the dependent variable?

2. During everyday speech we often use figurative phrases, such as "let the cat out of the bag" or "over the hill." Researchers are very interested in what phrases people use or are familiar with. One researcher selects a sample of 16- to 22-yr-olds as well as a sample of 66- to 72-yr-olds. The researcher interviews each subject for 5 minutes and records the number of figurative expressions each subject makes. The researcher finds that the older subjects use more figurative expressions than do the younger subjects.
   a. What is the dependent variable in this study?
   b. What is the independent variable? How many levels of the independent variable are there?
   c. Is the independent variable manipulated or selected?
   d. The researcher is tempted to conclude that, as a person gets older, he or she uses more figurative language. What are some other possible explanations for the results?

3. A television advertisement states that "scientific studies prove that this product works; and it will work for you, too."
   a. If a viewer believes this advertisement, what method of knowing is being used?
   b. Explain why a scientific study cannot *prove* that a product will work for an entire population.

4. In this chapter, five ways of knowing were described: superstition, intuition, authority, rational-inductive argument, and the scientific method. This book focuses on the scientific method, but that method is not always the best way of acquiring knowledge. Provide examples of situations in which intuition, authority, and rational-inductive argument would be an adequate or superior way of gaining information, and explain why you believe so.

5. What is the difference between objectivity and subjectivity, and why is it so important that scientific research be conducted objectively?

6. What is the difference between applied and basic research? Provide examples of research questions for an applied researcher and a basic researcher.

7. Which of the following is the best operational definition?
   a. Memory is the amount of information retained after a specified period of time.
   b. Memory is the process of encoding, storing, and retrieving information.
   c. Memory is the number of nonsense syllables recalled from a list of 50 nonsense syllables after 2 minutes of studying.

8. A good scientific theory should be parsimonious, precise, testable, and accurate.
   a. Explain the concept of parsimony, and create an example (other than the one provided in the chapter) comparing two theories on parsimony.
   b. Explain the value of precisely stated theories.

c. Explain the concept of testability in relation to theories. What is the difference between testing a theory and proving one? Why do I rant and rave when a student claims to have proved a theory?

d. Why is accuracy an important criterion for a theory to meet?

9. Describe a situation in which you and your classmates might make up a population and one in which you and your classmates might constitute a sample. As a sample, what populations could you represent?

10. How do you think you might use information from this course and textbook in the future? Answer this question again after you have completed the book.

2

Ethics in Research

F or psychologists ... one of their obligations is to use their research skills to extend knowledge for the sake of ultimate human betterment. Psychologists begin with the commitment that the distinctive contribution of scientists to human welfare is the development of knowledge and its intelligent application to appropriate problems. Their underlying ethical imperative, thus, is to conduct research as well as they know how (American Psychological Association 1982, p. 15).

Psychologists conduct research not only because they enjoy the process, but also because psychology as a discipline is defined by and depends on psychological research. However, conducting research doesn't simply require the development of a project that will yield interpretable results; it also requires awareness and consideration of a number of ethical concerns. There are two major areas of ethical considerations in research: treatment of the subjects while the research is being conducted, and treatment of the results of the research. Each of these areas will be discussed in this chapter.

ETHICAL TREATMENT OF THE SUBJECTS OF RESEARCH

The subjects of research in psychology are usually either animals or humans. How the subjects of psychological research are treated during the course of a research project is in part mandated by law, in part regulated by guidelines developed by psychologists, and in part determined by the researcher's own conscience. Together, the law, the guidelines, and the conscience lead to research projects that not only provide invaluable information about behavior but do so while respecting the dignity of the research subjects.

ETHICAL TREATMENT OF HUMAN SUBJECTS

Institutional Review Boards (IRBs) are committees of individuals from diverse backgrounds who review proposals for research with human subjects. Members of an IRB at a college may include faculty members from different academic departments as well as members of the community. The diverse backgrounds of the members help bring different perspectives to the review process. All federally funded research using human subjects must be reviewed by an IRB, but changes in the law in 1981 exempted many other types of research from review, including research that involves common educational practices or collects data in a manner such that the subjects remain anonymous (Department of Health and Human Services, January 26, 1981). Most colleges and universities, however, in an effort to guarantee the ethical treatment of human subjects, review all research proposals involving human subjects that will be carried out under their auspices.

Typically, a researcher completes an application form for the IRB that asks specific questions about the procedures to be used in a research project, whether there are any known risks or benefits related to the procedure, and how the subjects' confidentiality will be maintained. Often a detailed research proposal is supplied with the application. An important part of the application to the IRB is the informed consent form.

The **informed consent** form is given to each subject prior to participation in the project. It describes the purpose of the study and states what the subject will be asked to do. Any known risks or benefits related to the study are made clear to the subject. Even after the subject signs the informed consent form, that person remains free to stop participating at any point during the project. This is also clearly stated in the informed consent form. An example of an informed consent form is presented in Box 2.1.

SAMPLE INFORMED CONSENT FORM

Box 2.1

Bradley University
CONSENT FORM ON THE USE OF HUMAN SUBJECTS IN RESEARCH
Statement of Informed Consent
I, _____, am being asked to participate in a research project entitled _____.
This project is being conducted under the supervision of _____ and was approved by Bradley University's Committee on the Use of Human Subjects in Research on _____.

From this project the investigators hope to learn _____.
[EXPLAIN, IN LAY LANGUAGE, WHAT THE PURPOSE OF THE STUDY IS.]

As a participant in this project I shall be asked to _____. [IN THIS SPACE EXPLAIN TO THE SUBJECT WHAT PROCEDURES WILL BE FOLLOWED. WHAT IS THE DURATION OF THE RESEARCH PROJECT? BE CONCISE, BUT FULLY INFORM THE SUBJECT. BE SURE TO AVOID LANGUAGE THAT IS TECHNICAL.]

The nature of this study has been explained to me by _____. I understand that the anticipated benefits of my participation are _____. I understand that the known risks of my participation in this study are _____. [FOR BENEFITS YOU CAN INCLUDE BOTH DIRECT BENEFITS (E.G., EXTRA CRED-IT POINTS) AND INDIRECT BENEFITS (E.G., THE BENEFIT TO SOCIETY OF AN INCREASED UNDER-STANDING OF THIS AREA). FOR RISKS, INCLUDE POTENTIAL DISCOMFORTS. IF NO RISKS ARE APPARENT, STATE SO.]

The investigators will make every effort to safeguard the confidentiality of the information that I provide. Any information obtained from this study that can be identified with me will remain confidential and will not be given to anyone without my permission. [IF YOUR STUDY INVOLVES THE POSSIBILITY OF OBTAINING INFOR-MATION THAT YOU ARE OBLIGATED BY LAW OR ETHICS TO DISCLOSE (E.G., CHILD ABUSE, DANGER TO SELF OR OTHERS), INSERT A SENTENCE INDICATING THE SPECIFIC LIMITS OF CONFIDENTIALITY.]

If at any time I would like additional information about this project, I can contact _____ at _____. [GIVE THE NAME OF THE INVESTIGATOR, AND GIVE AN ADDRESS AND PHONE NUMBER.]

I understand that I have the right to refuse to participate in this study. I also understand that if I do agree to participate I have the right to change my mind at any time and stop my participation. I understand that the grades and services I receive from Bradley University will not be negatively affected by my refusal to participate or by my withdrawal from this project. [IF THE PROJECT IS TAKING PLACE AT SOME OTHER ORGANIZATION, STATE HOW REFUSAL TO PARTICIPATE OR WITHDRAWAL WILL AFFECT SERVICES RECEIVED FROM THAT ORGANIZATION.]

My signature below indicates that I have given my informed consent to participate in the above described project. My signature also indicates that:
* I have been given the opportunity to ask any and all questions about the described project and my participation, and that all of my questions have been answered to my satisfaction.
* I have been permitted to read this document and I have been given a signed copy of it.
* I am at least 18 years old.
* I am legally able to provide consent.
* To the best of my knowledge and belief,I have no physical or mental illness or weakness that would be adversely affected by my participation in the described project.

_____   _____
Signature of participant   date

_____   _____
Signature of witness   date

Although the consent form provides much information about the study, typically the study is also described to the subject orally and an opportunity for the subject to ask questions is provided. The goal is not to convince the subject to sign the consent form; the goal is to provide enough information so that the subject can make an informed decision about participating. The consent form simply documents that the subject has consented to participate, and the IRB's review of the form ensures that the subject receives adequate information to make an informed decision.

When a researcher has spent considerable time planning and developing a research project, review by an IRB can sometimes seem an unnecessary hurdle before one can actually collect data. However, the importance of an impartial review should not be underestimated. Ethical concerns are not always major and obvious; often they are subtle, inconspicuous, and easily overlooked by the researcher. I once used a procedure that involved rapidly presenting slides to the subject. During its development, I had tried the procedure on myself and a number of willing friends with no ill effects, but an impartial reviewer who experienced the procedure found that it gave him a headache. Of course mention of the risk of headache or other discomfort was added to the informed consent form; but if it had not been for the observation of that reviewer and the inclusion of that risk in the information provided to the subjects, subjects who subsequently experienced headaches from the procedure might have believed that I had intentionally withheld warning about this negative side effect. Ignoring ethical problems does not make them go away, but it can harm the reputation of the researcher as well as of psychology as a whole.

Concern for the welfare of the subjects does not start at the IRB, nor does approval of the procedure by the IRB free the researcher from responsibility for any ethical violations they may have missed. Ethical considerations must be addressed throughout the development of the project. To aid researchers in identifying important ethical concerns, the **American Psychological Association** (APA, a national organization of psychologists) has developed a set of ethical principles to be considered in the conduct of research with human subjects. These 10 principles are presented in Box 2.2.

ETHICAL PRINCIPLES IN THE CONDUCT OF RESEARCH WITH HUMAN PARTICIPANTS

Box 2.2

The decision to undertake research rests upon a considered judgment by the individual psychologist about how best to contribute to psychological science and welfare. Having made the decision to conduct research, the psychologist considers alternative directions in which research energies and resources might be invested. On the basis of this consideration, the psychologist carries out the investigation with respect and concern for the dignity and welfare of the people who participate and with cognizance of federal and state regulations and professional standards governing the conduct of research with human participants.

A. In planning a study, the investigator has the responsibility to make a careful evaluation of its ethical acceptability. To the extent that the weighing of scientific and human values suggests a compromise of any principle, the investigator incurs a correspondingly serious obligation to seek ethical advice and to observe stringent safeguards to protect the rights of human participants.

B. Considering whether a participant in a planned study will be a "subject at risk" or a "subject at minimal risk," according to recognized standards, is of primary ethical concern to the investigator.

C. The investigator always retains the responsibility for ensuring ethical practice in research. The investigator is also responsible for the ethical treatment of research participants by collaborators, assistants, students, and employees, all of whom, however, incur similar obligations.

D. Except in minimal risk research, the investigator establishes a clear and fair agreement with research participants, prior to their participation, that clarifies the obligations and responsibilities of each. The investigator has the obligation to honor all promises and commitments included in that agreement. The investigator informs the participants of all aspects of the research that might reasonably be expected to influence willingness to participate and explains all other aspects of the research about which the participants inquire. Failure to make full disclosure prior to obtaining informed consent requires additional safeguards to protect the welfare and dignity of the research participants. Research with children or with participants who have impairments that would limit understanding and/or communication requires special safeguarding procedures.

E. Methodological requirements of a study may make the use of concealment or deception necessary. Before conducting such a study, the investigator has a special responsibility to (1) determine whether the use of such techniques is justified by the study's prospective scientific, educational, or applied value; (2) determine whether alternative procedures are available that do not use concealment or deception; and (3) ensure that the participants are provided with sufficient explanation as soon as possible.

F. The investigator respects the individual's freedom to decline to participate in or to withdraw from the research at any time. The obligation to protect this freedom requires careful thought and consideration when the investigator is in a position of authority or influence over the participant. Such positions of authority include, but are not limited to, situations in which research participation is required as part of employment or in which the participant is a student, client, or employee of the investigator.

G. The investigator protects the participant from physical and mental discomfort, harm, and danger that may arise from research procedures. If risks of such consequences exist, the investigator informs the participant of that fact. Research procedures likely to cause serious or lasting harm to a participant are not used unless failure to use these procedures might expose the participant to risk of greater harm or unless the research has great potential benefit and fully informed and voluntary consent is obtained from each participant. The participant should be informed of procedures for contacting the investigator within a reasonable time period following participation should stress, potential harm, or related questions or concerns arise.

H. After the data are collected, the investigator provides the participant with information about the nature of the study and attempts to remove any misconceptions that may have arisen. Where scientific or humane values justify delaying or withholding this information, the investigator incurs a special responsibility to monitor the research and to ensure that there are no damaging consequences for the participant.

I. Where research procedures result in undesirable consequences for the individual participant, the investigator has the responsibility to detect and remove or correct these consequences, including long-term effects.

J. Information obtained about a research participant during the course of an investigation is confidential unless otherwise agreed upon in advance. When the possibility exists that others may obtain access to such information, this possibility, together with plans for protecting confidentiality, is explained to the participant as part of the procedure for obtaining informed consent.

SOURCE: American Psychological Association (1982). *Ethical Principles in the Conduct of Research with Human Participants*. Washington, D.C.: American Psychological Association.

According to the first ethical research principle, a researcher is obligated to make a careful ethical evaluation of the proposed methodology. If there is any question of an ethical violation, the researcher should seek ethical advice from others. Thus, even when an IRB review is not required, a researcher should not hesitate to ask advice of other individuals.

The primary ethical concern is whether the subjects of the experiment would be **at risk** or **at minimal risk**. Although the APA does not define "minimal risk" in Principle B, the definition used by IRBs reviewing biomedical and behavioral research is as follows:

> "Minimal risk" means that the risks of harm anticipated in the proposed research are not greater, considering probability and magnitude, than those ordinarily encountered in daily life or during the performance of routine physical or psychological examinations or tests (Department of Health and Human Services, January 26, 1981).

Thus, if the procedure involved in an experiment causes no more physical or psychological stress than one would expect to encounter in everyday life, or imposes no greater risk of harm than one usually faces, then a subject is "at minimal risk." A subject who participates in an experiment in which he or she spends an hour carrying out a very boring task may experience the discomfort of being bored, but this is not likely to be any more harmful or stressful to the individual than the boredom encountered in everyday life. Similarly, completing a pen-and-pencil psychological test, such as the Minnesota Multiphasic Personality Inventory (MMPI) which entails answering 200 true/false questions, can be a long and perhaps somewhat stressful endeavor. However, since it is not unusual for students to be tested with long, somewhat stressful paper-and-pencil examinations, student subjects completing the MMPI would probably be considered "at minimal risk." In a study in which subjects received painful but otherwise nonharmful shocks, the subjects might very well be considered "at risk" because the stress associated with the shocks might be deemed to be of greater magnitude than one would typically encounter.

It is the researcher's responsibility to assess whether the subjects are "at risk" or "at minimal risk." If the researcher believes the subjects may be "at risk", a decision must be made about whether the risks to the subjects outweigh the possible benefits of the knowledge gained. When the risks are relatively small compared to the gains to be had from the results then most advisory boards would allow the research to be conducted (with fully informed consent from the subjects, of course). The greater the risks to the subjects, the greater the obligation on the researcher to consider alternative procedures with smaller risks.

Regardless of whether an advisory board has given the go-ahead for a project or whether the researcher is the person who actually collects the data for the project, Principle C asserts that the researcher always remains responsible for conducting the project ethically. Often students or technicians will work for a researcher and will be the people actually conducting the research. If a research assistant behaves unethically, both the assistant and the primary researcher are responsible for that behavior and for alleviating any negative side effects caused by the unethical behavior.

Principle D makes clear that, in procedures in which a subject is deemed "at risk," it is important that the subjects be informed of the risks, as well as of the prospective benefits, prior to the subject's participation in the study. Additionally, the researcher should answer all of the subjects' questions about the study. This may require some special effort in cases where the subjects are children or are people with mental or physical limitations that hinder communication.

Another situation in which special effort is required to safeguard the subjects is when full disclosure of the purpose of a study or the procedure being used cannot be made prior to the investigation without compromising the validity of the results. For example, in an investigation studying subjects' reactions to emergency situations, the researcher cannot tell the subject that a staged emergency situation is about to occur and retain any confidence that the results reflect what the subjects would do in real life. According to the APA principles, studies involving deception or concealment should be conducted only when there is no known alternative procedure available. Furthermore, when studies involving deception or concealment are conducted, it is important that the subjects be informed of the true purpose of the study as soon as possible.

Even in studies that do not involve deception, the actual purpose of the study may not be fully explained at the time the procedures are described. This is because, when the subjects know the purpose of the study, they often try to "help" the experimenter by behaving in the way they think the experimenter wants. Thus, while the procedure, risks, and benefits may be described in detail, the reason for conducting the research may not be explained thoroughly before the subject participates. Principle H of the APA ethical guidelines, however, states that information about the purpose of the study should be provided as soon as possible after the data have been collected. This is called **debriefing** the subject. Often debriefing occurs immediately after an individual's data have been collected, but other times debriefing may be provided at a later date, after the data are collected from all the subjects. This may have to be done when there is a risk that knowledge of the purpose of the study might leak to other subjects before they participate.

Even when provided with the true purpose of an investigation, subjects will often create additional misconceptions of their own. As many psychology majors have noticed when they've mentioned their major to nonpsychology majors, people often have the mistaken notion that psychologists can see into their souls. When subjects were asked to rate figurative phrases such as "let the cat out the bag" for how often they have heard these used, some of them believed that how they rated a list of these phrases said something about their personalities. Misconceptions about the purpose of a research project should be removed so that the researcher and psychology in general do not suffer (or benefit) from them.

Even after signing the consent form, a subject has the right to quit the study at any time. Of course this can be very frustrating to an investigator; and if more subjects from one group than from another are quitting the project, it can affect the interpretability of the results (this is called a **mortality effect**). Nonetheless, as frustrated and disappointed as a researcher may be when a subject decides to discontinue participating in an investigation, no effort should be made to convince the subject to stay. As a volunteer, the subject has the right to terminate participation, and this right must be respected.

Similarly, no undue effort should be made to convince a person to serve as a subject in an investigation. The subject must be in a situation allowing **free consent**. Free consent is consent given without coercion or pressure to comply. While its clear that whining and pleading by the researcher are unacceptable, it is less obvious when a person feels coerced because the researcher is in a position of authority. For example, a student may feel pressure—imagined or real—to participate in an investigation being conducted by his or her advisor. Or a patient may wonder whether declining to participate in a study will affect the medical treatment he or she receives thereafter. An employee may wonder whether volunteering to serve as a subject might translate into a few more dollars in the next raise. Research in prisons is no longer conducted because it is impossible to remove even the perception of coercion. In a situation where the researcher is in a position of influence or authority, it is important that special effort be made to avoid any real or perceived coercion of potential subjects.

There is a fine line between providing incentives to participate and using coercion. Subjects should be told of benefits related to the research (such as that a project might help researchers better understand how people read), but these benefits should not be presented so that a subject who refuses to participate or quits during the study feels guilty about this decision. Similarly, incentives in the form of extra credit or money should be of a magnitude that is appealing to the subject but not so great that the subject can't turn down the offer. A $5.00 inducement might be appropriate for shoppers in a mall but might be coercive to a student with no regular income. The researcher must keep the benefits of participating on the side of incentives and avoid crossing the line into coercion. The input of colleagues or an IRB may be needed to help the researcher find this line.

If an investigation involves some risk of negative effects, these risks must be made clear to the subject. If the risks are serious, the investigator is obligated to consider alternative procedures. If there are no alternative procedures, an important decision must be made. Should research on the topic be scrapped, or do the potential benefits of the knowledge to be gained from the research outweigh the risks to the subjects? Research involving serious risks to the subjects should be undertaken only when there are *great* potential benefits, or when risks to the subjects would be even greater if the research were not conducted.

Principle I states that, in the course of a study, whether risks to the subjects are serious or minimal, it is the researcher's responsibility to detect any negative consequences of participating. Furthermore, the researcher must ameliorate these negative effects, even if they are long-term. This may require following up on subjects long after an investigation has been completed. Perhaps less obviously, Principle I also requires that subjects in the control condition be offered the treatment provided to those in the experimental condition should this be demonstrated to be beneficial.

Finally, Principle J makes clear that, unless arrangements have been made between the researcher and the subject prior to the data collection, all information collected in the course of the project is *confidential*. This is not a principle to be taken lightly. Offhand comments to others about some silly thing a subject did during a study serve only to undermine the respectability of the researcher, the research, and psychology as a discipline. In other cases, the information gained from a subject may be very sensitive and could cause the person great distress if learned by others outside the experiment. When the information is sensitive, plans for how to maintain confidentiality, such as by coding the data numerically or storing them in locked cabinets for which only the investigator has a key, should be discussed with the subject as part of the informed consent procedure.

ETHICAL DILEMMAS

Although these guidelines aid researchers in their decisions about how and when to conduct a research project, they are only guidelines, not laws; and researchers can stray from them with legal impunity. For example, a researcher who learns from a subject that he or she plans to commit a serious crime may be morally justified (and in some cases legally required) to breach confidentiality and report this information to the appropriate authorities. In fact, evidence supplied during the course of a research project can be subpoenaed by a court. Furthermore, these ethical guidelines were developed to apply to a broad array of research procedures and to reflect the ethical beliefs of a great number of psychologists. As such, they do not address ethical questions that some people find especially important—for example, when it is acceptable to observe behavior and when such observation constitutes a violation of privacy, or whether it is ever acceptable to use deception in research or whether such practices betray an ingrained disrespect for human dignity.

PRIVACY

Privacy refers to an invisible physical or psychological buffer zone or boundary around a person (Sieber & Stanley, 1988). Not uncommonly, research is designed to elicit information from within those boundaries, such as research on sexual behaviors, child-rearing practices, or personal relationships. In some cases the researcher is able to ask permission prior to gathering this information. When subjects voluntarily complete a questionnaire on their buying habits or religious beliefs, they demonstrate their willingness to share this private information. In other cases researchers may observe people who are unaware that they are being watched. For example, in one investigation men were observed by means of a periscope to study the effect of invasion of personal space on speed and rate of urination. In the condition in which the subject's personal space was invaded, a confederate (a person who knows about the experiment) in a public restroom would urinate in the urinal next to the subject. In the noninvasion condition, the confederate was not present (Middlemist, Knowles & Matter, 1976). Obviously, in this study there was no opportunity to gain informed consent from the subjects. If you were a member of an IRB reviewing a proposal for this study, what would your decision be? Would you allow the study to be conducted as described, would you suggest some modifications, or would you deny permission for it to be undertaken?

DECEPTION

In a now famous study of obedience by Stanley Milgram (1963), subjects were instructed to administer "shocks" to another person whenever that person made errors in a learning and memory study. The subjects in this study were 40 males of various backgrounds, aged 20 to 50, who had responded to a newspaper advertisement for subjects in a learning and memory study. The subjects were paid $4.50 on arriving at the laboratory and were told that the money was theirs no matter what happened in the study.

Each subject was led to believe that he would be the "teacher" and would be administering shocks to another subject, the "learner," whenever the learner made an error in memorizing lists of paired works. In actuality, the learner was a confederate who was only pretending to be shocked.

The subject sat in front of a control panel with 30 switches marked with voltage levels from 15 to 450 volts. The switches also had labels ranging from "Slight Shock" to "Danger: Severe Shock." The final two switches were each labeled "XXX." The learner was in a separate room.

All of the subjects gave shocks up to 300 volts, at which level the learner pounded on the wall and no longer made responses. Of the 40 subjects, 14 stopped before reaching the highest voltage level, and 26 continued to the highest level. The level of compliance was much greater than anticipated.

Milgram was criticized by colleagues, the press, and the general public for deceiving his subjects and causing them to experience the stress associated with a distasteful truth about themselves. However, based on immediate debriefings and one-year follow-up interviews with his subjects, Milgram (1977) reported that only about 1% of the subjects told him that they wished they had not participated in the study; Milgram also reported that most of the subjects said that they were very glad they had.

The positive reaction of Milgram's subjects to being deceived in a psychological research appears not to be unusual. Pihl, Zacchia and Zeichner (1981) interviewed subjects who had participated in research involving deception, shock, and alcohol. Of these subjects, only 19% reported being bothered by any part of the study; 4% (approximately one-fifth of this 19%) were bothered by the deception, whereas most were bothered by the consumption of the alcohol and the speed with which it was consumed. In another investigation, 464 subjects were asked their opinions of the research projects in which they had been involved (Smith & Richardson 1983). The subjects who had experienced deception in research projects reported that they had gained more educational benefits and had enjoyed those experiences more than was reported by the subjects who had not experienced deception.

Researchers investigating subjects' reactions to research suspect that debriefing is an important step in making subjects feel positive toward an experience that involved deception. In a replication of Milgram's obedience study, only 4% of debriefed subjects wished they had not participated, but approximately 50% of subjects who had not been debriefed wished they had not participated (Ring, Wallston & Corey, 1970).

In some research, however, debriefing itself may be unethical. In research in which subjects act cruelly or prejudicially, it may be worse to point out their behavior than not to debrief them. For example, imagine that a person with crutches stumbles in front of you and drops some books and that for whatever reason you choose not to assist the person. It may be more damaging to learn that your behavior was observed and recorded than it would be to simply go on your way without realizing that you were part of a research project.

Perhaps deception in research is more of a problem for researchers and ethicists than for the subjects of the investigations. And perhaps that is how it should be, since the goal of ethical treatment of research participants is that they not be discomforted by the procedures of the investigations. The evidence that most subjects are not distressed by the deception that they have faced in research suggests that researchers have succeeded in minimizing the negative effects of the deception.

This discussion should not be construed as an argument in favor of using deception in research. It is preferable to avoid deception, and some observers would say that the use of deception is never justified. Nonetheless, considering that roughly 44% of psychological research with human subjects involves deception (Leavitt 1991), it is unlikely that the use of deception will cease in the near future. It is important, though, that people who oppose deception in research remain vocal, because they play an important role in maintaining the diligent effort to minimize deception's negative effects on the subjects of psychological research.

ETHICAL TREATMENT OF ANIMAL SUBJECTS

Psychological research involving animals as subjects makes up approximately 7% of all research published by the APA (Miller, 1985). The results of animal research,

"WHAT'LL IT BE — A HYPOTHETICAL MOUSE IN A THEORETICAL MAZE, A SUPPOSITIONAL GUINEA PIG TESTING A HYPOTHETICAL DRUG, OR A THEORETICAL RHESUS MONKEY WITH A SUPPOSITIONAL DISEASE?"

Courtesy of Sidney Harris

however, laid the cornerstone of much of present-day psychology. Pavlov's research on classical conditioning, Thorndike's instrumental conditioning research, and Skinner's operant conditioning research have provided important foundations for our present-day understanding of animal and human learning.

Although specific requirements and regulations protect the welfare of animal research subjects, animal rights supporters have become quite vocal and active in recent years. Often these activists try to bring public attention to what they perceive as the mistreatment of animals in unnecessary or poorly conducted research. Unfortunately, some members of animal rights groups feel justified in breaking into laboratories to destroy equipment and data and to "liberate" animals. Between 1981 and 1990, 71 illegal acts against animal research facilities were committed, causing damage with an estimated cost of $10 million (Erikson, 1990).

Animal rights supporters differ in their assessment of the value of animal research. Some simply want to ensure that the animals are treated humanely and that only necessary research is conducted. Others demand a total ban on animal research (Erikson, 1990). In rebutting the arguments of critics opposed to animal research, many researchers have cataloged the advances and benefits that have directly resulted from animal research. In psychology, Neal Miller (1985) has connected the results of animal research to advances in psychotherapy; behavioral medicine; rehabilitation of neuromuscular disorders; understanding and alleviation of the effects of stress and of constant pain; drug treatment of anxiety, psychosis and Parkinson's disease; knowledge about drug addiction and relapse; treatment of premature infants in incubators; understanding of the relationship of aging and memory loss; and the treatment of anorexia nervosa, among others.

Animal rights activism has encouraged scientists to use animals more efficiently and to develop alternative methods that do not require the use of animals (Erikson, 1990). Partly as a reaction to public concern for the ethical treatment of animal subjects, the APA has developed a set of guidelines for animal researchers to use in their research; these are presented in Box 2.3.

In summary, the principles maintain that animals must be treated humanely; that treatments involving pain, stress, or privation be used only when absolutely necessary; and that surgical procedures be performed using anesthetics and techniques that avoid infection and minimize pain. The personnel that interact with the animals must be well-trained and must be supervised by a psychologist who is trained and experienced in the care of laboratory animals. And of course, the animals must be treated in accordance with local, state (or provincial), and federal laws.

The U.S. Department of Agriculture is responsible for regulating and inspecting animal laboratory facilities. In addition to mandating inspections, the Animal Welfare Act of 1985 requires institutions to establish Institutional Animal Care and Use Committees. These committees are similar to the IRBs for human research and must review proposals for animal research that will occur at the institution (Erikson, 1990). The goal of the Animal Care and Use Committees, as well as of the laboratory inspections, is to ensure that the animals are housed and treated humanely.

Animal research has played an important historical role in the development of psychology as a discipline, and it is continuing to contribute to psychological science and human betterment. Only time will tell if psychological research involving animal subjects will continue in the future or if other methods will replace it.

APA PRINCIPLES FOR THE CARE AND USE OF ANIMALS

Box 2.3

An investigator of animal behavior strives to advance understanding of basic behavioral principles and/or to contribute to the improvement of human health and welfare. In seeking these ends, the investigator ensures the welfare of animals and treats them humanely. Laws and regulations notwithstanding, an animal's immediate protection depends upon the scientist's own conscience.

a. The acquisition, care, use, and disposal of all animals are in compliance with current federal, state or provincial, and local laws and regulations.

b. A psychologist trained in research methods and experienced in the care of laboratory animals closely supervises all procedures involving animals and is responsible for ensuring appropriate consideration of their comfort, health, and humane treatment.

c. Psychologists ensure that all individuals using animals under their supervision have received explicit instruction in experimental methods and in the care, maintenance, and handling of the species being used. Responsibilities and activities of individuals participating in a research project are consistent with their respective competencies.

d. Psychologists make every effort to minimize discomfort, illness, and pain of animals. A procedure subjecting animals to pain, stress, or privation is used only when an alternative procedure is unavailable and the goal is justified by its prospective scientific, educational, or applied value. Surgical procedures are performed under appropriate anesthesia; techniques to avoid infection and minimize pain are followed during and after surgery.

e. When it is appropriate that the animal's life be terminated, it is done rapidly and painlessly.

SOURCE: American Psychological Association (1981). "Ethical Principles of Psychologists," *American Psychologist* 36: 638.

ETHICAL TREATMENT OF THE RESULTS OF RESEARCH

Another important area of ethical concern for researchers involves how the results of a research project are handled. Basically, a researcher wants to feel confident that another reseaarcher's article represents a research project that really occurred, that it occurred in the manner described, that the actual results are the ones given in the article, and that these results are presented in a clear, straightforward manner. Unfortunately, some individuals take shortcuts in the research process or attempt to present research results in a manner that allows them to fit the researcher's original expectations more closely than is objectively warranted.

In recent years more attention and publicity have been focused on misconduct in science than used to be in the past, in part because several cases of fraud in govenment-funded research have been uncovered. In 1988, Stephen Breuning, once considered an authority on the treatment of mental retardation with tranquilizers and stimulants, pleaded guilty to two counts of fraud. He had been charged with taking federal grant money for research and falsifying his "research" results.

Scientific misconduct is not new. Isaac Newton is said to have purposely adjusted his data to make a rival look worse; and Gregor Mendel is suspected of having tampered with his data, since some of his results match the ideal numbers to an improbable degree (*Discover*, 1988). Recently, even Freud has come under suspicion of having distorted facts to suit his theory (Raymond, 1991). The most infamous example in psychology is that of Cyril Burt, an early twentieth-century investigator of intelligence and heredity (Roman, 1988). It was learned after his death that Burt not only had fabricated data, but had invented subjects and research assistants.

Scientific misconduct can occur in a number of ways. A researcher can fabricate data, as Bruening and Burt did, or a researcher can alter data from actual studies, as Newton and Freud are accused of doing. There is general agreement that data altering and fabrication are serious breaches of ethics, but gray areas emerge when authorities discuss the proper way to make research findings public. Some researchers publish many articles from one large set of data, breaking the project into blocks of what is sometimes called the "least publishable unit." Critics perceive this as an inappropriate way to gain prestige and a wasteful use of journal space that could be used to present entirely new research. But others argue that journals often limit the number of pages that can be devoted to a single article, and results of large studies cannot always be presented within those limits. Moreover, tenure and promotion in the academic world often depend on the number of research articles published, as well as on their quality; thus a researcher's job may hinge on his or her publishing multiple papers on one topic.

Another bone of contention among researchers is that some researchers present results to the popular press before these results are published in the professional press. This is a problem because the quality of the research is not subjected to judgment by a panel of professionals when it appears in the popular press. Further, the popular press frequently fails to understand the full import and context of the research and consequently misrepresents the research to the public. The counterargument here is that the review process is too slow and that the public has a right to know about potential research breakthroughs as soon as possible (Grisso et al., 1991).

Although it has received more publicity in recent years, there is no evidence to suggest that scientific misconduct is on the rise. In general, researchers are conscientious and honest, presenting research as it was done and presenting results has they occurred. Inevitably, it is the rare case of misconduct that the public hears about.

ETHICAL CONSIDERATIONS IN THE SPONSORSHIP OF RESEARCH

A final area of ethical concern related to the ethical treatment of research results involves the sponsorship of research. Research can sometimes be very expensive, and it is not uncommon for researchers to apply for and receive grants from either the government or private industry to fund their projects. However, funding by an outside source introduces another area in which an individual's ethics can be compromised.

An organization that funds a project may expect to apply the results of that research. For example, NASA funds research on motion sickness so that it can apply the results to the motion sickness experienced by some astronauts. Because it is sometimes difficult to foresee what a study's results may be used for, the APA suggests that researchers familiarize themselves with a funding organization's mission and with how the organization has used the results of previous research (American Psychological Association, 1982).

Courtesy of Sidney Harris

This issue of the use of research leads to a final point—that knowledge is a double-edged sword. For every piece of information we gain that can be used for "good," we also gain knowledge that can be used for "bad." For example, information on how to defuse stereotyping also provides information on how to instill it. The skill to make material easier to read and more coherent is attended by the skill to make reading material incomprehensible and opaque. Knowledge of animal behavior can be used to teach a dog to be gentle or to teach it to attack.

We tend to believe that misuse of scientific information only occurs in science fiction. Yet, in the early twentieth century, Goddard, a psychologist, used the newly developed intelligence test to "demonstrate" that immigrating Jews, Italians, Poles, and Russians were of inferior intelligence and would cause the deterioration of the American intellect. This was based on the scores recorded for immigrants who were tested on Ellis Island as they arrived in America. The testing was done in English, regardless of the language spoken by the immigrant. By his arguments based on these results, Goddard helped convinced Congress to enact very strict immigration laws (Sieber & Stanley, 1988). There are no guidelines for dealing with the double edge of research; each individual must consider this question and make his or her own decision about whether or not to pursue research in a particular area, given the possible consequences.

CONCLUSION

Research in psychology can be a rewarding endeavor for the researcher, the subjects, the consumers of the research, and the beneficiaries of advances in science, but only when that research is conducted and reported in an ethical manner.

Psychological researchers are guided in their ethical decision-making by laws and by the APA guidelines for ethical treatment of human and animal research subjects. Ultimately, however, the researcher's own conscience determines whether the research is conducted and reported ethically.

Given the thousands of colleges, universities, and other institutions in America and around the world at which psychological and nonpsychological research is conducted, it is encouraging that so few complaints of unethical treatment are made. Scientists respect the dignity of their subjects and their disciplines.

IMPORTANT TERMS AND CONCEPTS

Institutional Review Board (IRB)

informed consent

American Psychological Association (APA)

APA Ethical Principles in the Conduct of Research with Human Participants

at risk/at minimal risk

debriefing

free consent

mortality effect

privacy

deception

APA Principles for the Care and Use of Animals

QUESTIONS AND EXERCISES

1. Define *informed consent* and *free consent*, and describe a situation in which informed consent might be given but free consent might be impossible to obtain.

2. Consider the role of deception in psychological research. How strictly do you define the term *deception*? Is deception used when a subject is misled about the purpose of a study, such as by being told that a study is being conducted to investigate how well a small child likes a toy when it really is being conducted to assess the interactions between the mother and the child? Is deception used when a subject is not given full information about the purpose of a project, such as by being told that the purpose is to investigate natural language usage when actually it is to identify the use of swear words in conversation? The line between providing enough information and providing too little information may be very fine. Determine for yourself what types of situations you would find acceptable and what types would be unacceptable to you as a researcher, as a subject, or as an IRB member.

For each of the following questions, explore your own feelings about the situation that is described and the issues that are addressed. There are no right and wrong answers to ethical questions, so don't focus on what you think you should say, but rather on your own attitudes. You may wish to share your answers with others; you may be surprised at the diversity of opinions.

3. You are a member of an IRB reviewing the following proposal. A researcher would like to determine how much of a person's casual conversation is composed of slang and figurative expressions. The results of this research would add to the body of knowledge in language comprehension, and would aid instructors and learners of English as a foreign language. To collect data on this topic, the researcher would like permission to tape-record conversations at restaurants, without the participants' knowledge. The participants would all be strangers to the researcher; the conversations would be coded for slang and figurative expressions only, and then the tapes would be destroyed. The participants would never know that they had been involved in this study.

    a. What questions would you ask the researcher?
    b. What alternative procedures might you suggest?
    c. Would you require changes in the proposal? If so, what would they be?
    d. What APA ethical principles are or might be violated by this project?
    e. Would you allow this project to be conducted? Why or why not?

4. With the advancement of the science of medicine has also come an increase in the number of survivors of closed head injuries and strokes. These individuals suffer brain damage as a result of some external or internal trauma to the brain. To study the effect of a drug that would be beneficial to these individuals, animal studies are conducted. You are on the Institutional Animal Care and Use Committee for a drug company that is conducting this research. An unpleasant aspect of the research is that the animals—in this case, cats—must suffer brain damage prior to testing of the drugs. Brain damage is induced under general anesthesia, when a small predetermined part of the brain is destroyed surgically.

    a. As a member of the Animal Care and Use Committee, what questions would you ask the researcher? Would you allow this research to be conducted? If not, why not? If so, would you ask the researcher for any modifications or additions to the procedure?
    b. Consider your own personal feelings about animal research. Do you feel that the type of research described here is necessary? Would you be comfortable con-

ducting this type of research? Would your feelings be any different if the animals involved were rats instead of cats? Why or why not?

5. An acquaintance approaches you about conducting a survey that would assess racist attitudes in your community. The organization this individual represents agrees that you may publish the results under your name, but it also reserves the right to use the results in its advertisements and literature.

a. Considering your own personal views, what information would you wish to know about this organization?

b. You discover that the organization's philosophy agrees with your own, but you also discover that the organization has distorted research results in the past to suit its own perceived interests. Given this information, would you still be willing to conduct their research? Why, why not, or on what conditions?

3

Observational Studies and Descriptive Statistics

PART I: OBSERVATIONAL STUDIES

Research in psychology can be carried out in a multitude of ways; a researcher investigating language comprehension, for example, may conduct memory experiments or reading time studies. The researcher may ask subjects to create their own sentences, or to solve anagrams and other word puzzles. The researcher might look at how different personality traits relate to the way the person uses language, or at how different characteristics of the language make it easy or difficult to understand. The researcher may have very sophisticated equipment—perhaps the capability to conduct a CAT scan of the brain as a person listens to language—or the researcher may have no equipment other than a pencil and paper. The number of ways research can be conducted is limited only by the researchers' imagination. In fact, new methodologies are being developed all of the time. Luckily, all of these different ways of conducting research can be categorized, and learning about each category of methodologies serves as a strong foundation for evaluating all of the different types of research in psychology.

In the table of contents for this book, the titles of chapters 3 through 12 reflect a way of categorizing methods of collecting data. In this chapter we will focus on observational research and on how to describe the data collected through observational research (as well as through other research approaches) by using statistics.

OBSERVATIONAL RESEARCH DESIGNS

"People watching" can be a very enjoyable and entertaining pastime. But scientific observations of people or animals involves more forethought and planning than does normal casual observation. When done carefully and correctly, however, observational studies can provide a wealth of information that casual "people watching" would miss.

Uses of Observational Studies   Observational research can be especially useful as a starting point for research on a new topic. Instead of simply jumping into a full-scale laboratory experiment, one can save much time and effort by first making some careful observations. For example, a researcher may be interested in how children play and in how interactions between and among children can be affected by the size of the group. Before delving into a complicated project in which children of various ages are combined into groups of various sizes, the researcher should have some sense of what to look for. Our researcher may wish to begin by conducting some observational studies, perhaps observing children at a playground or at a daycare center. Do boys and girls play differently? What types of play occur? Is it aggressive or peaceful? Is it independent or cooperative? Does the type of play vary with age? Does the same child stay with one activity or switch rapidly from one

Courtesy of Sidney Harris

type of play to another? By conducting an observational study initially, a researcher can learn what types of behavior are common and what types are unusual, and thus can do a better job of interpreting the results of later laboratory research.

Observational research need not be exclusively used as the starting place for a series of studies; it can also be helpful later in the process. Researchers who conduct most of their research in the laboratory can benefit by taking their studies to the field. By conducting observational studies later in the process, a researcher can learn whether the results from the laboratory also occur in the natural environment. If children's play behavior in the laboratory involves more cooperative play when there are more girls in the group than boys, does this also occur on the playground?

Observational studies, of course, can stand on their own merits. Often observation is the only way a particular hypothesis can be tested. To learn how the social order among a group of chimpanzees affects their behavior at feeding time, a researcher must observe. An observational approach may also be the best way to determine whether a new speed limit is being observed or ignored by drivers. Thus, although probably underutilized (during one 70-year period, less than 8% of the published research on children and adolescents involved observation of naturally occurring behaviors; Wright, 1960), observation can be a highly useful and informative research approach.

TYPES OF OBSERVATIONAL RESEARCH DESIGNS: NATURALISTIC OBSERVATION AND OBSERVATION WITH INTERVENTION

Observational studies can be divided into two types: naturalistic observation and observation with intervention. Observational studies can vary considerably along a continuum of intervention. In naturalistic observation, there is no intervention; but in a field experiment—a type of observational study with intervention—the researcher in effect conducts a laboratory experiment without the laboratory. Between these two extremes lie studies involving varying amounts of intervention. We will work our way through the continuum in this section.

Naturalistic Observation   Studies using **naturalistic observation** involve unobtrusively observing behaviors in the natural setting. In this type of research the investigator does nothing to interfere with the subjects' behavior. In fact, often the subjects do not realize they are being observed.

It is not always possible (or ethical) to observe subjects without their being aware of it. In these cases, the researcher may make some preliminary efforts to reduce the effect of his or her presence. One approach a researcher might use is called **desensitization**; it involves slowly moving closer and closer to the subjects until the researcher can sit near or even among them. This technique is often used by researchers investigating animal subjects. Another technique commonly used by animal researchers, but also by researchers with human subjects, is called **habituation**. When using a habituation procedure, the researcher appears in the setting numerous times until his or her presence no longer appears to affect the subjects' behavior.

Jane Goodall, the famous ethologist, studied chimpanzees in their natural setting in Africa. She used both habituation and desensitization to study her subjects. Initially, the chimpanzees would flee at the first sight of her. After several weeks, if she sat very still and was totally silent, she could sit within about 60 to 80 yards of the chimps. For the next 5-month period, when she was able to move closer to the chimps, they tended to act aggressive and hostile toward her, shaking sticks and barking at her aggressively. One chimp even came up behind her and hit her in the head. After Goodall spent more than 6 months observing the chimpanzees from a distance, the chimps came to realize that she was no threat and would let her get closer. Eventually some of the chimps even allowed her to touch them and tickle them. However, she and her co-observer realized that this was a mistake, not only because male chimpanzees are large and powerful animals that can easily hurt a human, but also because the interaction of humans with chimps interferes with collecting data on natural behavior (van Lawick-Goodall, 1971).

You will probably not find yourself in Africa observing primates. But the same techniques of habituation and desensitization can be used with humans, as well as with other animal subjects. As a college student conducting research on the role of sex role stereotypes in children's comprehension of stories, I worked with a third-grade class. The teacher suggested that I come to the class several Friday afternoons in a row before attempting to collect any data so that the children would get used to my presence in the classroom. She was suggesting that I use habituation.

Unfortunately, it is nearly impossible to ensure that an observer's presence is not affecting behavior, and the researcher would probably want input from other sources when available. For example, if the observer were in a classroom, the classroom teacher could probably be asked whether the students were still behaving differently. In this way, the researcher could avoid depending on his or her own potentially biased (or simply unknowledgeable) judgment.

Observation with Intervention   Although naturalistic observation studies can be very useful for gaining information about naturally occurring behaviors, in other situations some intervention on the part of the investigator can better answer the research question. Observation studies with intervention can be divided into three types: participant observation, structured observation, and field experiments.

Participant observation.   In **participant observation** studies, the researcher is an active participant in the situation in which the subjects are involved. The researcher may be a **disguised participant** or an **undisguised participant**. When the researcher is an undisguised participant, the other participants are aware that the person is observing their behavior. This a common research method used by anthropologists who join and work with a society while also observing it. If the researcher is a disguised participant, the other participants do not know that the researcher is observing their behavior.

One of the most famous disguised participant studies in psychology was conducted by Rosenhan (1973). Rosenhan wished to investigate whether insanity was functionally distinguishable from sanity. He chose to approach this question by testing whether sane people who had been admitted to psychiatric hospitals would be detected; if they were, this would suggest that insanity is distinguishable from sanity. On the other hand, if the pseudopatients were not be detected, this would support the thesis that insanity is not functionally distinguishable from sanity. The implication of the latter is that labeling people as mentally ill or as schizophrenic is useless at best and perhaps harmful, since these labels tend to follow people throughout their lives.

In this study eight sane individuals were admitted to 12 psychiatric hospitals. The pseudopatients told the admissions office that they had been hearing voices that said "empty," "hollow," and "thud." After being admitted to the psychiatric ward of the hospitals, each patient immediately ceased simulating any symptoms. The pseudopatients spent their time engaging others in conversation and taking notes on their observations. These notes were taken openly, since nobody seemed to care one way or the other.

The pseudopatients were discharged after an average of 19 days (the range of stay in the hospitals was 7 to 52 days). At discharge, each was given the diagnosis of schizophrenia in remission. None of the pseudopatients was ever detected as being sane by the hospital staff, although about one-third of the real patients realized that the observers were not really ill.

Rosenhan's study provides some food for thought about the nature of mental illness and the effect of diagnoses and labels. In addition, Rosenhan's study provides some interesting information about and insights into life on a psychiatric ward—information that probably could not have been gained without the disguised-participant research design.

Research involving participant observation can be very interesting and often makes fascinating reading, but a potential pitfall of this design is that the observations made by the participant observer are subject to bias. Kirkham (1975), a criminologist, served as an undisguised participant in his research on police work. He went through policy academy training and became a uniformed police officer in a high-crime section of a medium-size city. In his article he describes how his attitude and personality changed during the course of his time as a policeman:

> According to the accounts of my family, colleagues and friends, I began to increasingly display attitudinal and behavioral elements that were entirely foreign to my previous personality—punitiveness, pervasive cynicism and mistrust of others, chronic irritability and free-floating hostility, racism, a diffuse personal anxiety over the menace of crime and criminals that seemed at times to border on the obsessive (Kirkham 1975, p. 19).

In evaluating participant observation research, we need to be aware of the potential for personal biases to slip into the descriptions and observations. Researchers who decide that a participant observation study is the only way to address a particular research problem need to be aware of the possibility of sympathetic or hostile bias and must realize that they are not in a position to recognize bias in themselves. Although not all forms of bias can be avoided, some can be minimized by carefully defining the types of behaviors that will be observed and recorded before entering the observation setting.

Just as the observer can be affected by the situation, the other participants can be affected by the observer. The smaller the group, the more likely it is that the participation of the observer will affect the behavior of the group. Kirkham's participation as a police officer probably had no significant affect on the police force as a whole, although he may have influenced those around him in unknown ways. Similarly, Rosenhan's pseudopatients probably did not alter the psychiatric wards, but there is no way of measuring how (if at all) the presence of the pseudopatients affected the behavior of the staff or other patients around them. Since some of the patients recognized that the pseudopatients were not ill, it is clear that their presence did not go totally unnoticed. The ethical ramifications of a participant observation study must also be considered carefully before data collection begins. What if the real psychiatric patients had become very upset by the presence of the pseudo-patients in Rosenhan's work, or if the other police officers were negatively affected by Kirkham's joining the force? Should these studies have been continued if those adverse circumstances had arisen?

Participant observation studies have limitations that may affect the accuracy and usefulness of the observations being reported, but a researcher can limit the possible problems in a study through careful planning and attention to potential flaws. For example, by preplanning what observations to make and how to make them, the researcher can minimize observer bias. When conducted carefully, the participant observation study can provide invaluable information that could not be gained by any other means.

Structured observation.   Another type of observational study that involves some intervention on the part of the investigator has been called the structured observation study. In participant observation studies, the researcher directly intervenes in the situation being observed by participating in the situation. In **structured observation** studies, the researcher intervenes in a way other than (or in addition to) participating in the situation. These types of studies involve more control than a naturalistic observation, but they also allow the subjects considerable leeway in behaviors. This intervention can be quite extensive or very subtle, but the amount of intervention falls short of that used in a field experiment.

One example of research involving structured observation is work conducted by Piaget in his study of children's cognitive development. Piaget would typically present a child with a situation and then ask the child questions about the situation. Piaget's focus was not on whether the child answered the questions correctly, but rather on how the child reached his or her answers. A classic Piagetian task is the conservation problem.

To address whether a child had grasped the concept of conservation of volume, Piaget would present the child with two balls of clay of equal size. The child would be asked if the balls had the same amounts of clay, and the child would say that they did (if not, the amounts of clay could be changed until the child said that they were the same). Piaget would then change the shape of one of the clay balls, perhaps by rolling it out into a sausage shape, and he would then ask the child if the two shapes had the same amount of clay or different amounts. A child younger than 7 or 8 years is likely to say that they have different amounts of clay, and that the sausage-shaped clay is "bigger." Until a child is 7 or 8 years old, he or she is often misled by perceptual cues, such as shape; but after 7 or 8, the child's realization that no clay was added or taken away from the two pieces of clay becomes more important than their particular shape. Piaget's observations of children led to the development of one of the leading theories of cognitive development.

Piaget's type of research is a type of structured observation. A child's behavior is observed in a situation that was set up by the investigator, and the investigator also interacts directly with the child. The focus is on the child's responses, with the investigator tailoring questions to each child's responses. Thus, unlike an experiment in which efforts are made to extend identical treatment to all subjects within a group, in this type of structured observation each subject may be treated considerably differently.

Piaget's use of structured observation involved a substantial amount of intervention, but not all structured observation does so. Indeed, intervention can be quite minimal. For example, a researcher may add a toy to a preschool playroom and then observe how the children interact with it and with each other in relation to it. This research involves making observations in a natural setting after some minimal intervention.

Field experiments.   **Field experiments** are very controlled observational studies that occur in a natural setting. In a field experiment, the researcher manipulates an independent variable and measures its effect on a dependent variable. For example, a researcher may wish to study altruistic behavior by observing whether subjects will come to the aid of an individual who has dropped some books. Perhaps the researcher wants to know whether how the person is dressed affects helping behavior. In this study, a confederate (research assistant) may dress casually in one condition—perhaps in faded blue jeans, a t-shirt, and sneakers—and dress up more for the other condition—perhaps in a skirt, blouse, and heels. The mode of dress is the independent variable. The confederate then "stumbles" and drops a pile of books in the presence of the subject, and the subject's behavior is observed and recorded. The observations made are the dependent measure. Often in this type of study the subject does not realize that he or she has participated in a research project. Since informed consent cannot be obtained before making the observations, the ethical ramifications of such a project must be considered before it is carried out.

Field experiments are especially useful for conducting research that possesses greater external validity (more generalizability) than research conducted in the laboratory. The particular problems and pitfalls one may encounter in a field experiment are the same as those encountered in a laboratory experiment and will be discussed more thoroughly in Chapter 6.

CHOOSING THE TYPE OF OBSERVATIONAL DESIGN

The type of observational design chosen to study a particular issue depends on a number of factors and often requires the researcher to balance advantages and limitations. Naturalistic observations have the advantage of good generalizability beyond the specific investigation. Field experiments, on the other hand, allow the researcher more control over the environment. Participant observation studies offer an insider's view of a situation, but at the risk of biased observations and researcher influence on the situation being observed. Structured observation studies may represent a compromise among the flaws of other observational studies, but they enjoy neither the full strength of the conclusions of a field experiment nor the full generalizability of naturalistic observations. A researcher must weigh carefully the advantages and disadvantages of each technique, along with practical considerations such as the time, money, and assistance available, and the ethical ramifications of the research. With these factors in mind, the researcher proceeds to design a project that maximizes advantages and minimizes flaws.

CONCEPT QUESTIONS 3.1

A researcher is interested in how the elderly are treated in our society. She asks your advice regarding different observational methods. Together you consider a naturalistic observation study, a disguised participant observation study, and an undisguised participant observation study. Describe how each of these types of observational studies might be carried out.

DATA COLLECTION

In the process of designing an observational study, the researcher must also decide what behaviors to observe and how to record these behaviors. In other words, the researcher must decide what variable to measure and how to measure it. The primary concerns of data collection in any type of scientific research are that the dependent measure be **reliable** and that it be **valid**.

Reliability   **Reliability** is the consistency with which one gets the same results. Just as a reliable vehicle is a vehicle that will start over and over, a reliable procedure for collecting data is one that will yield the same results when repeated over and over. If I try to measure my backyard by the number of steps it takes me to walk across it, and sometimes it takes 20 steps and sometimes it takes 19, then my measurement technique—and hence the resulting measurements—are not especially reliable. However, my pacing method would be more reliable than a method consisting of asking five people to estimate the width of my yard by simply looking at it, assuming that each person provided estimates that differed by more than a few feet. If, however, I use a tape measure and find that the yard is 40 feet wide each time I measure it, then the tape measure technique is the most reliable of these three methods. To determine whether an observation technique is reliable, a researcher may calculate its **interobserver reliability**.

Interobserver reliability is the degree to which a measurement procedure yields consistent results when different observers use the procedure. For example, two observers may be watching children play and may be categorizing the play activity as independent play, parallel play (two or more children engaged in the same activity but with little interaction, such as coloring), cooperative play (two or more children engaged in the same activity with interaction, such as a board game), or aggressive play. They watch the same child for 5 minutes and categorize the play activity every 30 seconds. Each subject will have made 10 observations, but all of their observations may not agree; perhaps they disagreed on one occasion when one observer interpreted the play activity as parallel and the other interpreted it as cooperative. To determine how reliable the observers' measurements of play activity were, we can calculate their interobserver reliability. Here is one general formula for interobserver reliability:

$$\frac{\text{Number of agreement}}{\text{Number of opportunities for agreement}} \times 100$$

For our example, the interobserver reliability would be as follows:

$$\frac{9}{10} \times 100 = 90\% \text{ agreement}$$

The closer agreement is to 100%, the greater is the reliability of the measure. When the preceding formula for interobserver reliability is used, an agreement rate of over 90% is usually considered to be quite good, but the benchmark could be lower (or higher) for a given research project. We'll discuss interobserver reliability more thoroughly in the second half of this chapter.

Other types of reliability can also be measured, especially when the dependent variable is a score from a psychological measure. **Test–retest reliability** refers to the consistency of scores on a test when the same person takes the same test twice. **Equivalent forms reliability** refers to the consistency between scores when the same person takes two versions of the same test. **Split–half reliability** is the consistency within a test and is calculated by comparing scores on half of a test with scores on the other half of the test. These types of reliability, as well as techniques for calculating them, will be discussed more thoroughly in Chapter 4.

Validity   Although it is important, even essential, that a dependent variable be reliable, it is equally important that the measure be valid. Two observers can agree 100% when making observations and yet both could be making equally inaccurate observations. **Validity** is the extent to which a measurement tool or technique measures what it purports to be measuring. Measuring age by counting the number of years or months (or other unit of time) since birth is a valid measure. Measuring age by recording a person's shoe size is not a valid measure.

The reliability of a variable can often be established by looking at the results of other studies that have used the same measurement. If a particular technique has yielded consistent results, it is typically considered reliable. Validity is somewhat harder to determine. In general, the more direct the measure of behavior is, the more faith one can have in its validity. For example, observing what a person eats during a meal is a more valid indicator of calorie consumption than is asking the individual to recall what he or she ate. The individual's recollection could be colored by not wishing to appear a glutton, as well as by a simple inability to remember everything. In much psychological research, determining the validity of a measure entails careful consideration of possible alternative measures and an act of faith. Unfortunately, for lack of a better way to determine validity, measures are too often assumed valid until someone develops a good argument against them.

CONCEPT QUESTIONS 3.2	1. Two researchers attempt to judge whether individuals are reading, studying, writing, or visiting at library tables. They observe 45 people and agree 43 times. What is their interobserver reliability? What does this suggest about their measurement technique?
	2. A researcher attempts to judge the hunger of a dog by how much food the dog eats. Some researchers, however, believe that dogs eat even when they aren't hungry. If the second researcher is correct, is the measurement of food eaten a valid measure of hunger? Could this measure be reliable?

Operational Definitions   To enable the researcher (and other evaluators of the research) to determine a dependent measure's reliability and validity, exactly what the researcher measured must be clearly defined. As discussed in Chapter 1, this type of definition is called an *operational definition*. Operational definitions are of primary importance in observational studies, where only a very few specific behaviors are being observed. (Observational studies with a broader focus will be discussed more thoroughly in the section on narrative records.)

Suppose that you are interested in determining whether vehicle drivers stop fully at stop signs. The temptation might be simply to tell your observers to note whether the driver stops or does not stop. *Stop* is a word we've all known since we were tykes; it certainly doesn't need to be defined, right? Now, imagine that two observers watch the same driver approach the intersection. The driver slows down, coming very close to, but not quite making a complete stop. One observer records this behavior as not stopping, but the other (who perhaps has a tendency to roll through stop signs) records it as a stop. Even the most basic of behaviors must be operationally defined to avoid any confusion.

Categories of behavior may also need to be broken into subcategories to be useful to the investigator. Suppose that an individual drives through the intersection without slowing down. As our categories stand, this behavior would be recorded as "not stopping." But it may become more meaningful if "not stopping" is divided into such subcategories as rolling stops, slowing but not stopping, and driving through without slowing. Each of these new subcategories, of course, would need its own operational definition, too.

An operational definition should be sufficiently clear that a person who does not know what is being investigated can understand the definition without requiring additional information. A clear operational definition is one that you can come back to a day, a week, or a year later and understand and use in the same manner; that is, it will still be clear to you how the behavior was and is to be recorded, and the procedure will yield reliable recordings.

Even when operational definitions are clear, observers can still become confused. It is worth the effort to train observers so that all are using the operational definitions in the same manner.

TECHNIQUES FOR DATA COLLECTION

What will be observed and how it will be observed are determined by the research question. Thus, for instance, what and how you observe people in an airport would vary considerably depending on whether you are looking for security risks or for a pocket to pick. It is therefore impossible to describe a single best way to make observations. Following are several techniques that have been used in observational research; each has its pitfalls, but each has advantages, as well.

Narrative Records **Narrative records** are running records of behavior observed in a given situation. They can be very complete or rather sketchy. Narrative records can be created by audiotaping or videotaping a situation, or by writing notes by hand. Later these notes can be organized, and various hypotheses about them can be tested.

The subjectivity of narrative records can vary substantially, depending on the observer's inclinations. Especially with handwritten notes, a decision must be made early on about how much leeway the observer should have in drawing inferences about a situation. If the observer is watching people in a cafeteria, should the observer note that "a young couple distanced themselves from others and enjoyed a private conversation," or should the notes include "just the facts"—perhaps, "a male and female, each apparently of college age, sat at a table no closer than two tables from anyone else; at this table the two individuals talked with each other." The amount of subjectivity allowed in a record may be determined in part by the purpose of the data collection. A narrative record that is to serve as a source of research hypotheses may be more useful with subjective information; but a record that is to serve as a faithful reflection of the behaviors observed, so that specific hypotheses may be tested, may be best developed with rather strict objectivity.

As alluded to earlier, operational definitions are of less use in narrative records than in other types of research. The reason for this is that the focus of research in which narrative records are used as a means of data collection is often broad, and specific behaviors are not of primary interest. Of course, clear writing still mandates that all terms be defined; a researcher would not want to use a term such as *interaction* without explaining whether this was a verbal or nonverbal interaction between people, animals, inanimate objects, or some combination of the three. Operational definitions grow in importance as the research becomes focused on a few specific behaviors. Those behaviors must be carefully and precisely defined so that other researchers and consumers of research can understand what was being observed and can evaluate the conclusions drawn from the observations.

From a practical point of view, if narrative records are to be written, one must figure out a way to make notes in an unobtrusive manner. It may be possible to desensitize or habituate the subjects to the presence of the observer and to the observer's notetaking, but this takes considerable time—something that not all researchers have. The observer may have to make cryptic notes on scraps of paper to avoid disrupting the setting, or may even have to leave the setting on occasion to make notes in private. The notes' accuracy depends on their being made as soon after observing as possible; the longer the delay between observing and noting, the more likely the notes are to be contaminated by biases and memory distortions of the observer.

A practical problem with narrative records involves deciding what to do with them once they have been made. Narrative records provide lots of information, but organizing that information can sometimes be quite cumbersome. Perhaps a person has an audiotape and field notes of a verbal interaction between a child and a researcher. The researcher may be interested in the types of questions a child asks. To determine this, the researcher must first have the audiotape transcribed into a written record. Then the transcription must be coded, with each question categorized as one or another of the several types the researcher has recognized. This coding must be done by more than one person, to allow the reliability of the coding system to be assessed. The field notes must also be coded according to some system that the researcher has established. The coding of the notes and tapes serves to reduce the volume of information to a more manageable amount; this is referred to as a **data reduction** procedure. The data reduction process can be time-consuming, but it makes testing hypotheses and drawing conclusions from the observations considerably easier.

Narrative records do not always have to be coded; full narrative records in their original form can be an excellent source of information when a researcher is first investigating a possible area of inquiry. For example, a researcher with a hypothesis about the behavior of fans at sporting events may wish to observe several different sporting events and create a narrative record of behavior. This narrative record may allow the researcher to refine the hypothesis, as well as to develop operational definitions for projects with a more specific focus.

Checklists   In observational studies focused on a limited number of specific behaviors, operational definitions can be developed. Characteristics of the situation and the subjects of the observation are also likely to be important. To help in recording these specific types of information, a **checklist** can be used to guide observations and to save time by organizing the record-making procedure.

In general, two types of checklists can be designed. Often they are combined on the same sheet of paper. A **static checklist** is used to record characteristics that will not change in the course of the observation; these might include characteristics about the setting, such as where the observations are being made, what the weather is like (if relevant), and how many people are present. Also included on the static checklist are characteristics of the subjects, such as gender and age. Other characteristics may also be important depending on the type of study. Observations in a nursing home, for example, might include information about the subject's state of health. Observations of driving behavior might include indentification of the make and color of the vehicle.

An **action checklist** is used to record the presence or absence of specific behaviors and characteristics. An action checklist could be used to record the types of play behavior a child demonstrates on the playground over a period of time, or it could be used to record what a small group of people do in the library. Table 3.1 presents an action checklist containing data about driving behavior at a 3-way intersection.

TABLE 3.1   *Driving behavior at a 3-way intersection.*

Vehicle	Stop	Slow	Run
1. car		*	
2. car		*	
3. car		*	
4. bus	*		
5. car		*	
6. car		*	
7. car		*	
8. car	*		
9. truck	*		
10. car	*		

Depending on how an action checklist is organized, it can simply provide information about the frequency of different categories of behavior, or, when combined with time information, it can provide information about the order and duration of behaviors.

For either type of checklist, each characteristic or category of behavior must receive its own operational definition. For example, the operational definition of a vehicle slowing at an intersection might be that the tire rotation decreases as the vehicle approaches the intersection, reaching a minimum rate of rotation at or near the crosswalk, after which rotation increases. Stopping at the intersection might be defined as occurring when all four tires cease rotating within a half-vehicle length of the crosswalk. It is a good idea to make some practice observations with the operational definitions. Even when it seems that the definitions are clear and the observations are straightforward, surprises can cause ambiguity in the operational definitions. Suppose a red car stops behind three other cars at the intersection. The red car stops as each other car stops at the crosswalk, but then the red car rolls through the crosswalk when it reaches the stop sign. How would you code this behavior? An additional "miscellaneous" category is often included to accommodate surprises that emerge during the "real" data collection.

Checklists have the disadvantage of focusing on a relatively small subset of behaviors or characteristics and ignoring all others—a disadvantage that can be avoided by using a narrative record approach to data collection. On the other hand, checklists have the advantage that the data do not need to be reduced by coding; they are already organized and thus are easier to summarize.

CONCEPT QUESTIONS 3.3	Suppose that a researcher wishes to observe the frequency of three behaviors in the classroom: visiting, working alone, and watching the teacher. The researcher will observe this classroom for 1 hour and will note the behavior of a specific child once every 2 minutes. Other information about the child that must be recorded includes the child's gender, age, and seating position in the classroom. Design the checklist for this study. Is it an action checklist, a static checklist, or a combination of both?

TYPES OF DATA COLLECTED

Many different types of questions can be answered by referring to data from observational studies. Information about the existence of subject and situational characteristics can be obtained; and when the data are organized, they can provide information about what characteristics tend to occur together. These characteristics might have been recorded on a static checklist, or they might be gleaned from narrative records.

Observations of behaviors supply even more information. Simply recording whether a type of behavior occurs provides information about the frequency of its occurrence. For example, an observer may watch a classroom and note whether students talk to the other students at inappropriate times. This information would allow the researcher to estimate how often this behavior occurs on a given day.

How often a behavior occurs may not be sufficient in and of itself to a researcher. To give a context to frequency data, the researcher may also need information related to time, such as the duration of the behavior or the times of day at which it tends to occur. For example, an observer who watches a classroom for whole days might record not only whether a behavior occurs but at what time it occurs. Later analysis of the data may suggest a pattern to the behavior; for example, the students may be more apt to talk inappropriately before lunch, but less apt to do so immediately after recess. Information about the duration of behaviors can also be recorded and may supply additional important insights into a research area. Information about frequency, duration, and timing can be obtained about several subjects or about one subject. The information can be gained from narrative records, if they are complete enough, or from checklists designed to record this information directly.

Sometimes information is more useful if characteristics and behaviors have been rated rather than simply noted as existing or not. Consider the example of drivers at an intersection. Instead of noting whether vehicles stopped at, slowed for, or ran the stop sign, observers could rate each driver on how fast the vehicle was going—perhaps on a 5-point scale, where 1 = stops and 5 = runs sign without slowing. Characteristics can also be rated. Observers may rate each member of a couple on attractiveness to test the hypothesis that couples are composed of people of roughly equal attractiveness.

Ratings provide a more continuous, less categorical description of behavior or characteristics than do checklists. Unfortunately, because ratings require the making of subjective judgments, it is more difficult to obtain agreement between raters than between checklist markers.

Scales of Measurement   In psychology, researchers assume that anything that exists—be it a physical characteristic, such as a person's height, or a psychological construct, such as extroversion—exists in some amount and that amount can be measured. **Measurement** consists of systematically assigning numbers to objects, events, or characteristics according to a set of rules (Stevens, 1951). Rating how happy you feel today on a scale of 1 to 10 is a type of measurement. It entails identifying a characteristic (your happiness) and quantifying the amount of that characteristic (happiness) you are experiencing. The rules used in this example of measuring are that the number you assign to your happiness must be between 1 and 10, inclusive, where 1 = a minimum of happiness and 10 = complete bliss.

Not all measurement systems are equivalent. In some, measurements can be mathematically manipulated, such as by adding a constant or by taking the square root of each number, and the measurement system retains its primary characteristics. In others, there is no tolerance for mathematical manipulation. Measurement systems can be classified as belonging to one of four **scales** (or levels) of measurement, which vary in the degree of mathematical manipulation they can tolerate: **nominal, ordinal, interval**, and **ratio**.

Nominal scale. **Nominal scales** are considered the weakest scales of measurement. A nominal scale of measurement merely classifies objects or individuals as belonging to different categories. The order of the categories is arbitrary and unimportant. Thus, subjects might be categorized as male or female, with the male category assigned the number 1 and the female category assigned the number 2. These numbers suggest nothing about the relative importance of the two categories. The numbers assigned could just as arbitrarily and just as meaningfully be 17.35 and 29.46. Other examples of the use of nominal scales of measurement are numbers on players' basketball jerseys or numbers assigned by the department of motor vehicles to the license plates of cars. When used in a nominal scale of measurement, numbers serve as labels only and say nothing about the magnitude or amount of the characteristic being measured.

Ordinal scale. An **ordinal measurement scale** differs from a nominal scale in that the order of the categories is important. A grading system consisting of the grades 4.0, 3.0, 2.0, 1.0, and 0.0 is an ordinal scale. The order of the categories reflects a decrease in the amount of the stuff being measured—in this case, knowledge. However, the distance between the categories is not necessarily equal; that is, the difference between a 4.0 and a 3.0 is not necessarily the same as the distance between a 3.0 and a 2.0.

Rank order data are also measured on a ordinal scale. An observer may rank-order subjects according to their physical attractiveness, or a researcher may ask tasters to rank-order a number of crackers according to their saltiness. When your eyesight is tested and you are asked to choose which of two lenses yields a clearer image, you are being asked to provide ordinal data. Again, when data are rank-ordered, a statement is being made about the magnitude or amount of the characteristic being measured, but the intervals between units need not be equivalent. If seven people are rank-ordered on the basis of physical attractiveness, the difference in attractiveness between the first and second persons does not necessarily have the same magnitude as the difference beween the second and third persons. The first and second persons may both be very attractive, with only a slight difference distinguishing first from second, while the third person might be substantially homelier than the second.

Interval scale. An **interval scale** of measurement is characterized by equal units of measurement throughout the scale. Thus, measurements made with an interval scale provide information both about order and about relative quantity of the characteristic being measured. Interval scales of measurement, however, do not have a true 0 value. A true 0 represents a complete absence of the characteristic being measured. Measuring temperature in degrees Farenheit or in degrees Celsius (also called centigrade) makes use of interval scales of measurement. The distance between degrees is equal over the full length of the scale; the difference between 20 and 40 degrees is the same as the difference between 40 and 60 degrees. In neither scale, however, is there a true 0, because in neither scale does 0 degrees represent a total lack of heat energy. Because there is no true 0 on these scales, it is inaccurate to say that 40 degrees (Fahrenheit or Celsius) is twice as warm as 20 degrees (Fahrenheit or Celsius). In other words, ratios cannot be computed with interval-scale data. In contrast, the Kelvin temperature scale *is* based on a true 0 value that represents the absence of heat energy. One can compute ratios using degrees Kelvin; therefore, degrees Kelvin are measured not on an interval scale of measurement but on a ratio scale.

Before introducing ratio scales, I need to discuss a controversy among psychological researchers regarding the use of interval and ordinal scales as rating scales. In these scales, often referred to as Likert or Likert-type scales, a subject is asked to rate something on a scale with particular endpoints, such as 1 to 7 or 0 to 5. Often the end numbers have labels, but the middle numbers often do not. The controversy arises over whether the ratings should be considered ordinal data or interval data. What has never been ascertained is whether the scales people use in their heads have units of equal size. If the units are of equal size, the data can be treated as interval data; if they are unequal, the data should be treated as ordinal data. This is a point of contention because, as we shall see, interval data is preferable to ordinal data for statistical purposes.

No final answer has yet been made about the nature of rating scale data. In some research areas, ratings tend to be treated cautiously and are considered ordinal data. In other areas, such as language and memory studies, where subjects may be asked to rate how familiar a phrase is or how strong their feeling of knowing is, ratings tend to be treated as interval data. The particular philosophy toward ratings scales in any particular area of study is perhaps best ascertained by referring to previous research in that area.

Ratio scale.   A **ratio scale** of measurement provides information about order. All units on the ratio scale are of equal size, and there is a true 0 value representing an abscence of the characteristic being measured. The inclusion of true 0 allows ratios of values to be formed. Thus, a person who is 50 years old is twice as old as a person who is 25. Age in years is a ratio scale, with each year representing the same amount of time no matter where it occurs on the scale; a year between 20 years and 21 years of age is the same amount of time as a year between 54 and 55.

As you may have noticed, scales of measurement can be arranged hierarchically from nominal to ratio. Each scale possesses all the capabilities of the next lower scale plus something new. Thus, nominal scales are simply categorical, while ordinal scales are categorical and also include ordering of the categories. Interval scales of measurement involve ordered categories of equal size; in other words, the intervals between numbers on the scale are equivalent throughout the scale. Ratio scales also have equal intervals; but in addition, ratio scales begin at a true 0 score that represents complete absence of the characteristic being measured and thus allows for the computation of ratios.

Importance of Scales of Measurement   At this point, a discussion of scales of measurement may seem to be an abstract digression from the topic of observational studies. But observational studies can provide a researcher with various of types of data, running the full gamut of the scales of measurement. Records of gender or of the manner in which a person carries his or her books constitute nominal data. A child's description of a flattened ball of clay as being bigger than a round ball provides ordinal data. Ratings of speed or of attractiveness can be interpreted as being interval data; and the number of times a child hits a Bobo doll is measured on a ratio scale.

As was mentioned earlier, the statistical techniques that are appropriate for one scale of measurement may not be appropriate for another. Therefore, a researcher must be able to identify the scale of measurement being used so that appropriate statistical techniques can be applied. Sometimes a technique's inappropriateness is difficult to detect, but other times it can be quite obvious—and quite embarrassing to a researcher who lets an inappropriate statistic slip by. For example, imagine that 10 people are rank-ordered according to height. In addition, suppose that information about the individuals' weights in pounds and ages in years are recorded. The researcher, who has access to a computer, absentmindedly includes the height rankings along with other variables when commanding the computer to calculate arithmetic averages. The computer provides information that the average age of the subjects is 22.6 years, that their average weight is 135.6 pounds, and that their average height is 5.5. Calculating this type of average on the basis of ordinal data yields no useful information.

CONCEPT QUESTIONS 3·4	On what scale of measurement would each of the following types of data be measured? a. The number of dollars in one's wallet. b. The rated sweetness of a can of soda. c. The number of yes and no responses to a question. d. Height, measured in inches. e. The gender of individuals. f. Weight, measured as light, medium, or heavy.

SAMPLING TECHNIQUES

One primary advantage of an observational study is that the results are more readily generalizable to "real life" than are the results of a laboratory study. Yet the generalizability of observational data depends on where and when the observations are made. A researcher who is interested in the types of food people choose in the college cafeteria cannot observe all cafeteria customers all the time. Instead, only a sample of all the customers can be observed. The goal is to choose a sample that fairly represents the population. A sample that is unrepresentative of the population is called a **biased sample**. In psychological research, two sampling techniques that increase the generalizability of observational data and decrease the probability of creating a biased sample are behavioral sampling and situation sampling.

Behavior Sampling   If it is not possible to observe all the patrons in a cafeteria, then a sample of the patrons—or more precisely, a sample of the patrons' behaviors —must be chosen for observation. One technique for sampling behaviors is called **time sampling**. Time sampling involves choosing the times at which observations will be made in such a way that a representative sample of behaviors will be obtained. Time sampling may be done **randomly** or **systematically**. Random time sampling means that each interval of time is equally likely to be chosen. Systematic time sampling occurs when time intervals for observation are chosen purposefully. Often, random time sampling and systematic time sampling occur together within the same study. For example, it may not be particularly useful to choose hours for observing a college cafeteria at random, since it isn't in use much of the day. Instead, systematic time sampling can be used to choose particular hours during the morning, noon, and evening meal times. The observers may also decide (systematically) to make observations for 10 minutes at a time. Random time sampling could then be used to determine which 10-minute intervals would be used. One way to choose these intervals at random is to use a random numbers table, such as the one provided in Appendix B. Alternatively, the intervals can be chosen from a hat. To use a random numbers table, arbitrarily choose a row and column, and from that point record the numbers encountered in the table as you move through it either horizontally or vertically (but not both). For example, to determine when to begin observing, a researcher may decide that the number in the random numbers table will represent the number of minutes after the top of the hour. Perhaps the first number is 8; then at 8 minutes after the hour, the first 10-minute observation will begin. Suppose that the next number is 4. The observer would then wait 4 minutes after the last observation before beginning another 10-minute observation session. This would continue until all of the 10-minute intervals were used in the allotted time. There is no exact way to use a random numbers table other than by following the numbers as presented in the table once a starting point has been chosen.

Time sampling is appropriate when the behaviors of interest occur on a nearly continuous basis. But when the behaviors occur less frequently, it may not be feasible to identify an observation time, since no behaviors may occur during that time period. In this case **event sampling** may be useful. Event sampling consists of randomly or systematically sampling events that include the behavior of interest. A researcher interested in neighbors' reactions to a fire may need to sample among fires in the city. It would not be possible to use time sampling in this case, since there might be no fire during the appointed time.

Systematic event sampling involves purposefully choosing events to observe, such as deciding to attend every fifth fire announced on the police radio. Random event sampling involves choosing events to observe in such a way that each event is equally likely to be chosen—for instance, by using a random numbers table to determine which fires to attend. A risk of systematic event sampling is that observations may be made only when it is convenient for the researcher to make them; this can lead to an unrepresentative sample of events.

Situation Sampling   **Situation sampling** involves making observations in different settings and circumstances. Situation sampling can greatly enhance the generalizability of an observational study. A researcher who is interested in how children play together in a playground, for example, can make observations at a number of playgrounds in different neighborhoods. This approach increases the likelihood that the observed play behavior is representative of all children's play behavior and not just of the play behavior in a specific neighborhood.

CONCEPT QUESTIONS 3·5	A researcher is interested in the factors that affect whether an individual picks up litter or leaves it where it is. The researcher, who wishes to place some litter (a paper cup from a fast-food restaurant) on the ground to see if passersby will pick it up and dispose of it, asks you to assist in designing the study. How could the researcher use time sampling? Could the researcher use event sampling? If so, how? If not, why not? How could situation sampling be incorporated into this design? Would the sampling techniques employed be used randomly or systematically?

PROBLEMS AND PITFALLS OF OBSERVATIONAL STUDIES

A research project should have sound **internal validity** as well as good **external validity**. Internal validity depends on how well the study actually answers the research questions; it represents the degree to which we can be certain that the manipulation of the independent variable is responsible for the change noted in the dependent variable. A study with good internal validity has no confounds; consequently, it fairly addresses the research question or the researcher's hypothesis. External validity consists of the extent to which the results of an investigation can be generalized beyond the original study. To allow analysts to draw any conclusions, research must have good internal validity. To permit them to generalize those conclusions beyond the original investigation, research must have good external validity. Thus, a research project may be internally valid, but not externally valid; but not the other way around. A study with poor internal validity has no external validity either.

A primary advantage of the observational study is its potential for strong external validity. Because observational studies are usually conducted in natural settings, their results are more readily generalizable to the rest of the population in question. To make the most of this advantage, it is essential that observational studies also have strong internal validity.

Internal validity is gained by avoiding potential confounds. In observational studies, the two primary sources of confounds are the influence of the observer on the subjects, and biased observations.

Influence of the Observer on Behavior   The mere presence of an observer can affect the behavior of subjects, as Jane Goodall found out when she attempted to observe chimpanzees. In the social sciences, the effect of the observer on the behavior of the subjects is called the **Hawthorne effect**. In the 1920s and 1930s, the Western Electric Company conducted a series of studies on workplace behavior. Some of the research involved changing the illumination to see how it affected productivity. Two workers in this set of studies showed increased productivity even in illumination conditions equivalent to working in moonlight (Jones, 1992).

Another set of studies involved setting up a special experimental workroom for a small group of women who were wiring relays. The productivity of these women was monitored as the researchers varied a number of factors—adding small group incentives, increasing and decreasing voluntary rest times, changing the starting and stopping schedule, changing the workers' chairs, introducing problems with raw materials, and changing the number of days per week that the people worked. Some of these variables were studied because the researchers were truly interested in their effects; others were included because the hard economic times called for them.

The researchers at the Hawthorne plant noted that, over the course of the study, the workers' productivity improved. They hypothesized that the additional attention they received from researchers and management was responsible for the increased productivity. To the Hawthorne researchers, this finding was an interesting sidenote, but to researchers in the social sciences it was of great importance. Interestingly, a recent reanalysis of the raw data from the Hawthorne studies suggests that there may not have been any significant increase in productivity over the course of the project after all (Jones, 1992).

Whether or not there actually was a Hawthorne effect in the original studies, the effect of the observer on the behavior of the subjects remains a concern. Observers must assume that their presence will affect behavior and must then make efforts to minimize that effect, such as by making observations surreptitiously or by observing the subjects without their being aware of it.

If a subject's behavior changes because the subject is aware that he or she is being studied, the measurement is called a **reactive measure**. **Reactivity** is the change in behavior caused by the subject's knowledge that he or she is being studied. Reactivity can be a problem in observational research and can decrease a study's internal validity. As was mentioned earlier, the effects of reactivity can be minimized by allowing the subject of the observation to grow accustomed to the observer, either through desensitization or through habituation. Unfortunately, there is no way to ensure that measurements of the dependent variable have ceased to be reactive. Unobtrusive observation is the only method that allows the observer to be fairly confident that the act of observing is not changing the behaviors. Unobtrusive observation involves making observations without the subjects' knowledge. In some cases this is relatively easy to do: observations in a college classroom might be made in a notebook, and observations at an intersection might be made from a parked vehicle. In other situations, making unobtrusive observations may require some creativity.

Reactivity in participant observation studies is always a concern. Again, it is impossible to determine what effect the participant may be having on the behavior of the others. Efforts can be made, however, to minimize these effects. If the study is a disguised participant observation, it is important that notes be taken or data recording be done as unobtrusively as possible. If the study is an undisguised participant observation, the subjects may become accustomed to the observer over time, after which reactivity will be reduced.

Expectancy Effects   A second threat to the internal validity of observational research is bias in measurements of the dependent variable. Psychological researchers recognize that a person's conscious or unconscious preferences can affect his or her perception of a situation; this is called **observer bias**. To counter this tendency, researchers design their studies carefully so that any bias they may have cannot affect the research results.

A simple way to avoid observer bias is to train other observers to make the observations for a study, without discussing the expected results with them. Unless the results of an investigation are intuitively obvious, the observers are likely either to have no expectations about the results or to have expectations that are not systematic; in the latter case, with more than one observer, the expectations may cancel each other out. Some research on experimenters' expectations suggests that errors attributable to recording data in favor of experimenters' expectations occur in less than 1% of the data (Rosenthal, 1978), and that the effect of experimenter bias may be so small that it does not constitute a replicable phenomenon (Barber & Silver, 1968). Relatedly, if a research finding is considered important, it is going to be investigated repeatedly by other researchers. If the original result was caused by experimenter biases, this is likely to become evident as other researchers have difficulty replicating the result (Kantowitz, Roediger & Elmes 1991, p 425).

Biases Resulting from the Use of Nonhuman Observers   One way to avoid observer bias is to have a nonhuman "observer," such as an audio- or videotape, make the observations. The advantage of a human observer, however, lies in the human's flexibility. Humans can see, hear, smell, taste, and feel; machines can typically only perform a subset of these behaviors. An audiotape recorder can only record sounds, so anything that can only be perceived visually, for example, goes unrecorded when audiotape is used to collect data. Moreover, bias in interpretation can be introduced if some information from the tape is ambiguous. If a researcher is investigating language use and a pun is made, it may difficult to determine whether the pun was intentional in the absence of the nonverbal cues of smiling, winking, and so on that may accompany an intentional pun. A videocamera may record both auditory and visual information, but it does not have the same field of vision and peripheral vision as a human. If the videocamera is left unattended, all that will be taped is whatever happens to be in front of the camera. Activities occurring outside of the camera's view that might have helped explain some of the behaviors will not be available when the data are being coded; and it will be left to the human to interpret the situation in their absence. If the camera is guided by a human, then the biases of the human are reintroduced during data collection.

As we have noted, even when information is obtained on video- or audiotape, it usually must be interpreted and coded by a human. Thus, even though mechanical observers may reduce some of the observer bias, they do not eliminate it. Some bias remains in the data collection, and further bias may be introduced during data reduction.

Awareness is probably the best defense against the threats of reactivity and observer bias to the internal validity of an observational study. A researcher who recognizes the possibility that these problems may occur can take steps to minimize their effects and thus can minimize damage to the interpretability of the investigation. By minimizing these threats to internal validity and by maximizing the advantages, the researcher increases the likelihood that useful and important information will be gained as a result of the observational investigation.

CONCEPT QUESTIONS 3.6	Do males ask and answer questions in class more often than females? A researcher was interested in this issue and wished to observe student behavior as a means to address this question. The researcher carefully devised operational definitions of "asking and answering questions" so that the observer could categorize responses easily. The researcher suspected that males did speak up more often in class, but was concerned that this bias might affect the data collection. What advice would you give this person? How would you suggest that the data be collected? Should human observers be used, or should nonhuman means be used to collect the data? How can the researcher avoid or minimize observer bias (human or nonhuman)? Will the method of data collection involve a reactive measure? How can reactivity be minimized or avoided?

PART II: STATISTICAL ANALYSES OF OBSERVATIONAL DATA

Statistics are among the principal tools used in research for developing theories based on the results of previous studies, and for testing hypotheses and drawing conclusions from current investigations. They are the mathematical techniques used to guide the collection of data so that conclusions can be drawn from them. Thus, statistics and research methods go hand in hand. The appropriate design of a study depends on knowledge of the types and appropriate uses of statistical techniques. This section introduces some concepts and techniques that can be used to draw conclusions from data from observational studies, as well as from other types of research. The techniques described here do not come close to exhausting all that can be done with observational data, but they do provide a starting place.

PRESENTING AND SUMMARIZING DATA

To guide our discussion of statistical analyses, let's develop an observational study. Suppose that an investigator is interested in examining whether drivers obey the speed limit on the interstate highway. Using a radar gun, our researcher clocks 40 drivers along a highway that has a posted speed limit of 65 mph. (We will avoid some reactivity concerns by conducting our imaginary study in Virginia where radar detectors are illegal and therefore less likely to be used.)

One of the primary purposes of statistical analysis is to organize and summarize data so that meaningful conclusions may be drawn from them. Once our researcher

TABLE 3.2
Speeds of 40 drivers.

mph	mph
66	67
72	65
68	70
64	73
74	68
60	70
70	64
73	65
62	69
69	71
72	68
67	63
65	66
65	62
66	70
67	77
56	62
65	65
64	67
59	65

has observed 40 drivers, the data amounts to a list of 40 numbers; as they stand, they are not especially meaningful (see Table 3.2).

A first step toward extracting meaningful information from this data set would be to reorganize the scores, perhaps from lowest to highest (see Table 3.3). By arranging the numbers in this manner we can see more easily that the lowest speed recorded is a 56 and the highest speed is a 77.

Another way to organize this set of data would be to list all of the occurring scores and the frequency with which each occurs. This is called a **frequency distribution**. A relative frequency distribution can also be included; it is obtained by dividing each frequency by the total number of observations. The relative frequency distribution provides information about the proportion of the total observations included in each score. If the relative frequency is multiplied by 100, it can be read as a percentage. Table 3.4 presents a frequency distribution and a relative frequency distribution of the speed data.

A frequency distribution summarizes the data more usefully than does a simple list of the individual scores; but sometimes, with a large set of data, this type of frequency distribution itself can be unwieldy. An alternative procedure is to tabulate the data using **class intervals**. Using class intervals requires combining the individual scores into categories of scores. In our example, the scores cover a range of 22 values, from 56 to 77. If we combine the scores into categories (intervals) of two values each, there will be 11 categories. A rule of thumb is to choose between 10 and 20 intervals for your distribution; this will be a manageable number of intervals but will not overly simplify the distribution of scores (Hinkle, Wiersma & Jurs, 1988, p. 26). One way to determine the appropriate width for your intervals is to subtract the smallest score from the largest score and then divide by the number of intervals you would like. For example:

$$\frac{\text{Highest number} - \text{Lowest number}}{\text{Number of intervals}} = \frac{77 - 56}{10} = \frac{21}{10} = 2.1$$

The frequency distribution that is created by using class intervals with a width of 2 scores each is provided in Table 3.5. Frequency distributions that use class intervals summarize the data set and reduce the number of categories of scores. However, the process of combining data into class intervals also causes the loss of some information about the individual scores. For example, although we can see from the class interval frequency distribution that four individuals are included in the 62–63 mph class interval, we cannot tell from this table whether zero, one, two, three, or all four were driving 62 mph.

What if a driver is timed at 67.2 mph? Does this person's data go in the 66–67 interval or in the 68–69 interval? To address this question, we need to categorize data another way. Data may be classified as being either **discrete** or **continuous**. Roughly, **discrete data** sets usually consist of isolated whole numbers. If we were to count the number of children in a collection of families, for example, the data would consist of nonnegative integers: 0, 1, 2, ... No family could have 2.6 or −.67 children. **Continuous data** usually fall along a continuum or, for our purposes, an interval of numbers. In the case of continuous data, fractional units are theoretically possible. For example, the speeds of vehicles measured in miles per hour are continuous data: a vehicle could go 65.3 mph (even if measured in whole numbers). On the

TABLE 3.3
Speeds ordered from lowest to highest.

mph	mph
56	67
59	67
60	67
62	67
62	68
62	68
63	68
64	69
64	69
64	70
65	70
65	70
65	70
65	71
65	72
65	72
65	73
66	73
66	74
66	77

other hand, speed of vehicles measured as slow or fast would be discrete data. According to this discrete measurement system, a vehicle's speed belongs in one category or the other, but not both; a vehicle's speed cannot meaningfully be categorized as "slow and a half."

For class interval frequency distributions involving continuous data, we usually add two more bits of information to our distribution; exact limits and midpoints. Consider again the measurements of vehicle speeds. If the class intervals are as shown in Table 3.5, we need to know how to classify the vehicle being driven at 67.2 mph. Without the exact limits column, we would not know where to put this person's score. Should it go in the 66–67 interval or in the 68–69 interval? The **exact limits** extend the class intervals by one-half unit above and below the intervals of the scores, the **score limits**. Thus, for the interval with score limits 66–67, the exact limits are 65.5 to 67.5. Usually the score limits are presented in the units of the measurements. Our original measurements were made as whole numbers. The exact limits extend the score limits a half unit beyond the unit of measurement. The 67.2 mph speed, which would be unusual in its precision, would be included within this interval.

If a vehicle is clocked going exactly 67.5, a decision must be made. Should this score be included in the 65.5–67.5 interval or in the 67.5–69.5 interval? If the researcher makes this decision, there is the risk that a subtle bias will be introduced into the data. To avoid this risk, the numbers that fall exactly on the boundary between two intervals should be randomly assigned to either the higher or lower limit. A simple approach is to flip a coin. The score limits and exact limits allow for placement of the unusually precisely measured data point. Primarily, however, they accentuate the continuous nature of the data.

Two assumptions are related to the use of class intervals. One is that the scores in each interval are uniformly distributed throughout the interval; that is, if the interval 72–73 has four scores, it is assumed that two scores fall between 71.5 and 72.5 and two scores fall between 72.5 and 73.5 (inclusive). The second assumption is that, if we must use a single score to represent the entire interval (as we must when graphing the scores), the **midpoint** of each interval can serve as an adequate representation of the entire interval. The **midpoint** is the center of each interval. The class interval frequency distribution for our example, including the exact limits and midpoints, is presented in Table 3.6.

Other information can be added to frequency distributions and class interval frequency distributions. For example, a **cumulative frequency** (cf) column can be added to describe the number of observations that falling at or below a certain score or interval. This is calculated by starting with the lowest interval (or score, if class intervals are not being used) and determining its frequency. Then the frequency of the lowest interval is added to the frequency of the next lowest interval; this sum constitutes the cumulative frequency for the second lowest interval. Similarly, this cumulative frequency can be added to the frequency of the third lowest interval to calculate the cumulative frequency for the third lowest interval. This process is repeated until a cumulative frequency has been calculated for each interval. A quick glance at a cumulative frequency column informs you of the number of scores that occur at or below any given interval.

TABLE 3.4   *Frequency and relative frequency distributions of the speed data.*

Score	f (Frequency)	rf (Relative Frequency)
56	1	.025
57	0	.00
58	0	.00
59	1	.025
60	1	.025
61	0	.00
62	3	.075
63	1	.025
64	3	.075
65	7	.175
66	3	.075
67	4	.10
68	3	.075
69	2	.05
70	4	.10
71	1	.025
72	2	.05
73	2	.05
74	1	.025
75	0	.00
76	0	.00
77	1	.025
	40	1.00

TABLE 3.5   *A class interval frequency distribution of the speed data.*

Class Interval	f	rf
56–57	1	.025
58–59	1	.025
60–61	1	.025
62–63	4	.10
64–65	10	.25
66–67	7	.175
68–69	5	.125
70–71	5	.125
72–73	4	.10
74–75	1	.025
76–77	1	.025
	40	1.00

TABLE 3.6   *A class interval distribution including midpoints and exact limits.*

Class Interval	Exact Limits	Midpoint	f	rf
56–57	55.5–57.5	56.5	1	.025
58–59	57.5–59.5	58.5	1	.025
60–61	59.5–61.5	60.5	1	.025
62–63	61.5–63.5	62.5	4	.10
64–65	63.5–65.5	64.5	10	.25
66–67	65.5–67.5	66.5	7	.175
68–69	67.5–69.5	68.5	5	.125
70–71	69.5–71.5	70.5	5	.125
72–73	71.5–73.5	72.5	4	.10
74–75	73.5–75.5	74.5	1	.025
76–77	75.5–77.5	76.5	1	.025
			40	1.00

TABLE 3.7   *A class interval distribution including a cumulative frequency and cumulative percent column.*

Class Interval	Exact Limits	Midpoint	f	cf	rf	c%
56–57	55.5–57.5	56.5	1	1	.025	2.5
58–59	57.5–59.5	58.5	1	2	.025	5.0
60–61	59.5–61.5	60.5	1	3	.025	7.5
62–63	61.5–63.5	62.5	4	7	.10	17.5
64–65	63.5–65.5	64.5	10	17	.25	42.5
66–67	65.5–67.5	66.5	7	24	.175	60
68–69	67.5–69.5	68.5	5	29	.125	72.5
70–71	69.5–71.5	70.5	5	34	.125	85
72–73	71.5–73.5	72.5	4	38	.10	95
74–75	73.5–75.5	74.5	1	39	.025	97.5
76–77	75.5–77.5	76.6	1	40	.025	100

A **cumulative percent** (c%) column represents the percentage of scores at or below a given interval. It is calculated in the same manner as the cumulative frequency column, but using the relative frequencies instead of the frequencies. The obtained scores are then multiplied by 100 (the decimal is moved over two places) so that the numbers can be read as percentages. The class interval distribution with a cumulative frequency column (cf), a relative frequency column (rf), and a cumulative percent (c%) column is presented in Table 3.7.

Since the purpose of the frequency distribution is to assist the researcher in organizing and summarizing the data, the type of frequency distribution used and the columns included in it depend on the particular data that have been collected and the particular questions that the researcher is addressing. Similarly, depending on the questions being asked, the amount of data collected, and the range of scores the data cover, a researcher may or may not want to group data into classes.

CONCEPT	Refer to Table 3.7 to answer the following questions.
QUESTIONS	
3·7	1. Based on the information from this table, what would you predict was the most common recorded speed?
	2. What percentage of the vehicles were be driven at speeds of 71.5 mph or less?
	3. To what interval would a speed of 64.9 mph be assigned?
	4. How many vehicles were being driven at speeds faster than 66.5 mph?
	5. What percentage of the vehicles were being driven at speeds of between 61.5 mph and 65.5 mph?

GRAPHING DATA

Frequency distributions can provide considerable information to a researcher, but sometimes drawing a picture is the best way to describe a data set. The particular type of graph a researcher should use depends on the type of data that are being collected and the characteristics of the data the researcher wants to illustrate. The most common types of graphs used in psychological research are bar graphs, histograms, frequency polygons, and line graphs. In this section we will consider graphs that are used to illustrate frequency distributions. In subsequent chapters, graphs will be used to compare different groups within a study and to illustrate relationships between variables.

Most graphs have two coordinate axes: the horizontal ***x*-axis** and the vertical ***y*-axis**. By convention, the *y*-axis should be the shorter of the two—60 to 75% of the length of the *x*-axis. If one were to make the *y*-axis inordinately tall, the graph would suggest a greater frequency of scores than actually exists; an unduly short *y*-axis would suggest a lesser frequency than actually exists. The graphs in Figure 3.1 demonstrate these illusions.

In designing an appropriate graphical representation of data, one must determine whether a bar graph or a line graph is more appropriate. This decision should be based on whether the independent variable is discrete or continuous. Line graphs and histograms are drawn in a manner that suggests an underlying distribution and are thus appropriate for representing continuous data. A bar graph is appropriate for discrete data.

Bar Graphs   Suppose that as part of our driving behaviors study, we not only recorded speed, but also recorded type of vehicle and classified each vehicle as a motorcycle, a car, a pickup truck, a van, or a large truck, Figure 3.2 shows a **bar graph** of the fictitious data. The graph represents the frequency with which each of these types of vehicles was identified. Notice that the bars do not touch each other. This reinforces the discrete character of the data and does not falsely suggest that a vehicle might somehow be a combination of types. Instead, it accurately reflects the fact that the vehicles were of five distinct types.

Histograms   A **histogram** is a type of bar graph that can be used to represent the frequency distributions of continuous variables. A histogram may depict the fre-

FIGURE **3.1**

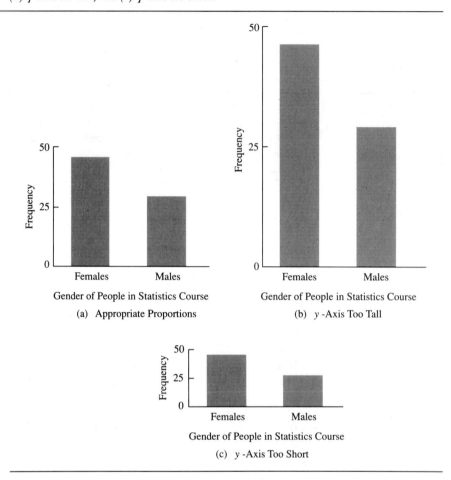

FIGURE **3.2**   Bar graph of vehicle types.

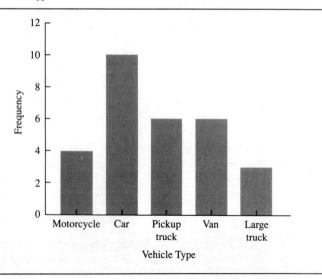

quencies of individual scores or of classes of scores from a class interval frequency distribution. Figure 3.3 shows two histograms, one representing the frequencies of individual speeds from Table 3.4 and the other representing the class interval distribution from Table 3.5. In a histogram, the bars are contiguous; that is, they touch each other. This reflects the fact that the underlying variable being measured is continuous.

In the histogram of the data for individual speeds, each bar represents one possible score; the width of each bar is one unit, starting $\frac{1}{2}$ unit above and ending $\frac{1}{2}$ below the whole-number value for a speed. For example, 55.5–56.5 is the one-unit interval for the speed 56 mph. In this histogram, the midpoint of each bar corresponds to each actual score.

In the histogram of the data for the class interval distribution, each bar represents one interval of scores. The exact limits of the intervals mark the beginning and the end of each bar, and the midpoint of the bar corresponds to the midpoint of each interval.

Frequency Polygons   The same data that were depicted by a histogram in Figure 3.3 can also be depicted by a line graph called a **frequency polygon**. Creating a frequency polygon involves plotting the frequencies of the individual scores (or for a class interval frequency distribution, plotting the midpoints of each class interval), and then connecting the dots. The frequency polygons for the frequency distribution of the individual speed scores and for the class interval frequency distribution for the speed scores are shown in Figure 3.4.

To reiterate, the continuous nature of frequency polygons and histograms make them most appropriate for representing continuous variables; in contrast, discrete variables are best represented by bar graphs.

CONCEPT QUESTIONS 3.8

1. Identify the flaws in the following histogram.

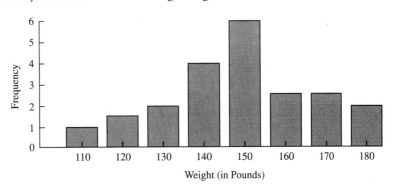

2. A researcher observes shopping behavior in a grocery store, noting the gender of the shoppers, how long they shop (measured in minutes), and the amount of money each shopper spends. The researcher wishes to represent the data in graphs but can't remember when to use bar graphs, histograms, or frequency polygons. Which graphs should be used to describe which data?

FIGURE 3.3   *Histograms of vehicle speed data: (a) individual scores; (b) class interval data.*

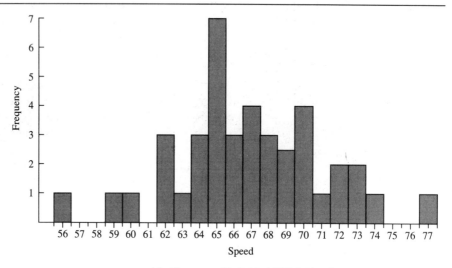

(a) Histogram of Individual Vehicle Speeds

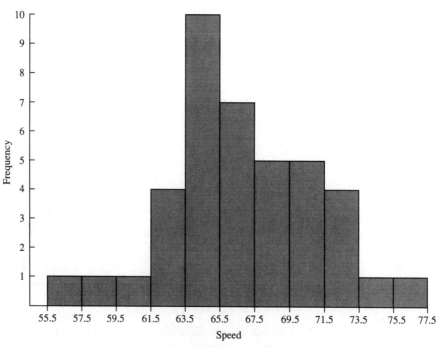

(b) Histogram of Vehicle Speeds, Based on Class Interval Data

FIGURE 3.4   *Frequency polygons of vehicle speed data: (a) individual scores; (b) class interval data.*

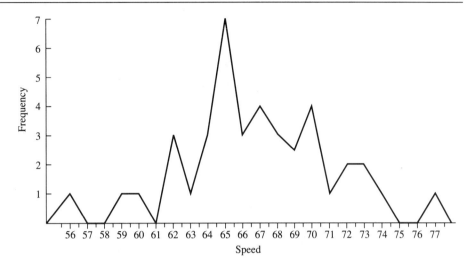

(a)   Frequency Polygon of Individual Vehicle Speeds

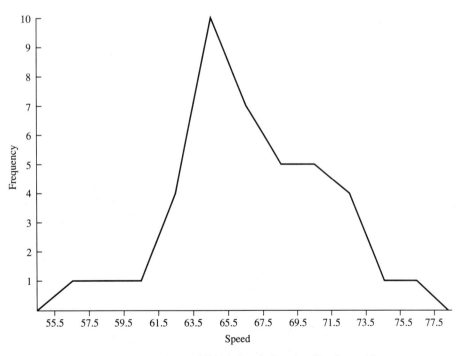

(b)   Frequency Polygon of Vehicle Speeds, Based on Class Interval Data

TABLE 3.8

Frequency distribution of speed data, including a cumulative frequency column.

mph	f	cf
56	1	1
57	0	1
58	0	1
59	1	2
60	1	3
61	0	3
62	3	6
63	1	7
64	3	10
65	7	17
66	3	20
67	4	24
68	3	27
69	2	29
70	4	33
71	1	34
72	2	36
73	2	38
74	1	39
75	0	39
76	0	39
77	1	40
	40	

DESCRIPTIVE STATISTICS

Tables and graphs can do much to make a set of data more meaningful, but interpretations of tables and graphs are not conclusive. For greater precision, numerical measures can be calculated. These measures supply information about the height and width of the distribution, as well as about whether it is symmetrical or whether it leans to one side or the other. Because these measures are used to describe the frequency distribution, they are called **descriptive statistics**.

If you are not familiar with summation notation—a shorthand for writing statistical formulas—you probably should take a break here and refer to Appendix D for a quick introduction to the topic.

Modes and Measures of Central Tendency   Perhaps the most commonly discussed characteristic of a data set is its average. However, three different averages can be calculated, each providing somewhat different information. These three measures are the mode, the median, and the mean.

The **mode** is the score in a set of discrete data that occurs most frequently. In a continuous distribution, the mode is where the tallest peak (the absolute maximum) occurs. For the vehicle speed data presented in Table 3.4, the mode is 65 mph. Sometimes a set of data will contain two (or more) scores that share the distinction of occurring most frequently. In such cases, the distribution is said to be **bimodal** (or **multimodal**). The mode is a very straightforward measure that can be used with nominal, ordinal, interval, or ratio scaled data.

The **median** is another type of average—a **measure of central tendency**; it provides information about the distribution of the scores by describing where the middle score for the data set lies. In fact, the median is defined as being the middle point in a set of scores—the point below which 50% of the scores fall. To determine the median of a distribution, we must first know the total number (N) of scores. For our speed data, $N = 40$. Furthermore, the scores must be presented in rank order from smallest to largest (or vice versa). The median of the distribution in this case is the point below which half of the 40 scores fall. A cumulative frequency column in a frequency distribution can be very useful for locating the median of the distribution. A cumulative frequency column (cf) is presented in the frequency distribution of the vehicle speed data in Table 3.8.

The median of the distribution in Table 3.8 is the score whose cumulative frequency includes $\frac{N+1}{2}$ scores. For this distribution, $N = 40$ and $\frac{N+1}{2} = \frac{41}{2} = 20.5$. Thus, the median in this case is the score whose cumulative frequency includes 20.5. Another way to think of the median is to imagine that all of the scores are lined up from lowest to highest; the median is then the score halfway between the 20th and the 21st scores. In this distribution, the 20th score is a 66; the cumulative frequency for 66 is 20. The 21st score is a 67; the cumulative frequency for 67 is 24, but it actually includes the 21st through the 24th scores. The median for this distribution, the 20.5th score, is halfway between 66 and 67; therefore, it is 66.5. This statistic means that half of the vehicles were driven at speeds of 66.5 mph or slower, and that half were driven at speeds of 66.5 mph or faster.

If the distribution contains an odd number of scores, the median is an actually occurring score. With an even number of scores, as in this example, the median lies midway between two occurring scores.

The median can also be calculated by using a class interval distribution. As we saw earlier, Table 3.7 shows the class interval distribution of the vehicle speeds, including a cumulative frequency column. We still have 40 observations; but if we focus on the class interval data, we are interested in the $\frac{N}{2}$ score—that is, the 20th score.

The 20th score falls somewhere in the interval of 60.5–67.5. This interval contains seven scores: the 18th through the 24th scores. We want to know what the score is for the 20th score. Because we know that this particular interval starts with the 18th score, we also know that the 20th score is the 3rd score within this interval. In other words, the 20th score is $\frac{3}{7}$ of the way into the interval. We now need to determine what score is $\frac{3}{7}$ of the way into the interval of 65.5–67.5. Remember, we assume that the scores are uniformly, or evenly, distributed throughout the interval. We also know that the interval is 2 scores wide (score 66 and score 67), and that the median must be greater than 65.5, which is the interval's lower exact limit.

To determine the median, we multiply $\frac{3}{7}$ times the interval width (2) and add that number to the lower exact limit (65.5):

$$\tfrac{3}{7}(2) + 65.5 = 66.357$$

The general formula for calculating the median (Mdn) when using class interval data is as follows:

$$\text{Mdn} = ll + \left[\frac{N(.50) - cf_b}{f_i}\right]w$$

where:

ll = Lower exact limit of the interval containing $N(.50)$

cf_b = Cumulative frequency of the interval *below* the one containing $N(.50)$

f_i = Frequency of the interval containing $N(.50)$

w = Width of the class intervals

Using this formula to calculate the median, we obtain the following calculation:

$$\text{Mdn} = 65.5 + \left[\frac{40(.50) - 17}{7}\right]2$$

$$= 65.5 + \left[\frac{20 - 17}{7}\right]2$$

$$= 65.5 + \tfrac{3}{7}(2)$$

$$= 65.5 + .8571$$

$$= 66.357$$

This number is a bit different from the median obtained from the data on individual vehicle speeds, primarily because of information lost as a result of grouping scores into intervals.

The median provides a measure of central tendency and some information about the rest of the data set. It can be used with ratio and interval scaled data, but not with all ordinal data; and it is inappropriate for use with nominal data.

Another measure of central tendency, the **mean**, is the arithmetic average of the scores in a distribution. The mean is calculated by adding up the scores in the distribution and dividing this sum by the number of scores. The formula for the mean is as follows:

$$\mu = \frac{\sum X}{N} \quad \text{or} \quad \bar{x} = \frac{\sum X}{N}$$

where:

$\sum$ means to sum.

X stands for the scores.

N is the number of scores.

μ is the symbol for the population mean.

$\bar{x}$ is the symbol for the sample mean.

If the scores do not represent an entire popplulation, but a sample from the population, the formula remains the same; however, the symbol for the sample mean is $\bar{x}$.

As a quick example of computing the mean, suppose that we have the following set of test scores: 100, 74, 92, 83, 61. The sum of these five scores is 410. Thus, we compute the mean test score as follows:

$$\mu = \frac{\sum X}{N} = \frac{410}{5} = 82$$

Again, if these scores were only a subset of a larger population of scores, the symbol for the mean would be $\bar{x}$.

Once more, let's look at the speed data. In Table 3.9, the speed scores are presented in the column labeled X. The symbol X is typically used to represent a score or set of scores, and we will be using it that way in this book. Remember that f stands for the frequency of observations for the individual scores. There is also an fX column, which stands for *frequency multiplied by score*. Summing the numbers in the fX column is the same, arithmetically, as adding all 20 scores individually. If this is not immediately clear to you, sum the scores in Table 3.2 so that the relationship becomes clear.

The sum of the fx column is 2671; therefore, $\sum X = 2671$. The mean of this set of scores (which we will assume are the scores of a small but complete population) is calculated as follows:

$$\mu = \frac{\sum X}{N} = \frac{2671}{40} = 66.775$$

The mean can also be calculated from class interval data by substituting the midpoint of the intervals for X. Table 3.10 presents the class interval speed data with

TABLE 3.9   *Frequency distribution of speed scores, including an fX column.*

X	f	fX
56	1	56
57	0	0
58	0	0
59	1	59
60	1	60
61	0	0
62	3	186
63	1	63
64	3	192
65	7	455
66	3	198
67	4	268
68	3	204
69	2	138
70	4	280
71	1	71
72	2	144
73	2	146
74	1	74
75	0	0
76	0	0
77	1	77
		$2671 = \sum X$

TABLE 3.10   *Class interval distribution, including midpoints.*

Interval	Exact Limits	Midpoint	f	f(Midpoint)
56–57	55.5–57.5	56.5	1	56.5
58–59	57.5–59.5	58.5	1	58.5
60–61	59.5–61.5	60.5	1	60.5
62–63	61.5–63.5	62.5	4	250.0
64–65	63.5–65.5	64.5	10	645.0
66–67	65.5–67.5	66.5	7	465.5
68–69	67.5–69.5	68.5	5	342.5
70–71	69.5–71.5	70.5	5	352.5
72–73	71.5–73.5	72.5	4	290.0
74–75	73.5–75.5	74.5	1	74.5
76–77	75.5–77.5	76.5	1	76.5
				$2672 = \sum X$

a new column, the f(midpoint) column. This column lists the product of the midpoint for each interval and the frequency of scores within each interval. The sum of the f(midpoint) column provides an estimate of the summed scores. The mean is then calculated by dividing $\sum X$ by the number of observations:

$$\frac{\sum X}{N} = \frac{2672}{40} = 66.8$$

Again, because of information lost as a result of grouping the data, this mean is close to but not exactly the same as the mean obtained from the individual scores.

The mean is probably the most commonly used measure of central tendency, in part because it is mathematically very manipulable and can be embedded within other formulas. However, like all the other measures of central tendency, it does have its limitations. For one thing, scores that are inordinately large or small (called **outliers**) receive as much weight as any other score in the distribution; this can skew the mean score—inflating it if the outlier is large, and deflating it if the outlier is small—relative to what it would have been without the outliers. For example, suppose that the scores on an exam were 80, 82, 80, and 20. The mean of these scores would be 65.5, a D. However, no one in the class received a D; in fact, all but one received a B. The one inordinately small score, the outlier 20, significantly deflated the mean. The mean can be used with interval and ratio scaled data, but it is not appropriate for use with data measured on either an ordinal or a nominal scale.

CONCEPT QUESTIONS 3.9

A researcher observes cars entering and leaving a parking lot and records the gender of the driver, the number of people in the car, they type of car (Ford, Chevrolet, Mazda, etc.), and the speed at which the car drives through the lot (measured with a radar gun in mph).

1. For each type of data measured, what would be an appropriate average to calculate (mode, median, and/or mean)?
2. One driver traveled through the parking lot 20 mph faster than any other driver. Which type of average would be most affected by this one score?

Measures of Dispersion   Another set of important descriptive statistics are **measures of dispersion** (also referred to as measures of variability or variation). Whereas measures of central tendency describe balance points where the data tend to fall together, measures of dispersion describe how spread out or compact the data are. Although they can be used with nominal and ordinal data, measures of dispersion are used primarily with interval or ratio scaled data.

The most straightforward measure of dispersion is called the **range**. The range identifies the number of possible values for scores in a discrete data set, or the interval of scores covered by a data set taken from a continuous distribution. The range is computed by subtracting the lowest score from the highest score and adding 1:

$$\text{Range} = \text{Highest} - \text{Lowest} + 1$$

The 1 is added so that the range will include both the highest value and the lowest value and not just one of these values.

Refer to Table 3.3, where the vehicle speed data are ordered from smallest score to largest score. The smallest value is a speed of 56 mph, and the largest is a speed of 77 mph. The range of this data set is $77 - 56 + 1 = 22$. The data are spread across a range of 22 values, from 56 to 77.

The range tells us over how many scores the data are spread, but it does not give us any information about how the scores are distributed over the range. Its value as a descriptive measure is limited because it relies on only two scores from the entire distribution.

Another approach to measuring dispersion involves measuring the distances that the scores fall from the mean score and then calculating the average distance (or mean distance) of each datum from the mean. We will call this measure of dispersion the **average deviation** (A.D.).

To calculate the average deviation from the mean, we must first know the mean. Then, for each score, we calculate its distance from the mean; this is called the deviation score:

$$X - \mu$$

We need to sum the deviation scores to obtain the mean deviation, but if we sum them as they are, they will add up to zero. So instead we take the absolute value of each deviation score and sum these:

$$\sum |X - \mu|$$

Finally, we calculate the mean deviation score by dividing the sum of the absolute values of the deviation scores by the number of deviation scores. Thus, the formula for the average deviation is as follows:

$$\text{A.D.} = \frac{\sum |X - \mu|}{N}$$

Table 3.11 presents the vehicle speed data and deviation scores. Using the information provided in Table 3.11 and the mean of 66.775 mph that we calculated earlier, we can compute the average deviation:

$$\text{A.D.} = \frac{\sum |X - \mu|}{N} = \frac{133}{40} = 3.325$$

For our speed data, the scores fall an average of 3.325 mph from the mean of 66.775 mph.

The average deviation is not especially useful for other statistical procedures, so it is not used as often as are two other measures of dispersion: the variance and the standard deviation.

Variance and standard deviation   When calculating the average deviation, we used the absolute values of the deviations from the mean to make all of the numbers positive (if we hadn't used the absolute values, the sum of the deviation scores would have been zero).

TABLE 3.11   *Calculations for the sum of the absolute value of the deviation scores.*

X	$X - \mu$	$|X - \mu|$	f	$f|X - \mu|$
56	-10.775	10.775	1	10.775
57	-9.775	9.775	0	0
58	-8.775	8.775	0	0
59	-7.775	7.775	1	7.775
60	-6.775	6.775	1	6.775
61	-5.775	5.775	0	0
62	-4.775	4.775	3	14.325
63	-3.775	3.775	1	3.775
64	-2.775	2.775	3	8.325
65	-1.775	1.775	7	12.425
66	$-.775$	.775	3	2.325
67	.225	.225	4	.90
68	1.225	1.225	3	3.675
69	2.225	2.225	2	4.45
70	3.225	3.225	4	12.90
71	4.225	4.225	1	4.225
72	5.225	5.225	2	10.45
73	6.225	6.225	2	12.45
74	7.225	7.225	1	7.225
75	8.225	8.225	0	0
76	9.225	9.225	0	0
77	10.225	10.225	1	10.225
			40	$133 = \sum|X - \mu|$

You may recall from an earlier algebra class that another technique for eliminating negative signs from a set of scores is to square each score. Thus, to eliminate the negative signs on the deviation scores, we could square each score. These scores could then be summed to a number greater than 0. (The sum of the squared deviation scores is also called the **sum of squares** for short, and it is often abbreviated SS). The average of the squared deviation scores can be determined by dividing SS by N. This procedure results in a statistic called the population **variance**. The formula for the variance is as follows:

$$\sigma^2 = \frac{\sum(X - \mu)^2}{N}$$

Table 3.12 presents the vehicle speed data with a column of squared deviation scores, a frequency column, and a column listing the products of the frequencies and the squared deviation scores.

Using the information provided in Table 3.12 and our mean of 66.775, we can calculate the variance (also called the mean squared deviation) for this distribution. We do this by dividing the sum of the squared deviation scores by the number of deviation scores:

TABLE 3.12   *Calculations for the sum of the squared deviation scores.*

X	$(X - \mu)$	$(X - \mu)^2$	f	$f(X - \mu)^2$
56	−10.775	116.1006	1	116.006
57	−9.775	95.5506	0	0
58	−8.775	77.006	0	0
59	−7.775	60.4506	1	60.4506
60	−6.775	45.9006	1	45.9006
61	−5.775	33.3506	0	0
62	−4.775	22.8006	3	68.4018
63	−3.775	14.2506	1	14.2506
64	−2.775	7.7006	3	23.1018
65	−1.775	3.1506	7	22.0542
66	−.775	.6006	3	1.8018
67	.225	.0506	4	.2024
68	1.225	1.5006	3	4.5018
69	2.225	4.9506	2	9.9012
70	3.225	10.4006	4	41.6024
71	4.225	17.8506	1	17.8506
72	5.225	27.3006	2	54.6012
73	6.225	38.7506	2	77.5012
74	7.225	52.2006	1	52.2006
75	8.225	67.6506	0	0
76	9.225	85.1006	0	0
77	10.225	104.5506	1	104.5506
				$714.8794 = \sum(X - \mu)^2$

$$\sigma^2 = \frac{\sum(X - \mu)^2}{N} = \frac{714.8794}{40} = 17.872$$

The variance is thus 17.872. To reconvert the variance into the original "unsquared" units, we take the square root of the variance. This new measure is called the **standard deviation** and is denoted by σ when it represents the standard deviation for an entire population:

$$\sigma = \sqrt{\sigma^2}$$

The standard deviation for our speed data is as follows:

$$\sigma = \sqrt{17.872} = 4.228$$

According to this measure, the scores fall approximately 4.228 mph, on average, from the mean. The standard deviation differs from the average deviation because the two scores are calculated differently, one using absolute values of deviation scores and the other using squared deviation scores. They each provide an estimate of the average distance of the scores from the mean.

The preceding symbols and formulas for variance and standard deviation apply to calculations of the **population** variance and standard deviation. If the scores a researcher is analyzing are a **sample** of a population, the appropriate formulas and symbols look like these:

$$s^2 = \frac{\sum(X - \bar{x})^2}{n - 1} \qquad s = \sqrt{s^2}$$

where:

s^2 = Sample variance

s = Sample standard deviation

n = number of scores in the sample

$\bar{x}$ = Sample mean

The formulas for the sample variance and the sample standard deviation differ from the formulas for the population versions of these statistics in two ways: the sample mean $\bar{x}$ is substituted for the population mean μ, and the denominator for the sample statistics contains $n - 1$ and not just by n (the equivalent of the population total N). Dividing by $n - 1$ provides better estimates of the population variance and the population standard deviation than does dividing by n alone, because it increases the values of the sample standard deviation and the sample variance. This is especially important if the sample is small, since dividing by n would tend to underestimate the sizes of the actual population variance and population standard deviation. For this reason, the sample standard deviation and the sample variance are called "unbiased estimators" of the population standard deviation and the population variance.

The preceding formula for the variance above is called the **deviation formula** because it involves calculating the deviation scores. Unfortunately, when the number of scores in a data set is large, the deviation formula becomes unwieldy. Consequently, for most purposes, researchers use a **raw-score formula** (also called a computational formula) when calculating the variance or the standard deviation by hand. These formula are the result of an algebraic transformation of the corresponding deviation formulas.*

The raw-score formula for the population variance looks like this:

$$\sigma^2 = \frac{\sum X^2 - \frac{(\sum X)^2}{N}}{N}$$

*This is the algebraic transformation for the top of the deviation formula to the top of the raw-score formula:

$$\sum(X - \bar{x})^2 = \sum(X^2 - 2\bar{x}X + \bar{x}^2)$$
$$= \sum X^2 - \sum 2\bar{x}X + \sum \bar{x}^2$$
$$= \sum X^2 - 2\bar{x}\sum X + \sum \bar{x}^2$$
$$= \sum X^2 - 2\bar{x}(N\bar{x}) + \sum \bar{x}^2$$
$$= \sum X^2 - 2N\bar{x}^2 + N\bar{x}^2$$
$$= \sum X^2 - N\frac{(\sum X)^2}{N^2}$$
$$= \sum X^2 - \frac{(\sum X)^2}{N}$$

Similarly, the raw-score formula for the population standard deviation looks like this:

$$\sigma = \sqrt{\sigma^2} = \sqrt{\frac{\sum X^2 - \frac{(\sum X)^2}{N}}{N}}$$

The raw-score formulas for the sample variance and standard deviation are as follows:

$$s^2 = \frac{\sum X^2 - \frac{(\sum X)^2}{n}}{n - 1} \qquad s = \sqrt{\frac{\sum X^2 - \frac{(\sum X)^2}{n}}{n - 1}}$$

The vehicle speed data are presented again in Table 3.13. We will use them to calculate the population variance and the population standard deviation, using the raw-score formulas. The first step in doing this is to square each score, so a column of squared scores is included in the table. A frequency column is not included in the table this time, and the values are not multiplied by their frequencies as was done earlier. The score values *could* be multiplied by their frequencies, but these formulas are so important that I want their operation to be very clear to you, and I believe that this can be seen more clearly without multiplying by the frequencies.

To calculate the population variance using the raw-score formula, we must sum all of the scores. For our data the sum of the scores ($\sum X$) is 2671. We also need to square each score and then sum the squared scores. The sum of the squared scores in our data ($\sum X^2$) is 179,071. We can now insert these numbers into our raw-score formula, along with the number of observations (40):

$$\sigma^2 = \frac{\sum X^2 - \frac{(\sum X)^2}{N}}{N} = \frac{179{,}071 - \frac{2671^2}{40}}{40} = \frac{714.975}{40} = 17.874$$

$$\sigma = \sqrt{17.874} = 4.228$$

If this set of data were from a sample of a population, we would calculate the following:

$$s^2 = \frac{\sum X^2 - \sum \frac{(\sum X)^2}{n}}{n - 1} = \frac{179{,}071 - \frac{2671^2}{40}}{39} = \frac{714.975}{39} = 18.333$$

$$s = \sqrt{18.333} = 4.282$$

Notice again that the only difference between the population parameter and sample statistic formulas is that the denominator becomes $n - 1$ when we calculate the sample statistics.

The variance and the standard deviation are probably the most commonly used measures of dispersion. They are used independently, and they are also embedded within other, more complex formulas. Because the variance and the standard deviation are based on the mean, they are appropriate for use with interval and ratio data, but not with ordinal and nominal data.

TABLE 3.13   *Speed data summed, and squared speed data summed.*

X	X^2
56	3136
59	3481
60	3600
62	3844
62	3844
62	3844
63	3969
64	4096
64	4096
64	4096
65	4225
65	4225
65	4225
65	4225
65	4225
65	4225
65	4225
66	4356
66	4356
66	4356
67	4489
67	4489
67	4489
67	4489
68	4624
68	4624
68	4624
69	4761
69	4761
70	4900
70	4900
70	4900
70	4900
71	5041
72	5184
72	5184
73	5329
73	5329
74	5476
77	5929
$2671 = \sum X$	$179{,}071 = \sum (X)^2$

CONCEPT
QUESTIONS
3.10

The weather report includes information about the "normal high temperature" for the day. Today's reported high temperature is 10 degrees above the normal high temperature for today's date. To determine whether today is a very strange day or not especially strange, we need to know the standard deviation. If we learn that the standard deviation is 15 degrees, what might we conclude about how normal or abnormal the weather is today? If the standard deviation is 5 degrees, what does that suggest about today's weather?

THE VARIOUS SHAPES OF FREQUENCY DISTRIBUTIONS

Descriptive statistics are used to add precision to the descriptions of frequency distributions, but another set of terms can be used to aid in making these descriptions.

Kurtosis refers to the relative peakedness or flatness of a distribution. A **leptokurtic** distribution has a tall thin peak; a **platykurtic** distribution has a short broad peak; and a **mesokurtic** distribution has a peak of medium height and breadth. Figure 3.5 presents examples of these curves.

Kurtosis is related to the degree of dispersion among the scores. Leptokurtic distributions have comparatively little dispersion; the scores are clustered together, and consequently the standard deviation and the variance for them are relatively small. At the other extreme, platykurtic distributions have comparatively great dispersion, and the standard deviation and the variance for them are relatively large.

When a distribution has the same shape on either side of the center line, the distribution is said to be **symmetric**. If there is one and only one peak and this is not at the center of the distribution, the distribution is said to be **skewed**. A **positively skewed** distribution has its peak to the left of the center line, and its tail trails off to the right. A **negatively skewed** distribution has its peak to right of the center line, and its tail trails off to the left. A **uniform** distribution has no peak; all scores occur with equal frequency. Figure 3.6 presents examples of these differently shaped frequency polygons.

For a unimodal, symmetric distribution of scores, the mode, the median, and the mean all have the same value. When the data are skewed, however, the direction

FIGURE **3.5**   *Types of distributions: (a) leptokurtic; (b) platykurtic; (c) mesokurtic.*

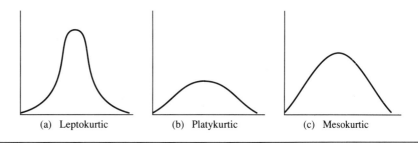

(a) Leptokurtic   (b) Platykurtic   (c) Mesokurtic

FIGURE 3.6   *Types of distributions: (a) symmetric; (b) uniform; (c) negatively skewed; (d) positively skewed.*

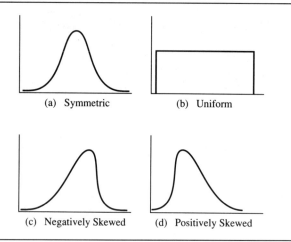

(a) Symmetric   (b) Uniform

(c) Negatively Skewed   (d) Positively Skewed

FIGURE 3.7   *Mean, median, and mode locations in different distributions: (a) symmetric; (b) bimodal; (c) negatively skewed; (d) positively skewed.*

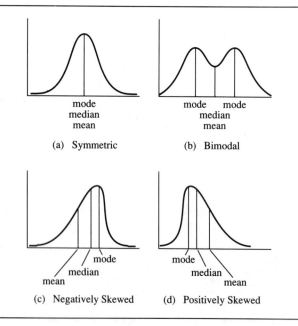

mode
median
mean
(a) Symmetric

mode   mode
median
mean
(b) Bimodal

mode
median
mean
(c) Negatively Skewed

mode
median
mean
(d) Positively Skewed

of the skew will affect the three averages. If the distribution is negatively skewed, the mean is usually smaller than the median, which is usually smaller than the mode. If the distribution is positively skewed, the mean is usually greater than the median, which is usually greater than the mode. If the distribution is symmetrical but also bimodal, the median and the mean will be the same, but the modes will be different. Figure 3.7 provides illustrations of these relationships.

For a more concrete example, let's consider our vehicle speed data again. The mode of this data set is 70. The median is 68.5. The mean is 68. Figure 3.8 shows the frequency polygon for these data, with the mode, the median, and the mean identified.

CONCEPT QUESTIONS 3.11	1. The mean number of times each student speaks in class is 5, the median number of times each student speaks is 4, and the mode number of times each student speaks is 3. What does this information tell you about the shape of the distribution of scores?
	2. The mean, median, and mode number of pages of notes students take in English class is 7; and the standard deviation is 2. In psychology class the mean, median, and mode is also 7; but the standard deviation is 4. Sketch these two distributions. Explain in words how they differ.

INTEROBSERVER RELIABILITY

One more statistic that helps researchers describe data needs to be introduced. Descriptive statistics describe the frequency distribution of a data set. **Interobserver reliability** describes the consistency of the technique used to collect the data.

Various techniques can be used to calculate interobserver reliability. The simplest, which was described earlier, is to determine the percent of agreement between two observers. Let's assume that two radar guns were used to measure the speeds of the vehicles in our example. In Table 3.14, the speeds are listed as measured by the two instruments. After comparing the data from each radar gun, we find that the guns measured differently 3 times out of 40 observations. Thus, they agreed 37 times. We can calculate interobserver reliability for the data from the two radar guns by using the following formula:

$$\frac{\text{Number of agreements}}{\text{Number of opportunities for agreement}} \times 100 = \frac{37}{40} \times 100$$

$$= .925 \times 100$$

$$= 92.5\% \text{ agreement}$$

The measurements of the two guns agreed 92.5% of the time.

Because the vehicles' speeds were measured on a ratio scale of measurement, another technique that could be used to calculate reliability is Pearson's product-moment correlation. This technique can be used with either interval or ratio scaled data. It will be discussed in Chapter 4.

FIGURE 3.8   *Mean, median, and mode locations noted on frequency polygons of vehicle speed data: (a) individual scores; (b) class interval data.*

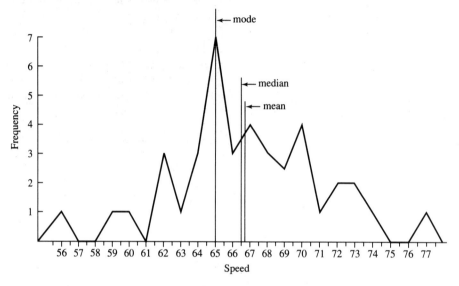

(a)   Frequency Polygon of Individual Vehicle Speeds

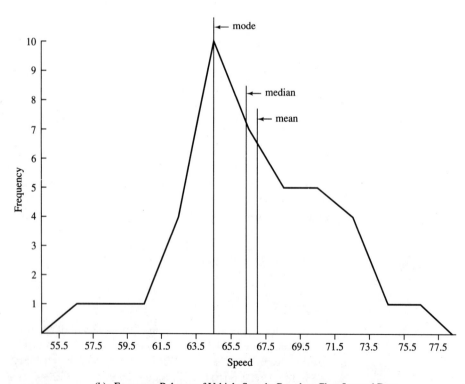

(b)   Frequency Polygon of Vehicle Speeds, Based on Class Interval Data

TABLE 3.14   *Speed data measured by two instruments.*

Vehicle	Radar Gun 1	Radar Gun 2
1	66	66
2	72	72
3	68	68
4	64	64
5	74	74
6	60	60
7	70	70
8	73	73
9	62	62
10	69	69
11	72	72
12	67	65
13	65	65
14	65	65
15	66	66
16	67	67
17	56	56
18	65	65
19	64	64
20	59	59
21	67	67
22	65	65
23	70	68
24	73	73
25	68	68
26	70	70
27	64	64
28	65	65
29	69	69
30	71	71
31	68	67
32	63	63
33	66	62
34	62	62
35	70	70
36	77	77
37	62	62
38	65	65
39	67	67
40	65	65

If only the existence or nonexistence of a behavior or characteristic is recorded, interobserver reliability can be determined by calculating **Cohen's kappa** (κ). Cohen's kappa goes a step beyond determining the proportion of agreements;

the proportion of agreements that would be expected just by chance is also considered in the calculations.

Suppose that, instead of measuring vehicle speeds in miles per hour, two researchers simply recorded whether cars exceeded the speed limit. The code sheet for this data collection might look something like the one presented in Table 3.15. The data from this code sheet can then be summarized on another table, called a **confusion matrix** (see Table 3.16). On the diagonal of the confusion matrix, from top left to bottom right, are the agreements between the two observers. Off the diagonal

TABLE 3.15   *Code sheet for data collection focused on speeding.*

	Observer 1		Observer 2	
	Speeding	Not Speeding	Speeding	Not Speeding
1.		×		×
2.		×		×
3.		×		×
4.		×	×	
5.	×		×	
6.	×		×	
7.		×		×
8.		×		×
9.		×		×
10.	×			×
11.		×		×
12.		×		×
13.		×		×
14.		×	×	
15.		×		×
16.	×		×	
17.	×		×	
18.	×		×	
19.		×		×
20.		×		×

TABLE 3.16   *Confusion matrix for calculating Cohen's kappa.*

		Observer 1	
		Speeding	Not Speeding
Observer 2	Speeding	5	2
	Not Speeding	1	12

are the disagreements. On this matrix, the top right quadrant identifies the number of cars recorded as speeding by observer 2 and recorded as not speeding by observer 1. Conversely, the bottom left quadrant lists the number of cars recorded as speeding by observer 1 and recorded as not speeding by observer 2.

On the basis of the confusion matrix, two proportions can be calculated. The first is the proportion of agreements (P_A), which is calculated by adding the numbers on the diagonal and dividing this figure by the total number of observations:

$$P_A = \frac{(\text{row}_1, \text{column}_1) + (\text{row}_2, \text{column}_2)}{\text{Number of observations}}$$

$$= \frac{5 + 12}{20} = \frac{17}{20} = .85$$

The second proportion that can be calculated is the proportion of expected agreement (P_O), which is calculated by multiplying the corresponding row and column totals, summing these numbers, and dividing this figure by the total number of observations squared:

$$P_O = \frac{(\text{row}_1 \times \text{column}_1) + (\text{row}_2 \times \text{column}_2)}{(\text{Number of observations})^2}$$

$$= \frac{(7 \times 6) + (13 \times 14)}{20^2}$$

$$= \frac{42 + 182}{400} = \frac{224}{400} = .56$$

These two proportions are then entered into the formula for Cohen's kappa. In this formula, the proportion of expected agreements is subtracted from the observed proportion of agreements, and this number is divided by 1 minus the proportion of expected agreements:

$$\kappa = \frac{P_A - P_O}{1 - P_O} = \frac{.85 - .56}{1 - .56} = \frac{.29}{.44} = .659$$

A rule of thumb suggested by Bakeman and Gottman (1989) is that a value for Cohen's kappa of greater than .7 suggests reasonable interobserver reliability. Thus, because our κ is less than .7, we would be wise to question the reliability of the researchers' measures in this study.

CONCEPT QUESTIONS 3.12

Calculate the interobserver reliability between the two observers in Table 3.15 using the following formula:

$$\frac{\text{Number of agreements}}{\text{Number of opportunities for agreement}}$$

Why is this number different from Cohen's kappa? About which assessment of reliability do you feel more confident, and why?

CRITIQUE OF OBSERVATIONAL STUDIES

When evaluating an observational study, one must consider the sample of subjects and the sampling techniques used, as well as the procedure for collecting observations, the statistics used to summarize and organize the data, and the conclusions drawn from the data. Considering these aspects of the study allows one to determine the internal and external validity of the observational study.

Quality of the Sample   One of the most important aspects of an observational study is the sample of subjects (and their behaviors) that were chosen for observation. Ideally, the sample is representative of the population. To obtain a representative sample, most researchers use systematic or random behavior sampling, including either time sampling or event sampling. To increase the generalizability of the results further, situation sampling may be used. If the manner in which subjects and their behaviors were chosen for observation creates a biased sample, this decreases the external validity of the results.

Procedure   Although the external validity of an observational study is important, the internal validity is essential. A primary consideration related to the internal validity of an observational study is the quality of the operational definitions used in the investigation. Ideally, definitions are clear and straightforward; but in actual practice they are sometimes rather complex. In such cases, the training procedures used to clarify the operational definitions for the observers should be explained, as should the criterion used to determine when the observers should begin collecting data.

The manner in which data were collected should be self-explanatory. If a narrative record was made, a portion of that record might be presented as an example of the types of information collected. If a checklist was used, it should be clearly described. When necessary, a sample checklist can be provided for additional clarification. In all cases, the types of behaviors being observed and the information being recorded should be clear to the reader of the research report.

Another consideration when evaluating the validity of the data collection procedures used is whether reactivity is a concern. Is there any reason to believe that the subjects were reacting to the observer and that this affected the behaviors being measured? If data collection involves a reactive measure, this circumstance decreases the validity of those measures.

The reliability of the measurement technique in an observational study is probably best described by an assessment of interobserver reliability. Interobserver reliability may be assessed by a simple comparison of agreements with the opportunity for agreement, by a Pearson's product-moment correlation between the ratings of the observers, or (for categorical data) by a calculation of Cohen's kappa. Whether the interobserver reliability is adequate depends on the assessment technique and the area of investigation. Comparing the study's calculated reliability with interobserver reliabilities presented in the research literature can assist in determining whether the reliability is adequate.

Observer bias is another potential confound in an observational study. The researcher should describe what measures were taken to avoid any observer bias. Were operational definitions of such a nature that observer bias was not likely? Did other observers who were unaware of the hypotheses of the study make the observations? The greater the possibility of observer bias, the greater the possibility of errors in data collection that might lead to unfounded results and conclusions.

Results and Discussion   Once the data have been collected, the researcher uses statistical techniques to find answers to the research questions. Thus far, you have learned about frequency distributions, graphs, and descriptive statistics. Frequency distributions are not likely to be included in a research article, but graphs and descriptive statistics are.

As the reader, you should assess the graphs for accuracy and for correct use. Was a bar graph used when a histogram should have been? Was a frequency polygon presented when the data would have been better represented by a bar graph. Are the x-axis and y-axis in correct proportion? Incorrect use of graphs can misrepresent the data and may suggest relationships that don't necessarily exist.

Descriptive statistics should be appropriate to the level of measurement of the data. Occasionally, a researcher will misuse descriptive statistics—typically by using statistics appropriate for interval or ratio data with nominal or ordinal data. A common error is to treat percentile ranks as interval data. Percentile ranks are ordinal data; the distance between each percentile and the next is not consistent throughout the scale.

Finally, the logic of the discussion should be assessed. In the discussion section of a research article, the researcher interprets the results of the investigation in light of past research and/or relevant theories. This section of the paper no longer depends on the scientific method per se; it also involves rational-deductive argument. Thus, this section is subject to researcher biases and flaws in logic. The reader must determine whether the arguments are consistent with the results. Are the results overgeneralized? Does the researcher try to read more into the results than is appropriate? Are some results ignored, or is their importance underestimated? A reader's reactions to a discussion section are often food for additional research on a topic.

IMPORTANT TERMS AND CONCEPTS

PART I:

naturalistic observation	interobserver reliability	action checklist
desensitization	test-retest reliability	measurement
habituation	split-half reliability	scales of measurement
participant observation	equivalent forms reliability	nominal scales
disguised participant	valid/validity	ordinal scales
undisguised participant	narrative records	interval scales
structured observation	data reduction	ratio scales
field experiments	checklist	biased sample
reliable/reliability	static checklist	behavior sampling

time sampling   situation sampling   Hawthorne effect

random sampling   internal validity   reactive measure/reactivity

systematic sampling   external validity   observer bias

event sampling

PART II:

frequency distribution   line graph   raw-score formula

discrete data   mode/bimodal/multimodal   kurtosis

continuous data   measure of central tendency   leptokurtic

class intervals   median   platykurtic

exact limits   mean   mesokurtic

score limits   measures of dispersion   symmetric

midpoint   range   skewed

cumulative frequency   average deviation   positively skewed

cumulative percent   sum of squares   negatively skewed

x-axis   variance   uniform

y-axis   standard deviation   interobserver reliability

bar graph   population   Cohen's kappa(κ)

histogram   sample   standard deviation

frequency polygon   deviation formula

QUESTIONS AND EXERCISES

1. Shopping malls have been described as the new town meeting places. A colleague of yours wants to study the people who congregate and the types of activities that occur at shopping malls; however, this person is unsure how to begin and comes to you for advice.

    a. What would you suggest that this person do first?

    b. What types of information would you suggest be collected, and how?

    c. After some initial observations, your colleague wishes to investigate whether people shop at the mall alone or in groups. What terms need to be operationalized? What definitions might you suggest?

    d. What type of observational study would you suggest to your colleague for study-

ing the question of shopping alone or in groups?

    e. How would data collection be done? Would you use a static checklist or an action checklist? If the latter, what would it look like?

    f. Would your design allow for an assessment of the reliability of the measurements? If so, how would you assess interobserver reliability?

    g. On what scale or scales of measurement would the data be measured?

2. Do males and females carry their books differently? Design and conduct an observational study to address this question.

    a. What is your operational definition of "carrying books"? What are the different ways books can be carried, and how have you defined them to ensure reliable observations?

b. Design your checklist. Is it an action checklist, a static checklist, or both?

c. Plan your data collection. Will you use behavior sampling? situation sampling? event sampling? Will your sampling be done randomly or systematically? Will you make observations for a specific period of time or until you have gathered a certain amount of data?

d. Will you be able to assess interobserver reliability? If so, how will it be assessed?

e. Collect your data.

f. Graph your data. What type of graph should you use? Why?

g. On what scale of measurement are your data recorded? Use the appropriate descriptive statistics to describe your data set.

h. Assess your interobserver reliability, if possible.

3. Following are final grades for an introductory psychology course. Using these data, create a frequency distribution that includes four columns: f, cf, %, and c%.

98 97 65 72 88 84 93 75 82 87 63 92 76 64 78

75 83 66 91 88 74 72 68 63 81 66 74 72 80 72

69 64 73 82 75 91 64 76 83 62 92 74 82 76 85

90 81 72 61 75 84 86

a. Draw a frequency polygon using the frequency distribution for the preceding data.

b. Determine the mode, the median, and the mean for these data.

c. What is the range for the data?

d. Create a class interval distribution, using intervals with a width of 5 units and beginning with the interval 61–65; use the following column headings:

class interval, exact limits, midpoint, f, cf, %, c%

e. Draw a histogram for this frequency distribution.

4. Following are data on the number of cups of coffee drunk in one day by members of the psychology department at Jittery U. Determine the mean, the median, the mode, the range, the variance, and the standard deviation for this set of data.

3 6 4 5 6 8 9 12 4 3 5 2

5. Two observers collect data on the behavior of people who come out of their homes when an emergency vehicle is in the neighborhood. The observers note whether the individuals approach the vehicle, stand alone, or stand with other neighbors. They make observations of 350 individuals, but disagree 28 times in their observations.

a. Based on this information, what is their interobserver reliability?

b. If they had reported an interobserver reliability of 87%, approximately how many times would they have disagreed in 350 observations?

c. Following is a portion of their checklist, where people are observed either standing alone or standing with others. Using the information from this checklist, calculate Cohen's kappa and interpret the result.

| | Observer 1 | | Observer 2 | |
| | | With | | With |
Observation	Alone	Others	Alone	Others
1	×		×	
2	×		×	
3		×		×
4		×		×
5		×	×	
6		×		×
7	×		×	
8		×		×
9		×		×
10		×		×
11	×			×
12		×		×
13	×		×	
14		×		×
15		×	×	
16	×		×	
17	×		×	
18		×		×

6. Following are several data sets representing the number of glasses or cups of liquid people drink on days with different general temperatures (hot, warm, cool, or cold) Draw a frequency polygon for each set. Calculate the mean, the median, the mode, the standard deviation, and the variance for each set. How do the sets differ, and what effect does this have on the frequency polygons?

Hot Day	Warm Day	Cool Day	Cold Day
8	6	8	6
9	7	6	6
7	6	3	5
8	6	2	7
4	7	7	7
6	6	4	8
5	5	5	8
5	5	1	8
8	3	9	6
8	3	5	9

4

Mail Surveys, Telephone Surveys, and Personal Interviews

In survey research, each respondent is asked to respond to a series of questions about a topic. The topic might be very specific, such as where and why the respondent purchased a particular brand of orange juice; or it may be very broad, such as the respondent's general philosophy of life. The purpose of the survey might be to provide answers to an applied research question or to advance basic research. Survey research is an especially appealing approach to data collection because it involves writing a series of questions to address a specific research issue and then finding the appropriate sample to answer these questions. Yet survey research must be done as carefully and conscientiously as any other type of scientific research if the results are to be useful and interpretable.

The terms *survey* and *questionnaire* are often used interchangeably, and will be treated so throughout this chapter. Nonetheless, some researchers make a distinction between the two by focusing on the types of questions surveys and questionnaires ultimately intend to answer. Survey researchers may be more apt to attempt to define distinctions among the subgroups answering the questions on their instrument, while questionnaire researchers may tend to be more interested in examining relationships between variables, such as whether people who report that they smoke also report that they tend not to wear their seat belt. However, this distinction is not clear and distinct, since survey researchers can look for relationships and questionnaire researchers often detect differences among subgroups of respondents.

Surveys can be presented to potential repondents in a number of ways, including verbally in person, verbally over the phone, or in writing by mail. The primary advantages and disadvantages of mail surveys, telephone surveys, and surveys conducted in person are discussed in Part I of this chapter, along with various practical concerns of designing a survey. Part II focuses on summarizing and analyzing the survey responses. The statistical analyses presented in this section are those used to identify relationships between variables. Statistical techniques for detecting differences between groups are provided in future chapters but are certainly applicable to data obtained from surveys and questionnaires. Finally, Part III offers a general critique of survey and questionnaire research.

PART I: SURVEYS: HOW AND WHY TO USE THEM

Surveys can be conducted orally and in person, or they can be read over the telephone, or they can be written and self-administered by the respondent. They may allow for in-depth answers to questions or simply for the choice of an option. The topics addressed may be as innocuous as opinions about a new ice cream product or as sensitive as details about personal sexual behaviors. Regardless of the topic or the format of a survey, however, the primary purpose is to gather reliable and valid information. Thus, it is important to design the survey and to conduct the study in a manner that maximizes truthful responses. Factors affecting whether a respondent will reply honestly to a survey vary with the types of surveys that can be used. In addition, some types of surveys are better suited for gaining some types of information than are others. For example, a mail survey may provide a researcher

Courtesy of Sidney Harris

with more information on sensitive topics than will the same questions posed during a personal interview. The many types of surveys, types of questions, and types of information a researcher can expect to obtain make surveys an important research tool.

MAIL SURVEYS

Mail surveys are written, self-administered questionnaires. As such, it is especially important that the survey be self-explanatory and that all questions be clearly worded. Ideally, the survey should also be interesting, so the recipient of the survey will be willing to respond.

Advantages of Mail Surveys   Mail surveys are a popular method for collecting data because they have several advantages over other methods of gathering data.

Mail surveys can reach a large number and a wide variety of potential respondents. Because mail surveys can be distributed widely, there is less chance for sampling bias with regard to who receives the survey. **Sampling bias** occurs when a sample overrepresents one or more subsets of the population and underrepresents other subsets, resulting in a sample that is not representative of the population. This might occur, for example, if more males than females are selected for a sample that should have equal numbers of each gender, or if minority groups are underrepresented in a sample of a city's population. Mail surveys can avoid sampling bias in part because they can be sent to neighborhoods where individual interviewers might be reluctant to go in person. Similarly, mail surveys can reach remote areas to which it would be impractical for interviewers to travel. Furthermore, an interviewer may miss a certain type of respondent—for example, by interviewing during particular times of the day—thus resulting in a sampling bias. Regardless of whether a respondent works at home, at an office, during the day or during the night, eventually the person will receive the mail and the mail survey.

It should be noted, however, that mail survey distribution is not perfect. Some individuals do not have mailing addresses, and thus will not be included in the sample. Those not fluent in English are less likely to complete—or complete accurately—a survey they receive in English. In addition, the illiterate will not be able to reply to a written survey.

Another advantage of the mail survey over the personal interview is that the self-administered questionnaire avoids the potential for interviewer bias. **Interviewer bias** occurs when an interviewer's behaviors, questions, or recording procedures yield data that are consistent with the interviewer's personal beliefs, but do not constitute an accurate record of the subjects' responses. Interviewers must be carefully trained to ask questions and record answers objectively. Yet bias can still be a problem when interviewers have expectations about the results of the survey, or when their own personal opinions are made apparent (even subtly) to the respondent. For example, Paul Erdos describes this incident of unintentional interviewer bias:

> [I]n one town where 6 interviewers administered a questionnaire to 400 people, 20 respondents stated that they liked a certain soap because '. . . it has a fragrance like lilacs.' All 20 interviews were made by the same interviewer. A check showed that she hadn't

been cheating. She just happened to like lilacs and had introduced this particular question with a little aside about the lilacs then in bloom" (Erdos, 1983, p. 8).

Mail surveys avoid even the subtlest forms of interviewer bias because no interviewer is present.

Mail surveys are likely to be completed at the respondent's convenience, and this can be advantageous for mail survey researchers. Because the respondents complete the survey according to their own schedules, the replies are likely to be complete. For example, a comparison was made between a mail survey and a telephone survey that both asked whether the respondents listened to the radio, watched TV, read the newspaper, or read magazines. In addition, both surveys asked for the names of the programs, newspapers, and magazines the respondents listened to, watched, or read. The mail and telephone survey results were comparable in the proportions of individuals who listened to, watched, or read the various forms of media; but the mail survey yielded more specific information about the programs, newspapers, and magazines involved (Erdos, 1983, pp. 8–9).

Another advantage of the mail survey over telephone surveys and personal interviews is its appropriateness for collecting sensitive information. A respondent can more readily believe that his or her responses are anonymous when no one is present recording the information. Some thought, though, must be given to the wording of questions that request sensitive information. These considerations and specific recommendations are discussed in the section on question writing.

Disadvantages of Mail Surveys   Although mail surveys have a number of advantages over telephone surveys and personal interviews, they also suffer from a number of disadvantages that must be recognized. A primary concern for researchers conducting mail surveys relates to the percentage of the sample who are willing to respond to the survey.

The extent to which people who receive a survey respond and complete the survey is called the **response rate**. It is determined for mail surveys by dividing the number of responses by the number of requests minus any requests that were made to ineligible people (such as a survey for students that may have been given to a faculty member) or were found to be undeliverable by the postal service. Multiplying this number by 100 will transform it to a percentage. A formula for response rate is as follows:

$$\frac{\text{Number of responses}}{\text{Number in sample} - (\text{Ineligible and undeliverable requests})} \times 100$$

Typically, if a mail survey is sent out only once, the researcher can expect that approximately 30% of the surveys will be completed and returned. To increase the response rate, a researcher may send out a second and even a third mailing of the survey to those who have not responded (Shaughnessy & Zechmeister, 1990, pp. 9–10). One risk of multiple mailings, however, is that it renders less believable to the people receiving the survey the researcher's assurance that their responses will be anonymous, since the researcher is obviously keeping track of who has and who has not completed the survey. To assuage such concerns, special efforts might be made, such as providing a postcard for respondents to mail at the same time as their completed survey. The postcard could be used for record keeping and an explanation of this procedure might reassure respondents that their responses are indeed anonymous.

The response rate to mail surveys is considerably lower than the response rate to other types of surveys, and this is a major disadvantage for mail surveys. A poor response rate can invalidate all the effort put into selecting a representative sample of the population. If only 30% of a carefully selected sample responds to a survey, it could very well constitute a subset of subjects with specific characteristics. Thus, the respondents may not represent the population, even though the original sample did. Only if the respondents cooperated randomly throughout the sample could the researcher be confident that the 30% of the sample that responded maintained the original characteristics of the sample.

It is typically impossible to determine how or why the particular subsample responded to the survey. The best way to reduce the possibility of a biased sample of respondents is to increase the response rate. A suggested minimum acceptable percentage of responses is 50%, unless there is some other form of verification that the nonrespondents and the respondents are similar (Erdos, 1983, p. 144).

Efforts must be made to increase the likelihood that a person will respond to the survey. Multiple mailings do increase the likelihood, as do personal touches such as a hand-addressed or hand-typed envelope and a personally signed cover letter. First-class postage may also increase the likelihood a response, but this is also significantly more expensive than mailing questionnaires at bulk-mail rates. Other ways to increase the response rate include giving advance notice that the survey is coming and supplying an incentive such as a free gift upon return of a completed questionnaire. A variation on offering a reward to everyone who responds is to offer a small incentive to all questionnaire recipients, in the hope that it will motivate some of the would-be nonrespondents to respond. Lately, for example, book publishers have been sending a quarter with their questionnaires, inviting recipients to have a complimentary cup of coffee while they complete the survey.

Obviously, a self-addressed, postage-paid envelope for the respondent to use is highly desirable. And finally, the appearance of a mail survey is very important in soliciting replies; every effort should be made to create a survey that is well organized, easy to understand, and easy to read.

Because they are self-administered, mail surveys must be self-explanatory. An interviewer will not be available to explain what a question means or to provide additional information. This may limit the amount of information that can be obtained by the mail survey, or it may yield incomplete information. Mail surveys are of little use in surveying the very old, the very young, or those simply uninterested in the topic. When choosing the type of survey design appropriate for a study, the researcher must consider whether the information is more likely to be provided on a mail survey or through solicitation by an interviewer.

TELEPHONE SURVEYS

Advantages of Telephone Surveys   Surveys conducted over the telephone have several advantages not shared by mail surveys or personal interviews. Unlike mail surveys, an interviewer can request clarifications of an answer or ask follow-up questions for additional information.

Telephone surveys also draw a higher response rate than do mail surveys. It is not unusual for telephone surveys to obtain response rates of between 59% and 70% (Groves & Kahn, 1979, p. 63). Compare this response rate to the 30% a researcher is likely to achieve with a single mailing of a mail survey. People are simply more likely to throw out a mail survey than to hang up on a telephone interviewer.

Perhaps one reason that telephone surveys enjoy a higher response rate than mail surveys is that the interviewer is able to establish a rapport with the respondent more easily than can be established on paper. The interviewer can also be supervised, and any practices that are likely to reduce the response rate can be corrected early.

Compared with personal interviews, telephone interviews are inexpensive; moreover, the interviewer need not travel and can complete more interviews over the phone in a given amount of time than can a face-to-face interviewer. Cost-effectiveness is less clear when comparing the cost of telephone surveys with mail surveys.

The cost of a mail survey depends on the costs of printing and postage, while telephone survey costs depend on the price of time on the telephone lines and the wages (if any) of the interviewers. For mail surveys, the cost differs little with distance, but distance can greatly increase the cost of a telephone call. Similarly, the length of a questionnaire has a minimal effect on postage costs (although it may affect the return rate), but it can increase the cost of a telephone call substantially. A small sample is likely to make a mail survey more expensive per survey than a larger sample (because bulk mailing discounts may be unavailable), but price per call is unaffected by sample size for the telephone survey. Therefore, a short survey designed for a small sample might be most cost-effectively conducted over the telephone rather than mailed, but longer surveys designed for a larger sample may be less expensively mailed to potential respondents.

Disadvantages of Telephone Surveys Although the telephone survey has a reputation for eliciting a relatively strong response rate, it also has some disadvantages.

There is always the possibility of a sampling bias. A sampling bias can occur in a telephone survey when all members of the population do not have telephones or when some people have telephones with unlisted numbers. The effect of unlisted phone numbers on sampling bias can be reduced by using random-digit dialing procedures, but this increases the chances of calling telephones you aren't interested in, such as those belonging to businesses when you are trying to reach residences. When the population of interest consists of businesses, few of which are likely to have unlisted phone numbers or no phone at all, then sampling bias is of little concern.

A concern in telephone surveys (and personal interviews) is the tendency of respondents to give **socially desirable** responses to questions. Socially desirable responses are those that reflect what the repondents consider is deemed appropriate by society, but do not necessarily reflect what they really think or do. For example, a respondent may say that he or she reads the newspaper everyday when the person actually reads the newspaper once a week, and then only the sports and the comics. The likelihood of receiving socially desirable responses increases as the questions become more threatening or more sensitive—that is, when the respondent feels the answer is more likely to affect the interviewer's impression or opinion of the respondent (Hochstim, 1967). Subjects may try to provide responses that are biased in the direction they think the interviewer wants to hear; for example, if the interviewer is a woman, the respondent might give more sympathetic answers to questions about women's rights, roles, and responsibilities than he or she would if the interviewer had been a man. The major problem with receiving socially desirable responses or responses biased toward what the respondent thinks the interviewer wants is that the responses then have little or no validity and thus are of little worth.

Another serious concern in telephone surveys is interviewer bias. Training before interviewing and supervision during the interviews can minimize this risk, but it must be recognized that, whenever two humans interact, there is the potential for biases to affect the responses and records.

PERSONAL INTERVIEWS

A third type of survey involves a personal interview with a respondent. This type of survey might be conducted on the street, in a shopping mall, door-to-door, or anywhere two people can talk.

Advantages of Personal Interviews   The personal interview has several advantages over the telephone survey and, in particular, over the mail survey. For telephone and mail surveys, a directory such as a telephone directory or a city directory of residents is often used for sampling purposes. These directories are almost never up-to-date, even when they first are published, since people inevitably have moved since the data were collected (Dillman, 1978, pp. 41–43). Personal interviews can avoid the bias potentially hidden in a directory by approaching the individuals who actually live at a particular address, and not the people who are merely listed as living there.

Another disadvantage of mail and telephone surveys is that you cannot be sure of the identity of the individual who responds to the survey. Especially with mail surveys, the researcher has no way of knowing if only one person responded or if the response was a collaborative effort. Did the head of the household respond, or did a bored child complete the survey? On the telephone it may not be easy to determine the situational status of the speaker and whether someone else is available who would be better suited to responding to the survey; for example, is the person on the telephone the manager of a business, the assistant manager, or a low-level employee? In a personal interview it is much easier to discern whom one is speaking to and what that person's role is in the family, the business, or whatever, because the interviewer can actually see the person.

Personal interviews typically yield a high response rate—often between 80% and 90% (Erdos, 1983, p. 141; Dillman, 1978, p. 51). Relatedly, in comparison to mail surveys and telephone surveys, personal interviews enable the researcher to determine more clearly the characteristics of nonrespondents (refusals), because the people are visible to the would-be interviewer. In addition, the nonrespondent typically must verbally refuse to participate and may provide a specific reason, such as being in a hurry or already being late for an appointment. Even without speaking with the nonrespondent, the researcher may be able to identify certain characteristics of the person—such as gender, approximate age, and perhaps even socioeconomic status and marital status—by looking at the individual or the individual's setting (Dillman, 1978, pp. 52–53). This information (although susceptible to bias and misinterpretation by the observer) can help the researcher determine whether the nonrespondents shared characteristics different from those of the sample of survey respondents.

People who are willing to be interviewed for a survey are often willing to devote a considerable amount of time to the interview. Therefore, the personal interview is often the method of choice when a survey is long as well as when its questions tend to be tedious (Dillman, 1978, pp. 54, 59–69).

Of course, since the interviewer is right there with the respondent, the opportunity exists to clarify questions for the respondent as well as to obtain complete answers to open-ended questions. The interviewer can use follow-up questions to encourage further elaboration and clarification of an incomplete answer—an opportunity unavailable with the mail survey.

Disadvantages of Personal Interviews   As useful as the personal interview is, it also has its share of disadvantages. As mentioned earlier, the tendency for respondents to make socially desirable responses can be a problem with personal interviews. Also, it may be more difficult to assure potential respondents that their responses will be anonymous when the interviewer is right there than it would be with a mail survey (Erdos, 1983, p. 9).

To obtain the most accurate information for a survey, it may sometimes be necessary for the respondent to consult with others. For instance, in a business setting, an employee may have to ask a manager about the average profit each month; or in a family setting, one member of the household may have to consult with others about the number of hours they spend watching television. With a personal interview, however, other are less likely to be available for consultation, and an interview may have to be rescheduled with the more knowledgeable person. A mail survey, completed at the respondents' convenience, allows more opportunity for ad hoc consulting.

Because the interviewer collects the information directly from the respondent and because it is difficult and inefficient to supervise individual interviewers closely, the personal interview method provides considerable opportunities for interviewer bias or outright subversion by the interviewer (Dillman, 1978, pp. 63–64). As with the telephone survey, subtle biases and expectations of the interviewer may be communicated to the respondent verbally or (with personal interviews) nonverbally. A smile or a nod may encourage one set of answers; a frown or silence may discourage another line of response. Another risk that is greater for personal interviews than for mail surveys or supervised telephone surveys is the potential for interviewers to out-and-out lie about the interviews, perhaps never conducting the interviews at all.

Assuming that the interviews are actually conducted, care must be taken to ensure that the responses to the survey do not lead to a response bias. If an interviewer conducts door-to-door interviews, people who work at home, are unemployed, or are retired may be overrepresented among the respondents. If interviews are conducted in a shopping mall, those who enjoy shopping and/or have money to spend may be overrepresented. This bias may also be affected by economic factors.

During a recession, a sample of shoppers may be considerably different from a sample of shoppers interviewed during healthier economic times.

On a practical note, personal interviews tend to be more expensive and time-consuming than other types of surveys. For small samples, the time and cost may not be prohibitive; but as the sample grows larger, either the time allotted for the study or the number of interviewers needed to carry out the study (or both) must be increased. Unfortunately, sometimes the monetary cost of a project determines the method used, regardless of what method would supply the most valid and reliable results.

CONCEPT QUESTIONS 4.1

What types of surveys would you recommend in the following situations?

a. Survey of sexual preferences, habits, and number of partners.
b. Long survey on the cleaners used by households.
c. Survey of car-buying history.
d. Survey of attitudes toward a recent presidential decision.

SAMPLING TECHNIQUES

If the results of a survey are to be interpreted accurately, the sample of respondents must adequately represent the population under investigation. The **population** consists of all of the members of a given group, and a **sample** is a subset of that population. The sample is chosen from a **sampling frame**, which is a list of all of the members of a population; thus, the telephone directory is a sampling frame for all of the residents of a particular geographical area. The sampling frame serves as the operational definition of the population. The **elements** or members of the sample are then chosen from the sampling frame. If you wanted to select a sample of students from your college, the student directory might serve as your sampling frame, and the individual names chosen from the directory would be the elements of your sample.

The goal of sampling is to create a sample that is representative of the population. One way to obtain a representative sample is to select the sample randomly. **Random selection** means that all members of the population are equally likely to be chosen as part of the sample. This should not be confused with haphazardly choosing or arbitrarily choosing elements for a sample. Haphazard or arbitrary selection is open to the subtle biases of the person doing the selecting. Random selection avoids these biases and results in a **random sample** whose elements were randomly chosen from a sampling frame.

Choosing a random sample often involves using a random numbers table, such as the one provided in Appendix B of this book. A starting place on the table is chosen arbitrarily; then, based on the numbers on the random numbers table, elements are chosen from the sampling frame. For example, if the first number on the random numbers table at the chosen starting place is a 3, the researcher should count down three people in the sampling frame and then include the third person as an element in the sample. If the next number on the table is 8, the researcher would count down eight more people and then include the eighth person as an element. This continues until the required number of elements are included in the sample. For large sampling frames, different parts of the frame might need to be randomly chosen to avoid selecting an entire sample from, for example, the Smith section of the phone book. Another technique that can be used when the sampling frame is not too large is to number each element in the sampling frame and then use the random numbers table to identify the numbers of the elements to be chosen for the sample.

Similar to (but not the same as) random sampling is systematic sampling. In **systematic sampling** elements are not chosen randomly; instead, they are chosen according to some specific plan or strategy. For example, if every third person on a list of registered students was chosen to be a part of a sample, this would be systematic sampling. A combination of random and systematic sampling might involve randomly choosing a starting point and then choosing every kth item to be an element in the sample, such as every tenth element or every third. This method is considerably less time-consuming than simple random sampling.

Sometimes a population is made up of members of different categories, such as a college that may have only recently begun accepting male students and thus may consist of 80% female students and 20% male students. To constitute a representative sample of a population consisting of individuals who fall into distinct categories, the sample must include members of those categories in the proportions in which they are present in the population. In these cases the researcher may not be willing to leave category membership up to chance in random or systematic sampling; instead, the researcher may choose to use stratified sampling.

Stratified sampling is done to guarantee that the sample accurately represents the population on specific characteristics. The sampling frame is divided into sub-samples or strata on the basis of specific, important characteristics. Elements of the sample are then chosen from the strata, either systematically or randomly. If they are chosen randomly, the technique is usually called **stratified random sampling**. To guarantee a sample representative of a population that is 80% female and 20% male, a researcher using stratified random sampling would divide the sampling frame according to gender. The researcher would then randomly select 80% of the sample from the female strata and 20% of the sample from the male strata.

When the population is too large for simple random sampling, or when there is no sampling frame available for the population, cluster sampling may be used. In **cluster sampling**, clusters of elements that represent the entire population are identified, and then all of the elements in those clusters are included in the sample. Recently, two researchers wished to collect survey information about date rape. At their university, two English composition courses are required of all students: a freshman composition course and a junior-level composition course. The researchers chose to solicit responses to their survey from the composition classes during one semester, because these two courses were required to be taken by all students at the university and each class tended to be representative of the population of university students. The composition classes thus served as representative clusters of the elements from the population (Finley & Corty, 1993).

Obtaining a representative sample is one of the most crucial aspects of conducting survey research, since the results of the research are only meaningful if they can be generalized to the population. However, only with a 100% response rate will the representativeness of the sample be transferred to the group of respondents. Almost always there are fewer responses than individuals sampled, and that introduces the possibility of distortion in the responses, since these may not be a totally accurate representation of the population's attitudes, beliefs, thoughts, or behaviors. This makes it all the more imperative that the researcher at least begin with a representative sample; then, through efforts to maximize the response rate, distortions caused by a less than perfect response rate can be minimized.

CONCEPT QUESTIONS 4.2	1. The student body of a college is composed of 20% science majors, 75% social science majors, and 5% art majors. Which sampling technique would you recommend for selecting a representative sample of the college's population? 2. What if the population of interest were a city of 150,000 people—79% white, 12% black, 6% Hispanic, 2.5% Asian, and .5% other? How would you suggest that a researcher sample this population?

SURVEY CONSTRUCTION

Developing a survey requires careful planning if the information it obtains is to be reliable and valid. The type of survey being conducted—be it telephone survey, personal interview, or mail survey—also plays a role in determining what questions are asked and in what order.

Layout of Questions   In a survey that the subjects will see, such as a mail survey, or in a survey that is to be conducted in a large group, such as a classroom, the appearance of the survey is especially important. It should strike the respondent as being easy and (ideally), interesting to complete. For a mail survey, the shorter the survey, the higher the percentage of returns (Erdos, 1983, p. 39). As mentioned earlier, respondents to personal interview surveys seem more tolerant of longer surveys.

   Demographic questions are descriptive questions about the respondent's socioeconomic statistics, such as gender, age, income level, and so on. These questions are usually as important to the researcher as any other questions on the survey, but the respondent may find them boring or too personal. For this reason authorities often recommend that the demographic questions be placed at the end of the questionnaire, where they are more likely to be completed since the respondent has made something of a commitment to the survey by this point (Dillman, 1978; Sudman & Bradburn, 1982). However, this is not a hard and fast rule. In some cases, especially when a personal interview or telephone survey is being conducted, the demographic questions, or a subset of them, may serve as an icebreaker that allows the interviewer to establish a rapport with the respondent before getting to the meatier questions.

Wording of Questions   Writing the questions for a survey takes considerable thought and planning so that the answers provided will be useful to the researcher. Unfortunately, when not enough effort has been spent on the wording of the questions, the result often is ambiguous questions that are misunderstood by the respondents.

In determining how to write questions, the researcher must decide what specific information is needed and then must ask for that information. If you want to know how many years a person has lived in an area, it is best to ask specifically for the number of years. Asking "How long have you lived in Centerville?" may elicit responses such as "Since I was a child," "I moved here after I got married," or "For many years." A better approach would be to ask "How many years have you lived in Centerville?" or "How long have you lived in Centerville? _____ yrs." (Erdos, 1983, p. 66).

The questions that appear in surveys can be divided into two types: open-ended questions and closed questions. **Open-ended questions** provide room or time for the respondent to formulate his or her own response. **Closed questions** ask the respondent to choose from a limited number of preformulated alternative answers.

Open-ended questions have the advantage of allowing the subject to provide complete information, including any explanatory information that may be necessary. On the other hand, open-ended questions are much more difficult to score for statistical analysis. Typically, some type of coding system must be designed, and two or more judges must code the responses. The reliability of the coding system can then be assessed by comparing the extent of agreement among the judges, much as with interobserver reliability (discussed in Chapter 3).

Closed questions do not require that the responses be coded, but they do limit the responses to the alternatives listed. Unless the researcher is very careful, alternatives that respondents would have used may be omitted, such as in a case where the researcher provides only yes or no as options but a subset of respondents would prefer to indicate that they don't know. Another problem is that the respondent does not have the opportunity to expand on or explain answers. Thus, closed questions may lead to less complete information than might be obtained from open-ended questions.

Because the options provided in closed questions may be incomplete, a respondent may not have an option that accurately reflects his or her answer. For example, a question may ask:

On average, how many hours per day do you watch television?

a. 0–1 hr   b. 2–3 hrs   c. 4–5 hrs   d. 6 or more hrs

The respondent who wishes to reply that he or she watches an average of 3.5 hours of television per day has to choose between option b and option c, neither of which is entirely accurate.

As a question is read, the respondent is likely to begin immediately to formulate an answer, even before the sentence has been completed. For this reason it is important that any conditional information be placed at the beginning of a question. Here are two questions, one with the conditional information first and the other one with it second:

Poorer construction:

Do you believe that abortion is permissible if the woman's life is at risk?

Better construction:

If the woman's life is at risk, do you believe that abortion is permissible?

When the conditional information is given first, the reader encounters all relevant hypothetical conditions before the key question is asked. This same principal holds true when the conditional information is a definition of a term or the description of a setting. It is important and logical to present the relevant conditional information before asking the specific question.

The specific words used in a question are also important in developing a clear, unambiguous question. To be avoided are loaded questions, leading questions, and double-barreled questions. **Loaded questions** are ones that include nonneutral or emotionally laden terms. An example of a loaded question is: "Do you believe that radical extremists should be allowed to burn our country's flag?" The term "radical extremist" is loaded and suggests the writer's opinion of flag-burners. Loaded questions invite biased responses that reflect what the questioner wanted to hear, not necessarily what the repondents believe.

Leading questions bias the presentation of information within the question, to incline the respondent to answer in a desired manner. An example is: "Most people believe that recycling is an important way to help conserve our resources; do you agree?" By suggesting what "most people" believe, the writer encourages the respondent to respond in a similar manner. Both loaded and leading questions suggest to the respondent what the "correct" reply is, instead of soliciting an unbiased reply.

Double-barreled questions ask more than one question at the same time. Often double-barreled questions include the word *or*. For example: "Do you find your job interesting or exciting?" It is unclear from this question whether the researcher wants to divide responses into the categories "either interesting or exciting" and "neither interesting nor exciting" or whether the researcher has implicitly assumed that no job could be found to be both interesting and exciting and therefore wants the respondent to choose between the categories "interesting" and "exciting." One way to test whether a question is double-barreled is to try to imagine how a person who could answer yes to part of the question and no to the other part might respond. A person who had an interesting job, but a job that wasn't very exciting, would have difficulty answering this question.

In writing questions for a survey, the goal is to write straightforward, unambiguous, and unbiased questions that elicit usable, reliable, and valid information. Not only are the specific words important within the questions, but the order of the questions themselves is important. The questions should be ordered logically. To prevent respondents from having to answer irrelevant questions, filter questions might be used. A **filter question** instructs the respondent or interviewer what the next question should be, depending on the answer to the filter question. An example of a filter question is:

Do you smoke cigarettes, cigars and/or a pipe? _____ yes _____ no

[If you answered NO to this question, please skip to question 5.]

Funnel questions may also be used in a survey. **Funnel questions** are a set of questions ordered from most general to most specific. Funnel questions serve to introduce a topic and then gradually focus on the more specific questions. A major function of funnel questions is to prevent earlier responses from biasing later responses (Kahn & Cannell, 1957, as cited in Sudman & Bradburn, 1982, pp. 219–20).

With careful planning and attention to wording and layout, a survey can provide meaningful and interpretable information. Unfortunately, it is very easy to write confusing questions or to present the questions in an illogical order that leads to ambiguity and uninterpretable data.

CONCEPT QUESTIONS 4·3

What is wrong with the wording of this question?

> How many individuals in the United States do you believe have AIDS or are HIV positive?

How might it be better worded?

Development Process   To maximize the probability that a survey will be useful, it is important not to skimp during the development stage. The first step is to determine exactly what information is needed and then to ask for that specific information. Do not waste your time or your respondents' time with irrelevant questions. After the questions are written, develop a first draft of the survey, but do not immediately put it into service to collect your data. Instead, you should carry out a **pilot study** in which you give your survey to a small group of people for them to complete. Solicit comments from these individuals. Were the questions straightforward, or were some difficult to understand? How long did it take each person to complete the survey? Then look at the responses to your questions. Did the questions elicit the type of responses you anticipated, or were some questions ambiguous and thus led to responses you hadn't expected? A pilot study can help you identify problems with the survey design before you collect your data.

After the survey has been modified in light of the pilot study results, the final version of the survey should be taken for a test run before being put to work. It should be presented to a small sample of subjects to be completed, using the same procedures the larger sample will use. This helps the researcher ascertain that the changes made were adequate and that no new problems have emerged. If the survey survives this final test, it is ready to be put to use.

PART II: SOME APPROPRIATE ANALYSES FOR SURVEY AND QUESTIONNAIRE DATA

Once the survey is developed and the data are collected, the data must be organized and summarized to be useful. Many of the statistical techniques discussed in Chapter 3 are applicable for use with survey data as well. This section reviews some statistics described earlier and introduces some new techniques that can be of use when interpreting survey data.

DESCRIPTIVE STATISTICS

Descriptive statistics serve an important role in all research by providing the researcher and the reader of the report with important summary information. These statistics provide a picture of the sample as a whole, as well as of any important subgroups of the sample, such as the number of males and females. Descriptive statistics are also useful for determining whether a sample of responses is representative of the population.

A survey requesting that respondents rate the familiarity of 97 common phrases, called idioms, was sent to 3816 residents of a small midwestern city. There were 1049 usable responses. Of these responses, 487 were from males and 525 were from females (and 37 respondents did not indicate their gender). The number of males and females can also be described in terms of percentages by dividing the number in each category by the total number of respondents. Thus, 46.42% of the respondents identified themselves as male $\left(\frac{487}{1049} \times 100 \right)$ and 50.05% identified themselves as female $\left(\frac{525}{1049} \times 100 \right)$.

Percentages are sometimes easier for a reader to interpret, but they can also be misleading. When a sample is very small, reporting percentages alone can suggest that a difference is substantial when in reality it is quite small. For example, if 6 of 25 respondents answer in one way and 8 others answer in a different way, there is a difference of only 2 respondents. But, if this were reported in terms of percentages, we would have $\frac{6}{25} \times 100 = 24\%$ and $\frac{8}{25} \times 100 = 32\%$, a difference of 8 percentage points. This sounds like a much more substantial difference than does a figure of only 2 respondents. To avoid inadvertently misleading the reader, it is good practice to present the actual number of responses along with the percentages of total responses.

In addition to presenting percentages of responses, researchers can use the mode and measures of central tendency to describe both the sample and the responses to individual questions. Important to consider when using these measures, however, is the scale of measurement of the data being described. For example, in the idiom familiarity survey, the age of the respondents was measured in years. Age in years uses a ratio scale of measurement, and thus the mean, the median, or the mode would be appropriate for describing the age of the respondents.

In this particular study, the mean was chosen to describe the age, primarily because the standard deviation could then be meaningfully used as a measure of dispersion. (Remember, the standard deviation is a measure of the average deviation of the scores from the mean.) The mean age of the respondents was 51.63 years, with a standard deviation of 16.16. Often this information would be written as $M = 51.63$ (SD = 16.16). It is a good idea to present the standard deviation whenever a mean is presented, because this supplies the reader with important additional information about the variability in the responses. Other measures of dispersion, such as the range, can also be useful to the evaluator of a research project.

The median is a second common measure of central tendency for describing samples and responses to questions. It is particularly useful when the data are measured on an ordinal scale, when the responses are to be divided into two groups of equal size, or when the data include outliers that would affect the mean.

In the idiom survey, the respondents were asked to estimate their annual household income level. The options were: less than $10,000, $10,000–$15,000, $15,000–$20,000, $20,000–$30,000, $30,000–$40,000, $40,000–$50,000, $50,000–$60,000, and over $60,000. This question supplied ordinal data, because the options provided information about income level; but the interval sizes for the categories are not consistent. Because the data are ordinal, use of the mean would be inappropriate, but use of the median would be proper. The median income level for this survey was the category of $30,000–$40,000 per year. [What's wrong with the set of options provided in this closed question? What improvements would you suggest?]

To compare responses among respondents of the upper income level with those among respondents of the lower income level, we would assign those above the median to the high income group and those below the median to the low income group. We would assign those who identified themselves as being in the $30,000–$40,000 category to the high or low income groups at random. This technique is called a **median split**, and serves to divide a sample into two equal groups. A median split can be conducted on ordinal, interval, or ratio data.

The mode, another descriptive statistic that can be used with survey data, is especially useful for nominal data—data that identify categories of responses for which order is not an issue. An example of a nominally scaled question is one that asks for the gender of the respondent. The mode of the gender responses could be reported (the mode for the idiom survey was females, 525); however, since there are only two options, it is just as easy to report the number of both male and female respondents. The mode would be more useful when a nominally scaled set of categories includes three or more possible options.

In survey research it is very important that a description of the sample of respondents include information about response rate. Response rate may be calculated slightly differently depending on the type of survey conducted (mail, telephone, or personal interview), but in general it is a ratio of the number of responses to the number of individuals approached. The following general formula was presented earlier in this chapter:

$$\frac{\text{Number of responses}}{\text{Number in sample} - (\text{Ineligible and undeliverable requests})} \times 100$$

The denominator in the fraction refers to the number of requests for responses made minus the number that should not have been made because they did not fulfill the requirements of the survey. For example, in a personal interview setting, if a researcher is only interested in interviewing residents of a town, people who are approached to complete the survey but who are not residents of the town should not be counted as refusals. These inappropriate subjects should therefore be subtracted from the total number of people approached. Similarly, in a telephone interview survey, all phone calls that are not answered or that are answered by someone who does not fulfill the standards set for a respondent (such as a small child) should be subtracted from the total number of calls made. And in a mail survey, all surveys that are returned as undeliverable should be subtracted from the total number of surveys sent. Although the inappropriate requests do not count toward the response rate, the number of such requests should be recorded, since this information may supply another researcher with important information about which techniques work and which don't work when soliciting responses.

For the idiom survey, 3837 surveys were mailed, but 21 surveys were returned as undeliverable by the postal service. Of the surveys that were delivered, 1049 were completed and returned. Thus, the response rate would be calculated as follows:

$$\text{Response rate} = \frac{1049}{3837 - 21} \times 100$$

$$= \frac{1049}{3816} \times 100$$

$$= .2749 \times 100$$

$$= 27.49\%$$

As an evaluator of research, you would want to determine whether this response rate is reasonable or too low. Should you be concerned about the representativeness of this sample? To answer questions about representativeness, the researcher should provide descriptive information about the sample, such as number of males and females, or perhaps the number of respondents of different races. This information can then be compared with the population.

The respondents to the idiom survey were 93% white ($N = 977$), 2.85% African-American ($N = 30$), and 1.33% members of other races ($N = 14$); 2.67% ($N = 28$) of the respondents did not indicate their race. Considering that approximately 12% of the residents of the city from which this sample was drawn are African-American, the sample of respondents appears not to represent the population of that city adequately.

CONCEPT QUESTIONS 4.4	1. Researchers distributed 188 surveys designed for student respondents, but one was mistakenly given to a faculty person, who did not complete it. The researchers received 122 completed surveys. What was their response rate? 2. A researcher sent out 1000 surveys to a random sample of a city's residents. The postal service returned 23 surveys as undeliverable. The researcher subsequently received 313 completed surveys. What was the researcher's response rate? What are some possible ways a response bias may have occurred?

A STANDARD SCORE—THE z-SCORE

Descriptive statistics are important for describing the sample of scores and respondents, but sometimes we want information about a single score. For example, if a respondent to a survey reports an annual income level of $65,000, the researchers may wish to know how this figure compares with the income level of other respondents. Is it higher than that of most other people? Lower than most? Perhaps a second survey is conducted in a different neighborhood. How does a reported annual income of $65,000 compare with the income level of respondents on the second survey? How do the two incomes compare with each other? Perhaps in the first survey the respondent with a $65,000 income was making more money than 90% of the respondents, but in the second survey an income of $65,000 is higher than only 25% of the respondents. This difference may have a substantial effect on the interpretation of the responses. A single raw score by itself is thus of little value without additional information about where it lies in relation to the rest of the scores.

Imagine that a test is given in an English class and that the mean score ($\bar{x}$) on the test was a 73, with a standard deviation (s) of 3 points. One of the students in the English class is also in a psychology class, where the $\bar{x}$ test score was a 68, with an s of 4 points. The student earned a 75 on the English test and a 73 on the psychology test. Compared with the other students' performances, on which test did this student perform better? At first glance it might appear that the student performed better on the English exam, because the English test score is higher. But notice that the mean for the English test is also higher than the mean for the psychology test; this needs to be taken into account. In essence, we are trying to compare apples and oranges: a test grade in English from one sample with a test grade in psychology from another sample. To compare these scores, we need to find some common ground. For example, degrees Kelvin and degrees Centigrade can be compared by transforming both scales into degrees Fahrenheit. When we transform scores to a score on a common scale, the new numbers are called **standard scores**. We use standard scores to describe IQs by transforming the raw scores from different IQ tests to a standard score that has a mean of 100 and standard deviation of 15 (or 16 in the case of the Stanford Binet). College entrance exam scores (the ACT and the SAT) are also transformed into standard scores. In research, a commonly used standard score is the z-score.

The **z-score** transformation translates raw scores into numbers that describe how far each test score falls from the mean scores. This distance can be measured in standard deviations. The formula for making this transformation is

$$z = \frac{X - \bar{x}}{s} \quad \text{or} \quad \frac{X - \mu}{\sigma}$$

where z is the symbol for the new standard score.

The z-scores are standard scores that indicate the number of standard deviations a raw score lies above or below the mean. It is a statistical technique that is appropriate for use with data measured on a ratio or interval scale of measurement (a scale on which it would be appropriate to calculate a mean). Let's return to our student with the English and psychology test scores. The following chart lists the necessary information for transforming the student's English and psychology test scores into z-scores:

Subject	X	$\bar{x}$	s
English	75	73	3
Psychology	73	68	4

To compute the z-score for the English test, we must calculate the difference between the score and the mean, and then divide that number by the standard deviation. The same process is used to determine the z-score for the psychology test. We obtain the following results:

English:
$$z = \frac{X - \bar{x}}{s}$$
$$= \frac{75 - 73}{3}$$
$$= .667$$

Psychology:
$$z = \frac{X - \bar{x}}{s}$$
$$= \frac{73 - 68}{4}$$
$$= 1.25$$

The student's z-score for the English test was .667, and the z-score for the psychology test was 1.25; that is, the student scored .667 standard deviations above the mean on the English exam and 1.25 standard deviations above the mean on the psychology test. Therefore, although the student answered a greater percentage of the questions correctly on the English exam than on the psychology exam, relative to the others in the classes this student performed better on the psychology exam than on the English exam.

When the mean of the z-scores is calculated, it is always 0; and the variance (and standard deviation) is always 1. Transforming raw scores to z-scores, however, does not have any effect on the shape of the distribution of the scores. If the distribution of the psychology test's raw scores was negatively skewed, the distribution of the psychology test's z-scores would also be negatively skewed.

THE NORMAL DISTRIBUTION

If a distribution of scores is mesokurtic, symmetric, and unimodal, we say that the distribution is a **normal distribution**. The normal distribution is not one single distribution, but a family of distributions with different means and standard deviations. All normal distributions, though, share the properties of being unimodal, mesokurtic, and symmetric, or what is often called "bell-shaped." Normal distributions reflect the frequencies of a continuous variable rather than of a discrete variable, and the distribution is *asymptotic* to the x-axis; that is, as the distribution moves farther from the mean on either side, it gets closer and closer to the x-axis but never

FIGURE 4.1   *Normal distributions with different means and standard deviations: (a) different means; (b) different standard deviations.*

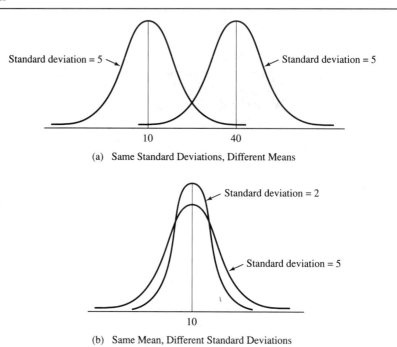

(a)   Same Standard Deviations, Different Means

(b)   Same Mean, Different Standard Deviations

touches it. In Figure 4.1, several normal distributions are presented, each with a different mean and a different standard deviation.

Recall from the last section that any distribution of scores transformed into z-scores will have $\mu = 0$ and $\sigma = 1$. If that distribution of scores is normally distributed, the distribution of z-scores is called the **standard normal distribution**. The frequency polygon illustrating this distribution is called the **standard normal curve**.

The standard normal curve is actually a theoretical distribution defined by a specific mathematical formula. Other normal curves approach the standard normal curve to greater or lesser degrees. The standard normal curve can be very useful for interpreting data because it can provide information about the proportion of scores that are higher or lower than any other particular score. Relatedly, by using the standard normal curve, a researcher can determine the probability of occurrence of a score that is higher or lower than any other score, assuming the distribution of raw scores is relatively normally distributed. Transforming scores that are negatively skewed to z-scores will not make the distribution normal.

To understand how the standard normal curve can be used by researchers, first consider the histograms we discussed in the previous chapter. In a histogram, the frequencies of a continuous variable are represented by a series of contiguous bars. Figure 4.2 displays a histogram representing some hypothetical test grade data. Each

FIGURE 4.2   *Histogram of hypothetical test scores.*

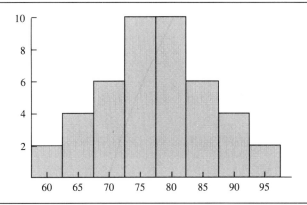

FIGURE 4.3   *Historgram of hypothetical test scores, where each score is represented by a square area.*

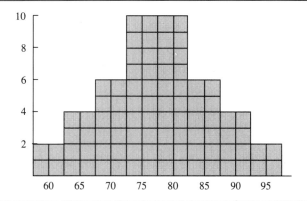

bar in the histogram can be broken up into equal-size squares representing each person's score so that each person's score takes up the same amount of area in the histogram as everyone else's (see Figure 4.3).

If the histogram is divided along its mean score, what proportion of the scores lie above the mean? This question could be answered the hard way—by counting all the scores above the mean and dividing this sum by the total number of scores— or we could reason that, in a symmetric and unimodal distribution, the mean and the median (and the mode) are the same. Thus, since the median divides the distribution of scores into two equal parts, so does the mean. This implies that half of the scores lie above the mean and half below, so the proportion of scores above the mean is .50. This proportion can also be thought of in terms of probabilities. If half of the scores lie above the mean, what is the probability of randomly choosing a score that falls above the mean? The probability is .50. Thus, the probability is equal to the proportion. We can determine the proportion of scores that lie between any two scores, if we are willing to count the squares between them (and thus also

FIGURE **4.4**   *Frequency polygon of test scores, with both z-scores and raw scores noted.*

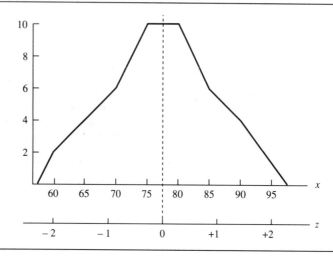

determine the probability of randomly choosing a score between any other two scores). Luckily, as we shall see, a table provides this information for us, already calculated.

Now, let's connect the midpoints of our histogram and erase the squares. In Figure 4.4 the frequencies of our scores are represented as a frequency curve for a normal distribution. Each score is still represented by an equal-size area, but we can no longer see the squares. A line corresponding to the x-axis has also been added to this distribution to show where the z-scores would lie in relation to the raw scores.

Because this graph is a direct transformation from the histogram in Figure 4.3, the proportion of scores lying above the mean (or below the mean) is still .50. But a researcher may wish to know about other, more interesting proportions. For example, if we suppose that this distribution of scores is the distribution for the psychology test mentioned earlier, we might wish to know what proportion of the scores lie above and below a score of 73, the score our student had. This information is gleaned from Table Z in Appendix B. A portion of Table Z has been reproduced in Table 4.1.

The columns along the top of Table Z are labeled z, *Area Between $\bar{x}$ and z, Area Beyond z*, and *Ordinate*. The z refers to the z-scores. *Area Between $\bar{x}$ and z* refers to the area under the curve between the mean of the distribution (where $z = 0$) and the z-score in the first column. This also represents the proportion of scores (or the probability of randomly choosing a score) between the mean and the z-score in column 1. *Area Beyond z* refers to the area under the curve from the z-score out to the tail. As with the area between $\bar{x}$ and z, the area also corresponds to the proportion of scores (or the probability of randomly choosing a score), beyond the z-score. The entire table goes only as far as a z-score of 4.00 because it is very unusual (although theoretically possible) for a normally distributed population of scores to include scores larger than this. The table only reports information about positive

TABLE 4.1   *A portion of the normal curve table.*

Areas Under the Standard Normal Curve for Values of z

z	Area Between $\bar{x}$ and z	Area Beyond z	Ordinate	z	Area Between $\bar{x}$ and z	Area Beyond z	Ordinate
0.00	.0000	.5000	.3989	0.42	.1628	.3372	.3653
0.01	.0040	.4960	.3989	0.43	.1664	.3336	.3637
0.02	.0080	.4920	.3989	0.44	.1770	.3300	.3621
0.03	.0120	.4880	.3988	0.45	.1736	.3264	.3605
0.04	.0160	.4840	.3986	0.46	.1772	.3228	.3589
0.05	.0199	.4801	.3984	0.47	.1808	.3192	.3572
0.06	.0239	.4761	.3982	0.48	.1844	.3156	.3555
0.07	.0279	.4721	.3980	0.49	.1879	.3121	.3538
0.08	.0319	.4681	.3977	0.50	.1915	.3085	.3521
0.09	.0359	.4641	.3973	0.51	.1950	.3050	.3503
0.10	.0398	.4602	.3970	0.52	.1985	.3015	.3485
0.11	.0438	.4562	.3965	0.53	.2019	.2981	.3467
0.12	.0478	.4522	.3961	0.54	.2054	.2946	.3448
0.13	.0517	.4483	.3956	0.55	.2088	.2912	.3429
0.14	.0557	.4443	.3951	0.56	.2123	.2877	.3410
0.15	.0596	.4404	.3945	0.57	.2157	.2843	.3391
0.16	.0636	.4364	.3939	0.58	.2190	.2810	.3372
0.17	.0675	.4325	.3932	0.59	.2224	.2776	.3352
0.18	.0714	.4286	.3925	0.60	.2257	.2743	.3332
0.19	.0753	.4247	.3918	0.61	.2291	.2709	.3312
0.20	.0793	.4207	.3910	0.62	.2324	.2676	.3292
0.21	.0832	.4268	.3902	0.63	.2357	.2643	.3271
0.22	.0871	.4129	.3894	0.64	.2389	.2611	.3251
0.23	.0910	.4090	.3885	0.65	.2422	.2578	.3230
0.24	.0948	.4052	.3876	0.66	.2454	.2546	.3209
0.25	.0987	.4013	.3867	0.67	.2486	.2514	.3187
0.26	.1026	.3974	.3857	0.68	.2517	.2483	.3166
0.27	.1064	.3936	.3847	0.69	.2549	.2451	.3144
0.28	.1103	.3897	.3836	0.70	.2580	.2420	.3123
0.29	.1141	.3859	.3825	0.71	.2611	.2389	.3101
0.30	.1179	.3821	.3814	0.72	.2642	.2358	.3079
0.31	.1217	.3783	.3802	0.73	.2673	.2327	.3056
0.32	.1255	.3745	.3790	0.74	.2704	.2296	.3034
0.33	.1293	.3707	.3778	0.75	.2734	.2266	.3011
0.34	.1331	.3669	.3765	0.76	.2764	.2236	.2989
0.35	.1368	.3632	.3752	0.77	.2794	.2206	.2966
0.36	.1406	.3594	.3739	0.78	.2823	.2177	.2943
0.37	.1443	.3557	.3725	0.79	.2852	.2148	.2920
0.38	.1480	.3520	.3712	0.80	.2881	.2119	.2897
0.39	.1517	.3483	.3697	0.81	.2910	.2090	.2874
0.40	.1554	.3446	.3683	0.82	.2939	.2061	.2850
0.41	.1591	.3409	.3668	0.83	.2967	.2033	.2827

z-scores although a normal distribution of scores actually ranges from approximately −4.00 to +4.00. Because the distribution is symmetric, however, the areas between the $\bar{x}$ and z and beyond the z-scores are the same whether the z is positive or negative. Thus, the table information represents absolute values of the z-scores.

Our student has a score of 73. To use Table Z, we must first transform the raw score to a z-score. This was done earlier, and we obtained a z-score of 1.25. From Table Z we find that the proportion of scores lying above the z-score is .1056. This is obtained from the *Area Beyond z* column. This number can also be interpreted to mean that 10.56% of the scores were greater than our student's score, or that the probability of randomly choosing a score with a z-score greater than 1.25 is .1056. To determine the proportion of scores lying below this z-score, we need to determine the area between $\bar{x}$ and z and then add .50. Why? Because Table Z supplies information about only one side of the normal distribution. To include the other side of the distribution, we must add the proportion of scores on that side, which is always .50 (see Figure 4.5). The proportion of scores falling below a z-score of 1.25 is .3944 + .50 = .8944. Thus, 89.44% of the scores are below our student's score, and the probability of randomly choosing a score below our student's is .8944.

Suppose that another student earned a test score of 65. What proportion of the scores are less than this student's? First, we calculate the z-score:

$$z = \frac{X - \bar{x}}{s}$$

$$= \frac{65 - 68}{4}$$

$$= \frac{-3}{4}$$

$$= -.75$$

Next, we must determine which column to use in Table Z. Figure 4.6 shows a picture of the standard normal curve, with this z-score and the z-score of 1.25 marked. The area corresponding to each column in Table Z is also indicated. To

FIGURE 4.5   *Determining the proportion of scores falling below a z-score of 1.25.*

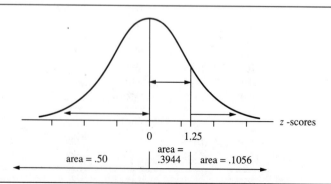

FIGURE 4.6   *Standard normal curve with z-scores of −.75 and 1.25 indicated, as well as the relevant areas under the curve.*

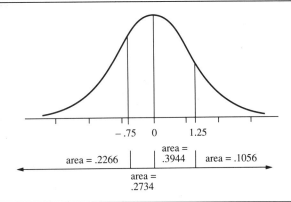

area = .2266

area =
.3944

area = .1056

area =
.2734

−.75   0   1.25

determine the proportion of scores falling below a z of −.75, we must look under the *Area Beyond z* column. There we find that the proportion is .2734.

What proportion of scores fall between our two students' scores? The z-scores are −.75 and 1.25. If we look at Figure 4.6, we see that, by consulting the *Area Between $\bar{x}$ and z* column for each z-score and summing the numbers, we can obtain the proportion of scores between the two z-scores. For $z = -.75$, the area between the mean and z is .2734. For $z = 1.25$, the area between the mean and z is .3944. So the area between a z of −.75 and a z of 1.25 is .2734 + .3944, or .6678.

The standard normal curve can also be used to determine the percentile at which a score falls (or what score falls at a given percentile). If I have taken an IQ test and have an IQ score of 117, I can use the normal curve table to determine my **percentile rank**. A percentile rank is the percentage of scores equal to or below the given score. First, I must transform my IQ score into a z-score. As mentioned earlier, IQ scores have a μ of 100 and a σ of 15. Therefore:

$$z = \frac{X - \mu}{\sigma} = \frac{117 - 100}{15} = \frac{17}{15} = 1.1333$$

By looking in the *Area Between $\bar{x}$ and z* column for a z-score of 1.13 we find the area .3708. Since we want to count all of the area below the z-score, we must add .50 (the other half of the area under the curve) to .3708. Thus, .8708 describes the entire area below a z-score of 1.13. If we multiply this by 100, we can describe my IQ as being at the 87.08th percentile.

What if we wanted to determine the IQ score at the 90th percentile? This can be done by following the logic in the last example backwards. Since we want to know which score has 90 percent of the scores at or below it, we must first find the z-score for that score. We find that z-score by looking for .40 in the column *Area Between $\bar{x}$ and z*. (Why .40 and not .90? Because the table describes only half of the curve, so we must subtract .50 from .90.) The closest area we can find is .3997, and that has a z-score of 1.28. Now we must solve for X, given that $z = 1.28$, $\mu = 100$, and $\sigma = 15$. Our z-score formula is as follows:

$$z = \frac{X - \mu}{\sigma}$$

The formula for X, therefore, is this:

$$X = z\sigma + \mu$$

We can determine what score is at the 90th percentile by using this formula for X:

$$X = z\sigma + \mu$$
$$= 1.28(15) + 100$$
$$= 19.2 + 100$$
$$= 119.2$$

Because the standard normal distribution always has a mean of 0 and a standard deviation of 1, the curve and its proportions always remain constant. Figure 4.7 represents the standard normal distribution, with the z-scores from ±1 to ±3 indentified and the areas between those z-scores indicated. As the figure shows, 68.26% of the scores in a normal distribution fall within 1 standard deviation of the mean; 95.44% of the scores fall within 2 standard deviations of the mean; and 99.74% of the scores fall within 3 standard deviations of the mean.

The table for the standard normal distribution is very useful for determining how a single score compares with the population of scores, or for determining the probability of choosing a score within a particular range. This greatly expands the information that can be gleaned from a single raw score. In the next chapter we examine how z-scores can be used to compare the scores in a sample to an entire population.

FIGURE 4.7   *Standard normal curve, with important areas under the curve indicated.*

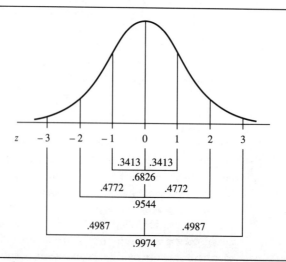

CONCEPT QUESTIONS 4·5	A researcher asks people about their caffeine consumption and finds that the number of cups of coffee drunk per day is normally distributed, with $\mu = 2$ cups and $\sigma = .33$ cups.

    a.   What is the proportion of scores greater than 2.5 cups of coffee?
    b.   What is the proportion of scores less than 1.8 cups of coffee?
    c.   How many cups of coffee does a person scoring at the 80th percentile drink?
    d.   How many cups of coffee does a person scoring at the 30th percentile drink?

CORRELATIONS

Another set of statistical techniques that can be especially useful for analyzing the results of survey data consists of correlation techniques. A **correlation** is a measure of the degree of relationship between two variables. For example, if data were collected on the number of hours students studied for a midterm exam and the grades they received on that exam, a correlation may be calculated between hours studied and midterm grade. Suppose that those with higher midterm grades studied more hours, and that those with lower midterm grades studied fewer hours. This correlation would be described as a positive correlation. With a **positive correlation**, as one variable increases, the other variable also increases. With a **negative correlation**, as one variable increases, the other variable decreases. A negative correlation might occur between hours of television watched the night before an exam and the score on the exam. Here, as the number of hours of television watching increases, the exam score decreases.

A mathematical formula is used to calculate a correlation coefficient, and the resulting number lies somewhere between -1.00 and $+1.00$. The closer the number is to either $+1.00$ or -1.00, the stronger is the relationship between the variables. The closer the number is to 0.00, the weaker is the correlation. Thus, $+.85$ represents a fairly strong positive correlation, but $+.03$ represents a very weak positive correlation. Similarly, $-.91$ represents a strong negative correlation, but $-.12$ represents a rather weak negative correlation. The *strength* of the relationship is represented by the absolute value of the correlation coefficient. The *direction* of the relationship is represented by the sign of the correlation coefficient. Therefore, $-.91$ represents a *stronger* correlation than does $+.85$.

A particular type of graph, called a **scattergram**, is used to demonstrate the relationship between two variables. The two variables (typically called the X and the Y variables) are plotted on the same graph. The X variable is plotted along the horizontal x-axis, and the Y variable is plotted along the vertical y-axis. Figure 4.8 presents a scattergram of the hypothetical data for number of hours studied and midterm exam scores.

Each point on the scattergram in Figure 4.8 represents the values of the two variables for each person. To calculate a correlation, we must be working with *pairs* of scores generated by one set of subjects, *not* with two separate sets of scores generated by separate sets of subjects. Notice that the points tend to form a pattern from the lower left corner to the upper right corner. This lower-left-to-upper-right

FIGURE 4.8   *Scattergram representing pairs of midterm exam scores and numbers of hours spent studying for the exam.*

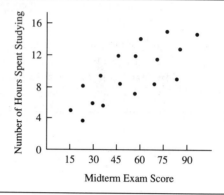

FIGURE 4.9   *Scattergrams representing correlations of different strengths and directions: (a) strong positive; (b) strong negative; (c) weak positive; (d) weak negative; (e) none.*

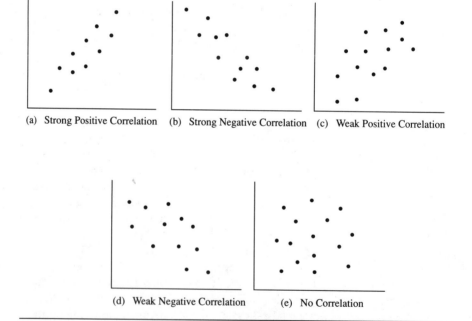

pattern indicates a *positive* correlation. In a *negative* correlation pattern, the points tend to be distributed from the top left corner to the bottom right corner. The closer the points are to falling along a straight line, the stronger is the correlation between the two variables. Figure 4.9 presents several scattergrams representing positive and negative correlations of various strengths.

The survey presented in Box 4.1 was completed by undergraduate students in a psychology course for nonmajors as an initial step in a larger project. It asks some questions about study habits and preferences for activities in the classroom.

SURVEY OF STUDY SKILLS AND CLASSROOM PREFERENCES

Box 4.1

Do not write your name on this survey. Your responses are anonymous and confidential and will have no bearing on any course grade.

1. How much time would you typically spend studying for a midterm exam in a lecture course?

   _____ hours per day for _____ day(s)

2. What do you typically do during a classroom lecture? (check one)

   _____ listen only

   _____ listen mostly—occasionally taking notes

   _____ take general notes on important concepts

   _____ take detailed notes

   _____ other _____

3. If you could design a course to fit your own preferences, which of the following would you include? (check all that apply)

   _____ complete lecture notes by the instructor

   _____ outlines of the lectures

   _____ outlines of important terms and concepts, with room for additional notes

   _____ handouts for important, complex topics

   _____ I'd prefer to take my own notes

   _____ I'd prefer the lectures be audio-taped

   _____ I'd prefer the lectures be video-taped

4. Please rank the following according to how important you believe this item would be to helping you learn lecture material. Use a number 1 for the most important item, number 2 for the second most, and so on.

   _____ listen attentively/no additional notes

   _____ complete lecture notes by the instructor/plus my own notes

   _____ complete lecture notes by the instructor/no additional notes

   _____ outlines of the lectures/plus my own notes

   _____ outlines of the lectures/no additional notes

   _____ outlines of important terms and concepts, with room for notes

   _____ outlines of important terms and concepts/no additional notes

   _____ taking my own notes

5. How many semester hours of college coursework have you completed?

   _____ semester hours

6. Are you male or female? (circle one)

TABLE 4.2   *Hours spent studying and number of semester hours completed for a sample of 14 subjects.*

Subject	X (# of Hours Studying)	Y (# of Semester Hours)
1	14	24
2	6	60
3	4	125
4	28	30
5	9	14
6	9	31
7	12	33
8	18	55
9	8	93
10	5	45
11	10	56
12	18	13
13	16	87
14	10	112.5

FIGURE 4.10   *Scattergram of number of semester hours completed and number of hours of study devoted to a midterm exam.*

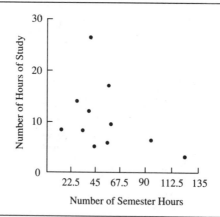

The researchers wanted to know whether there was a correlation between the number of semester hours of coursework a student had completed and the number of hours the student reported studying for a midterm exam. Table 4.2 presents the data for number of hours studied and number of semester hours completed for a sample of 14 students. A scattergram can be made for these data, to indicate the type of relationship (if any) that exists between these two variables. The scattergram is presented in Figure 4.10.

Because both variables—number of semester hours and number of hours spent studying—are measured on either a ratio or an interval scale, the appropriate

TABLE **4.3**   *Hours spent studying (X) and semester hours completed (Y) plus the scores squared and the scores' crossproducts.*

X	X²	Y	Y²	XY
14	196	24	576	336
6	36	60	3600	360
4	16	125	15,625	500
28	784	30	900	840
9	81	14	196	126
9	81	31	961	279
12	144	33	1089	396
18	324	55	3025	990
8	64	93	8649	744
5	25	45	2025	225
10	100	56	3136	560
18	324	13	169	234
16	256	87	7569	139
10	100	112.5	12,656.25	1125
167	2531	778.5	6017.25	6854

correlation to compute is the **Pearson's product-moment correlation coefficient**, often referred to more simply as **Pearson's r**. This correlation coefficient, symbolized by the letter r, was developed by Karl Pearson, an English statistician. It is the correlation coefficent most often used by behavioral scientists. To compare two sets of scores that are often measured in different units, Pearson developed his formula for the correlation coefficient by using z-scores. His formula looks like this:

$$r = \frac{\sum z_x z_y}{n}$$

If the z-scores have already been calculated, this formula is quite easy to use. But typically the z-scores have not been calculated, in which case a more complicated looking **raw score formula** can be used. The raw score formula for Pearson's r is an algebraic transformation of Pearson's original formula:

$$r_{xy} = \frac{n\sum XY - \sum X \sum Y}{\sqrt{[n\sum X^2 - (\sum X)^2][n\sum Y^2 - (\sum Y)^2]}}$$

In Table 4.3 the data for semester hours completed and the hours spent studying are presented again, along with columns for X^2, Y^2, and the crossproduct of X and Y (the XY column).

We calculate Pearson's r, using the raw score formula for these data, as follows:

$$r_{xy} = \frac{n\sum XY - \sum X \sum Y}{\sqrt{[n\sum X^2 - (\sum X)^2][n\sum Y^2 - (\sum Y)^2]}}$$

$$= \frac{14(6854) - 167(778.5)}{\sqrt{[14(2531) - 167^2][14(60,176.25) - 778.5^2]}}$$

$$= \frac{95,956 - 130,009.5}{\sqrt{(35,434 - 27,889)(842,467.5 - 606,062.25)}}$$

$$= \frac{-34,053.5}{\sqrt{7545(236,405.25)}}$$

$$= \frac{-34,053.5}{\sqrt{1,783,677,600}}$$

$$= \frac{-34,053.5}{42,233.698}$$

$$= -.8063$$

We have thus calculated an r_{xy} of $-.8063$. What does this tell us?

We know that correlations vary from -1.00 to $+1.00$. Our correlation coefficient is relatively close to -1.00. This would typically be interpreted as a moderately strong negative correlation between X and Y. In other words, the more semester hours these students had under their belts, the fewer hours they spent studying. Whether a correlation coefficient should be interpreted as reflecting a strong, moderate, or weak correlation can vary from topic to topic and from project to project. In some situations anything less than a correlation of .60 would not be considered worthwhile; in others, .40 might be considered quite an impressive level of correlation.

Another way that a correlation coefficient can aid in the interpretation of a data set is by indicating the amount of variation among the scores that is accounted for in the study. Here the subjects did not all study exactly the same number of hours and had not all completed exactly the same number of semester hours. That is to say that there is variation in the X scores and in the Y scores. The variation in X (hours spent studying) is associated with variation in Y (semester hours), but it is also associated with other undefined factors, such as the difficulty of the course, the general intelligence of the student, and the student's motivation to perform well. The more the variation in X and the variation in Y are associated, the larger grows the absolute value of the correlation coefficient. If the correlation coefficient is squared, the resulting number represents the *proportion* of variance in Y associated with variance in X. Thus, $-.8063^2 = .6501$ means that approximately 65% of the variance in hours spent studying is associated with semester hours completed, while 35% of the variance is associated with other factors.

Whether the amount of variation among the scores accounted for is viewed as being considerable or modest, again, depends on the area of research. Pearson's correlation coefficient and r^2 supply descriptive information, but researchers must supply the interpretation.

Alternative Correlation Coefficients The Pearson's product moment coefficient is appropriate for use when X and Y are measured on a ratio or an interval level of measurement. Other correlation coefficients may be used for other situations.

Spearman's rho (ρ) is a special case of Pearson's r that is appropriate for use with data that have been ranked. For example, suppose that we were interested in

TABLE 4.4   *Ranked performance in a course and hours spent studying for an exam:*
Data for calculating Spearman's rho.

Class Rank	Hours Spent Studying	Hours Ranked	d	d^2
1	15	2	-1	1
2	18	1	1	1
3	10	6	-3	9
4	7	9	-5	25
5	12	4	1	1
6	13	3	3	9
7	11	5	2	4
8	8	8	0	0
9	9	7	2	4
10	6	10	0	0
11	4	12	-1	1
12	5	11	1	1
13	3	13	0	0
14	2	14	0	0
				56

the correlation between a person's ranked performance in a course and the number of hours they typically spent studying for an exam. These data are presented in Table 4.4; the data for hours spent studying in this table have already been ranked, and columns for differences (d) between the ranks and for the differences squared (d^2) are also included.

The formula for Pearson's r can be used to calculate the Spearman's rho, but the following simpler formula can be used instead:

$$\rho = 1 - \frac{6\sum d^2}{n(n^2 - 1)}$$

Using this formula and the information from Table 4.4, we can calculate Spearman's rho as follows:

$$\rho = 1 - \frac{6\sum d^2}{n(n^2 - 1)}$$

$$= 1 - \frac{6(56)}{14(14^2 - 1)}$$

$$= 1 - \frac{336}{14(195)}$$

$$= 1 - \frac{336}{2730}$$

$$= 1 - .1231$$

$$= .877$$

We interpret the Spearman's rho in the same manner as we do the Pearson's *r*. In this example, we have calculated a strong positive correlation of .877. This suggests that class rank and hours spent studying are related such that those with a higher class rank tend to spend more time studying (the greatest number of hours was ranked 1, the second greatest 2, and so on).

In the preceding example of the Spearman's rho calculations, one variable was already rank-ordered and the other variable needed to be transformed into rank-ordered data. Ranking can be done from smallest to largest or from largest to smallest, whichever makes most sense to the researcher. A problem may arise, however, in the case of tied ranks. **Tied ranks** occur when two or more observations for one variable are the same. Suppose that we wished to rank the following numbers from smallest to largest:

TABLE 4.5   *Gender and hours spent studying for an exam.*

X (Gender)	X²	Y (Hours Spent Studying)	Y²	XY
0	0	4	16	0
1	1	4	16	4
0	0	2	2	0
1	1	12	144	12
0	0	4	16	0
1	1	6	36	6
0	0	7	49	0
1	1	9	81	9
0	0	10	100	0
1	1	5	25	5
1	1	14	196	14
0	0	8	64	0
1	1	8	64	8
0	0	10	100	0
1	1	7	49	7
0	0	6	36	0
0	0	6	36	0
1	1	10	100	10
0	0	9	81	0
0	0	5	25	0
0	0	9	81	0
0	0	12	144	0
0	0	4	16	0
0	0	21	441	0
0	0	7	49	0
0	0	8	64	0
0	0	6	36	0
9	9	213	2067	75

X:		5	8	7	6	9	4	6	3	2

The number 2 would receive a rank of 1; the number 3, a rank of 2; the number 4, a rank of 3; and the number 5, a rank of 4. Next, however, are two number 6 observations that would have been ranked 5 and 6 if they hadn't been identical numbers. Instead, we give these two observations the average of the ranks they would have received; that is, each 6 receives a rank of 5.5. The next higher observation is a 7; this number receives a rank of 7—the next rank after 5 and 6, which the two number 6 observations would have been ranked if they hadn't been tied. The next higher number then receives a rank of 8, and so on. Thus, we have

X:		5	8	7	6	9	4	6	3	2
Ranks:		4	8	7	5.5	9	3	5.5	2	1

When tied ranks occur, the ties cause the Spearman's rho never to equal a positive or negative 1.00. If more than one pair of tied ranks occur within a data set, an alternative approach is to use the Pearson's r formula. This yields a more accurate measure of the actual correlation when there are tied ranks in the data (Howell 1982).

When both variables are rank-ordered or can be transformed into rank-ordered data, a Spearman's rho is appropriate. But **point-biserial correlation** is appropriate when a data set involves one variable measured on a ratio or interval scale and another variable measured on a true dichotomy. A **truly dichotomous variable** is a discrete, nominal variable with only two possible alternative values and no underlying continuum between the two values. An example of a truly dichotomous variable is gender: a person or animal is either male or female, but not both.

Suppose that the researcher now wishes to investigate whether gender is related to the number of hours a student typically studies for a midterm exam. The data we will use to calculate the point-biserial correlation are presented in Table 4.5. Here, the dichotomous variable is coded as 0 for one response and 1 for the other.

The same formula as is used for the Pearson's r can be used to calculate the point-biserial correlation, but the symbol used is r_{pb}. For our example, the point-biserial correlation would be calculated like this:

$$r_{pb} = \frac{n\sum XY - (\sum X)(\sum Y)}{\sqrt{[n\sum X^2 - (\sum X)^2][n\sum Y^2 - (\sum Y)^2]}}$$

$$= \frac{27(75) - (9)213}{\sqrt{[27(9) - 9^2][27(2067) - 213^2]}}$$

$$= \frac{2025 - 1917}{\sqrt{[243 - 81][55,809 - 45,369]}}$$

$$= \frac{108}{\sqrt{(162)10,440}}$$

$$= \frac{108}{\sqrt{1,691,280}}$$

$$= \frac{108}{1300.4922}$$

$$= .083$$

The resulting correlation coefficient, .083, indicates that these data demonstrate virtually no correlation between gender and the reported number of hours studied for a midterm exam. [By the way, these responses were gathered from volunteers from an actual introductory psychology class.]

Some statistics books provide different formulas for the point-biserial correlation. All, however, are derived from Pearson's product-moment correlation formula, so all provide the same result. I don't detail these formulas here, because I find that Pearson's formula is fairly easy to calculate once the dichotomous variable has been coded as 0s and 1s.

TABLE 4.6   *Gender and pet ownership (female = 0, male = 1; ownership = 0, nonownership = 1).*

X (Gender)	Y (Pet Ownership)	XY
0	0	0
0	0	0
1	0	0
1	1	1
1	1	1
1	0	0
0	0	0
0	0	0
0	0	0
1	1	1
0	0	0
0	1	0
1	1	1
0	0	0
1	0	0
0	0	0
1	1	1
1	1	1
0	0	0
0	0	0
0	0	0
0	0	0
0	1	0
1	1	1
1	0	0
0	0	0
11	9	7

Another correlation that constitutes a special case of the Pearson's product moment correlation is called the phi coefficient (ϕ). The **phi coefficient** is calculated when both the X and the Y variables are measured on true dichotomies. For example, ϕ would be calculated if a researcher were correlating marital status (married versus single) with home ownership (own versus don't own). As an example, we will correlate gender with whether the respondent reported owning a pet. The data are presented in Table 4.6. Females are coded as 0, males are coded as 1; pet ownership is coded as 0, and not owning a pet is coded as 1.

Using the information from Table 4.6 and the formula for the Pearson's r, we can calculate ϕ. Table 4.6 does not include X^2 or Y^2 columns, because $1^2 = 1$ and $0^2 = 0$, so $X^2 = X$ and $Y^2 = Y$. Our calculations are done in this way:

$$\phi = \frac{n\sum XY - (\sum X)(\sum Y)}{\sqrt{[n\sum X^2 - (\sum X)^2][n\sum Y^2 - (\sum Y)^2]}}$$

$$= \frac{26(7) - (11)9}{\sqrt{[26(11) - 11^2][26(9) - 9^2]}}$$

$$= \frac{182 - 99}{\sqrt{(286 - 121)(234 - 81)}}$$

$$= \frac{83}{\sqrt{(165)(153)}}$$

$$= \frac{83}{\sqrt{25,245}}$$

$$= \frac{83}{158.887}$$

$$= .5224$$

Our obtained ϕ coefficient is .5224, suggesting that these (hypothetical) data show a moderate correlation between gender and pet ownership such that females are more apt to own pets.

As with the point-biserial correlation, other formulas for the ϕ coefficient are presented in some statistics books. But since all scores can be coded as 0s and 1s, calculating ϕ by using the Pearson's r formula is quite easy.

In this section we have discussed four correlation coefficients: Pearson's r, Spearman's rho, the point-biserial, and the phi coefficient. Each is used in different situations, but all assume that the relationship between X and Y is a **linear relationship** not a **curvilinear relationship**. Looking at a scattergram of a data set will help you determine whether the relationship between X and Y is linear or not. The scores in a linear relationship are scattered in a cigar shape. The scores in a curvilinear relationship are scattered in more of a J or U shape, or even in a more complex shape.

Although several correlational techniques have been described in this chapter, still others are appropriate in situations not discussed. Should you be faced with a situation not discussed here and need to determine the relationship between two variables, you might read the appropriate sections in Hinkle, Wiersma & Jurs (1988), Howell (1982), or another advanced statistics text.

Correlation versus Causation   An important point must be stressed about interpreting all correlation coefficients. Although correlations describe the degree and direction of relationship between two variables, the correlation provides no information about the cause of that relationship. *Correlation does not imply causation.* A strong relationship may exist between X and Y, but that does not mean that X caused Y—any more than it means that Y caused X. For example, a substantial positive correlation exists between ice cream consumption and violent crimes. As ice cream consumption increases, so does the incidence of violent crimes, but that certainly does not mean that ice cream consumption causes violent crimes, nor that violent crimes cause ice cream consumption. In this case, a third variable— perhaps heat—may simultaneously cause an increase in ice cream consumption and an increase in violent crimes. Be ever vigilant for erroneous interpretations of correlations.

CONCEPT QUESTIONS 4.6	A popular psychology magazine had a cover story a few years back on the correlation between exercise and a satisfactory sex life. Researchers had found a significant correlation according to which, as exercise level increased, so did satisfaction with (and frequency of) sex. This correlation continued up to a point, but associated with a high level of weekly exercise, a decrease in satisfaction with and frequency of sex was reported. The author's conclusion was that a moderate increase in one's exercise level would increase one's frequency of and satisfaction with sex; that is, moderate exercise *caused* sexual satisfaction. How many alternative explanations for the reported correlation can you think of?

Correlations and Measures of Validity and Reliability   Correlations provide important information about the relationship between two variables. One way to use this information in research is in establishing the reliability and validity of psychological measures, as well as of the judgments made by two or more observers or raters. In Chapter 3, the concepts of reliability and validity were introduced. These measures of reliability and validity are usually established for paper-and-pencil tests in psychology. For example, a researcher would want to establish the reliability and validity of a set of questions meant to assess eating disorders. The stronger the reliability and validity of a psychological measure, the greater the confidence researchers can have that it will yield meaningful results. Several types of reliability and validity can be assessed by using correlations.

   Test-retest reliability is the degree to which people score the same way on a measure when completing the measure a second time. If a group of subjects completes a psychological test or a survey and then completes the same test or survey a second time, the scores from time 1 and time 2 can be correlated. To the extent that the correlation is strong (and positive), the measure has test-retest reliability. Weak test-retest reliability may suggest that the measure yields different results over a short period of time. For most measures, this is detrimental.

Split-half reliability measures the degree of consistency within a test; that is, do the subjects respond in the same manner throughout the survey or test, or do their responses change considerably? For example, perhaps on a 10-item survey about attitudes toward date rape there is no correlation between the responses to 5 randomly chosen items and the responses to the other 5 items. This might suggest a **response set**, where the subject responds in a manner related more to the options (such as choosing all A options, and avoiding all C options) than in a manner related to the questions. Split-half reliability can be calculated by correlating the scores on one half of a measure with the scores on the other half. The stronger the correlation, the greater the split-half reliability.

Criterion validity is the degree to which a measure correlates with other established measures of the same concept or construct. There are two types of criterion related validity: predictive validity and concurrent validity.

Predictive validity is the degree to which a score on a test accurately predicts some future outcome. A score on an intelligence test is predictive of future school success. This can be confirmed by correlating intelligence test scores taken previously with a measure of school success, such as GPA. In a survey of shopping behaviors, a researcher hopes that the survey responses correlate well with the respondent's actual behavior. To assess the predictive validity of the survey, the researchers would need to conduct a separate investigation in which the subsequent shopping behaviors of a subset of respondents were monitored in some manner. The survey responses and the actual behaviors could then be correlated to yield a measure of predictive validity.

Concurrent validity is the extent to which the new measure and an established measure are correlated. This differs from predictive validity in that both the new and the established measures are elicited in the present. Suppose that a new method for diagnosing depression has been developed, based on the amount of chocolate a person eats at one sitting. If this new chocolate depression assessment method correlates strongly with scores on an established measure of depression, such as the Beck Depression Inventory, the chocolate method would be said to have strong concurrent validity.

Construct validity is a type of validity related to the measurement of some concept, also called a construct. If we are attempting to measure depression, then depression is the construct. An IQ test attempts to measure the construct of intelligence.

For a researcher developing a set of questions to assess how stingy people are, stinginess is the construct of interest. To determine the construct validity of this new measure, the researcher needs to determine whether scores on this measure correlate positively with other measures and manipulations of the same construct. For example, suppose that a group of people complete the stinginess survey, and their scores are negatively correlated with how much money they spend in a department store (as stinginess goes up, spending goes down). This would suggest that the construct measured by the survey and the construct measured by how much money a person spends in a department store overlap. This lends support to the measure's construct validity. However, if the responses on the stinginess survey correlate with something the researcher would not expect them to be correlated with, such as amount of money given to charities or even scores on a sense-of-humor measure, this would detract from the construct validity of the stinginess measure, suggesting that the survey may be assessing some different concept.

A final type of validity to be considered is called **face validity**. Face validity is the extent to which a test appears to measure what it is purported to measure. An English literature exam has face validity if it asks questions about literature read for the course. A personality test has face validity if it asks questions about behaviors, beliefs, and attitudes. Face validity could be calculated (though it rarely is) by correlating the topics of test or survey items with the topics that a group of subjects say they would expect to see given the purpose of the measure. Face validity, however, is of little worth for evaluating research; some would argue that face validity is no validity at all. Anyone can sit down and write a paper-and-pencil test and say that it measures something; for example it could purport to measure work satisfaction. The test may involve 25 questions about how the respondent feels about his or her job and co-workers. The test may have great face validity, it may appear to measure what it purports to measure, but it may have absolutely no other reliability or validity. Relatedly, it is not unusual for the purpose of a psychological test to be disguised, in which case a reliable and valid measure may have no face validity. However, while researchers find face validity to be of little value, respondents might demand it. My aunt recently sent me a survey she received in the mail but didn't complete because "the questions didn't seem relevant" to her.

To assess any of these types of validity or reliability, each respondent must be measured twice, to produce pairs of scores that can be correlated. Pearson's product-moment correlation coefficient is probably the most commonly used correlation coefficient, but—depending on the scales of measurement of the test or survey responses—another coefficient might be more appropriate.

PART III: CRITIQUE OF SURVEY AND QUESTIONNAIRE RESEARCH

Survey research is very popular in psychology and other social sciences. But as with any other type of research, the results are only useful if the research is carried out carefully and correctly. A reader of survey research needs to consider the quality of the sample of respondents, the survey itself, the statistical techniques used to analyze the survey results, and the conclusions drawn about those results.

QUALITY OF THE SAMPLE

Because survey research usually involves generalizing from the actual responses of a sample to the inferred responses of a population, it is essential that the sample represent the population as accurately as possible. The evaluator of survey data should consider the quality of the sample. How was the sample of potential respondents chosen? Was the sampling technique used likely to yield a representative sample or a biased sample? If the original sample of potential respondents is biased, the results—no matter how interesting—may not be generalizable.

Another important piece of information in determining the representativeness of the responses is the response rate for the survey. A response rate of less than 50%

is probably suspect, and the results from such a survey should be interpreted with some caution.

THE SURVEY

Another area requiring special attention is the actual survey. Ideally, a copy of the survey is provided as part of the research report. The general layout of the survey should be logical and easy to follow, and the questions should be written clearly and concisely. The responses to loaded, leading, or double-barrelled questions must be interpreted carefully, if at all. Poorly written questions yield responses of questionable reliability and validity.

PROCEDURE

How the responses were actually elicited can provide a research evaluator with important information about potential confounds. Mail surveys may result in low response rates, and thus limit the generalizability of the results. Telephone surveys and personal interviews are subject to interviewer bias. Information about the types of supervision provided for the interviewers and about the degree of standardization in the manner questions were asked can alleviate some of these concerns.

Procedures describing how open-ended questions were coded are also important in permitting a complete evaluation. Only with this information can an evaluator determine whether the coding procedure was likely to be unaffected by the researchers' expectations.

RESULTS

The responses to the survey or interview must be organized and summarized to be useful. The manner in which these statistical analyses are conducted is important. If inappropriate statistical techniques are used, the results of the analyses may be misleading.

As described in Chapter 3, the appropriate descriptive statistics to use depend on the scale of measurement of the variable. Similarly, the appropriateness of other statistics depends on the scale of measurement of the variables being summarized. Pearson's r is appropriate with interval or ratio data, while Spearman's rho is used with rank-ordered data. The point-biserial correlation coefficient is appropriate when one variable is measured on an interval or ratio scale, and the other is measured on a nominal scale with two categories. Finally, the ϕ coefficient is suitable for calculating the correlation between two nominally scaled variables, where each variable has only two categories. In all cases of the correlation coefficients described in this chapter, the variables are assumed to be linearly related. Curvilinear relationships would be underestimated by these correlational techniques.

DISCUSSION

The discussion section of a research report is where the researchers provide their explanation for the statistical results they obtained. The quality of the discussion section depends on the quality of thought that went into its development. A common error made when explaining correlational results is to assume that one variable caused the change in the other variable. It is perfectly acceptable to propose a causal relationship as food for future research, or to hypothesize a causal relationship as the basis for additional arguments. But it is important that the researcher and the reader of the research be aware that the mere existence of a correlation between two variables provides no sound evidence that a causal relationship exists.

Surveys are an exceedingly useful tool for researchers to use in their search for knowledge about human behavior. The process of developing and using a survey, however, is deceptively simple. Great care must be taken in developing the survey, sampling the population, and drawing conclusions from the survey results, if the survey research is to be worthy of consideration.

IMPORTANT TERMS AND CONCEPTS

sampling bias

interviewer bias

response rate

socially desirable response

population

sample

sampling frame

elements

random selection

random sample

systematic sampling

stratified sampling

stratified random sampling

cluster sampling

demographic question

open-ended question

closed question

loaded question

leading question

double-barreled question

filter question

funnel question

pilot study

median split

z-score

normal distribution

standard normal distribution

standard normal curve

percentile rank

correlation

positive correlation

negative correlation

scattergram

Pearson's product-moment correlation coefficient (Pearson's r)

raw score formula

Spearman's rho

tied ranks

point-biserial correlation

truly dichotomous variable

phi coefficient

linear relationship

curvilinear relationship

test-retest reliability

split-half reliability

response set

criterion validity

predictive validity

concurrent validity

construct validity

face validity

QUESTIONS AND EXERCISES

1. A survey is conducted by asking every third person entering the Student Center to participate. What type of sampling is being used?

   Would this procedure yield a random sample? Why or why not?

2. A colleague wishes to conduct a survey to

investigate the attitudes of the residents of a state toward the creation of a storage site/dump for nuclear waste in their state. The researcher would like to get responses from 3000 individuals such that the sample is representative of the state's population. One city in the state comprises 25% of the state's population; another 10% live in the suburbs of this city; three other cities of roughly equal size together account for 35% of the state's population; and the remaining 30% of the population live in rural areas of the state. The researcher has access to all of the city and town directories in the state, as well as all of the phone books.

a. In what possible ways could this researcher sample the population; that is, how could this person use random sampling, stratified sampling, systematic sampling, cluster sampling, or some combination of the above?

b. The planned number of questions on this survey is quite small: some demographic questions and about 10 questions related to the topic. Given the topic and the length of the survey, what are the advantages and disadvantages of a mail survey, a phone survey, and a personal interview? Which would you suggest to the researcher?

3. You are creating a survey to address people's attitudes toward people with AIDS. Rewrite the following questions and/or options so that the wording and choices are more appropriate for a survey.

AIDS is a plague affecting millions of Americans either directly or by afflicting loved ones. To what extent do you think AIDS research money should be devoted to counseling those with AIDS and their loved ones?

How many people do you know who have AIDS?

a. <1 b. 1–10
c. 10–20 d. >20

Do you have unsafe sex or worry about contracting the AIDS virus?

a. yes
b. no
c. sometimes

4. The results of a survey indicate that the average home in Peoria was sold for $75,000 (the mean) in 1992, with a standard deviation of $15,500. The prices of these homes is normally distributed.

a. Suppose that someone bought a home for $86,500. What proportion of the homes were bought for an amount equal to or greater than this?

b. Suppose that someone bought a home for $55,000. What proportion of the homes were bought for an amount equal to or greater than this?

c. What proportion of the homes were sold for an amount between $55,000 and $86,500?

d. At what percentile rank is a home that sold for $26,900?

e. At what percentile rank is a home that sold for $77,800?

5. A survey of college students was conducted the day before final exams began. Respondents were asked to rate their level of stress on a 10-point scale, where 1 was not stressed and 10 was exceedingly stressed. The mean stress rating was 4.5, with a standard deviation of 1.25. (The researcher chose to use this rating data as interval scale data.) The stress scores are also normally distributed.

a. What stress rating would the person at the 85th percentile have?

b. What stress rating would the person at the 25th percentile have?

c. What is the percentile rank for a person with a stress rating of 5.7?

d. What ratings fall exactly 1 standard deviation above and below the mean?

6. In a separate survey, college students rated their stress levels and also indicated the number of exams, presentations, papers, and projects that were due during the next week. The resulting data are presented next.

Projects, etc.	Stress
4	5
2	3
5	4
6	8
4	2
1	1
7	9
3	4

a. Conduct a Pearson's *r* to determine the degree of the relationship between final exams, projects, etc., and stress.
b. How much variability in stress scores is accounted for by final projects, etc.?
c. Draw a scattergram for these data.

7. Using the data in Exercise 6, rank-order the data and conduct a Spearman's rho. How do the results of the Spearman's rho and the Pearson's *r* compare?

8. Stress during finals was assessed during finals week for both faculty members and students. In the accompanying data, students are coded with a 1 and faculty with a 0.

Faculty/Student	Stress
0	6
1	7
0	5
0	3
1	9
1	6
0	4
1	8
1	6
0	3

Calculate the point-biserial correlation for these data. What is your interpretation of the data?

9. A telephone interview was conducted in which people were asked whether they had voted in the last mayoral election. The respondents were futher identified as owning a home or not owning a home. The resulting data are shown next. Calculate the ϕ coefficient, and interpret the results.

Voted	Owns Home
1	1
0	1
1	1
0	0
0	0
0	1
0	1
1	1
1	1
1	1
0	0
0	0
1	0
1	1

[1 = voted, 0 = did not vote; 1 = owns home, 0 = does not own home]

10. A survey conducted by a walking-related magazine finds that, among the magazine's readers, there is a positive relationship between exercise and health. The magazine article suggests that these data "prove that increasing exercise will increase your health." What is wrong with this statement?

5

Hypothesis Testing and the Single-Group Design

Observational studies and surveys are often used to describe how a single group of subjects behaves or believes. This information can be very useful to researchers who are trying to understand an area of research more fully. Another strategy for investigating a topic is to compare one group of subjects to another group of subjects or to other information about a population. The differences that appear (or do not appear) can be very enlightening to researchers.

Research involving comparisons is designed to answer specific questions in such a way that, if a difference emerges between the groups, this suggests an answer to the question. For instance, if a program for preparing for the Scholastic Aptitude Test (SAT) has any beneficial effects, then, a representative sample of people who complete the program should score higher on the SAT than do members of the remaining population of people taking the SAT. Thus, a difference in SAT scores between the general population and the group of people who completed the SAT preparation program would suggest that the program was beneficial. If those who took the preparation program actually performed worse than the general population, that would suggest that the program was detrimental. A finding of no difference between the general population and those completing the preparation program supplies inconclusive information. It could be that the program does not have any effect, or it could be that there is an effect that for some reason did not emerge in this particular study. We'll discuss interpreting the results of a study more thoroughly throughout this chapter.

Research is typically designed to address a specific research question, such as "does the SAT preparation course have any effect on

SAT scores?" The answers to the research question are called **hypotheses**. **Hypothesis testing** is the process of determining whether the hypothesis is supported by the results of a research project.

HYPOTHESES

Suppose that a researcher is interested in the relationship between summer programs and the intelligence of grade-school children. In particular, this researcher wishes to know whether children who choose to participate in a summer program where they can choose from among sessions on learning a foreign language, learning about dinosaurs, learning how to use a computer, and other topics are smarter than most other children. This is the research question. Based on this question, the researcher forms one or more hypotheses; in this case, the researcher may hypothesize that the students in the summer program have higher IQ scores than the population in general.

Most intelligence tests are standardized so that the mean score (μ) is 100 and the standard deviation (σ) is 15. In order for the research to support the hypothesis that the children in the summer program have higher IQ scores than the general population, the students in the summer program, as a group, must score above 100.

In any effort, to test a hypothesis, *two* hypotheses are actually involved because there are two sides to every question: what the researcher expects, and what the researcher does not expect. One of these hypotheses is called the **null hypothesis** (H_0), and the other is called the **alternative hypothesis** or sometimes the **research hypothesis** (H_1 or sometimes H_A). The null hypothesis is the prediction that there is *no difference* between the groups being compared. It is what one expects if the population from which the sample is drawn is the same as the population with which it is being compared. The null hypothesis is typically what the researcher does *not* expect to find; a researcher does not usually predict the null hypothesis, although in certain cases he or she may. In our example, the null hypothesis is that the IQ of the summer program students does not significantly differ from the IQ of the general population; that is, the null hypothesis is that the population of summer program students is the same as the general population. The null hypothesis can be written like this:

$$H_0: \mu_0 = \mu_1$$

The alternative hypothesis is the prediction that the researcher is making about the results of the research; it is the prediction that there is a difference between the groups being compared. There are two types of alternative hypotheses. In one type the researcher simply predicts that the two groups being compared differ, without predicting the direction of that difference. That is, the researcher does not predict which group will score higher or lower. This is called a **two-tailed hypothesis**. To help clarify why this is called two-tailed, consider the normal curve in Figure 5.1. In the middle of the curve lies the population mean (μ); in the case of the IQ example, $\mu = 100$. If a sample mean were very much higher than 100, it would fall far to the right of the mean, in the positive *tail* of the distribution. If a sample mean were very much lower than 100, it would fall far to the left of the mean, in the

FIGURE 5.1   *Normal distribution of IQ scores.*

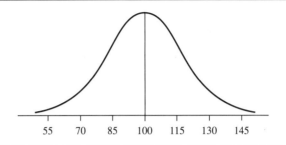

negative tail of the distribution. If a researcher wishes only to predict that a sample mean will differ from the population mean, but does not wish to predict whether it will be higher or lower, the researcher simply predicts that the sample mean will fall in one of the *two tails* of the distribution. That is why an alternative hypothesis that does not predict the direction of the difference is called a two-tailed hypothesis.

On the other hand, if the researcher predicts the direction of the difference, such as by predicting that the mean IQ of college students is higher than the population mean, this type of alternative hypothesis is called a **one-tailed hypothesis**. Here the researcher predicts the tail of the distribution in which the sample mean is expected to fall. The two-tailed hypothesis and both possible one-tailed hypotheses can be written as such:

$$H_1: \mu_0 \neq \mu_1 \quad \text{(two-tailed hypothesis)}$$

$$H_1: \mu_0 < \mu_1 \quad \text{(one-tailed)}$$

$$H_1: \mu_0 > \mu_1 \quad \text{(one-tailed)}$$

CONCEPT QUESTIONS 5.1	A researcher hypothesizes that a sample of families from the Midwest differs in size from the national average family size. What are the researcher's null and alternative hypotheses?

HYPOTHESIS TESTING

Although the research is designed to determine whether the alternative hypothesis is supportable, hypothesis testing actually involves testing the null hypothesis, not the alternative hypothesis. If the difference between the groups being compared is sufficiently large that it is unlikely that the difference was caused by chance occurrences alone, the null hypothesis is *rejected*. If the null hypothesis is rejected, the alternative hypothesis in turn is *supported*. On the other hand, if the difference between the groups is so small that it may have occurred by chance, we *fail to reject the null hypothesis.* If the null hypothesis is not rejected, the alternative hypothesis cannot be supported.

In our example, the researcher predicted that the mean IQ scores of summer program students exceeds the population mean of 100. This is a one-tailed alternative hypothesis. [What would be the two-tailed alternative hypothesis, and what would be the other one-tailed hypothesis?] The null hypothesis is always that there is no difference between the groups being compared. In this case, the sample mean will not be different from the general population mean. If we collect our data and find a mean that is significantly greater than 100 (we'll discuss what is meant by "significantly" in the ensuing pages), we can *reject the null hypothesis.* When we do this, we are concluding that the null hypothesis—that there is no difference between the sample mean and the population mean—is wrong. Because we reject the null hypothesis, we *support* our alternative hypothesis that the sample mean is greater than the population mean. In other words, the evidence suggests that the sample of summer program students does indeed represent a population that scores higher on the IQ test than the general population.

However, if the mean IQ score for our data is *not* significantly different from the population mean, we *fail to reject the null hypothesis,* and thus we fail to support our alternative hypothesis.

ERRORS IN HYPOTHESIS TESTING

Researchers carefully design their studies to answer their research question by either supporting or failing to support the alternative hypothesis. But, because statistical analysis is not infallible, researchers can sometimes reject a null hypothesis even though it is really true. This happens when a researcher finds a difference in a study that suggests that two populations differ when in fact they do not. Another possible error involves failing to find a difference in a study when a difference between the populations truly exists.

In any research problem there are two possibilities: the null hypothesis is correct, and there is no difference between the populations; or the null hypothesis is false, and there is a difference between the populations. The researcher, however, never knows the TRUTH. Look now at Figure 5.2. Along the top is the truth (which the researcher can never know), and along the left side are the researcher's two choices in making a decision: to reject the null hypothesis or not to do so. This allows four possible outcomes, consisting of two ways for the researcher to be correct, and two ways to be wrong.

The two ways to be correct are straightforward. First, the researcher can reject the null hypothesis when, in reality, it is false; that is, the researcher can identify a true difference between the groups being compared. Second, the researcher can fail to reject the null hypothesis when, in fact, the null hypothesis is true. In this case, the researcher has not detected a difference between the groups being compared and, in reality, there is no difference between the groups.

Mirroring the two ways to be correct are the two possible errors: rejecting the null hypothesis when it is true is called a **Type I error**; and failing to reject the null hypothesis when it is false is called a **Type II error**.

FIGURE 5.2   *The four possible outcomes of a research decision.*

THE TRUTH

	The null hypothesis is true.	The null hypothesis is false.
THE DECISION Reject H_0	Type I error (α)	Correct $(1 - \beta)$
Fail to reject H_0	Correct $(1 - \alpha)$	Type II error (β)

The Type I error consists of rejecting the null hypothesis when it is true—that is, finding a difference between the groups being compared that does not truly exist. Sometimes, regardless of how well designed a study might be, a difference is detected between groups that does not exist outside the study. For example, we might find that the sample summer program students do have, on average, a higher mean IQ score than the general population. But perhaps our sample of summer program student just happened to be bright students, and there truly isn't a difference between the IQ scores of the entire population of summer program students and those of the general public. Because a difference was identified that does not truly exist between the populations, we have made a Type I error. To the extent that the results of a study have immediate ramifications, such as motivating important changes in the curriculum based on the results of the IQ differences, Type I errors can be very serious indeed.

The Type II error consists of failing to reject the null hypothesis when it is false—in other words, failing to detect a difference between the groups being compared when a difference truly does exist between the populations. For example, a Type II error would occur if our sample of summer program students did not have a mean IQ score significantly greater than the mean IQ for the general population, but the entire population of summer program students *did* have a significantly higher IQ than that of the general population. Our study would have failed to detect a difference that actually existed. This can happen for a number of reasons. Perhaps our sample includes the less intelligent among the summer program students, or our IQ test was administered in a nonstandard way (a way different from the manner used for the general population, and one that caused greater variation in the scores). Another possibility is that more students were needed in our sample to enable us to detect the difference. We will discuss this last possiblity further in the section of this chapter on sample size.

Type II errors are often viewed as being less serious than Type I errors. If a difference truly exists but is not identified in a research project, continued research is likely to detect the difference. An analogy to the United State's justice system may make the relationship of null and alternative hypotheses with Type I and Type II errors easier to remember. Consider the case of a person accused of a crime. The null hypothesis is that an accused person is not guilty; that is, the accused person is no different from the general population. The alternative hypothesis is that the accused is guilty; the accused person is different from the general population. In America it is considered a more serious error to convict a person who is not guilty than to acquit a person who is guilty; in other words, it is more serious to find a difference that does not exist than to fail to find a difference that is really there.

CONCEPT QUESTIONS 5.2	A researcher collects information on family size and, based on the data, concludes that Midwestern families are larger than the average family in the United States. However, unbeknownst to the researcher, the sample includes several unusually large families, and in reality, Midwestern families are no larger than the the national average. What type of error was made?

PROBABILITY OF MAKING A TYPE I ERROR

The probability of making a Type I error is called **alpha** (α). The alpha level is typically specified, and in the social and behavioral sciences the acceptable probability of making a Type I error (or α-level) has traditionally been set at .05. This standard indicates that researchers in the social and behavioral sciences are willing to accept a 5% risk of making a Type I error. Another way to say this is that, with α set at .05, a difference between the groups large enough to justify rejecting the null hypothesis will occur by chance only 5 times out of 100. A difference this large is said to be a **significant difference**.

Let's consider our summer program example again. Figure 5.3 shows a normal distribution, which represents the sampling distribution of IQ scores in the general public. (The **sampling distribution** is the distribution of sample $\bar{x}$'s, as opposed to individual scores; this will be discussed more thoroughly later in the chapter.) If the null hypothesis is true, the mean IQ score for the summer program students will be included as part of this distribution. However, if the alternative hypothesis is

FIGURE 5.3   *Region of rejection for a one-tailed alternative hypothesis when $\alpha = .05$.*

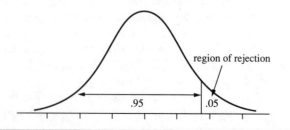

FIGURE 5.4   *Regions of rejection for a two-tailed alternative hypothesis with α = .05.*

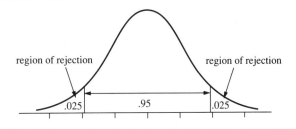

correct—in this case, that the population mean of the summer program students is greater than the mean for the general population—the mean for our sample better represents a different distribution (that of the sampling distribution of summer program students' IQ scores). To determine whether the population mean of the summer program students is greater than or equal to the mean of general public, we compare our sample mean to the population mean of the general public. If our sample mean is so great that it falls in the top 5% of the distribution for the general public (because α = .05), this indicates that sample mean had only a 5% chance of being drawn by chance from that population. We then reject H_0 and support H_1. The 5% of the distribution marked in Figure 5.3 represents α and is called the **region of rejection**. If a score falls within the region of rejection, then H_0 is rejected.

In our previous example, the alternative hypothesis was one-tailed. For a one-tailed hypothesis, the region of rejection all lies in one end of the distribution. For a two-tailed hypothesis, the region of rejection is split equally between the two tails—2.5% in one tail and 2.5% in the other tail, when α = .05. This is demonstrated in Figure 5.4.

PROBABILITY OF MAKING A TYPE II ERROR

The probability of making a Type II error is called **beta** (*β*). This is a measure of the likelihood of finding a difference that truly exists. The opposite of *β* is called **power** and is calculated as 1 − *β*. In general, researchers want to design studies that are high in power and have a low *β*. However, *β*, α, and power are interconnected; and increasing one decreases the others. Figure 5.5 presents a representation of *β*, α, and power.

In Figure 5.5, the distribution on the left represents the distribution of scores when the null hypothesis is correct. The distribution on the right represents the distribution of scores when the alternative hypothesis is correct. In terms of our summer program example, the distribution on the left is the distribution of IQ scores for the general public; this distribution would include the summer program students if they were not significantly different from the general public. The distribution of scores on the right represents the IQ scores of the summer program students, assuming that they do score significantly higher than the general public.

The shaded area labeled α represents the top 5% of the null hypothesis distribution. If the sample's mean is so large that it falls in the top 5% of the null hypothesis

FIGURE 5.5   *Representation of β, α, and power.*

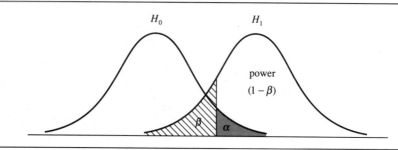

distribution, we say that it is unlikely to belong to that distribution, and we reject the null hypothesis.

The striped area of the alternative hypothesis distribution to the left of α represents β. This is the probability of making a Type II error. If a mean is too small to land in the region of rejection, but actually does belong to a separate population, it will fall within the β region. The researchers will fail to reject H_0, even though it is false, and thus will commit a Type II error. Another way to think of β is as the proportion of scores in the alternative hypothesis distribution that, if obtained, would result in a Type II error. Power $(1 - \beta)$ is the proportion of scores in the alternative hypothesis distribution that, if obtained, would result in rejecting the null hypothesis correctly. Whenever possible, a researcher attempts to increase the power of a project.

Consider Figure 5.5 again. Power can be increased by reducing β, and β can be reduced by increasing α. Increasing α, however, is often not a realistic option. Only rarely will a researcher—and perhaps more importantly, the researcher's colleagues—trust the results of a study in which α is greater than .05. Luckily, a set of facts known about distributions, called the Central Limit Theorem, can aid a researcher in dealing with this problem.

To consider the Central Limit Theorem, you must be somewhat familiar with a **sampling distribution of the mean** (which is usually shortened to *sampling distribution*). A sampling distribution is a theoretical frequency distribution of all the possible sample means of a certain sample size that can be taken from a given population. Suppose that samples of a given size were repeatedly drawn from a population until all members of the population had been sampled. The means of those samples could be plotted to form a frequency distribution, just as single scores can be plotted. The resulting frequency distribution of scores is the sampling distribution of the mean.

The **Central Limit Theorem** states that, for a population with a mean (μ) and a variance (σ^2), the sampling distribution of the mean has a mean equal to μ and a variance equal to $\dfrac{\sigma^2}{N}$. In addition, the sampling distribution approaches the normal distribution as N increases. Of importance to us now is the fact that the variance of the sampling distribution equals $\dfrac{\sigma^2}{N}$, which also means that, as N increases, the

FIGURE 5.6   *The relationship of α, β, and power when the variance differs.*

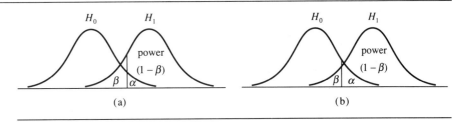

(a)   (b)

variance decreases. However, even though the variance changes as N changes, the mean (μ) remains the same. Figure 5.6 presents two sets of distributions. In the first set, N is smaller than in the second set. Throughout, α remains set at .05; but with the larger N, β is smaller, and thus the power is greater. Therefore, a relatively simple way for a researcher to increase the power of a study is to increase the sample size.

WHY WE DO NOT "ACCEPT" THE NULL HYPOTHESIS

You may be wondering why we use the convoluted speech of saying that we "fail to reject" the null hypothesis, instead of just "accepting" the null hypothesis. If you reject the null hypothesis, you do so because your finding was relatively unlikely to have occurred by chance alone. But if you do not reject the null hypothesis, what does that mean? The null hypothesis says that there is no significant difference between the sample mean and the population mean. If you do not reject the null hypothesis, does that mean that your sample's scores are equal to the population's scores? Not necessarily. By failing to reject the null hypothesis, you have failed to find a significant difference, but that does not mean that you have found an equality. There can be a number of reasons for failing to find a difference (that is, for failing to reject the null hypothesis). It could be because you made a Type II error— perhaps because your method of data collection was not sensitive enough to detect the difference, or because you needed a larger sample to detect the difference consistently. Or perhaps your sample, simply by chance, was such that its mean wasn't significantly different from the population's score. Or perhaps a confound in your study is causing your results to come out differently from what you expected. Any of these reasons and more could cause you to make a Type II error and fail to reject the null hypothesis when it is false. Of course, there is also the possibility that you failed to reject the null hypothesis because the null hypothesis is actually true. How can you tell whether the null hypothesis is true or whether you have made a Type II error? You can't; and for this reason it is risky to "accept" the null hypothesis as true when no difference is detected. Similarly, it is risky to predict that no difference exists between your sample and the population. If you find no difference, you cannot know from this one study whether it is because your prediction was accurate or because you made a Type II error. Additional research, however, may permit you to clarify the issue.

If a researcher does find sufficient evidence to reject the null hypothesis and support the alternative hypothesis, how much support is that? Support for the alternative hypothesis means that the identified difference was so large that it was unlikely to have occurred by chance. If the difference didn't occur by chance, why did it occur? Explaining the difference is the job of the researcher. One researcher may believe that summer program students are smarter than the general public from the outset, while another researcher may think that the summer program serves to increase students' IQ scores. Based on their beliefs, both of these researchers are likely to predict that the mean IQ score for a sample of summer program students will be greater than 100. Suppose that both researchers collect and analyze some data, and both find results that are consistent with their predictions. Each researcher can be sure that only 5 times out of 100 would the mean of the summer program students' IQ scores be significantly greater than the population mean by chance, but neither can be totally confident that his or her explanation for the results is correct. Rejection of the null hypothesis and support of the alternative hypothesis lend confidence to the results found, but not to the explanation given. The explanation may or may not be correct; it is vulnerable to all of the subjectivity, wishful thinking, and faulty reasoning that humans are heir to. The best explanation will emerge only after other carefully designed investigations are conducted.

SINGLE-GROUP DESIGNS

Finally, we get to the application of hypothesis testing: data collection and analysis. Perhaps the simplest type of investigation involving hypothesis testing is the **single-group design**.

In a single-group design, the mean score from a sample of subjects is compared to a population mean. The null hypothesis is that there is no difference between the sample's mean score and the population's mean score. We have been using a single-group design as an example throughout this chapter. In our example, the mean IQ score for a sample of summer program students is compared with the mean IQ score of the general population. Our null hypothesis is that there is no significant difference between the scores of students and the average IQ test score; that is, the sample of summer program students is from a population that does not differ from the general population. This null hypothesis could be written as

$$H_0: \mu_1 = 100$$

because we know that the population mean is 100. Or it could be written more generally as

$$H_0: \mu_0 = \mu_1$$

Our alternative hypothesis is that the sample mean IQ of the summer school students is significantly greater than the population mean IQ; that is, the sample of summer school students represents a population of summer school students that differs from the general population. This could be written as

$$H_1: \mu_1 > 100$$

PROBABILITY

IF YOU HAVE 5 DOGS, 3 WILL BE ASLEEP

Courtesy of Sidney Harris

Or it could also be written more generally as

$$H_1 : \mu_0 < \mu_1$$

Of course, comparing students with the general population on IQ is not the only investigation you can conduct with a single-group design. A sample may be compared with a population any time you know the population mean. Information about populations can sometimes be difficult to find, but it may be acquired from previous literature, from standardized tests (such as the ACT, SAT, or IQ exams), from reference books, from the census bureau, from administrative offices, or from other reliable sources.

After you have found the population mean (and if available, the population standard deviation), it is time for you to collect data from a sample. As we discussed in Chapter 4, the goal of sampling is to acquire a sample that is representative of the population. You cannot generalize results based on data from a biased sample. Because the results of a single-group design are based on the data from a single sample, the sample must be representative of its population. You might want to refer to Chapter 4 to refamiliarize yourself with the different sampling techniques.

One practical concern involves determining how large your sample should be. We discussed sample size in the previous section of this chapter, in relation to the probability of making a Type II error and judging the power of a study. In general, the greater the sample size, the greater is the power of the study and the smaller is the probability of making a Type II error. More advanced statistics books provide a more detailed discussion of power, as well as tables to assist researchers in determining an appropriate sample size for their investigation. For additional information on this topic you may wish to read the appropriate sections of texts by Hinkle, Wiersma, and Jurs (1988), Howell (1987), and Kirk (1990). As a rule of thumb, however, if the difference between the sample mean and the population mean is at least as large as $\frac{1}{2}$ standard deviation (in the case of IQs, that would be a 7.5-point difference), a sample size of approximately 30 subjects will provide a researcher with enough power to reject the null hypothesis 80 times out of 100 (assuming that the null hypothesis is false). More subjects will be needed to detect smaller differences, and a decrease in the number of subjects will increase the researcher's likelihood of making a Type II error.

The data may be collected in any appropriate nonreactive manner so that simply collecting the data does not cause them to change. For example, data may be obtainable from file records or from the results of a survey or from testing. The subjects might simply be asked straight out for a piece of information, if that is appropriate. Of course, the ethical ramifications of the data collection must always be considered, and informed consent must be obtained whenever appropriate.

After selecting the sample and collecting the data, the researcher can begin analyzing the data and testing the hypotheses. Three tests are presented in this chapter that can be used to analyze data from single-group designs. We will start with the z-test and the t-test. These tests are called **parametric tests** because they involve making assumptions about estimates of population characteristics called *parameters*. We will also consider a **nonparametric test** called the chi-square goodness-of-fit. Nonparametric tests do not involve any population parameters, and the data do not have to fulfill as many assumptions as for parametric tests. Nonparametric tests, however, tend to be less powerful than parametric tests.

THE z-TEST

Let's assume that the following IQ scores were collected from a random sample of 100 students at a summer studies program. Our null and alternative hypotheses are as follows:

$$H_0: \bar{x} = \mu$$

$$H_1: \bar{x} > \mu$$

The population mean (μ) and the population standard deviation (σ) are known; they are

$$\mu = 100 \qquad \sigma = 15$$

We already know how to calculate a z-score for any single data point; this was introduced in Chapter 4. For example, the z-score for an IQ score of 120 would be

$$z = \frac{X - \mu}{\sigma} = \frac{120 - 100}{15} = \frac{20}{15} = 1.333$$

This score of 120 is 1.333 standard deviations above the mean on a frequency distribution of single scores. By referring to the normal curve table, we see that only 9.18% of the scores exceed 120.

In a single-group design, we are not interested in where the individual subjects' scores lie in relation to the mean on a frequency distribution of single scores. Rather, we want to know where the sample mean lies on the sampling distribution of the means. This distribution, according to the Central Limit Theorem introduced earlier, has a mean equal to μ and a variance equal to $\frac{\sigma^2}{N}$. The standard deviation for the sampling distribution is the square root of the distribution's variance and is called the **standard error of the mean**. The symbol for the standard error of the mean is $\sigma_{\bar{x}}$, and the formula for this statistic is

$$\sigma_{\bar{x}} = \frac{\sigma}{\sqrt{N}}$$

Suppose that, for a sample of 100 summer program students, $\bar{x} = 104$. The standard error of the mean for the sampling distribution, based on samples of 100 subjects, is

$$\sigma_{\bar{x}} = \frac{\sigma}{\sqrt{N}} = \frac{15}{\sqrt{100}} = \frac{15}{10} = 1.5$$

Figure 5.7 illustrates the sampling distribution with $\sigma_{\bar{x}} = 1.5$ and $\mu = 100$. The position of $\bar{x} = 104$ is also identified.

To test our hypothesis that the sample of summer program students represents a population with a mean IQ greater than the mean IQ for the general population, we need to determine whether the probability of a sample mean as large as 104 is likely or unlikely to be randomly chosen from this sampling distribution. In other words, with $\alpha = .05$ (unless otherwise stated, α will always be .05 in this textbook), does $\bar{x} = 104$ fall in the region of rejection of the sampling distribution? Our next steps are to determine what score marks off the region of rejection and to determine whether our $\bar{x}$ falls within that region.

Because our sampling distribution is normally distributed, we can use the standard normal curve table in solving this problem. In Chapter 4 we saw that the

FIGURE 5.7   *The obtained mean in relation to a normal distribution of IQ scores.*

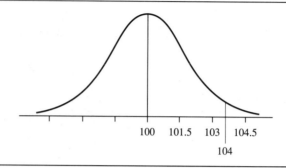

100   101.5   103 | 104.5
                  104

table provides information about the likelihood of scores falling between μ and some z-score, or beyond the z-score. We can think of our problem in terms of identifying the area under the curve where the chance of a score's occurring is 5% or less. Because we are only concerned with whether our mean is *greater* than the population mean, we need look only at the right tail of the distribution.

From the standard normal curve table, we find that the z-score that marks off the top 5% of the distribution is 1.645; it is called the **z critical value** (z_{cv}). Recall that the z-score denotes distance measured in standard deviations from the mean. To determine whether our sample mean is significantly greater than the population mean, we need to know whether the sample mean lies more than 1.645 standard deviations above the mean; that is, we need to determine the z-score for the sample mean.

As introduced in Chapter 4, the formula for calculating the z-score for a single score is

$$z = \frac{X - \mu}{\sigma}$$

The formula for determining the z-score for a sample mean is quite similar, but with two small changes. Because we are finding a z-score for a mean instead of for a single score, we exchange $\bar{x}$ for X. And because the standard deviation for the frequency distribution for a sample mean is the standard error of the mean, we exchange $\sigma_{\bar{x}}$ for σ. Thus, the formula is

$$z = \frac{\bar{x} - \mu}{\sigma_{\bar{x}}}$$

For $\bar{x} = 104$, we can compute

$$z = \frac{\bar{x} - \mu}{\sigma_{\bar{x}}}$$

$$= \frac{104 - 100}{1.5}$$

$$= \frac{4}{1.5}$$

$$= 2.6667$$

The z-score for our sample mean, 2.6667, falls within the region of rejection; this means that there is less than a 5% chance of our having randomly chosen a sample with a mean so great (see Figure 5.8). Thus, we reject the null hypothesis (H_0) that the sample mean represents the general population mean, and support our alternative hypothesis that the sample mean represents a population of summer program students whose mean IQ is greater than 100. We have just conducted the z-test for comparing a sample mean to a population mean.

Let us now consider the z-test for different alternative hypotheses. For example, in the preceding problem the alternative hypothesis was

$$H_1: \mu_0 < \mu_1$$

The z_{cv} was 1.645 and the region of rejection was in the right tail. But what if the alternative hypothesis were in the opposite direction:

$$H_1: \mu_0 > \mu_1$$

Here the region of rejection would be in the left tail, because we expect the sample mean to be smaller than the population mean, and the z_{cv} would be -1.645. A rule of thumb for rejecting H_0 when H_1 is one-tailed is that H_0 should be rejected when both z_{cv} and the calculated z (often called **z obtained**, and symbolized z_{obt}) have the same sign (positive or negative) and $|z_{obt}| > |z_{cv}|$. When this is true, z_{obt} will fall within the region of rejection.

A third possibility is that the alternative hypothesis is two-tailed. In this case a difference between the sample mean and population mean has been predicted, but not the specific direction of that difference:

$$H_1: \mu_0 \neq \mu_1$$

In the case of a two-tailed alternative hypothesis, the region of rejection is divided equally between the two tails of the sampling distribution, with 2.5% of the area in each part constituting the region of rejection. The z_{cv} now changes. From the

FIGURE 5.8   *The z critical value and the z obtained for the z-test example.*

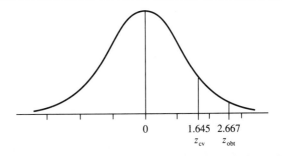

FIGURE **5.9**   *Regions of rejection and critical values for one- and two-tailed alternative hypotheses: (a) region of rejection for $z_{obt} > z_{cv}$; (b) regions of rejection for $z_{obt} < z_{cv}$; (c) regions of rejection for $|z_{obt}| > |z_{cv}|$.*

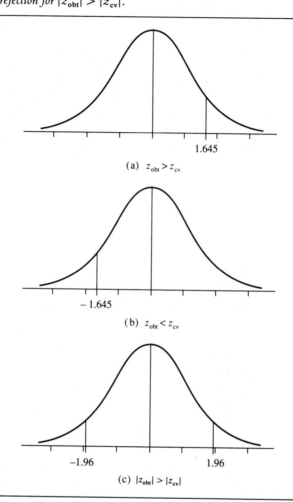

(a) $z_{obt} > z_{cv}$

(b) $z_{obt} < z_{cv}$

(c) $|z_{obt}| > |z_{cv}|$

standard normal curve table, we find that the z-score marking off the top (and bottom) 2.5% of the distribution is 1.96. Thus, $z_{cv} = \pm 1.96$. To justify rejecting H_0 when H_1 is two-tailed, $|z_{obt}| > |z_{cv}|$; when this is true, z_{obt} will fall within the region of rejection. Figure 5.9 illustrates the regions of rejection and critical values for these three different alternative hypotheses.

Assumptions and Appropriate Use of the z-Test   The z-test is called an inferential test or a parametric procedure for hypothesis testing. Parametric tests involve population characteristics, or parameters, that are either known or estimated from sample statistics. Because it is a parametric procedure that involves calculating a sample mean, the z-test is appropriate for interval and ratio scale data, where a mean is a meaningful statistic (a variant of the z-test presented here is also appropriate for nominal and ordinal data). In addition, to calculate a z-score, both the population mean and population standard deviation must be known. When the sample size is small ($N < 30$) or the population standard deviation is not known, the researcher may need to conduct a single-sample t-test instead of the z-test.

THE t-DISTRIBUTION AND THE t-TEST FOR SINGLE SAMPLES

William Sealey Gossett, a chemist, worked in quality control for the Guinness Brewing Company of Dublin, Ireland, at the beginning of the twentieth century. Gossett found that, when samples he chose for quality-control testing were small, the sampling distribution of the means was symmetrical but not normal. As the size of the samples increased, however, the distributions approached the normal distribution. In 1908, he published his findings under the pseudonym Student (company policy forbade the publication of trade secrets). Thus, the members of this family of symmetric distributions are referred to as **Student's t distributions**. With the assistance of mathematician Karl Pearson, Gossett developed a general formula for the t-distributions that was published in 1926 (Hinkle, Wiersma, & Jurs, 1982; Spatz, 1993).

The t-distributions are a family of distributions that, like the normal distribution, are symmetric and bell-shaped. And as z is used to indicate the number of standard deviations from the mean μ, t also indicates the number of standard deviations from the mean. However, unlike the normal distribution, the t-distributions involve different distributions for each sample size. Thus the critical value marking off the region of rejection changes for different sample sizes (see Figure 5.10).

Appendix B includes a table labeled "t Critical Values" (Table t). This table supplies the t_{cv} values for one- and two-tailed alternative hypotheses for a broad range of α levels and sample sizes. However, there is no column labeled n for sample size; instead, there is a column labeled "df," which stands for **degrees of freedom**.

Assume that you are given four numbers: 3, 6, 8, and 11. The mean of these numbers is 7. Now you are told that you can change the numbers as you wish, but you must keep the mean at 7. How many numbers can you change arbitrarily? The answer is that you can only change three of the four numbers arbitrarily, because, as soon as three numbers have been changed, the value of the fourth is determined by

FIGURE 5.10   *Three different t-distributions, each with a different number of degrees of freedom.*

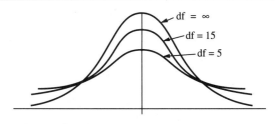

the restriction that the mean must equal 7. Given four numbers and one restriction, only three numbers are free to vary; consequently, there are three degrees of freedom.

Most statistical tests involve setting one or more restrictions on the data set. In the case of the single-sample t-test, we need to estimate the population standard deviation. It may not be obvious, but in the course of estimating the standard deviation we have also estimated the population mean, and thus set a restriction on our set of numbers. For that reason, for the single-sample t-test, $df = N - 1$.

Looking at Table t, we see that sample size is reflected in the df column, and that for different df's (and thus different sample sizes) the critical values for t vary. However, the very bottom line of the table, where $df = \infty$, shows that $t_{cv} = z_{cv}$. When $\alpha = .05$, 1.645 is the t_{cv} for a one-tailed hypothesis, and 1.96 is the t_{cv} for a two-tailed hypothesis. This underscores what was stated earlier—that, as N increases, t approximates the normal distribution.

Let's consider an example using the single-sample t-test. The mean ACT score for students admitted to a certain university is 23. This is the population mean, but the population standard deviation is not known. A member of the psychology department thinks that students who decide to be psychology majors may differ on ACT scores from the population of students at the university in general. The null and alternative hypotheses are thus as follows:

$$H_0: \mu_0 = \mu_1$$

$$H_1: \mu_0 \neq \mu_1$$

The researcher then obtains ACT scores for a sample of psychology majors. These data are provided in Table 5.1.

The mean ACT score for the sample of psychology majors is 25.3333 points. This serves as our estimate of the mean ACT score for the population of psychology majors. We now must determine whether this score differs significantly from the university mean of 23. Because we do not know σ, we must conduct a t-test instead

TABLE 5.1   *ACT scores for a sample of psychology majors.*

X
20
25
32
27
21
30
28
23
22

$$\sum X = 228 \qquad \bar{x} = \frac{\sum X}{N} = \frac{228}{9} = 25.3333$$

of a z-test. The formula for t is

$$t = \frac{\bar{x} - \mu}{s_{\bar{x}}}$$

This is very similar to the formula for z:

$$z = \frac{\bar{x} - \mu}{\sigma_{\bar{x}}}$$

with the only difference being the substitution of $s_{\bar{x}}$ for $\sigma_{\bar{x}}$. The symbol $s_{\bar{x}}$ represents the estimated standard error of the sampling distribution, where the sample standard deviation s is used as an estimate of σ. Thus, the formula for $s_{\bar{x}}$ is

$$s_{\bar{x}} = \frac{s}{\sqrt{N}}$$

Once again, the formula for s is

$$s = \sqrt{\frac{\sum X^2 - \frac{(\sum X)^2}{N}}{N - 1}}$$

The next step in conducting our t-test is to calculate s. To do so, we need the additional column for X^2 in Table 5.2, as well as the sums for $\sum X^2$ and N. Now we find s as follows:

$$s = \sqrt{\frac{\sum X^2 - \frac{(\sum X)^2}{N}}{N - 1}}$$

$$= \sqrt{\frac{5916 - \frac{228^2}{9}}{9 - 1}}$$

TABLE 5.2   *ACT scores and squared values for these scores for a sample of psychology majors.*

X	X²
20	400
25	625
32	1024
27	729
21	441
30	900
28	784
23	529
22	484
$\sum X = 228$	$5916 = \sum X^2$ $N = 9$

$$= \sqrt{\frac{5916 - \frac{51984}{9}}{8}}$$

$$= \sqrt{\frac{5916 - 5776}{8}}$$

$$= \sqrt{\frac{140}{8}} = \sqrt{17.5} = 4.1833$$

The standard deviation for this sample is 4.1833. We now use the sample standard deviation to calculate the standard error of the sampling distribution, by dividing $s_{\bar{x}}$ by $\sqrt{N}$. Thus,

$$s_{\bar{x}} = \frac{s}{\sqrt{N}}$$

$$= \frac{4.1833}{\sqrt{9}}$$

$$= \frac{4.1833}{3} = 1.3944$$

Now that $s_{\bar{x}}$ has been obtained, t may be calculated:

$$t = \frac{\bar{x} - \mu}{s_{\bar{x}}}$$

$$= \frac{25.3333 - 23}{1.3944}$$

$$= \frac{2.3333}{1.3944} = 1.6733$$

Our sample mean falls 1.6733 standard deviations above the population mean of 23. Our question now is whether this puts it within the region of rejection.

Because ours is a two-tailed alternative hypothesis, the region of rejection is divided evenly between the positive and negative tails of the sampling distribution. With $\alpha = .05$, the region of rejection consists of the top and bottom 2.5% of the distribution. Whether our t-value falls within the region of rejection depends on whether the obtained t (t_{obt}) falls beyond t_{cv}. We determine the critical value by referring to Table t.

In Table t we can find the t_{cv} that corresponds with a two-tailed alternative hypothesis, where $\alpha = .05$ and $df = N - 1 = 9 - 1 = 8$. Using this information, we find that $t_{cv} = 2.306$. The t_{obt} is, therefore, not within the region of rejection. We do not reject H_0, and thus cannot support H_1; that is, we have insufficient evidence to allow us to conclude that the population of psychology majors differs significantly on ACT scores from the rest of the student body at this university.

Assumptions and Appropriate Use of the Single-Sample t-Test   The t-test, like the z-test, is a parametric procedure; and as such, its validity depends on its meeting certain assumptions. The data should be measured on an interval or ratio scale; and the sample should be randomly selected to ensure that the sample is representative of the population. The observations should also be independent, meaning that the observation of one subject has no effect on the performance or observation of another. Finally, the population distribution of scores should be normal. Violating these assumptions weakens the power of the *t*-test, making it more difficult to detect differences between the sample and the population.

The *t*-test, however, has the reputation of being a "robust" test, which means that it can tolerate some violation of the assumption of normality, especially if $N > 30$. With smaller samples, normality becomes more of a concern.

The single-sample *t*-test is used to compare a sample mean to a population mean when a *z*-test cannot be done. Primarily, this occurs when the population mean is known but the population standard deviation is not known. When neither a *z*-test nor a *t*-test is appropriate, the researcher may wish to consider a nonparametric test.

CONCEPT QUESTIONS 5·3	A researcher wishes to compare a sample mean with a population mean. The sample includes 25 elements, and the sample standard deviation is known. Which should be calculated—a *z*-test or a single-sample *t*-test?

THE χ^2 GOODNESS-OF-FIT TEST

A nonparametric test is a statistical test that does not test a hypothesis about a parameter of the sampled population; that is, no population parameters need to be known or estimated. Nonparametric tests tend to be based on fewer assumptions about the data set or about the population from which the data were sampled, and for this reason nonparametric tests are also called assumption-free tests (although *assumption-freer* would be more accurate, because they are not totally free of assumptions). Nonparametric tests are often easier to calculate than parametric tests, but they also tend to be less powerful, making it more difficult to reject the null hypothesis when it is false.

The χ^2 (spelled chi-square and pronounced "kie-square") **goodness-of-fit test** is a nonparametric test that is useful for comparing categorical information to what one might expect to encounter by chance (or what one might expect to encounter based on some other information). It is a nondirectional test; that is, the alternative hypothesis is neither one-tailed nor two-tailed. Instead, the alternative hypothesis is simply that the obtained data do not fit the expected frequencies. Let's consider an example where the χ^2 goodness-of-fit test would be appropriate.

Stories are often told of animals that find their way back home across many miles. Some researchers have wondered if people also have a "homing" instinct, an internal compass that may help them maintain their orientation in unknown places. In one particular study, the subjects were shown which way north was; then each subject was blindfolded, spun around several times, and asked to point in an arbitrarily chosen direction (north, south, east, or west). Subjects were allowed 45° of

TABLE 5.3   *Obtained and expected frequencies for χ^2 goodness-of fit example.*

Frequencies	Correct	Incorrect
obtained	9	10
expected	4.75	14.25

error on either side of the direction. Each subject's response was recorded as either correct or incorrect. In this study, 19 subjects were tested, of which 9 responded correctly and 10 incorrectly.

According to chance, each subject had a 25% chance of being correct and a 75% chance of being incorrect. Another way to think of this is that, for a group of subjects responding with random guesses, one would expect 25% of the subjects to be correct and 75% of the subjects to be incorrect. Hence, for 19 subjects, we would expect 4.75 subjects to be correct, and 14.25 subjects to be incorrect. The expected frequencies are calculated by multiplying the number of observations (N) by the probability of category membership's occurring.

To conduct a χ^2 goodness-of-fit test, we need to compare our obtained frequencies of correct and incorrect responses to our expected frequencies of these responses. The obtained and expected frequencies are presented in Table 5.3.

Now how can we tell whether our obtained frequencies fit the expected frequencies or differ significantly from the expected? We must calculate χ^2, according to the following formula:

$$\chi^2 = \sum \frac{(O - E)^2}{E}$$

where O is the obtained frequency and E is the expected frequency.

The null hypothesis is rejected if the χ^2_{obt} is *greater than* χ^2_{cv}. The value for χ^2_{cv} is obtained from Table C in Appendix B. The degrees of freedom for the χ^2 goodness-of-fit test is the number of categories minus 1 [In this example, 2 (correct and incorrect) minus 1 equals 1.] In the table we find that, for $\alpha = .05$ and 1 degree of freedom, $\chi^2_{cv} = 3.84$. We can reject the null hypothesis if our χ^2_{obt} is greater than 3.84. The χ^2_{obt} is calculated as follows:

$$\chi^2 = \sum \frac{(O - E)^2}{E}$$

$$= \frac{(9 - 4.75)^2}{4.75} + \frac{(10 - 14.25)^2}{14.25}$$

$$= \frac{4.25^2}{4.75} + \frac{-4.25^2}{14.25}$$

$$= \frac{18.0625}{4.75} + \frac{18.0625}{14.25}$$

$$= 3.8926 + 1.2675 = 5.1601$$

The χ^2_{obt} is greater than 3.84, so we can reject the null hypothesis and state that the frequencies of the obtained correct responses are significantly greater than expected by chance. By comparing the obtained frequencies with the expected frequencies for each category we can see that the subjects correctly identified North more frequently than expected.

Assumptions and Appropriate Use of the χ^2 Goodness-of-Fit Test The χ^2 goodness-of-fit test is a nonparametric test, which means, from a practical standpoint, that it is less restrictive than a parametric test; it does, however, have its own assumptions that must be met.

To be generalizable to the population, the sample must be randomly selected. Perhaps even more importantly, the observations must be independent. This means that each observation must be generated by a different subject, and the observation of one subject has no effect on the observations of the other subjects. For example, in the example of blindly pointing toward a requested direction, the observations would not be independent if each subject took the test more than one time.

Another important issue in the χ^2 test is that the expected frequencies should not be very small. A small expected frequency has a greater impact on the total χ^2 value than does a large expected frequency; this is especially problematic when the expected frequency is smaller than five. In fact, the χ^2 goodness-of-fit test should probably not be conducted if even one expected frequency is less than five. If this problem arises more data should be collected to increase the expected frequencies.

Assuming that these assumptions and criteria have been met, the χ^2 goodness-of-fit test can provide useful information. This test is appropriate when the data are frequencies measured on a nominal scale. This means that the data are categorical. Data that have been originally measured on a higher-level scale of measurement (ordinal, interval, or ratio) can typically be transformed into categorical data. For example, test scores expressed in percentages of questions answered correctly can be transformed into letter grades, and the frequencies of students with A's, B's, C's, D's, and F's can be assessed and compared to some expected frequencies.

CRITIQUING THE SINGLE-GROUP DESIGN

When evaluating research reports that describe the results of single-group designs, the reader should pay special attention to the sampling technique used by the investigators. Because the results are based on a comparison of a single sample to a population, an investigation using a single-group design is only as good as the sample. Efforts must be made to obtain a sample that is representative of the population. If the population is assumed to be a homogeneous group, simple random sampling is adequate; and cluster sampling can be used in some cases. If the population is known to be composed of distinct subpopulations, however, stratified random sampling is probably more appropriate. Random sampling is important if a parametric test is used to test the hypothesis.

Another concern is the manner in which the data were collected. Of particular concern is any indication that the measurements taken may have been reactive (so that the process of making the observations changed the behavior or the reporting of the behavior). The evaluator must consider how the data were collected. If they were collected directly from the subjects, does it seem clear that the subjects reported the data accurately, or might the subjects have been motivated to modify their responses—perhaps in order to make themselves appear more socially appropriate? This is more likely to be a concern when sensitive or embarrassing information is requested. People may overreport or underreport information in an effort to present themselves as they would like to be perceived.

Another issue to consider is how the collected data compare with the population data. Is the same information obtained about the sample and from the population? For example, an insurance company may have data on the number of accidents per insuree, and a sample of subjects may be asked about the number of car accidents they have had while driving. Although at first it may appear that these data are comparable, they may not be at all. The insurance company and the subjects may have two different definitions of a car accident. The insurance company may only count accidents that resulted in over $300 worth of damage, while the subjects may report less expensive incidents. Thus the means for the sample and for the population may be different in large part because they are measuring two different things.

Assuming that appropriate sampling and data collection were performed, the next area of interest is the statistical treatment of the data. Three tests for data from single-group designs have been introduced in this chapter: the z-test, the t-test, and the χ^2 goodness-of-fit. The z-test and the t-test may be used with interval or ratio data, but not with ordinal or nominal data. This error is most commonly made when ordinal data are treated as if they were interval data, and the most common error of this type involves treating percentile ranks as if they were measured on an interval scale. Percentile ranks are ordinal data; a difference of five percentile points may be equivalent to one raw score point at one place on the scale and equivalent to two or three raw score points somewhere else on the scale. For this reason, it is inappropriate to conduct t-tests or z-tests with percentile ranks. On the other hand, it is perfectly acceptable to transform interval or ratio data into ordinal or nominal data and then to perform a nonparametric test such as the χ^2 goodness-of-fit.

The last thing to evaluate is the researchers' interpretation of their results. Did they interpret the results of statistical tests correctly? Occasionally, researchers may overinterpret their results, reading more into a rejection of the null hypothesis than they should. In the case of single-group designs, the most likely mistake is to make causal inferences about the results. For instance, consider our example of the mean IQ score from a sample of summer program students compared to the population mean IQ score. If the sample mean is significantly larger than the population mean, we can be fairly confident that the population of summer program students score higher on the IQ tests than do the general population, but we do not know why this is so. It may be that the students have higher IQs to begin with, or they may have learned how to take IQ tests during the summer program, or perhaps the information and thinking strategies employed during the program actually do increase students' IQ scores. While it is acceptable and correct to postulate possible causes for this difference, it is unwise simply to assume a cause. Unfortunately, this is an error more easily detected in others than in oneself.

IMPORTANT TERMS AND CONCEPTS

hypothesis/hypotheses

hypothesis testing

null hypothesis

alternative (research) hypothesis

two-tailed hypothesis

one-tailed hypothesis

Type I error

Type II error

alpha (α)

significant difference

sampling distribution
(sampling distribution of
the mean)

region of rejection

beta (β)

power

Central Limit Theorem

single-group design

parametric tests

nonparametric tests
(assumption-free tests)

standard error of the mean

z critical value

z obtained

Student's t distributions

degrees of freedom

χ^2 goodness-of-fit test

QUESTIONS AND EXERCISES

1. It was hypothesized that college students have higher IQ scores than the general population.
   a. What are the null hypothesis and the alternative hypothesis?

   $$H_0:$$

   $$H_1:$$

   For IQ in the general population, $\mu = 100$ and $\sigma = 15$. Assume that 90 college students are sampled and that $\bar{x}$ for this sample is 103.5.
   b. What is $\sigma_{\bar{x}}$ for this problem?
   c. What is z_{obt} for this problem?
   d. What is z_{cv} for this problem?
   e. Should the null hypothesis be rejected? What should a researcher conclude from the results of this test?

2. Assume that the average household income (μ) in America is $35,353, with $\sigma = \$14,900$. Members of a sample of 150 midwestern residents are surveyed, and their average income is calculated. The researchers hypothesized that the μ income of midwesterners would be different from that of Americans in general.
   a. What are the null hypothesis and the alternative hypothesis?

   $$H_0:$$

   $$H_1:$$

   b. What is $\sigma_{\bar{x}}$ for this problem?
   c. The calculated $\bar{x}$ for the midwesterners was $36,188. What is z_{obt} for this problem?
   d. What is z_{cv} for this problem?
   e. Should the null hypothesis be rejected? What should a researcher conclude from the results of this test?

3. The mean number of children per family in the United States was 3.26 in 1982. A researcher hypothesizes that family size has decreased in the last 10 years. Data are collected on number of children in the family from a random sample of 12 families, with the results shown in the accompanying list. Is the researcher's hypothesis supported?

X
3
3
0
2
1
2
2
0
2
2
0
1

4. Assume that the average smoker (μ) in America smokes one pack (20 cigarettes) per day. You want to determine whether college students who smoke do so more heavily than the average American smoker. Below are data collected from some smokers.

X
20
25
30
15
40
35
25
30

a. What are the null hypothesis and the alternative hypothesis for this example?
b. What is $s_{\bar{x}}$ for this sample?
c. What is t_{cv} for this sample?
d. What are the degrees of freedom?
e. What is t_{cv}?
f. Should the null hypothesis be rejected? What conclusions should you draw from these results?

5. According to the U.S. Bureau of the Census, 34.6% of adults smoked cigarettes in 1982. An investigator predicts that fewer adults smoke now than smoked then. A sample of 90 adults are asked about their current smoking habits: 20 adults report smoking, and 70 report not smoking.

a. What is χ^2_{obt}?
b. What is (are) the degree(s) of freedom?
c. What is χ^2_{cv}?
d. What conclusion should be drawn from these results? Should the investigator conclude that the incidence of cigarette smoking is less now than it was in 1982?

6. A researcher is asked by a news reporter to determine whether the unemployment rate in their city is greater than the national unemployment rate. At the time, the national unemployment rate was 9%. The researcher collects information from a random sample of 100 people.

a. What statistical test should be conducted —a z-test, a single-sample t-test, or a χ^2 goodness-of-fit test?
b. The researcher finds that, in the sample of 100 people, 7 qualify under federal accounting standards as unemployed. Conduct the appropriate statistical test, and decide what the researcher should tell the reporter.

6

Introduction to Experimentation

NONPARAMETRIC TESTS FOR THE TWO-GROUP BETWEEN-SUBJECTS DESIGN: THE WILCOXON'S RANK-SUM TEST AND χ^2 TESTS

THE WILCOXON'S RANK-SUM TEST

χ^2 TEST OF HOMOGENEITY OF PROPORTIONS AND TEST OF INDEPENDENCE

CRITIQUING THE TWO-GROUP STUDY

EXPERIMENTS VERSUS CORRELATIONAL STUDIES

Research investigations can be divided into three types: descriptive studies, correlational studies, and experiments. In **descriptive studies**, variables or phenomena are described in objective and, perhaps, statistical terms. In **correlational studies**, relationships between or among variables can be identified, but causal inferences cannot be made, because of the possible effects of uncontrolled variables. In **experiments**, two (or more) equivalent groups of subjects are treated exactly the same in all ways except the independent variable. Differences in measurements of the dependent variable can then be attributed to differences in the independent variable. In experiments, one can make causal inferences.

One simple type of experiment uses two groups of subjects. A two-group experiment is one type of a broader category of studies using a **between-subjects research design**. Research designs are outlines or general models for setting up a research project. In a between-subjects design, the performances of subjects in one or more groups are compared with the performances of subjects in another group. In an experiment, the groups are made up of very similar subjects and are treated in the same manner *except* with respect to the independent variable. The independent variable is manipulated by the experimenter so that one group of subjects receives one level of the independent variable and the other group receives a second level. For example, if a researcher is testing a new pain reliever, one group would receive a dose of the pain reliever and one group would receive a dose of a **placebo**—an inert substance or treatment that has no effect.

Sometimes the group of subjects receiving the placebo is called the control group, and the one receiving the test treatment is called the experimental group (or the treatment group). Both groups are measured on a dependent variable; in this case, they may be asked to rate the severity of their pain. If the control group and the experimental group differ on the dependent measure, the difference is inferred to have been *caused* by the change in the independent variable. If the experimental group reports less pain than the control group, the pain reliever ingested by the experimental group is assumed to have caused the difference in severity of pain.

Designing an experiment so that causal inferences can be made requires careful planning and full consideration of all factors that might affect the dependent variable. For a study to yield causal results, two requirements must be met: the groups being compared must be equivalent before the independent variable is introduced, and there must be no other potential confounds in the design that might provide alternative explanations for the results. Meeting one or the other of these requirements is not sufficient to permit the experimenter to make causal statements about the results; both requirements must be met.

EQUIVALENT GROUPS

Equivalent groups are necessary in an experiment, and an important method for obtaining equivalent groups is by using **random assignment**. This involves randomly determining the condition to which each subject will be assigned. When subjects are randomly assigned to one of two groups, each subject is equally likely to be assigned to either of the groups; consequently, subject characteristics that may affect the dependent variable can be expected to be distributed evenly between the experimental groups. To do a random assignment, one might draw names or numbers from a hat or identify numbers on a random numbers table. For example, subjects matched with an odd number on the random numbers table may be assigned to one group, and even numbers may be assigned to the other.

Random assignment allows the researcher to be reasonably confident that the groups are equivalent, although it does not *guarantee* that the groups are equivalent in all ways. Any differences between the groups, however, will be caused by chance, will not be systematic, and will probably have little or no effect on the experiment.

Another approach to creating equivalent groups involves matching subjects on important variables. This approach requires a different statistical treatment than random assignment and will be discussed more thoroughly in Chapter 8.

In an experiment involving two groups of subjects, one group (often the control group) is used as a standard of comparison to assess the effect of the independent variable. If members of a group of subjects take a depression test, are then given an antidepression treatment, and are then retested, any change in their depression scores could be due to the treatment or due to anything else that occurred between the first and second testing, including the simple passage of time. By comparing the scores of the experimental group with a comparable control group that receives no treatment, the experimenter can determine whether the people in the experimental group improved because of the effects of the treatment.

Not all two-group experiments have a clear control group that does not receive the treatment. Sometimes research is conducted to compare two different treatments with each other. For example, a researcher may wish to compare one antidepressive medication with another; or a memory researcher may want to compare one type of mnemonic technique, such as the peg-word mnemonic, with another technique, such as the chain mnemonic.

CONTROL OVER EXTRANEOUS VARIABLES

To be able to draw a causal conclusion from the results of an experiment, the experimenter must control variables that could affect the outcome of the study. A variable capable of affecting the dependent variable is called an **extraneous variable**. If an extraneous variable is present for one group in an experiment but not for the other (or not to the same degree), we can no longer feel confident that change in the independent variable caused the difference measured in the dependent variable. It could be that differences between the groups on the dependent variable were caused by change in the extraneous variable, by change in the independent variable, or by the combined effects of change in both variables.

To be controlled, an extraneous variable can be held constant across all groups. As a result, all groups in the study will have the same level or amount of the extraneous variable. Perhaps gender is identified as an extraneous variable in a study that compares the effect of room temperature on productivity. This extraneous variable could be eliminated from the study by limiting the study to subjects of one gender; in this way gender cannot serve as an alternative explanation for observed changes in the dependent variable, and (assuming that no other extraneous variables are present) any difference in productivity must be attributed to temperature. An alternative method for controlling this extraneous variable is to ensure that the genders occur in similar proportions within each group. For example, if the control group is 60% male and 40% female, the experimental group should also be 60% male and 40% female.

When extraneous variables covary or change with the independent variable, they provide alternative explanations for the results of the study. When more than one explanation for the results is possible because of the presence of extraneous variables, the results are said to be *confounded*. For instance, suppose that a researcher is studying the effects of noise on memory performance. The subjects are randomly assigned to either the noise condition or the no-noise condition. Each subject puts on a set of headphones through which those in the noise condition hear static and those in the no-noise condition hear nothing. After putting on the headphones, the subjects in the no-noise condition study a list of 25 words for two minutes, and those in the noise condition study a different list of words for two minutes. Later, when the researcher tries to interpret the results of this study there is a problem: is the difference in performance of subjects between the noise and no-noise conditions a result of the independent variable, noise, or is it a result of the difference between word lists, or is it perhaps due to a combination of the two? There is no way for the researcher to know at this point. To avoid this problem, the experimenter must plan ahead to identify potential confounds and control their effects. We discuss some common extraneous variables that can confound results—and consider ways to control them—in the section on internal validity.

EXPERIMENTER MANIPULATION OF THE INDEPENDENT VARIABLE

A final important aspect of experiments relates to the nature of the independent variable. The independent variable in an experiment is manipulated by the experimenter: the experimenter determines which group receives which level of the independent variable. For example, a researcher investigating the effect of ingested alcohol on reaction times may wish to compare a group of sober subjects with a group of subjects with blood alcohol levels (BAL) at .10. The experimenter randomly assigns subjects to the two groups; one group receives drinks containing alcohol and one group receives a placebo (a drink, such as grapefruit juice, that tastes as if it could have alcohol in it but does not). The subjects' reaction times are then measured, and any differences between the groups are attributed to the effect of the alcohol. This study is an experiment.

Now consider an alternative investigation. A researcher throws a large party where both alcoholic and nonalcoholic beverages are available. After several hours, the researcher measures the BAL of the party-goers and identifies a group of sober subjects and a group of subjects with BAL at .10. The reaction times for these subjects are then measured, as in the first example. In this study, however, the researcher cannot assume that any difference in reaction time between subjects in the sober and intoxicated groups is attributable to the alcohol. The researcher did not manipulate the independent variable; the subjects, in essence, assigned themselves to either the sober or the intoxicated condition. Although the researcher may note a relationship between reaction time and BAL, the researcher cannot assume that a causal relationship exists. One explanation is that the subjects who chose to become intoxicated had slower reaction times before the party began than the subjects who chose to remain sober. Can you think of any other possible explanations? This investigation is not an experiment; it is a correlational study.

In the preceding situation, the manner in which the study was conducted determined whether the independent variable was manipulated by the experimenter or not. A situation in which the experimenter has no power to manipulate the independent variable is when this variable is a subject variable. **Subject variables** are measurable characteristics of the subject such as height, weight, gender, extroverted or introverted, motivated or unmotivated, and energetic or lethargic. Because an experimenter cannot randomly assign subjects to levels of these variables, the experimenter cannot manipulate this independent variable. For instance, a comparison of the replies of males and females to a question on sexual harassment can be very informative, but any difference between the genders on the replies *cannot* be assumed to be *caused* by gender. Other factors that correlate with gender, such as past experiences, socialization, and awareness of sex roles, may actually be causing the difference in replies.

Experiments differ from correlational studies primarily on two related characteristics: equivalent groups of subjects are compared, and the independent variable is manipulated by the experimenter. Nonequivalent groups make it difficult or impossible to determine whether a difference between the groups on the dependent measure is attributable to the independent variable. An independent variable that is not manipulable by the experimenter, such as a subject variable, leads to nonequivalent groups (males versus females, extroverts versus introverts). Thereafter, any differences on the dependent variable cannot readily be attributed to the independent variable, but may instead be related to some variable correlated with the independent variable.

Correlational studies are important contributors to the body of psychological knowledge and are the only way to study many important issues such as gender differences, or the effects of early child abuse on development. In fact, many of the most interesting psychological questions are about the role and influence of subject variables on behavior. The contributions of correlational studies should not be underestimated. And when interpreting the results of a correlational study, it is always appropriate to suggest *possible* causal explanations for the results. Only true experiments, however, yield results that can be causally interpreted with confidence.

CONCEPT QUESTIONS 6.1

Researchers identified individuals who regularly saved money and individuals who rarely if ever saved money; they then asked these individuals to rate their marital satisfaction. The results were that the money savers expressed more satisfaction with their marriages. The researchers concluded that saving money causes this increase in satisfaction.

1. Are the researchers conclusions well-founded?
2. Are there other explanations for the results?
3. How might the researchers design an experiment that would test their hypothesis that saving money effects marital satisfaction?

INTERNAL VALIDITY AND CONFOUNDS

Internal validity is the extent to which the design of an experiment ensures that the independent variable, and not some other variable or variables, caused the measured difference on the dependent variables. In other words, an internally valid study has no extraneous variables or other problems that would confound the results. **Confounds** are extraneous variables or other flaws in the research design that permit alternative explanations for the results and thus limit a study's internal validity. Internal validity, therefore, is maximized by eliminating confounds. Experienced researchers automatically watch for some common confounds and design their studies to avoid or control these confounds. Several of the most common threats to internal validity are presented here.

NONEQUIVALENT GROUPS

A primary concern to a researcher conducting an experiment is that the groups of subjects be equivalent to each other before the independent variable is introduced. As discussed earlier, if the groups differ on some extraneous variable before the independent variable is introduced, any difference between the groups on the dependent measure might be caused by either the extraneous variable or the independent variable or both. Whether the groups are equivalent or not depends on how the subjects are selected for the study. If subjects are randomly assigned to the experimental conditions, the experimenter and evaluator of the research can be fairly confident that the groups are equivalent.

EXPERIMENTER BIAS AND DEMAND CHARACTERISTICS

Clever
Hons
(Pfungst 1911)

A researcher who has spent considerable time conceptualizing, developing, planning, and undertaking an experiment—no matter how objective he or she attempts to be—hopes that the results will be meaningful and useful. The problem is that the experimenter may unconsciously (or even consciously) affect the results of the experiment. For instance, the researcher may reinforce certain responses by the subject and ignore others; or when coding data, the researcher may consistently code ambiguous data so that it complies with the hypotheses being tested. When the experimenter's expectations affect the outcome of a study, this confounding variable is called **experimenter bias**.

Subjects who participate in a study are not blank slates; they develop their own ideas about the purpose of the study and how they think the experimenter wants them to behave. Often these ideas about how they should behave are based on information provided by the experimenter, as well as by the setting of the experiment and by any rumors the subjects may have heard about the study. If these cues (called **demand characteristics**) are too powerful, they can influence the outcome of an experiment.

Clearly, a researcher wishes neither demand characteristics nor experimenter bias to affect the outcome of an experiment. Avoiding these problems can often be accomplished by using a single-blind or a double-blind procedure. In a **single-blind procedure**, either the subjects do not know which experimental condition they are in or the experimenter does not know. In a **double-blind procedure**, neither the experimenter nor the subject is aware of the subject's experimental condition.

Imagine that a new toothpaste is being compared with another brand. If the subjects know that they are using the new toothpaste, they may be more attentive to their dental hygiene—brushing more, flossing more, eating fewer sweets—and then they may score higher on the dependent variable, number of cavities. Similarly, if the subjects know that they are "only" in the control group, they may be disappointed and pay less attention to their teeth than they otherwise would. If the subjects are unaware of the type of toothpaste they have been assigned, the effect of the demand characteristics will be greatly diminished.

It may be just as important to keep the experimenter blind to the condition of the subject. The experimenter who expects the new toothpaste to perform better than the old toothpaste may be apt to identify more cavities among users of the old toothpaste than among users of the new toothpaste. By using a double-blind procedure, where neither the subject nor the experimenter knows whether the subject is in the experimental or the control condition, the researcher can minimize or eliminate the effects of both demand characteristics and experimenter bias.

SUBJECT MORTALITY

Although people volunteer to participate in experiments and provide their informed consent before the experiment begins, they sometimes quit a study partway through. This is known as **subject mortality** (or **subject attrition**).

Subject mortality can be categorized as either nonsystematic or systematic. **Nonsystematic subject mortality** occurs when subjects terminate their participation or when their data cannot be used for reasons unrelated to the experiment itself. For example, a subject may leave a study because it took more time than had been anticipated; or a subject's data may not be used because of equipment problems during the experimental session. Nonsystematic subject mortality is more of an annoyance than a threat to internal validity.

Systematic subject mortality involves the termination of participation by subjects in one experimental group more so than in another. This type of subject mortality is a threat to the internal validity of the experiment, because the groups of subjects that remain as participants in the experiment may no longer be equivalent. Perhaps smokers are asked to participate in an experiment investigating a new way to quit smoking. The subjects are randomly assigned to either the experimental group, which receives nicotine-releasing patches to wear, or the control group, which is to quit smoking "cold turkey." The groups of subjects are relatively equivalent; they include some people who are highly motivated to quit, some who are moderately motivated, and some who are only appeasing friends and family. Many of the low-motivation subjects may have volunteered for the study because they thought they'd have the opportunity to try the nicotine patches. Of these subjects, those who were assigned to the "cold turkey" control group are no longer interested in the study and quit. Now the groups are no longer equivalent; while the experimental group still contains people of various levels of motivation, the control group has lost many of the people with low motivation, leaving primarily those highly motivated to stop smoking.

COMPARABLE TREATMENT OF GROUPS

To maximize the internal validity of an experiment, the researcher must treat the experimental groups as similarly as possible, except in relation to manipulation of the independent variable.

When an experiment involves testing many subjects individually, it can often be too time-consuming to be conducted by one experimenter. In these cases, multiple experimenters are used to conduct the experiment. The use of multiple experimenters affects the internal validity of the experiment if different experimenters test the different experimental groups. For example, if one experimenter tests the subjects in the control group and one experimenter tests the subjects in the experimental group, the experimenter becomes an extraneous variable that covaries with the independent variable. In other words, the use of two experimenters in this manner

Courtesy of Sidney Harris

confounds the results; any difference between the groups could be attributable either to change in the independent variable or to the different experimenters.

This does not mean that all studies need to be conducted by a single experimenter. Instead, the effect of the experimenter must be controlled by **balancing** or distributing its effect evenly across the experimental conditions. When multiple experimenters are used in an experiment, the experimenters need to be distributed equally across the experimental groups; that is, experimenter 1 would test half of the experimental group and half of the control group, and experimenter 2 would test half of the experimental group and half of the control group. When experimenters are balanced across groups, any differences in the experimenters that might affect the dependent variable occur in both the experimental and the control groups.

The experimenter needs to be alert to other, less obvious variables covarying with the independent variable, for they also can confound the results of the experiment. These variables may include (among other possibilities) the time of day when the groups are tested, the way the experimenter is dressed, the weather conditions, the day of the week, and the point during the academic term. If any of these, or any other variables, differ significantly from one group to the other, the experimenter should consider the possibility that the results have been confounded. With some foresight, however, the effects of extraneous variables can at least be distributed across conditions.

SENSITIVITY OF THE DEPENDENT VARIABLE

Balancing potential confounding variables helps maintain the internal validity of an experiment, but it may cause another problem. Because balancing allows an experimenter to distribute the effect of an extraneous variable instead of eliminating the effect, this procedure can actually make it more difficult to reject the null hypothesis.

Consider the z-test and t-test formulas from Chapter 5:

$$z = \frac{\bar{x} - \mu}{\sigma_{\bar{x}}} \quad \text{and} \quad t = \frac{\bar{x} - \mu}{s_{\bar{x}}}$$

In both cases, the number on the bottom of the formula is the standard error. The standard error is an estimate of the average distance the sample means fall from μ within the population, *before* the change in the independent variable has been introduced. Thus, among the general population, the means of samples of 100 people will fall an average of 1.5 points from μ because, with $\sigma = 15$ and $N = 100$, the value of $\sigma_{\bar{x}} = 1.5$. The difference from the mean is the result of **sampling error**; that is, just by chance, some samples score higher because they happen to have more intelligent people in the sample, and some samples score lower because they happen to have less intelligent people; similarly, some samples have good testing days, and some samples have bad testing days. This natural, random fluctuation in scores is called **error variance**.

To reject the null hypothesis with either the z-test or the single-sample t-test, the obtained value must exceed the critical value. If there is very little error variance, the standard error will be smaller than when there is more error variance; and when the denominator of a fraction is smaller, the resulting answer will be larger. Therefore, distributing the effect of an extraneous variable across conditions can actually make it more difficult to reject the null hypothesis, because distributing the effect may increase the error variance among the data.

When designing an experiment, in addition to minimizing error variance to increase the probability of rejecting the null hypothesis, the researcher tries to choose a dependent variable that will be sensitive to the differences between the experimental conditions. An insensitive measure will fail to detect a difference between the experimental groups, even when there is one. For example, measuring the weights of premature and full-term infants to the nearest pound, instead of to the nearest ounce, may not be sensitive enough to detect differences between the groups.

When a dependent variable yields high scores near the top limit of the measurement tool for one or all groups, the experimenter is said to have found a **ceiling effect**. Similarly, if the dependent variable yields scores near the lower limit of the measurement tool for one or all groups, the experimenter is said to have found a **floor effect**. Ceiling and floor effects are not desirable, because they demonstrate the limited sensitivity of the measurement instrument. If the experimental group and the control group recall approximately the same number of words, and neither group recalls many words at all (or both recall virtually all of the words), the task was probably too difficult (or easy) for both groups, and any effect of the independent variable cannot be determined.

CONCEPT QUESTIONS 6.2

A researcher investigates the effectiveness of a new diet program. Subjects wishing to lose weight are randomly assigned to either the control group or the diet program group. The control subjects are told to try to lose weight on their own. The diet program group is provided with educational material, complete menus, and free diet-program foods. After one month each subject is weighed, and the number of pounds lost is recorded.

What potential confounds might affect the results of this study? What improvements would you propose?

EXTERNAL VALIDITY

An experiment or a correlational study *must* have good internal validity to supply interpretable and meaningful results. Another goal of research projects is to maximize external validity. **External validity** refers to the generalizability of the results of an investigation beyond the specific subjects and laboratory of the experiment. First and foremost, an investigation must have internal validity if it is to have any external validity. An experimenter has little leeway regarding internal validity, since a study must be internally valid to be interpretable. There is more flexibility, however, with external validity.

Any investigation needs to have some external validity; an experiment whose results are irrelevant beyond the subjects in the study is of little or no worth. But the controls needed to create an internally valid study can limit the external validity of the study.

Suppose that an investigator wishes to research the effect of hypnosis on pain tolerance. In the experimental group, each subject is hypnotized and given the suggestion that he or she cannot feel pain; then each subject submerges his or her arm in a bucket of ice water. Members of the control group will also be told that they cannot feel pain, but they will not be hypnotized. These subjects will also submerge their arms in the ice water. The dependent variable is the length of time each subject keeps his or her arm in the water.

The gender of the experimenter and the gender of the subjects are extraneous variables that might affect the outcome of this study. The gender of the experimenter might affect how long the subject is willing to tolerate the pain of the ice water. For instance, male subjects may withstand the pain longer in front of a male experimenter than in front of a female (or vice versa); and male subjects may feel honor-bound to sustain pain longer than female subjects would. The experimenter has some alternatives to consider in dealing with this problem. Should both male and female experimenters be used, balancing gender of experimenter across the control and experimental groups, while also making sure that half of the subjects in each group are tested by a person of the same gender and half by a person of the opposite gender? Should both male and female subjects be involved in the study, or should it be limited to only one gender? Using both male and female subjects and both male and female experimenters increases the external validity of the experiment; but as noted earlier, balancing these variables can also decrease the sensitivity of the test and complicate the design of the study. There is no correct answer to this problem. Some researchers choose to balance the extraneous variable, while others opt for controlling it. Those who choose to balance the extraneous variable have access to statistical procedures that can account for the effect of the extraneous variable. This procedure is discussed in Chapter 9.

Another factor that can affect the external validity of a study is the manner in which the subjects are selected for the project. The ideal solution is to use random selection to identify subjects from a population. **Random selection** requires randomly drawing sample elements from a sampling frame, and it typically yields a representative sample. When necessary, variations on random sampling, such as stratified random sampling, can be used to increase the probability of generating a representative sample. These are appropriate techniques to use when a sampling frame is available, but that is not always the case.

More often than not, the subjects for investigations in psychology come from a readily available subject pool: it is very common for researchers to solicit volunteers from introductory psychology classes. This type of sample is called an **accidental sample**. Accidental sampling occurs when subjects are not randomly chosen from a sampling frame, but instead happen to be in the right place at the right time to participate.

Does accidental sampling automatically reduce external validity? It depends on the research. If a researcher wants to investigate the political concerns of 18- to 22-year-olds, then using only 18- to 22-year-old college students will limit the external validity of the study, since the results will not be generalizable to 18- to 22-year-old noncollege students. On the other hand, if physiological or perceptual processes are being studied that are assumed to be pretty much the same whether one is in college or not, the research is likely to have reasonable external validity even though it is conducted exclusively with college students. Finally, the external validity of a study is open to testing. One need only repeat the work in a different context to see whether the results can be generalized.

TWO-GROUP BETWEEN-SUBJECTS DESIGN

In the two-group between-subjects design, two independent groups of subjects that differ on one independent variable are compared. The two-group between-subjects design is called an **experimental design**, because it can be used as a standard arrangement for an experiment; experimental designs, however, can also be used to design correlational studies. The two-group design might involve manipulating an independent variable, and thus (assuming equivalent groups and no confounding factors) would be an experiment. Or the two-group design might involve comparing groups on a subject variable such as age, gender, or experience. This type of study would be correlational. Regardless of whether the project is an experiment or a correlational study, the statistical analyses are the same. In this section, we discuss some of the particulars involved in analyzing the two-group between-subjects design.

A researcher wishes to investigate the effect of light on mood. Light, or lack of it, has been associated with mood in research on Seasonal Affective Disorder (SAD). Two randomly assigned groups of subjects participate. One group is assigned to the fluorescent lighting condition, and the other group is assigned to the full-spectrum lighting condition. The latter type of lighting emits light of wavelengths from the full range of visible light. Fluorescent lighting emits only a subset of visible light wavelengths. Each subject is asked to sit quietly in the lit room for 10 minutes. After 10 minutes, each subject rates his or her mood on a 10-point scale, where 0 is very depressed, 10 is very happy, and 5 is neutral.

This is an example of a two-group between-subjects design. It is characterized by two independent groups of subjects, each assigned to a different experimental condition (also called *different levels* of the independent variable). In this example, the independent variable is type of lighting, and the two levels of type of lighting are the fluorescent lighting and the full-spectrum lighting. The dependent variable in this example is the subjects' mood ratings.

HYPOTHESIS TESTING AND THE TWO-GROUP BETWEEN-SUBJECTS DESIGN

Hypothesis testing is an integral part of the two-group study. The hypothesis testing of this and all other types of experimental designs is essentially the same as that described in Chapter 5. The only element of hypothesis testing that varies is what is being compared. In the examples given in Chapter 5, single samples were being compared to populations (in the case of the z- and t-tests) and to some expected results (in the case of the χ^2). In the two-group design, two samples representing two populations (the population receiving level one of the independent variable, and the population receiving level two of the independent variable) are compared. The null hypothesis is that the populations represented by the control group and by the experimental group do not differ:

$$H_0: \mu_1 = \mu_2$$

The alternative hypothesis is either that the populations represented by the control and experimental groups differ (without predicting the direction of the difference, making this a two-tailed test),

$$H_1: \mu_1 \neq \mu_2$$

or that they differ in a specific direction (a one-tailed test):

$$H_1: \mu_1 < \mu_2 \qquad \text{or} \qquad H_1: \mu_1 > \mu_2$$

The criterion for a "significant" difference depends on the alpha level (typically, $\alpha = .05$) and the specific statistical test being conducted.

As with the one-group design, the appropriate statistical test for the two-group design depends on the scale of measurement of the data and on whether the data meet the assumptions of the test. We will discuss several statistical tests that could be used with a two-group between-subjects design: the independent-samples *t*-test, the χ^2 test of homogeneity of proportions, and Wilcoxon's rank-sum test.

INTERVAL OR RATIO DATA: THE INDEPENDENT-SAMPLES *t*-TEST

A graduate student is interested in determining whether noise is a help or a hindrance when studying. This student notes that there are a number of ways to define *noise*, including such possibilities as rock music, traffic sounds, and other people talking. This researcher decided to define *noise* operationally as radio static, and expected to find that subjects who were required to study a list of words in the static condition would recall fewer words than subjects who studied in a quiet condition. For this study, the null and alternative hypotheses are as follows:

$$H_0: \text{Quiet condition} = \text{Noise condition}; \quad \mu_q = \mu_s$$

$$H_1: \text{Quiet condition} > \text{Noise condition}; \quad \mu_q > \mu_s$$

The researcher solicited the assistance of 20 volunteers who were then randomly assigned to either the control (silence) condition or the experimental (static) condition. Each subject was tested individually. The subject sat at a desk in a quiet room and was fitted with a set of headphones. The headphones served to block out all other extraneous noise for those in the control group, or to present the radio static from an attached receiver for those in the experimental group. Each subject was presented with a list of 50 words randomly chosen from a dictionary. The subjects studied this list for 10 minutes and then completed a free recall task in which they tried to write down as many of the words as they could. The numbers of words correctly recalled by the subjects are presented in Table 6.1.

TABLE 6.1   *Number of words recalled under silent and static environmental conditions.*

Silence	Static
20	12
15	17
22	18
19	12
17	11
21	13
18	15
21	16
18	11
19	14
$\bar{x}_1 = 19$	$\bar{x}_2 = 13.9$

Now the researcher needs a way to determine whether the mean of the silence condition is significantly greater than the mean for the static condition. In the single-sample *t*-test discussed in Chapter 5, a single sample mean was compared to a population mean. To compare two sample means, we also use a *t*-test, but this one is called the **independent-samples** *t*-test. The general formula for the independent-samples *t*-test is

$$t = \frac{(\bar{x}_1 - \bar{x}_2) - (\mu_1 - \mu_2)}{s_{\bar{x}_1 - \bar{x}_2}}$$

In essence, this resembles a double version of the single-sample *t*-formula. Instead of comparing a single sample with a single population, however, here the difference between two sample means is compared with the difference between two population means. In most research involving the independent-samples *t*-test, the null hypothesis is that there is no difference between μ_1 and μ_2; that is, the difference is 0.* For example, if the heart rates of two randomly chosen groups of subjects were compared, we would not expect any difference between the mean heart rates *unless* an independent variable, such as biofeedback training, had been manipulated. Thus, we can simplify this formula somewhat by dropping the difference between the populations:

$$t = \frac{\bar{x}_1 - \bar{x}_2}{s_{\bar{x}_1 - \bar{x}_2}}$$

The standard error used in the independent-samples *t*-test is officially called the **standard error of the differences between means**. It is the standard deviation for the sampling distribution composed of differences between sample means (instead of for a sampling distribution composed of sample means). Imagine that a sample was

---

* Actually, a difference between the populations can be other than 0, but we will address only this most commonly formulated null hypothesis.

FIGURE 6.1   *Sampling distribution of differences between means.*

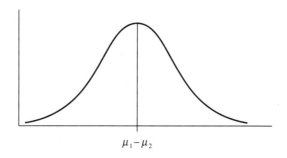

$$\mu_1 - \mu_2$$

taken from population 1 and another sample from population 2, after which their means were calculated and the difference was plotted on a frequency distribution. This was done over and over for all of the samples in populations 1 and 2. The result would be a sampling distribution of differences between means, as in Figure 6.1. The mean of this distribution would be equal to the difference between the population means ($\mu_1 - \mu_2$), and the standard deviation for this distribution would be the standard error of the differences between means ($s_{\bar{x}-\bar{x}}$; usually called the *standard error*).

In the course of conducting the independent-samples t-test, we are determining how far from the difference between the population means lies the difference between our sample means. If the difference between our sample means is relatively large, the difference will fall in one of the tails of the distribution—far from the difference between the population means, which our null hypothesis says is 0. To determine the distance of the difference between sample means from the difference between the population means, we need to convert our mean differences to standard errors. As with the single-sample t-test, the difference between the means is divided by the standard error. The formula for the standard error for a single sample, as you may recall, is

$$s_{\bar{x}} = \frac{s}{\sqrt{N}}$$

Algebraically, this is the same as

$$s_{\bar{x}} = \sqrt{\frac{s^2}{N}}$$

The standard error for the independent-samples t-test is similar to this version of the standard error for a single sample. The formula for the standard error for the independent-samples t-test is as follows:

$$s_{\bar{x}_1-\bar{x}_2} = \sqrt{\frac{s_1^2}{n_1} + \frac{s_2^2}{n_2}}$$

Thus, the formula for the determining t is

$$t = \frac{\bar{x}_1 - \bar{x}_2}{\sqrt{\dfrac{s_1^2}{n_1} + \dfrac{s_2^2}{n_2}}}$$

In the preceding formulas, n refers to the number of scores in each group, whereas N has been (and continues to be) used to refer to the total number of scores in the entire study.

Let's use this formula to determine whether a significant difference occurs between the silent and static conditions described earlier. Table 6.2 reviews the data calculated thus far. Now let's compute the other variables of interest:

$$\bar{x}_1 = \frac{\sum X_1}{n_1} = \frac{190}{10} = 19 \qquad\qquad \bar{x}_2 = \frac{\sum X_2}{n_2} = \frac{139}{10} = 13.9$$

$$s_1^2 = \frac{\sum X_1^2 - \dfrac{(\sum X_1)^2}{n_1}}{n_1 - 1} \qquad\qquad s_2^2 = \frac{\sum X_2^2 - \dfrac{(\sum X_2)^2}{n_2}}{n_2 - 1}$$

$$= \frac{3650 - \dfrac{190^2}{10}}{9} \qquad\qquad = \frac{1989 - \dfrac{139^2}{10}}{9}$$

$$= \frac{3650 - 3610}{9} \qquad\qquad = \frac{1989 - 1932.1}{9}$$

$$= \frac{40}{9} = 4.4444 \qquad\qquad = \frac{56.9}{9} = 6.3222$$

$$t = \frac{\bar{x}_1 - \bar{x}_2}{\sqrt{\dfrac{s_1^2}{n_1} + \dfrac{s_2^2}{n_2}}}$$

$$= \frac{19 - 13.9}{\sqrt{\dfrac{4.4444}{10} + \dfrac{6.3222}{10}}}$$

$$= \frac{5.1}{\sqrt{1.0767}}$$

$$= \frac{5.1}{1.0376} = 4.915$$

Our $t_{obt} = 4.915$. We now consult Table t in Appendix B to find t_{cv}. Our alternative hypothesis was one-tailed, and $\alpha = .05$. The degrees of freedom for the independent-samples t-test are $(n_1 - 1) + (n_2 - 1)$ or $n_1 + n_2 - 2$; because two estimates of the standard deviation are being made: one with $n_1 - 1$ degrees of freedom, and one with $n_2 - 1$ degrees of freedom. In this case, the degrees of freedom are 18. For a one-tailed test with 18 degrees of freedom, $t_{cv} = 1.734$, so our t_{obt} falls beyond the critical value and in the region of rejection. Thus, we reject the null hypothesis and support the alternative hypothesis that more words can be recalled after studying in the quiet condition than in the noise condition. These

TABLE 6.2   *Data for the silence and static noise example.*

Silence	X_1^2	Static	X_2^2
20	400	12	144
15	225	17	289
22	484	18	324
19	361	12	144
17	289	11	121
21	441	13	169
18	324	15	225
21	441	16	256
18	324	11	121
19	361	14	196
190	3650	139	1989

statistical results would be written in an article as $t(18) = 14.55$, $p < .05$. This tells the reader the obtained t value, the degrees of freedom, and that the t was significant with α at .05. The phrase "$p < .05$" can be translated as "the probability of making a Type I error (α) is less than .05."

The preceding formula for the independent-samples t-test is appropriate for use when the samples have equal n values. However, it needs to be modified for situations where there are more subjects in one group than in the other. In the case of unequal values n, the variances of the two samples are averaged together, with each average weighted by its degrees of freedom. This new measure is called the **pooled variance**. The formula for the pooled variance is as follows:

$$s_p^2 = \frac{(n_1 - 1)s_1^2 + (n_2 - 1)s_2^2}{n_1 + n_2 - 2}$$

The formula for the t-statistic now looks like this:

$$t = \frac{\bar{x}_1 - \bar{x}_2}{\sqrt{\dfrac{s_p^2}{n_1} + \dfrac{s_p^2}{n_2}}} = \frac{\bar{x}_1 - \bar{x}_2}{\sqrt{s_p^2\left(\dfrac{1}{n_1} + \dfrac{1}{n_2}\right)}}$$

This formula may be used when the samples are of equal size; it will not affect the value of the standard error. It must be used when the samples are of unequal size.

EXAMPLE INVOLVING UNEQUAL *n*'S

A kindergarten teacher has read an article on the self-esteem of boys and girls. She suspects that children with high self-esteem would name more children as their friends than would children with low self-esteem. She wonders whether boys and girls differ on the number of friends they think they have. The teacher predicts a difference, but she is not sure of its direction. Consequently, she adopts the following null and alternative hypotheses:

$$H_0: \mu_{\text{girls}} = \mu_{\text{boys}}$$

$$H_1: \mu_{\text{girls}} \neq \mu_{\text{boys}}$$

The teacher asks each child individually to name his or her friends, and the teacher records the number of friends listed. The resulting data are presented in Table 6.3. Because the groups are of unequal size, the formula for the t-statistic involving the pooled variance must be used:

$$t = \frac{\bar{x}_1 - \bar{x}_2}{\sqrt{\dfrac{s_p^2}{n_1} + \dfrac{s_p^2}{n_2}}} = \frac{\bar{x}_1 - \bar{x}_2}{\sqrt{s_p^2 \left(\dfrac{1}{n_1} + \dfrac{1}{n_2} \right)}}$$

The raw data scroes and their squared values are given in Table 6.4. We now use these to compute the values of the following variables:

$$s_1^2 = \frac{\sum X_1^2 - \dfrac{(\sum X_1)^2}{n_1}}{n_1 - 1} \qquad s_2^2 = \frac{\sum X_2^2 - \dfrac{(\sum X_2)^2}{n_2}}{n_2 - 1}$$

$$= \frac{196 - \dfrac{40^2}{9}}{8} \qquad = \frac{132 - \dfrac{26^2}{6}}{5}$$

$$= \frac{196 - 177.7778}{8} \qquad = \frac{132 - 112.6667}{5}$$

$$= \frac{18.2222}{8} = 2.2778 \qquad = \frac{19.3333}{5} = 3.8667$$

$$s_p^2 = \frac{(n_1 - 1)s_1^2 + (n_2 - 1)s_2^2}{n_1 + n_2 - 2}$$

$$= \frac{(9 - 1)2.2778 + (6 - 1)3.8667}{9 + 6 - 2}$$

$$= \frac{18.2224 + 19.3335}{13} = 2.8889$$

$$t = \frac{\bar{x}_1 - \bar{x}_2}{\sqrt{s_p^2 \left(\dfrac{1}{n_2} + \dfrac{1}{n_2} \right)}}$$

$$= \frac{4.4444 - 4.3333}{\sqrt{2.8889 \left(\dfrac{1}{9} + \dfrac{1}{6} \right)}}$$

$$= \frac{.1111}{\sqrt{.8025}} = \frac{.1111}{.8958} = .124$$

Thus, $t_{\text{obt}} = .124$. For a two-tailed hypothesis with 13 df $(9 - 1 + 6 - 1)$, the t_{cv} is 2.160. Our obtained value does not fall within the region of rejection. We fail to

TABLE 6.3   *The hypothetical number of friends reported by boys and girls.*

Girls	Boys	
4	5	
2	3	
6	3	
4	7	
3	2	
5	6	
4	—	
7	26	$\bar{x}_2 = \dfrac{26}{6} = 4.3333$
5		
—		
40		$\bar{x}_1 = \dfrac{40}{9} = 4.4444$

TABLE 6.4   *Data for the number-of-friends survey.*

Girls	X_1^2	Boys	X_2^2
4	16	5	25
2	4	3	9
6	36	3	9
4	16	7	49
3	9	2	4
5	25	6	36
4	16	—	—
7	49	26	132
5	25		
—	—		
40	196		

reject the null hypothesis and do not support the alternative hypothesis that girls and boys report a different number of friends. These statistical results might be written as $t(13) = 2.16$, $p > .05$. Or $p > .05$ might be replaced with the letters N.S., which stand for "not significant." Often the numerical details of nonsignificant results are not reported at all. The fact that the test was conducted and that the results weren't significant might simply be stated in the text of the report.

GRAPHING MEANS

When a significant difference is detected between the means of two groups, it is quite common (but not necessary) to graph those means for a pictoral representation of the relationship between the independent and the dependent variables. Two types

FIGURE **6.2** *Mean numbers of words recalled under silence and static conditions.*

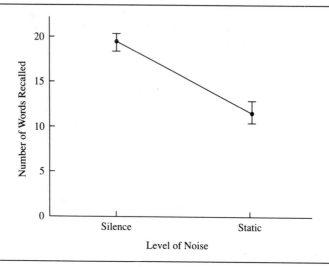

FIGURE **6.3** *Number of friends claimed by boys and girls.*

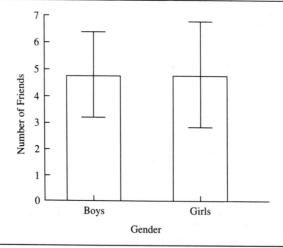

of graphs are typically used: line graphs and bar graphs. The type of graph used is determined by whether the independent variable is continuous or discrete.

Let's revisit our example with the two noise conditions, silence and static. An argument can be made that the independent variable is continuous—that there is a smooth increase in fractional units of some type from silence to static. Thus, a line graph would be appropriate to demonstrate the relationship between the noise conditions and memory performance.

In creating this graph, we customarily place the independent variable on the *x*-axis and the dependent variable on the *y*-axis. Each mean is plotted, and a line connects the two means, as shown in Figure 6.2. The vertical lines at each point on the line represent the standard deviation of the scores for that group of subjects; these lines are called **error bars**. The information they convey can be very useful for interpreting data. As in other graphs, the *y*-axis should be 60% to 75% of the length of the *x*-axis so that the representation is not distorted.

Although the difference between the boys and the girls in our hypothetical kindergarten class was not significant, we can use those means to provide an example of a bar graph (see Figure 6.3) because the independent variable, gender, is discrete. As on the line graph, the vertical lines extending above and below the bars are error bars.

ASSUMPTIONS AND APPROPRIATE USE OF THE INDEPENDENT-SAMPLES *t*-TEST

The assumptions of the independent-samples *t*-test are the same as those for the single-sample *t*: that the data are interval or ratio scale, that the underlying distribution is normal, and that the observations are independent. An additional assumption of the *t*-test for independent samples is that the variances of the two populations are homogeneous (that is, the same). Statisticians have demonstrated that, if the sample sizes are equal, heterogeneity of variance is not a problem; however, it is a concern if the sample sizes are not equal. In that case a correction needs to be made. The actual correction is beyond the scope of this text, but it can be found in more advanced statistics textbooks such as Hinkle, Wiersma, and Jurs (1988) and Howell (1987). Should the independent-samples *t*-test be inappropriate for use with data from a two-group between-subjects design—perhaps because the data are not measured on an interval or ratio scale, or because the variances in the two groups are very different—one of a number of nonparametric tests may be more appropriate.

NONPARAMETRIC TESTS FOR THE TWO-GROUP BETWEEN-SUBJECTS DESIGN: THE WILCOXON'S RANK-SUM TEST AND χ^2 TESTS

Several nonparametric tests may be used to compare data from two independent samples. Presented here are the Wilcoxon's rank-sum test for use with ordinal data, and the χ^2 tests of homogeneity of proportions and of independence for use with nominal data. Even if a researcher has collected data on an interval or ratio scale of measurement, if parametric tests would be inappropriate, interval and ratio data can always be transformed into a lower scale of measurement and nonparametric tests may then be conducted.

THE WILCOXON'S RANK-SUM TEST

In the independent-samples t-test, the null hypothesis is that μ_1 and μ_2 are equal, with the same σ^2, and that they therefore come from the same population. The **Wilcoxon's rank-sum test** also tests the null hypothesis that the scores of both groups were drawn from the same population, but it is not restricted by the assumptions of normally distributed scores or homogeneity of variance.

To understand the logic behind the Wilcoxon's rank-sum test, imagine two samples of equal size with scores on some measure for which the null hypothesis is false (because the groups differ on these scores). If we rank all of the scores without regard to group membership, the members of one group should tend to have higher ranks than the members of the other group. Thus, the sum of the ranks in one group should be substanially greater than the sum of the ranks for the other group. If the null hypothesis were true and the groups do not differ, the sum of the ranks of the members of each group should be approximately equal.

The test statistic for the Wilcoxon's rank-sum test is the sum of the ranks of the *smaller* of the two samples or, if $n_1 = n_2$, the *smaller* of the two sums. The null hypothesis is then tested by comparing this number with the appropriate number in Table W of Appendix B.

Example Using the Wilcoxon's Rank-Sum Test   Two colleagues from different academic departments were comparing ailments when they began to wonder whether there is a difference between the numbers of physical complaints made by psychology professors and by English professors. To avoid experimenter effects, a colleague from a third department was recruited to poll the members of the English and psychology departments for the number of physical complaints each had suffered during the prior three months. The researchers chose to conduct a nonparametric test instead of an inferential test because they were not convinced that number of physical complaints should be treated as ratio data. Although a score of 0 meant no complaints, they were not convinced that all intervals along the scale were equivalent; for instance, three hangnails probably should not be treated as equivalent to two migraines and appendicitis. Moreover, it is difficult to conceive of a fractional score for number of physical complaints. The collected data are presented in Table 6.5.

The first step for conducting the Wilcoxon's test is to rank the numbers from lowest to highest, assigning tied ranks to tied scores. For example, there are three 4's among the data; if they were not tied, they would have been ranked fourth, fifth, and sixth. We take the average of these ranks and assign this to all of the 4's; thus each of the three 4's is assigned a rank of 5. The ranks and their sums for these data are presented in Table 6.6. As a check to confirm that the ranking has been done correctly, we can inquire whether the highest rank is equal to $n_1 + n_2$ (in this case, 13), as it should be; also, the sum of the ranks should equal $\dfrac{N(N + 1)}{2}$. Here, $75 + 16 = 91$ and $\dfrac{13(14)}{2} = 91$, so the ranking was done correctly.

The sum of the ranks of the smaller group, the English professors, is 16. We now compare that number to a number from Table W. To permit us to reject the null hypothesis, the obtained sum must be *less than or equal to the table value*.

TABLE 6.5   *Hypothetical number of physical complaints reported by members of a psychology department and an English department.*

Psychology	English
8	4
6	3
9	4
10	2
4	1
6	
5	
7	

TABLE 6.6   *Ranked data for the Wilcoxon's test example.*

Psychology	Ranks	English	Ranks
8	11	4	5
6	8.5	3	3
9	12	4	5
10	13	2	2
4	5	1	1
6	8.6		—
5	7		16
7	10		
	75		

In our example, we did not predict which group would have the fewer complaints; thus, we have a two-tailed hypothesis. In this particular table, with $\alpha = .05$, we must look in the .025 column for a two-tailed test. Remember, the .05 is divided in half for a two-tailed test, with .025 in each tail, and this table looks only at the lower tail values.

We now find the portion of the table devoted to $n_1 = 5$, and look down the first column to find $n_2 = 8$ (n_1 is always the n of the smaller group). The critical value for W_s is 23. Our obtained value of 16 is smaller than 23, so we reject the null hypothesis that the populations are identical on number of physical ailments. According to our data, the psychologists reported more physical ailments than did the English professors. The results of this analysis might appear in a report as W_s ($n_1 = 5$, $n_2 = 8$) = 16, $p < .05$.

The Wilcoxon's rank-sum test with ranking from lowest to highest leads to rejection of the null hypothesis only if the smaller ranks congregate in the smaller group. It is possible, however, that the larger ranks might congregate there, such as

TABLE 6.7   *Wilcoxon's test example data for number of papers assigned.*

Psychology	Ranks	English	Ranks	
6	7	12	12	
3	4	10	10.5	
4	5	15	13	$n_1 = 5$
7	8	8	9	
5	6	10	10.5	$n_2 = 8$
1	2		—	
0	1		55	
2	3			
	—			
	36			

if the English professors had had more physical complaints. One solution is to rerank the scores from highest to lowest instead of from lowest to highest; then the smaller ranks (associated with the larger scores) would congregate in the smaller group. An alternative (and perhaps easier) technique is to calculate W'_s:

$$W'_s = 2\overline{W} - W_s$$

where $2\overline{W} = n_1(n_1 + n_2 + 1)$ (Howell 1982).

Let's consider another example. Suppose that the number of papers assigned by English professors and psychology professors are compared. Our alternative hypothesis will be two-tailed for this example. The data, their ranks from lowest to highest, and the rank sums are presented in Table 6.7.

W_s is 55, but we need to calculate W'_s for the smaller group, too, and then use the smaller of the two numbers:

$$2\overline{W} = n_1(n_1 + n_2 + 1) = 5(5 + 8 + 1) = 5(14) = 70$$

$$W'_s = 2\overline{W} - W_s = 70 - 55 = 15$$

W'_s is smaller than W_s, so we will compare 15 to the critical value from Table W, which is 23. Our obtained value is smaller than the critical value, so we reject the null hypothesis that both populations assigned the same number of papers. The English professors assigned more.

Table W in Appendix B is suitable for sample sizes up to 25. When n exceeds 25, the distribution of W_s approaches the normal distribution. For a more accurate test of the null hypothesis, we should use the standard normal distribution; but to do so, we must transform W_s to a z-score. We accomplish this by using the following formula:

$$z = \frac{W_s - \dfrac{n_1(n_1 + n_2 + 1)}{2}}{\sqrt{\dfrac{n_1 n_2(n_1 + n_2 + 1)}{12}}}$$

Just to demonstrate the computations, let's use the data from the last example to compute a z-score:

$$z = \frac{W_s - \dfrac{n_1(n_1 + n_2 + 1)}{2}}{\sqrt{\dfrac{n_1 n_2 (n_1 + n_2 + 1)}{12}}}$$

$$= \frac{55 - \dfrac{5(5 + 8 + 1)}{2}}{\sqrt{\dfrac{5 \times 8(5 + 8 + 1)}{12}}} = \frac{55 - 35}{\sqrt{46.6667}}$$

$$= \frac{20}{6.8313} = 2.9277$$

Thus, $z_{obt} = 2.9277$, which falls beyond the z_{cv} of 1.96 for two-tailed tests of 1.96 and within the region of rejection.

Here is a final note related to the Wilcoxon's rank-sum test. As you read research reports, you may run across a reference to another test, the **Mann-Whitney** U, which is used in some situations where the Wilcoxon's test would be equally appropriate. Wilcoxon developed his tests at approximately the same time Mann and Whitney developed theirs (1945 and 1947, respectively). Both are nonparametric tests that compare data from two independent samples. In fact, the Mann-Whitney U and the Wilcoxon's rank-sum test are so closely related that the sum of W_s and U equals a constant:

$$W_s + U = \frac{n_1(n_1 + n_2 + 1)}{2}$$

If a value for U is available but a value for W_s is preferred (perhaps to permit easy comparison with the test statistics from previous research), you need only subtract U from $\dfrac{n_1(n_1 + n_2 + 1)}{2}$. Similarly, U can be obtained by subtracting W_s from the same constant.

The Wilcoxon's rank-sum test is a nonparametric procedure that is analogous to the independent t-test. It is used in situations where scores are available for two independent samples. It can be used with ratio, interval, or ordinal data, all of which must be converted into ranks before the test can be conducted. If frequency data on a categorical variable (nominal data) are collected from two samples, neither the t-test nor the Wilcoxon's rank-sum test will be appropriate, although χ^2 may be.

χ^2 TEST OF HOMOGENEITY OF PROPORTIONS AND TEST OF INDEPENDENCE

The χ^2 **test of homogeneity of proportions** and the closely allied χ^2 **test of independence** are extensions of the χ^2 goodness-of-fit test described in Chapter 5. In fact, the formula is the same:

$$\chi^2 = \sum \frac{(O - E)^2}{E}$$

It is used when frequency data for two (or more) samples (or one sample divided into two or more groups) have been collected on a categorical variable—that is, when there are no quantitative scores for the individuals in each group, but only a frequency count for each subcategory.

The χ^2 test of homogeneity of proportions and the χ^2 test of independence use the same formula and critical values, but they differ on how subjects are chosen. When two (or more) random samples are chosen and each subject's response is classified as belonging to one of two or more categories, the χ^2 test is called the test of homogeneity of proportions. The test is called the χ^2 test of independence when one random sample is chosen and the subjects are classified as belonging to two (or more) groups. The subjects' responses are also classified as belonging to one of two or more categories.

An example may clarify this difference. Imagine that a single sample of drivers are asked whether the car they most often drive was produced by an American company or by a foreign company, and whether they are satisfied or dissatisfied with their car's performance. Because one sample of subjects is grouped according to the subjects' responses, the appropriate test to conduct is the χ^2 test of independence.

Now assume that a sample of owners of foreign cars and a sample of owners of American cars are asked to indicate whether they are satisfied or dissatisfied with their cars' performance. Because two separate samples were chosen, the appropriate χ^2 test is the test of homogeneity of proportion.

CONCEPT QUESTIONS 6.3

Teenagers in a randomly chosen sample are categorized as having been employed as a babysitter or as having never babysat before. These two groups are asked whether they have ever taken a Red Cross first aid course. The researcher wishes to determine whether babysitters are more likely to have taken first aid than nonbabysitters. Which χ^2 test would be used under these circumstances?

Example Using the χ^2 Test of Homogeneity of Proportions Suppose that I am interested in the career goals of psychology majors who are planning to go to graduate school. Specifically, I want to know whether the plans of sophomore majors differ from those of senior majors; that is, do the sophomores change their minds? I randomly select 50 sophomore majors and 50 senior majors, all of whom have indicated a desire to go to graduate school. I ask each individual whether they plan to enter a clinical psychology program, an experimental psychology program, or some other type of psychology program. I then organize my data in a **contingency table** (see Table 6.8).

To calculate the expected frequencies for these data, we need to take into account that plans for attending a clinical program are more prevalent than plans to attend the other types of programs. This means that the probability of choosing the clinical program is greater than the other two probabilities. We need to take these probabilities into consideration when calculating our expected values. This is

TABLE 6.8   *Frequencies at which senior and sophomore psychology majors indicated preference for particular graduate programs.*

Class Standing	Type of Psychology Graduate Program			
	Clinical	Experimental	Other	Row Totals
Seniors	30	8	12	50
Sophomores	36	5	9	50
Column Totals	66	13	21	100

TABLE 6.9   *Contingency table for psychology majors' preferences, including expected frequencies in parentheses.*

Class Standing	Type of Psychology Graduate Program			
	Clinical	Experimental	Other	Row Totals
Seniors (expected frequencies)	30(33)	8(6.5)	12(10.5)	50
Sophomores (expected frequencies)	36(33)	5(6.5)	9(10.5)	50
Column Totals	66	13	21	100

done by incorporating the column and row totals. The formula for calculating the expected frequency for each cell is

$$E = \frac{(RT)(CT)}{N}$$

where RT is the row total, CT is the column total, and N is the total number of observations.

For the uppermost left cell, the expected frequency would be computed as

$$E = \frac{50(66)}{100} = \frac{3300}{100} = 33$$

The contingency table, with the expected frequencies included, is given as Table 6.9. Now χ^2 is calculated in the same manner as for the χ^2 goodness-of-fit test:

$$\chi^2 = \sum \frac{(O - E)^2}{E} = .2727 + .3462 + .2143 + .2727 + .3462 + .2143 = 1.6664$$

The df for a contingency table equals $(r - 1)(c - 1)$, where r stands for the number of rows and c stands for the number of columns. Thus, in this example, df = $(2 - 1)(3 - 1) = 2$. We now use Table X in Appendix B to identify the χ^2_{cv} for 2 df and $\alpha = .05$, and we find $\chi^2_{cv} = 5.991$. Our obtained value of 1.6664 therefore does not exceed the critical value, so we fail to reject the null hypothesis, which is that the proportion of students who plan to attend a certain type of graduate program is *independent* of the students' sophomore or senior standing. If reported in an article, this result might be presented as χ^2 (2, $N = 100$) = 1.67, $p > .05$ (or N.S.).

The Null and Alternative Hypotheses   The null hypothesis for the test of homogeneity of proportions is that the proportions of subjects from each sample choosing each category of response are equivalent. In other words, the null hypothesis for our example is that the proportion of seniors indicating a preference for a clinical program is roughly the same as the proportion of sophomores indicating a preference for a clinical program, and that this is also true for the proportions of students preferring an experimental program or some other program. The alternative hypothesis is that these proportions are not equivalent across the samples, and therefore that class standing is *associated* with preference for a type of graduate program.

The null hypothesis for the test of independence is somewhat different. Imagine that members of a large random sample of students are asked to indicate whether they are science majors or not, and whether the last book they read for pleasure was fiction or nonfiction. The χ^2 test of independence would be appropriate for analyzing these data. The null hypothesis, informally stated, is that these factors are not associated—that they are *independent* factors. More formally, the null hypothesis is that the probability of a respondent's having read one or the other type of book is independent of the probability that the respondent holds a particular major. The alternative hypothesis is much like that for the test of homogeneity of proportions: that major and type of book read are associated with one another.

Assumptions of the χ^2 Test   The assumptions underlying the χ^2 test of homogeneity of proportions and the χ^2 test of independence are the same as those discussed in Chapter 5 for the χ^2 goodness-of-fit test: the sample must be random, and the observations must be independent of each other. Particular to the tests of independence and of homogeneity of proportions, though, is a requirement related to sample size. If any of the expected frequencies are less than 10, the **Yate's correction for continuity** should be used.

The Yate's correction for continuity simply involves subtracting .5 from the difference between each observed and each expected frequency while calculating the χ^2 statistic. The χ^2 formula including the Yate's correction is as follows:

$$\chi^2 = \sum \frac{(|O - E| - .5)^2}{E}$$

There is some controversy about the appropriate use of the Yate's correction. A paper by Camilli & Hopkins (1978) suggests that it should *not* be used with 2×2 contingency tables because of the reduction in the power of the χ^2 test under these conditions. Kirk (1990), on the other hand, recommends using it whenever the $df = 1$ (as would be the case with a 2×2 contingency table) and any expected frequency is not much greater than 10. To avoid the area of controversy, whenever possible, collect enough data so that the expected frequencies are greater than 10.

Finally, a point should be made about including nonoccurrences in the χ^2 contingency table. In the case of a response variable that has two options—such as yes or no, or agree or disagree—it is important that both responses be included in the contingency table. Do not be tempted to create a table that includes only the positive (or only the negative) responses, for this will distort the data and invalidate the test.

As an example, suppose that a researcher asked subjects whether they would vote for the current United States' President if there were an election tomorrow, and also asked the subjects if they considered themselves to be a Democrat, a Republican, or other. If the researcher looked only at the data of those who said they would vote for the President, the data might look like this:

	Democrat	Republican	Other
Would vote for	50	50	35

The researcher might then conduct a χ^2 goodness-of-fit test, resulting in a χ^2 of 3.968. The researcher would fail to reject the null hypothesis, concluding that there was no evidence of a difference in support for the President among Democrats, Republicans, and others. But if the data of those who would not vote for the President are also included, the data might look like this:

	Democrat	Republican	Other
Would vote for	50	50	35
Would not vote for	25	150	20

Now the researcher appropriately conducts the χ^2 test of independence and calculates a χ^2 of 53.276. This time the null hypothesis is rejected; evidently, support for the President is associated with the respondent's political party. The moral of this story is to include all of the data, not just the positive or just the negative responses.

CRITIQUING THE TWO-GROUP STUDY

In evaluating a study that involves comparing two groups, several factors are worth considering. The first is the composition of the groups. How were the subjects assigned to groups? Was the method of assignment likely to yield equivalent groups? Random assignment of an accidental sample is the most often-used method for obtaining equivalent groups. It is also amenable to statistical analysis. There are, however, other workable methods, such as matching, or combining matching with random assignment. No method guarantees equivalent groups, but random assignment decreases the likelihood of creating systematic differences between the groups.

Every bit as important as subject selection and subject assignment is the procedure used in conducting the investigation. The internal validity of the study depends on the researcher's having used a procedure devoid of confounds. For example, is it possible that the subjects' behaviors were affected by demand characteristics? Were there opportunities for experimenter effects? Could the experimenter's expectations have affected the results? Were the groups treated differently in any manner other than with respect to manipulation of the independent variable? Only when there are no alternative explanations can the experimenter be confident that the investigation has good internal validity.

Because the conclusions of the study are based on the results of the statistical analyses, the appropriate tests must be conducted. As with the single-group design, probably the most common mistake involves using parametric procedures with ordinal or nominal data. For example, conducting a t-test on ranked data would be inappropriate because ranks are ordinal and thus uniformly (not normally) distributed. The t-tests should be used with only interval or ratio data. In the case of the χ^2 test, a common error is for single subjects to contribute more than once to the data, which would mean that the scores are not independent.

Finally, what conclusions did the researchers draw from their work? Did they make causal statements about their results? If so, were they warranted? Only if they conducted a true experiment can researchers properly draw causal conclusions. Less controlled studies involving two groups, or studies where the independent variable is a subject variable, yield correlational (not causal) information.

The two-group between-subjects design is a classic design for true experiments, as well as for correlational studies, in the behavioral sciences. Luckily, in science the worth of a project is not determined by the complexity of its design. The two-group between-subjects design can provide a simple but elegant way to gain very important information.

IMPORTANT TERMS AND CONCEPTS

descriptive studies

correlational studies

experiments

between-subjects research design

placebo

random assignment

extraneous variable

subject variable

internal validity

confound

experimenter bias

demand characteristics

single-blind procedure

double-blind procedure

subject mortality (subject attrition)

nonsystematic subject mortality

systematic subject mortality

balancing extraneous variables

sampling error

error variance

ceiling effect

floor effect

external validity

random selection

accidental sample

experimental design

independent-samples t-test

standard error of the differences between means (standard error)

pooled variance

error bars

Wilcoxon's rank-sum test

Mann-Whitney U

χ^2 test of independence

χ^2 test of homogeneity of proportions

contingency table

Yate's correction for continuity

QUESTIONS AND EXERCISES

1. Two methods for teaching statistics were compared by one instructor. During the fall semester, this instructor taught the statistics course using a lecture/discussion format. In the spring semester, the instructor taught the statistics course using a self-paced, independent-study approach. Each class was given the same final exam, and the results of an independent-samples t-test suggested that the students in the self-paced class performed better than did those in the lecture/discussion class. The instructor concluded that the superior performance of the self-paced class was caused by the teaching technique and decided to teach statistics in this manner from then on.

   a. Was this a true experiment? Why or why not?

   b. Are there any confounds and alternative explanations for these results? If so, what are they?

2. Two college students are investigating whether males or females spend more money in an average week. The students solicit information from a random sample of males and females from their campus. The data are presented in the accompanying list.

Males	Females
40	80
60	30
50	20
30	60
50	30
20	50
40	

   a. What statistical analysis would you suggest be conducted?

   b. What are the null and the alternative hypotheses?

   c. Conduct the appropriate analysis, and determine whether the null hypothesis should be rejected.

   d. What conclusions can the researchers draw from these results?

   e. Is this a correlational study or a true experiment? Why?

3. Hayfever sufferers volunteer to participate in a study testing a new antihistamine. Subjects are randomly assigned to either the control condition, which receives a competitor antihistamine, or the new drug condition, which receives the new antihistamine. As one measure in the study, the subjects are asked to record how many times they sneezed in a 24-hour period. The researchers have no evidence to suggest that sneezing is normally distributed.

   a. How would you suggest that the data be analyzed?

   b. Calculate the Wilcoxon's rank-sum test using the accompanying data.

Control	New Drug
12	8
10	6
8	4
9	13
7	9
5	3
7	11

   c. What conclusions can the researchers draw from these results?

   d. Based on the information provided, is this a correlational study or a true experiment?

4. An employee in the University Security Office is responsible for sending out letters regarding the results of an appeal of the individual's parking or traffic ticket. The employee, a student in an experimental psychology course, wonders whether there is any relationship between the tone of the appeal and the ultimate decision. The tone of each of 114 appeals was categorized as angry, apologetic, or neutral; the result of each appeal was either that the appeal had been granted or that it had been denied. The data are presented next.

	Angry	Apologetic	Neutral
Granted	10	16	25
Denied	17	18	28

Tone

Results

a. Which χ^2 test is appropriate in this situation?
b. Calculate the appropriate χ^2 test. What do the results suggest?

5. According to some research, males have better spatial skills than do females; and according to other research, females have better reading skills than males. A student is interested in determining which gender performs better on a word-search puzzle (a puzzle in which words are hidden vertically, horizontally, and diagonally within an array of letters), since this type of puzzle involves both spatial and reading skills. A sample of males and females volunteer to participate and are given 10 minutes to work on a 50-word puzzle. The number of words correctly recognized is recorded for each subject, and the resulting data are as follows:

Males	Females
12	15
8	12
9	11
11	18
10	13
12	14
7	17
15	

a. The student researcher conducts an independent samples t-test with these data. What are the null and the alternative hypotheses made by this researcher?
b. Calculate t_{obt} and find t_{cv}. Assuming that a t-test was an appropriate statistical test to do, what should the researcher conclude?
c. Out of curiosity, the researcher reanalyzes the data using the Wilcoxon's rank-sum test. Calculate W_s to see what the researcher found. What would the researcher conclude now? In what way do the results obtained using W_s differ from those obtained using the independent-samples t-test?

6. A random sample of homeowners and a random sample of renters are polled and asked whether they voted in the last mayoral election. The results are listed here.

	Voted	Didn't Vote
Homeowner	65	43
Renter	52	47

a. Which χ^2 test should be conducted?
b. Conduct the χ^2 test.
c. Should the null hypothesis be rejected? What do the results indicate?

7

Between–Subjects Design with One Independent Variable Containing Three or More Groups

The classic, two-group design, with an experimental group and a control group, may be the first type of experimental design that comes to the minds of most people. But several alternatives to that design are equally useful, or perhaps even more useful. The two-group design serves as a strong foundation upon which to build other more complex designs. In this chapter I will introduce studies involving one independent variable with three or more levels, the advantages and disadvantages of this design, and typical statistical tests for it.

THE EXPERIMENTAL DESIGN

Imagine an investigation where the researcher is interested in the effects of caffeine on the number of errors made while performing an eye-hand coordination task. One way to design this study would be to assign one group of subjects to the caffeine condition and another group to the no-caffeine condition, and then have both sets of subjects conduct the eye-hand coordination task. This design would allow the experimenter to determine whether there was an effect for caffeine, assuming that the amount of caffeine in the caffeine condition was great enough to cause an effect. If the researcher continues to use the two-group design and wishes to decrease the amount of caffeine given to the subjects in the caffeine condition, a control group will be needed for each experiment. A more efficient design, however, would be to compare several levels of caffeine with one no-caffeine control condition all at once.

Suppose that our researcher designs a study in which the volunteer subjects, who typically drink no more than two caffeinated drinks per day, are randomly assigned to one of four groups. One group receives caffeine in an amount equivalent to that contained in three cans of cola; this is the high caffeine condition. The second group receives caffeine in an amount equivalent to that in two cans of cola; this is the medium caffeine condition. The third group receives caffeine in an amount equivalent to that in one can of cola; this is the low caffeine condition. The fourth group receives no caffeine; this is the no caffeine condition, or the control group. All four groups of subjects are treated in the same manner. Each subject receives a beverage that contains the appropriate amount of caffeine (or no caffeine); each beverage tastes the same, so the subjects do not know which condition they are in. In fact, the experimenter has another person assign subjects to condition and serve the beverage, so even the experimenter does not know which condition each subject is in. [Do you remember the name for a study design in which neither the subject nor the experimenter is aware of the subject's experimental condition? If not, see Chapter 6.]

Each subject in each condition performs the same task, and each subject's error rate is measured. Now, not only can the experimenter compare each caffeine condition with the control condition (as would be the case with a series of two-group studies), but the experimenter can also compare each caffeine condition with each other caffeine condition. By comparing caffeine conditions with each other, the researcher can determine whether errors increase or decrease significantly between conditions. In other words, by designing one experiment with four conditions, the experimenter is able to answer many more questions than could be answered with a series of simpler experiments.

Investigations designed to measure the effects of several levels of one independent variable are not substantially more difficult to design than an investigation with only two levels. As with a two-group study, a multigroup study must be designed so that no extraneous variables or other confounds are present to muddy the interpretation of the results. The confounds that can affect a multigroup study are the same as those that can affect a two-group study, and these vary from study to study. The experimenter, while designing the study, needs to be careful to minimize the effects of demand characteristics, to avoid experimenter bias, and to treat subjects in each condition as similarly as possible, except with regard to manipulation of the independent variable. As with the two-group between-subjects design, the between-subject design with three or more groups is referred to as an experimental design, because it can be used as the outline for developing true experiments. Yet the between-subjects design with three or more groups is also an important design for investigating the effects of subject variables in correlational studies. A well-designed and carefully conducted multigroup study, either experimental or correlational, is likely to be a rich source of information.

CONCEPT **QUESTIONS** **7.1**	A colleague wishes to determine the effect of mood on subjects' perceptions of their bodies. Your colleague is thinking of conducting two experiments: one comparing the body image of subjects induced to a depressed mood with that of a control group of subjects induced to a neutral mood, and another comparing the body image of subjects induced to an elated mood with that of a second control

group of subjects induced to a neutral mood. [Mood is induced by having subjects read a series of either depressing, elating, or neutral words. Body image is measured by using a test of body image distortion.] Describe a single, more efficient experiment design. What possible confounds may have to be controlled or balanced by the experimenter?

INFERENTIAL ANALYSIS: ONE-WAY ANALYSIS OF VARIANCE

Let's assume that our researcher has conducted the proposed investigation into the effects of high, medium, and low levels of caffeine on number of errors. The hypothetical data are presented in Table 7.1.

Given what you have learned so far about statistics, it might seem reasonable to compare the groups with each other by conducting a series of independent-sample t-tests. Unfortunately, several factors make that approach undesirable. First, with four means (one for each group), six t-tests would have to be conducted to compare each mean with each other mean. This can be tiresome when calculations are done by hand, but dangerously easy when a computer performs the calculations. This leads to the second, and more important problem: as the number of t-tests increases, the probability of making a Type I error also increases.

When multiple comparisons are made, the Type I error rate for the whole set of comparisons can be calculated as follows:

$$1 - (1 - \alpha)^c$$

where:

α = Level of significance for each test

c = Number of comparisons

If all six comparisons were made with $\alpha = .05$, the Type I error rate would be

$$1 - (1 - .05)^6 = .265$$

Thus, the probability of making a Type I error would not be 5 in 100, but 26.5 in 100. This is called the **familywise** or **experimentwise error rate** (Howell, 1992);

TABLE 7.1 *Data for caffeine example: number of errors made by each subject.*

High Caffeine	Medium Caffeine	Low Caffeine	Control
2	2	2	2
3	3	2	3
4	3	3	2
4	2	2	1
3	3	2	2

it is the probability of making *at least one* Type I error among a set of related comparisons, such as among the group means within an experiment.

Instead of calculating multiple *t*-tests, we can conduct another statistical analysis, called analysis of variance. **Analysis of variance (ANOVA)** is an inferential statistical test for comparing the means of three or more groups. ANOVA has the additional advantage over multiple *t*-tests of being more powerful and thus less likely to make a Type II error, because all of the scores from all of the groups are included in the analyses—not just the scores from two groups at a time. ANOVA is very flexible, as you will see, and it can be used when an experimenter is comparing three groups that vary on one independent variable, or multiple groups that vary on more than one independent variable. ANOVA can be used for very simple designs or very complex ones. In this chapter, I will introduce you to the logic, rationale, and use of ANOVA for analyzing simple designs with one independent variable.

Let's continue with our example of the experiment comparing the number of eye-hand coordination errors made after ingesting high, medium, or low levels of caffeine, or no caffeine. The mean for the high caffeine condition is 3.20 errors; for the medium caffeine condition, 2.60 errors; for the low caffeine condition, 2.20 errors; and for the control condition, 2.00 errors. When all of the data are combined, the mean error rate for all participants (the **grand mean**) is 2.50 errors. Clearly, not every (nor indeed any) subject made 2.50 errors. Similarly, not every subject in the caffeine conditions obtained an error rate score equal to the mean of that subject's condition. In other words, variability exists among the scores. The trick is to determine whether the variability is primarily attributable to the differences in caffeine conditions or to random error variance. **Error variance**, as mentioned in Chapter 6, is the amount of variability among the scores of the individuals assigned to each condition caused by chance and uncontrolled variables.

We can estimate the amount of error variance in our set of data by considering the amount of variability *within* each experimental condition. Because every subject in the high caffeine condition has ingested the same amount of caffeine, any differences in their scores is attributed to random fluctuations and factors that are of little interest to the researcher, such as that some subjects are better at eye-hand coordination tasks than others, some are more motivatd, some are stiff from playing volleyball, some are distracted by thoughts of a recent date, and some are hungry—in other words, error variance. Thus, **within-groups variance** is an estimate of the population error variance.

The means between the groups also differ from the grand mean, as we would expect if different levels of the independent variable affect the number of errors. However, even if the independent variable had no effect on the dependent measure, we would still expect some differences among the group means, simply because of error variance. For example, if subjects were randomly assigned to four groups and their reaction times were measured, few (if any) of the subjects' scores would be equal to the grand mean; and similarly, the group means would differ from each other, too. This would occur simply because of individual differences among the subjects and the effects of variables not controlled (or controllable) by the experimenter. Therefore, the **between-groups variance** is an estimate of the effect of the independent variable *plus* error variance.

We now have two measures of variability: within-group variance, which is an estimate of error variance; and between-group variance, which is an estimate of the variability attributable to the effect of the independent variable plus error variance. What the experimenter wants to know is whether most of the variability in the study is attributable to the independent variable or to random factors. This question can be answered by forming a ratio called an **F-ratio**. The F-ratio is a ratio of the between-groups variance to the within-groups variance:

$$F = \frac{\sigma^2_{Between\text{-}groups}}{\sigma^2_{Within\text{-}groups}} = \frac{\sigma^2_{Error} + \sigma^2_{Effect}}{\sigma^2_{Error}}.$$

If the variability among the scores that is attributable to the independent variable (the number on top) is substantially greater than the error variance (the number on the bottom), the F-ratio will be significantly greater than 1.00. Conversely, if the null hypothesis is true and there is no effect of the independent variable, the between-groups variance will be about the same as the within-groups variance; consequently, the F-ratio of between-groups variance to within-groups variance will be approximately 1.00.

ANOVA uses the F-ratio (named in honor of statistician R. A. Fisher) to determine the effect of the independent variable on the dependent variable. The null hypothesis for ANOVA is that the sample means represent the same population (H_0: $\mu_1 = \mu_2 = \mu_3 = \mu_4$). The alternative hypothesis is that the sample means represent different populations (H_1: at least one $\mu \neq$ another μ). When an experimenter rejects the null hypothesis, this suggests that the independent variable did affect the dependent measure sufficiently for at least one sample mean to differ significantly from another sample mean. An inability to reject the null hypothesis indicates that there is not enough evidence to suggest that the sample means represent at least two different populations. Let's continue with our caffeine example and see how a researcher would calculate the F-ratio.

CONCEPT QUESTIONS 7.2	Which F-ratio is most likely to suggest that the independent variable affected the dependent variable?

a. $\dfrac{.806}{.704}$ b. $\dfrac{.704}{.806}$ c. $\dfrac{.239}{.667}$ d. $\dfrac{.667}{.239}$

CALCULATING THE ONE-WAY ANOVA

The data for our caffeine study are presented once again in Table 7.2. To calculate the F-ratio, we must divide (or partition) the total variability among the data into two sources of variation: the variation within the groups (variation due to random error), and the variation between the groups (variation due to the treatment plus random error).

To partition the variability among the scores, we must have some information about that variability. This is gleaned by computing **sums of squares (SS)**, which

TABLE 7.2   *Data for caffeine example: number of errors made by each subject.*

High Caffeine	Medium Caffeine	Low Caffeine	Control
2	2	2	2
3	3	2	3
4	3	3	2
4	2	2	1
3	3	2	2

are the squared deviation scores $[\sum(X - \bar{x})^2]$. This expression might look vaguely familiar to you; it is the top of the first variance formula you learned back in Chapter 3. We will use sums of squares as our measure of the variability among the scores. Because we want to split the total variability into variability within the groups and variability between the groups, we are interested in three different sums of squares. These sums of squares are typically denoted SS_{Total} for sum of squares total, SS_B for sum of squares between groups, and SS_W for sum of squares within groups.

Before we begin making calculations, let me introduce three symbols. N, as we have been using it, stands for the number of scores. In ANOVA, we must distinguish between the number of scores in the entire study, and the number of scores in each group. N (uppercase) stands for the number of scores in the entire study, and n (lowercase) stands for the number of scores in each group. The number of groups of scores in the study is also important in the calculations. We denote the number of groups of scores by the letter k.

We are now ready to calculate the sums of squares. We'll begin with SS_{Total} and then calculate its two subparts, SS_B and SS_W. The formula for SS_{Total} is

$$SS_{Total} = \sum X^2 - \frac{(\sum X)^2}{N}$$

You may have noticed that this formula is the same as the top of the variance formula. That's because SS_{Total} is the top of the variance formula we use when calculating the variance among all of the scores in the data set. SS_B and SS_W are parts of that total variance; when summed, they will equal SS_{Total}.

The formulas for SS_B and SS_W are as follows:

$$SS_B = \sum \frac{(\sum X_g)^2}{n_g} - \frac{(\sum X)^2}{N}$$

$$SS_W = \sum \left[(\sum X_g)^2 - \frac{(\sum X_g)^2}{n_g} \right]$$

where X_g refers to each score within each group, and n_g refers to the number of scores in each group.

If you have relatively little mathematics background, these formulas may look a bit formidable. However, they each involve nothing more complicated than

TABLE 7.3   *Data and squared scores for caffeine and error rate example.*

High Caffeine	X^2	Medium Caffeine	X^2
2	4	2	4
3	9	3	9
4	16	3	9
4	16	2	4
3	9	3	9
16	54	13	35

Low Caffeine	X^2	Control	X^2
2	4	2	4
2	4	3	9
3	9	2	4
2	4	1	1
2	4	2	4
11	25	10	22

$$N = 20 \qquad \sum X = 50 \qquad \sum X^2 = 136$$

$$n = 5 \qquad (\sum X)^2 = 2500$$

squaring, summing, dividing, and subtracting scores. Their use will be clearer after we have calculated an example.

To calculate the sums of squares for SS_{Total}, SS_B, or SS_W, we must square the scores in our data set. After each score is squared, we must also calculate the sums of those squared scores for each group and for the whole data set. The original scores must be summed both for each group and for the total. These summed scores and squared scores are presented in Table 7.3.

Using these data, we calculate SS_{Total} by squaring the sum of the scores, dividing this number by N, and subtracting the answer from the sum of the squared scores. The calculations are as follows:

$$SS_{Total} = \sum X^2 - \frac{(\sum X)^2}{N}$$

$$= 136 - \frac{2500}{20}$$

$$= 136 - 125$$

$$= 11.00$$

Next we calculate SS_B. The formula for SS_B is

$$SS_B = \sum \left[\frac{(\sum X_g)^2}{n} \right] - \frac{(\sum X)^2}{N}$$

Let's walk through this formula. First, notice that the last element of the formula, $\frac{(\sum X)^2}{N}$, is the same element that appears at the end of the SS_{Total} formula. This is calculated by squaring the sum of all the scores and dividing this preliminary figure by N. The first element is the squared sum of the scores in each separate group, divided by their respective n's and summed together. If the n's in the groups are all the same (such as when all the groups consist of 8 scores), the squared sums of each group may be summed together and then divided by n. Regardless of which way the first element is calculated, the second element is now subtracted from it. The result is SS_B. The SS_B for our example is calculated as follows:

$$SS_B = \sum \left[\frac{(\sum X_g)^2}{n} \right] - \frac{(\sum X)^2}{N}$$

$$= \left[\frac{16^2}{5} + \frac{13^2}{5} + \frac{11^2}{5} + \frac{10^2}{5} \right] - \frac{2500}{20}$$

$$= 51.2 + 33.8 + 24.1 + 20 - 125$$

$$= 129.2 - 125$$

$$= 4.20$$

SS_W remains to be calculated. Its formula is

$$SS_W = \sum \left[\sum X_g^2 - \frac{(\sum X_g)^2}{n} \right]$$

Look carefully at the portion of the formula within the brackets. This should remind you of the top of the variance formula again. SS_W is the sum of the SS for each group, and it is calculated as follows:

$$SS_W = \sum \left[\sum X_g^2 - \frac{(\sum X)^2}{n} \right]$$

$$= \left[54 - \frac{16^2}{5} \right] + \left[35 - \frac{13^2}{5} \right] + \left[25 - \frac{11^2}{5} \right] + \left[22 - \frac{10^2}{5} \right]$$

$$= 2.80 + 1.20 + .80 + 2.00$$

$$= 6.80$$

Notice that $SS_W + SS_B = SS_{Total}$ [6.80 + 4.20 = 11.00]. If the calculated SS values for between-groups and for within-groups do not sum to SS_{Total}, there is an error in the calculations.

Although calculating the SS is an important step in the ANOVA, it is not sufficient for determining the effect of the independent variable. The sums of squares must be transformed to something called **mean squares (MS)**, which are usually denoted as $\mathbf{MS_B}$ for mean squares between groups and $\mathbf{MS_W}$ for mean squares within groups. The term *mean square* is an abbreviation of *mean squared deviation scores*, which is simply a description of how variance is calculated. Thus, the MS values are the estimates of the variance between and within the groups of scores. MS is calculated by dividing each SS by the appropriate df, which means that we need to consider the degrees of freedom for each source of variation.

When calculating SS_{Total}, we based our calculations for the deviations around the grand mean. In other words, we have set one restriction on our data—the grand mean—leaving us with $N - 1$ total degrees of freedom (df_{Total}). For our example,

$$df_{Total} = N - 1 = 20 - 1 = 19$$

SS_B is the variability of k means (the number of groups) around the grand mean. Therefore, the degrees of freedom for the between-groups variance (df_B) is the number of groups (k) minus 1 ($k - 1$). There are four groups in our example, so df_B is $4 - 1$, or 3. Now let's consider the degrees of freedom for the within-groups variance (df_W). The variability within any one group is based on the deviation of the group scores from the group mean. The degrees of freedom for a single group would then be $n - 1$; but since there are k groups, the df_W is equal to $k(n - 1)$ or ($N - k$). Therefore, the df_W in our example is $20 - 4$, or 16. Notice once again that the sum of the within-groups and between-groups degrees of freedom (16 and 3) is equal to the total degrees of freedom (19). If they do not sum to the total degrees of freedom, there is an error someplace in the calculations.

Now that we have calculated both the sum of squares and the degrees of freedom for each source of variation among our data, we can calculate our estimates of the between-groups and within-groups variances. As mentioned earlier, these variance estimates are called mean squares, and they are calculated by dividing each sum of squares by its respective degrees of freedom. Therefore,

$$MS_B = \frac{SS_B}{df_B} = \frac{4.20}{3} = 1.40$$

$$MS_W = \frac{SS_W}{df_W} = \frac{6.80}{16} = .425$$

MS_{Total} is rarely calculated (although it could be, easily enough) simply because we don't need to use it. However, it is the variance among all the scores in the data set:

$$MS_{Total} = \frac{SS_{Total}}{df_{Total}} = \frac{11}{19} = .5789$$

Finally, because we have our MS_B and MS_W, we can calculate the F-ratio by creating a ratio of MS_B to MS_W:

$$F = \frac{MS_B}{MS_W} = \frac{1.40}{.425} = 3.294$$

Our F-ratio is equal to 3.294. Although our F_{obt} is greater than 1.00, we do not know whether it is a large enough margin to allow us confidently to reject the null hypothesis (with $\alpha = .05$), or whether it is larger than 1.00 simply as a function of error variance. To make this decision, we must compare our obtained F with an F_{cv}.

As with the z-score and the t-score described in previous chapters, there is an underlying distribution of the F-ratio, called the F-distribution. The F-distribution is actually a family of distributions, each based on the degrees of freedom between

Courtesy of Sidney Harris

and within each group. The *F*-distribution is positively skewed; its tail points toward the higher positive numbers. The practical significance of this is that we do not test one- or two-tailed hypotheses. Without exception, the alternative hypothesis is that the population means represented by the sample means are not from the same population. Table F in Appendix B is a table providing the *F* critical values (F_{cv}) for the family of *F*-distributions when $\alpha = .05$ or $\alpha = .01$. To read the table, look for the df_B at the top of the table, and look for the df_W along the left side of the table; the F_{cv} is found by tracing these rows and columns to their intersection.

In our example, $df_B = 3$ and $df_W = 16$. With $\alpha = .05$, the $F_{cv} = 3.24$. The obtained *F*-score is 3.294; thus, the obtained score falls beyond the critical value and within the region of rejection (See Figure 7.1). The null hypothesis is rejected; at least two means among the four groups differ from one another, suggesting that these sample means represent at least two different populations.

The results of the ANOVA need to be reported to people interested in the study, and there is a standard format for doing this. Usually, the researcher describes what data were collected, identifies what the means and the standard deviations

FIGURE 7.1   *The F-distribution for the caffeine experiment, with the F obtained value of 3.294 and the F critical value of 3.24 indicated.*

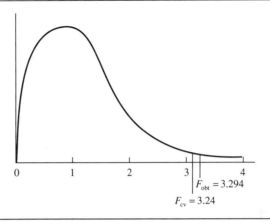

TABLE 7.4   *ANOVA summary table, including formulas.*

Source	df	SS	MS	F
Between groups	$k - 1$	$\sum \dfrac{(\sum X_g)^2}{n_g} - \dfrac{(\sum X)^2}{N}$	$\dfrac{SS_B}{df_B}$	
				$\dfrac{MS_B}{MS_W}$
Within groups	$N - k$	$\sum \left[(\sum X_g)^2 - \dfrac{(\sum X_g)^2}{n_g} \right]$	$\dfrac{SS_W}{df_W}$	
Total	$N - 1$	$\sum X^2 - \dfrac{(\sum X)^2}{N}$		

were, and notes that an ANOVA was conducted to identify significant differences among the means. The standard notation for describing the results of an ANOVA is as follows: $F(df_B, df_W)$ = the F-ratio, $p < \alpha$; so, for our example, the researcher would report that $F(3, 16) = 3.294$, $p < .05$.

We have now conducted an ANOVA to calculate an F-ratio. The calculations for the F-ratio are not especially difficult, but there are a number of them, so a summary table is often created to organize the results of the calculations. In fact, computer programs that calculate ANOVA print a summary table routinely so that all of the information is available to the researcher. You will often find summary tables of ANOVA calculations published in articles describing research results. A summary including the formulas presented in this section appears in Table 7.4. The results of the calculations for SS, MS, and F-ratio in our caffeine experiment are presented in the summary table in Table 7.5.

TABLE **7.5**   *Completed summary table for hypothetical caffeine data.*

Source	df	SS	MS	F
Between groups	3	4.20	1.40	
Within groups	16	6.80	.425	3.294
Total	19	11.00		

The *F*-ratio in our example was significantly larger than 1.00, which means that the independent variable (caffeine) had an effect on the dependent variable (an eye-hand coordination task). Basically, the effect was sufficiently consistent that significantly more variability occurred between the groups than within the groups. But, it would be useful to know how much of the variability among the scores can be attributed to the independent variable; this would serve as a measure of the magnitude of the effect. One such measure is called eta-squared; the symbol for it is η^2, and it is calculated as follows:

$$\eta^2 = \frac{SS_B}{SS_{Total}}$$

In our example η^2 would be $\frac{4.20}{6.80} = .6716$. In other words, approximately 67% of the variability among the scores can be attributed to the caffeine condition to which the scorer was assigned.

PICTORIAL REPRESENTATION OF MEANS

Graphing the means of the groups is an important way to present the relationships among the groups visually. The means for each group are graphed in Figure 7.2. A line graph is used because the levels of the independent variable represent values of a continuous variable (amount of caffeine). When the independent variable is discrete, a bar graph should be used.

MULTIPLE COMPARISON PROCEDURES: TUKEY'S HSD AND THE NEWMAN-KEULS TEST

If the results of the ANOVA suggest a difference among the means, the next step is to attempt to identify that difference (or those differences). Because such analyses are conducted after the data have been collected, these tests are called **a posteriori** or **post hoc analyses**. A first thought might be, "We can use the independent samples *t*-test here," but we shouldn't. The chance of any two randomly selected samples' having significantly different means is about .05. But recall that the familywise error rate increases as the number of comparisons increases. Testing differences among means with a series of independent-samples *t*-tests and with a table critical value

FIGURE 7.2   *Line graph of the means (and standard deviations) of the number of eye-hand coordination errors made at each level of caffeine consumption.*

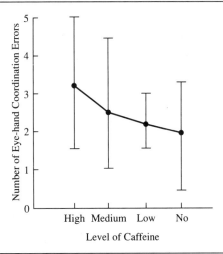

Where $\alpha = .05$ does not maintain the probability of making a Type I error at .05. Instead, the probability of making a Type I error is greater.

Sometimes researchers compute multiple t-tests and apply a correction so that α remains at .05 or lower. This technique is called protecting α. An experimenter who wishes to maintain α at approximately .05 can identify α' by dividing .05 by the number of t-tests he or she plans to make. If the experimenter is going to conduct four t-tests, then $\frac{.05}{4} = .0125$. This new number, α', reflects the α-level of the critical value from the t-distribution table that should be used to maintain α at .05 for all four t-tests.

Unfortunately there are two serious problems with protecting α: first, it is very conservative and will likely decrease the power of the experimenter's analyses; and second, a table of t_{cv} for the specific α' needed may not be available. However, many other techniques have been developed to permit comparisons among the means in a multigroup study and still maintain α at .05. I will present two here: Tukey's Honestly Significant Difference test and the Newman-Keuls test.

Tukey's HSD   Tukey's **Honestly Significant Difference** (HSD) is designed to enable the researcher to make all pairwise comparisons among the sample means in a study while maintaining α at the desired level (usually .05 and/or .01). In other words, the researcher can compare all the possible pairs of means. Different textbooks describe the calculation and procedure for using Tukey's HSD somewhat differently, although all are only algebraic variations on the same test. The procedure I describe here is one that my students understand readily.

The smallest difference between any two means that is still significant with $\alpha = .05$ is the HSD. The formula for the HSD is

$$HSD = Q_{.05}(r, df_W)\sqrt{\frac{MS_W}{n}}$$

where Q is the studentized range statistic and can be found in Table Q in Appendix B. The studentized range statistic is actually a variation of the t statistic; in fact, $Q = \sqrt{2}t$. To find the correct Q in Table Q you need two pieces of information: r and df_w. The df_w can be found in the ANOVA summary table; for our example it is 16. The r changes from one post hoc test to another; for Tukey's HSD, r is equal to the number of means in the study. For our example, $r = 4$.

For our example of the investigation of the effects of caffeine on the number of errors, HSD is calculated as follows:

$$HSD_{.05} = Q(r, df_W)\sqrt{\frac{MS_W}{n}}$$

$$= Q(4, 16)\sqrt{\frac{.425}{5}}$$

$$= 4.05(.2915)$$

$$= 1.181$$

This calculation tells us that any pair of means differing by 1.181 errors or more differ significantly with $\alpha = .05$. Such means would be so different that they would be unlikely to represent the same population.

HSD can also be calculated with α set at .01. The second half of Table Q provides these values, and this HSD is calculated as follows:

$$HSD_{.01} = Q_{.01}(r, df_W)\sqrt{\frac{MS_W}{n}}$$

$$= Q_{.01}(4, 16)\sqrt{\frac{.425}{5}}$$

$$= 5.19(.2915)$$

$$= 1.513$$

Any pair of means differing by 1.513 errors or more differ significantly with $\alpha = .01$.

We have identified four sample means from our investigation of the effects of caffeine on the number of errors:

High caffeine: $\bar{x}_{hc} = 3.20$

Medium caffeine: $\bar{x}_{mc} = 2.60$

Low caffine: $\bar{x}_{lc} = 2.20$

Control: $\bar{x}_c = 2.00$

A table of differences between each pair of the four means can now be made (see Table 7.6). This is useful for ascertaining that all pairwise comparisons have been made and that none has been overlooked. The differences in this table can then be compared with the $HSD_{.05}$ and the $HSD_{.01}$.

TABLE 7.6   *Differences between each pair of means in the caffeine study.*

	High Caffeine 3.20	Medium Caffeine 2.60	Low Caffeine 2.20	No Caffeine (Control) 2.00
3.20	——	.60	1.00	1.20
2.60		——	.40	.60
2.20			——	.20
2.00				——

In this example, only one pair of means has a difference greater than $HSD_{.05}$ (but not greater than $HSD_{.01}$). Those in the high caffeine condition made significantly more errors than those in the no-caffeine control condition. All of the other comparisons were not significant, thus not providing enough evidence to allow us to reject the null hypothesis.

The Newman-Keuls Test   Another post hoc test for comparing means after finding a significant *F*-ratio is called the **Newman-Keuls test**. In this test, pairs of means are again compared.

To begin with, we must order our means from largest to smallest:

High Caffeine	**Medium Caffeine**	**Low Caffeine**	**No Caffeine**
3.20	2.60	2.20	2.00

For our example, this happens to be the order of amount of caffeine, but it needn't be so.

We want to compare each mean with each other mean, to determine whether the difference between the two means is large enough to permit us to reject the null hypothesis that they represent the same population. We label the critical difference value as *D*; the general formula for *D* is as follows:

$$D = Q_{.05}(r, \mathrm{df}_W)\sqrt{\frac{MS_W}{n}}$$

Does this look familiar? It is the same formula we used for Tukey's HSD. The difference between Tukey's HSD lies in the *r*. For Tukey's HSD, *r* equals the number of means. For the Newman-Keuls test, *r* equals the *range* of means involved in that specific comparison. For example, with the means ordered from largest to smallest, if the largest and the second largest means are compared, the range of means involved is 2. Similarly, if the smallest and the second smallest means are compared, the range of means is 2 again. If the smallest mean is compared with the *third* smallest mean, now the range of means involved in the comparison is 3. If five means are calculated in a study and the largest mean is compared with the smallest, the range of means is 5.

In our example, we have four means; thus, when comparing the largest mean (the mean for the high caffeine condition) with the smallest mean (the mean for the no-caffeine control condition), the range of means is 4 and $r = 4$ in the formula for D.

To find Q, we need r, which we have just discussed, and df_W, which we can obtain from the ANOVA summary table. We then consult Table Q in Appendix B. There we find that, for a comparison with a range of 4 means and 16 degrees of freedom, $Q = 4.05$. Let's now compute D for the comparison of the high caffeine mean with the no caffeine mean:

$$D = Q_{.05}(r, df_W)\sqrt{\frac{MS_W}{n}}$$

$$= Q_{.05}(4, 16)\sqrt{\frac{.425}{5}}$$

$$= 4.05\sqrt{\frac{.425}{5}}$$

$$= 4.05\sqrt{.085}$$

$$= 4.05(.2915)$$

$$= 1.181$$

The minimum difference between the high caffeine and no caffeine groups that can occur and still constitute a significant difference with $\alpha = .05$ is 1.181. However, because this is the only pair of means separated by two other means, it is the only pair of means that would use an r of 4 and thus yield this particular D.

Let's make our comparisons in a more systematic way. First, let's compile our means into a table of differences much like the one we used for Tukey's HSD (see Table 7.7). The difference between the high caffeine and no caffeine conditions in Table 7.7 is starred, because it is significantly different at the .05 level.

Let's now consider the comparisons that have a range of three means. Those would be the comparison of the medium caffeine and no caffeine conditions, as well as the comparison of the high caffeine and low caffeine conditions. D is calculated in the same manner, but now r is equal to 3 instead of 4, which yields a different value

TABLE 7.7   *Differences between each pair of means in the caffeine study.*

	High Caffeine 3.20	Medium Caffeine 2.60	Low Caffeine 2.20	No Caffeine (Control) 2.00
3.20	—	.60	1.00	1.20*
2.60		—	.40	.60
2.20			—	.20
2.00				—

for Q:

$$D = Q_{.05}(r, \mathrm{df}_W)\sqrt{\frac{MS_W}{n}}$$

$$= Q_{.05}(3, 16)\sqrt{\frac{.425}{5}}$$

$$= 3.65(.2915)$$

$$= 1.064$$

The smallest difference needed to permit us to reject the null hypothesis that the means are from the same population is 1.064. Neither the difference between the medium caffeine and no caffeine conditions nor the difference between the high and low caffeine conditions is equal to or greater than 1.064. Therefore, neither difference is significant.

The last comparisons are between means that are adjacent to each other and thus have a range of two means: high with medium, medium with low, and low with control (no caffeine). Now when we calculate D, the r equals 2:

$$D = Q_{.05}(r, \mathrm{df}_W)\sqrt{\frac{MS_W}{n}}$$

$$= Q_{.05}(2, 16)\sqrt{\frac{.425}{5}}$$

$$= 3.00(.2915)$$

$$= .875$$

Again, no difference among the comparisons of adjacent means is equal to or greater than D; and thus, the null hypothesis cannot be rejected. Table 7.8 presents a summary of our results using the Newman-Keuls test.

Again, the difference between the high caffeine condition and the no-caffeine control condition is significant, such that those in the high caffeine condition made

TABLE 7.8 *Summary of differences between each pair of means in the caffeine study, with values assessed by the Newman-Keuls test.*

	High Caffeine 3.20	Medium Caffeine 2.60	Low Caffeine 2.20	No Caffeine (Control) 2.00
3.20	——	.60	1.00	1.20*
2.60		——	.40	.60
2.20			——	.20
2.00				——

*$p < .05$.

TABLE 7.9   *Differences between each pair of means in the memory performance study.*

	Neutral 22	Elated 17.5	Depressed 16.2
22	——	4.5	5.8
17.5		——	1.3
16.2			——

more eye-hand coordination errors than did those in the no caffeine condition. Because the research was described as an experiment, and assuming that there were no subtle confounds in the design of the study, the results of the ANOVA and the post hoc analyses suggest that ingestion of a high level of caffeine caused the subjects to make more errors than were made by those who had ingested no caffeine.

In our caffeine example, the Newman-Keuls test yielded the same results as the Tukey's HSD, but this is not always the case. The Newman-Keuls test tends to be somewhat less conservative than the Tukey's HSD test, which means that you may find more significant differences among the means by using Newman-Keuls than by using Tukey's. In exchange, however, the probability of making a Type I error increases slightly.

Let's consider a second example to compare Tukey's HSD and Newman-Keuls. Suppose that a researcher compared the memory performance of three groups: subjects who had been induced to a depressed mood, an elated mood, or a neutral mood. The researcher asked each subject, after the mood induction, to study a list of 30 words for a set period of time. Their memory performance yielded a mean of 22 words for the neutral group, 16.2 words for the depressed group, and 17.5 words for the elated group. The ANOVA yielded a significant F-ratio; MS_W was 1.271, df_W was 18, and $n = 7$. Let's conduct both Tukey's HSD and Newman-Keuls as post hoc analyses on these data.

First, let's create a table of differences between the means, as shown in Table 7.9. Now, let's calculate HSD:

$$\text{HSD} = Q_{.05}(r, df_W)\sqrt{\frac{MS_W}{n}}$$

$$= Q_{.05}(3, 18)\sqrt{\frac{1.271}{7}}$$

$$= 3.61\sqrt{.1816}$$

$$= 3.61(.4261)$$

$$= 1.538$$

According to our calculations, a difference of 1.538 is needed to justify rejecting the null hypothesis that the two means being compared come from the same population. Referring to our table of differences, we see that the difference between the neutral condition and the elated condition and between the neutral condition and the depressed condition are both significant with α at .05. However, the difference between the elated and the depressed conditions is not signficant.

Now let's conduct the Newman-Keuls test. We need to calculate two D's—one for a comparison involving a range of 3 means, and one for the two comparisons involving a range of 2 means. The D with $r = 3$ is the same as the HSD we just calculated, so we know that D is 1.538. The comparison involving a range of 3 means is the comparison of the largest mean (that for the neutral condition) with the smallest mean (that for the depressed condition). That difference is equal to 5.8 words, which is larger than 1.538. Thus, the difference between the neutral and the depressed conditions is significant.

We must now calculate D for the two comparisons involving a range of 2 means:

$$D = Q_{.05}(r, df_W)\sqrt{\frac{MS_W}{n}}$$

$$= Q_{.05}(2, 18)\sqrt{.1816}$$

$$= 2.97(.4261)$$

$$= 1.266$$

There are two comparisons involving a range of two means: neutral with elated, and elated with depressed. The difference between the mean for the neutral condition and the mean for the elated condition is 4.5 words. This is greater than 1.266 and thus is signficant. The difference between the elated condition and the depressed condition is 1.3 words. This is also greater than 1.266, and thus this difference is also significant. Therefore, according to the Newman-Keuls test, all of the means are significantly different from each other. Those in the neutral condition remembered more words than those in either the elated or the depressed condition, and those in the elated condition recalled more words than those in the depressed condition. Notice, however, that, according to the Tukey's HSD (which we did first), the only significant differences were those between the neutral and depressed conditions and between the neutral and elated conditions. No significant difference appeared between the elated and depressed conditions when we conducted Tukey's HSD. This demonstrates that, because Tukey's HSD is somewhat more conservative than the Newman-Keuls test, it may not detect as many probable differences.

REPORTING THE RESULTS OF THE ANOVA AND POSTTESTS

Let's return to our example of the effect of caffeine on the number of errors in an eye-hand coordination task. If the results of this research were to be written into a report, the researcher would want to supply readers with enough information to enable them to evaluate the project and statistical analyses. Typically, the researcher would report descriptive statistics, such as the means and the standard deviations for each condition, any statistical tests that were conducted, and the results of those tests. The researcher might write something like this:

The numbers of errors on the eye-hand coordination task were recorded for the subjects in each of the four caffeine conditions. The means and the standard deviations for these data are presented in Table 1.

Insert Table 1 about here.

An analysis of variance (ANOVA) conducted on these data was significant, $F(3, 16) = 3.294$, $p < .05$. The results of Tukey's HSD indicated that the only significant difference between the conditions was between the no-caffeine control condition and the high caffeine condition ($p < .05$).

The table that the researcher creates would include the means and standard deviations for the four conditions and could be typed on a separate page:

Table 1
The Means and Standard Deviations for the Four Caffeine Conditions

Condition	M	SD
High	3.20	2.8
Medium	2.60	1.2
Low	2.20	0.8
No Caffeine	2.00	2.0

NOTE: $n = 5$ in each condition.

ASSUMPTIONS UNDERLYING THE ANOVA

As with all parametric procedures, several assumptions should be met to ensure proper use of the between-subjects ANOVA:

1. *Normality*: The scores are normally distributed within each population.
2. *Homogeneity of variance*: The variances among the populations being compared are equal.
3. *Interval scale of measurement*: The dependent variable is measured on an interval or a ratio scale of measurement.

ANOVA is said to be a "robust" statistical technique, which means that violations of these assumptions do not always affect the results. In particular, if the dependent variable is not normally distributed, but is instead somewhat skewed, this often does not affect the results of the ANOVA. When the dependent variable departs severely from the normal distribution, another type of statistical analysis should probably be used.

ANOVA also tends to be robust in regard to violations of homogeneity of variance. However, this is only when the sample sizes are equal. Advanced statistical texts, such as Kirk (1990) and Howell (1992) can suggest ways to transform the data or modify the F-ratio when samples demonstrate heterogeneity of variance.

Another way to analyze data when it does not meet the assumptions of ANOVA is to use a nonparametric procedure called the Kruskal-Wallis one-way analysis of variance.

NONPARAMETRIC ANALYSIS: KRUSKAL-WALLIS ONE-WAY ANALYSIS OF VARIANCE

The **Kruskal-Wallis analysis of variance** (or the **Kruskal-Wallis *H*-test**) is a nonparametric test that compares two or more independent groups of scores. It is a direct extension of the Wilcoxon's rank-sum test described in Chapter 6. The null hypothesis for the Kruskal-Wallis is that there are no differences among the scores of the different groups, meaning that the groups all have the same central tendencies. The alternative hypothesis is that there is a difference between at least two of the populations represented by groups' scores, or that some combinations of these populations differ so that the central tendencies differ.

To calculate the Kruskal-Wallis, we first rank the scores without consideration of group membership; we then sum the ranks of each group. The relationship among these summed ranks is identified through use of the following formula:

$$H = \frac{12}{N(N + 1)} \sum \frac{R_g^2}{n} - 3(N + 1)$$

where R_g is the sum of the ranks for each group.

The underlying distribution of H is the χ^2 distribution. The obtained H is comparable to χ^2_{cv} with $k - 1$ df.

Suppose that a German-language instructor wishes to determine which of three teaching techniques leads to the highest language acquisition: watching videos in German, listening to German-language tapes, or engaging in one-on-one conversation in German. Students agree to be randomly assigned to one of these conditions, and after five weeks they are all given the same test on German-language comprehension and production. After looking at the scores, the instructor is concerned that the variance is not equal across the three conditions; and observing that this difficulty is compounded with unequal n's, the instructor believes (correctly) that the Kruskal-Wallis analysis of variance should be conducted. The data and ranks for the analysis are provided in Table 7.10. Notice that tied ranks are dealt with in the same manner as they were with the Wilcoxon rank-sum test.

We then calculate H as follows:

$$H = \frac{12}{N(N + 1)} \sum \frac{R_g^2}{n} - 3(N + 1)$$

$$= \frac{12}{14(15)} \left[\frac{40.5^2}{5} + \frac{11^2}{4} + \frac{53.5^2}{5} \right] - 3(15)$$

$$= \frac{12}{210} [328.05 + 30.25 + 572.45] - 45$$

TABLE 7.10   *German-language test scores and ranked scores and calculations for Kruskal-Wallis example.*

Videos		Tapes		Conversation	
Score	**Rank**	**Score**	**Rank**	**Score**	**Rank**
81	6	75	5	90	11
85	8.5	40	1	97	14
92	12	72	3	85	8.5
87	10	71	2	95	13
73	4	—	—	82	7
	40.5		11		53.5

$$= .0571(930.75) - 45$$

$$= 53.1458 - 45$$

$$= 8.146$$

Further, we can find from Table C in Appendix B that, with $k - 1 = 2$ df and $\alpha = .05$, $\chi^2_{cv} = 5.99$.

The obtained H is 8.146, which is greater than the χ^2_{cv} of 5.99; thus, the null hypothesis is rejected. The teaching techniques lead to different German-language test scores. By inspection of the data, it appears that the German-language tapes lead to the poorest test scores of the three techniques. Various post hoc analyses exist for making multiple comparisons after rejecting the null hypothesis with the Kruskal-Wallis technique. These can be found in statistics books that focus on nonparametric statistics.

The Kruskal-Wallis analysis of variance is a nonparametric technique appropriate for comparing two or more independent samples of scores. It may be used whenever data can be rank-ordered. The Kruskal-Wallis analysis of variance is especially useful when the parametric analysis of variance is inappropriate, such as when the distributions of scores are not normally distributed or when the variances among the populations are feared to be unequal. As with most nonparametric tests (in comparison to parametric tests), the Kruskal-Wallis is less powerful than ANOVA and thus has a greater probability of making a Type II error.

NONPARAMETRIC ANALYSIS OF NOMINAL FREQUENCY DATA

As with the two-group design, three or more groups consisting of nominal, frequency data can also be compared, as described in Chapter 6, by using the χ^2 test of independence or the χ^2 test of homogeneity of proportions. If there is more than one category on the dependent measure, the χ^2 test of independence or test of homogeneity of variance should probably be used. Whether the test would be called the test of independence or the test homogeneity of proprotions depends on how the subjects were sampled.

TABLE 7.11   *Data for the exercise and health study.*

| | Exercise Condition | | |
Health	High	Medium	Low
Sick	14	8	17
Well	6	12	3

For example, suppose that a researcher is interested in the effect of exercise on health. The researcher randomly assigns 60 volunteers to three conditions. In the high exercise condition, the subjects run 3 miles four times a week; in the moderate exercise condition, the subjects walk 3 miles four times a week; and in the low exercise condition, the subjects walk 1 mile once a week. The numbers of subjects in each condition who reported having a cold or other virus within a three-month period were recorded. The data are presented in Table 7.11. Which type of χ^2 test should be conducted in this situation?

The χ^2 test of homogeneity of proportions would be used to test the null hypothesis that the proportion of well and sick people is equivalent across the three exercise conditions. This test is calculated exactly as described in Chapter 6; refer to that chapter for specifics about these calculations. Try to work the problem yourself. The answer is given at the end of this chapter.

CRITIQUE OF THE BETWEEN-SUBJECTS DESIGN WITH THREE OR MORE GROUPS

Investigations that compare three or more independent samples are quite common in the behavioral sciences. They can test more predictions and make more comparisons simultaneously than can a two-group experimental design, but they are also more susceptible to flaws within the experimental design.

A good place to begin an evaluation of a study using a between-subjects design with three or more groups is with the composition of the individual groups. To be appropriate for manipulation by the statistical techniques described in this chapter, the groups must represent independent samples. Either the samples should be randomly selected from different populations or (more commonly) subjects should be randomly assigned to one of the experimental conditions if the dependent variable is manipulated by the experimenter and the experimenter makes causal statements about the results. Other techniques, such as allowing the subjects to choose their own condition or even arbitrarily assigning every third subject to a specific condition, allows biases to slip into the sample selection process and decreases the likelihood that the groups are independent and equivalent before the independent variable is introduced.

Between-subject designs with three or more groups are also conducted when the dependent variable is a subject variable such as gender or background—variables that cannot be manipulated by the experimenter. These designs yield important information about the relationship between the independent and the dependent variables.

The procedure used in the investigation should also be evaluated carefully, regardless of whether the study is experimental or correlational. As with all research designs, there is always the possibility of confounds in the design. Demand characteristics can often confound the results of multigroup experiments, but other extraneous variables—such as the use of multiple experimenters, testing on different days, testing during different times of day—or experimenter biases can affect the results, making them uninterpretable.

Of course, for the results of the study to be valid, the appropriate statistical techniques must be used. If parametric analysis of variance was used, were the data appropriate for this technique? Were the data normally distributed within each population? Were variances homogeneous? Were data measured on an interval or ratio scale? If ANOVA was used and the null hypothesis was rejected, what technique was used to compare the means within the study? Were multiple t-tests used? If so, was α protected? Tukey's HSD and the Newman-Keuls test were introduced in this chapter as techniques for making multiple comparisons, but other similar approaches could be used instead, such as the Scheffé test and Fisher's Least Significant Difference. The Scheffé test has the advantage that complex combinations of means can be compared, such as comparing two alcohol conditions together against a no–alcohol control condition. This test, though, is even more conservative than Tukey's HSD. The HSD test in turn is more conservative than the Newman-Keuls test; this gives Tukey's the advantage of reducing its probability of making a Type I error, but it also increases its probability of making a Type II error. Fisher's Least Significant Difference, the least conservative of all the tests mentioned, may increase the risk of making a Type I error beyond what many researchers are willing to permit.

In the discussion section, researchers draw conclusions from the results of their statistical analyses. The evaluator's job is to determine whether these conclusions are logical. Are they warranted? As with the two-group design, causal statements should be made only when a true experiment has been conducted. Thus, causal statements may be made only if the independent variable was manipulated by the experimenter. Correlational statements are always warranted when the null hypothesis has been rejected.

Multigroup experiments offer an efficient way to answer many related research questions simultaneously. When designed, conducted, and analyzed appropriately, these studies can be the source of considerable information and fuel for future research.

IMPORTANT TERMS AND CONCEPTS

familywise (experimentwise) error rate

analysis of variance (ANOVA)

grand mean

error variance

within-groups variance

between-groups variance

F-ratio

sums of squares (SS)

sum of square total (SS_{Total})

sum of square between groups (SS_B)

sum of square within groups (SS_W)

mean squares (MS)

mean squares between groups (MS_B)

mean squares within groups (MS_W)

a posteriori analyses (post hoc analyses)

Tukey's Honestly Significant Difference (HSD)

Newman-Keuls test

Kruskal-Wallis analysis of variance (Kruskal-Wallis H-test)

QUESTIONS AND EXERCISES

1. Subjects were randomly assigned to one of three conditions: earned money, suprise earnings, or gift money. In the earned money condition, the subjects read a scenario that described the subject earning $50.00. In the surprise earnings condition, the subjects read a scenario in which the subject voluntarily did some work and was later suprised by being paid $50.00 for the work. In the gift money condition, the subjects read a scenario in which the subject won $50.00 in a raffle. After reading the appropriate scenario, each subject indicated how much of the $50.00 he or she would save.

   a. What predictions, if any, do you have about the outcome of this study?

   b. The resulting data are provided in the accompanying chart. Use them to calculate the one-way analysis of variance and to fill out the summary table that follows.

Earned	Surprise	Gift
50	40	40
30	50	20
40	40	25
45	30	30
45	45	35

Summary Table

Source	df	SS	MS	F	F_{cv}
Between groups					
Within groups					
Total					

   c. Is the null hypothesis rejected? What does this tell you about the differences among the means?

   d. If the null hypothesis is rejected, what is the next step? If appropriate, conduct a post hoc analysis.

   e. The researcher argues that the experimental conditions represent increasing surprise at being given money. Draw a line graph of the four group means, including error bars.

2. In a study investigating the effects of sleep on cognitive processes, each of 40 subjects is randomly assigned to one of four conditions: 8 hours of sleep, 6 hours of sleep, 4 hours of sleep, and 2 hours of sleep. After sleeping for the requisite number of hours, each subject is given a list of 30 anagrams to solve in 15 minutes. The number of anagrams correctly solved is recorded.

   a. Is this a true experiment? Why or why not?

   b. After collecting the data (which are reproduced in the accompanying chart), the investigators discover that the variances among the groups are not equivalent. They decide to use the Kruskal-Wallis analysis of variance.

8 Hours	6 Hours	4 Hours	2 Hours
18	25	6	9
29	21	7	6
24	9	5	3
30	27	9	2
19	8	10	7
26	14	16	10
16	22	6	4
28	17	5	3
23	12	12	3
15	13	10	0

c. Is the null hypothesis rejected? What do the results of the analysis of variance tell you about the effect of sleep on ability to solve anagrams?

3. Twelve rats are trained to press a bar. After the initial training, each rat is randomly assigned to one of three reinforcement schedules: a continuous reinforcement schedule, a fixed interval reinforcement schedule (reinforced every 2 minutes as long as at least one appropriate response has occurred), and a fixed ratio reinforcement schedule (reinforced every 4 responses). After a period of 10 minutes, during which the reinforcement schedules are established, a 10-minute test period is run. The number of responses that occur during those 10 minutes is recorded, and a response per minute score is calculated for each rate. The data are provided in the accompanying chart.

Continuous	Fixed interval	Fixed ratio
3.5	1.3	.60
4.0	.90	.30
3.8	1.5	.70
4.2	2.0	.50

a. Using the parametric ANOVA, determine whether the types of reinforcement schedules affected the number of responses per minute.

Summary Table

Source	df	SS	MS	F	F_{cv}
Between groups					
Within groups					
Total					

b. Is the null hypothesis rejected? If it is, conduct the next step, using one of the post hoc analyses introduced in this chapter.

c. Which type of graph would be appropriate for representing the means? Draw a graph of the three group means, including error bars.

d. Using the Kruskal-Wallis analysis of variance, reanalyze these data.

e. Do you obtain the same results with both analyses of variance?

4. A student wishes to test the hypothesis that individuals who pay their own way through college have higher GPAs than do those whose tuition is paid by parents or who receive financial aid. This student asks a number of friends and acquaintances in her class which category they fit in and what their GPA is. She then conducts an ANOVA with the GPA data but fails to reject the null hypothesis.

a. Did this student conduct an experiment or correlational study?

b. There are several flaws in the design of this investigation; name as many as you can.

5. A researcher is interested in the effect of room temperature on cognitive processes. Three room temperatures will be used in the researcher's study: 85°, 72°, and 60°. The subjects will be required to sit in the room and complete a series of math problems for 20 minutes. Three experimenters will conduct this study. Describe how you would organize the assignment of subjects and researchers to the conditions. Imagine that you will actually conduct this study; what are some practical concerns you need to take into account to avoid confounding the results?

The answer to the χ^2 problem presented in the chapter is

$$\chi^2_{obt} = 8.420 \qquad df = 2 \qquad \chi^2_{cv} = 5.99$$

The null hypothesis is rejected. The proportions of well and sick people are not equivalent across the three conditions. It appears that fewer people reported illness in the moderate exercise condition than in the other two exercise conditions.

8

Within-Subjects Design

W hen a researcher conducts an experiment in which two independent groups of subjects receive different levels of the independent variable, the researcher looks for differences *between* the groups on the dependent variable. But as we saw in Chapter 7 when discussing the F-ratio, the experimental groups differ not only on the independent variable, but also on a number of uncontrolled variables that contribute to the error variance. The greater the amount of error variance among the data, the more difficult it is to detect a significant effect for the independent variable.

Researchers can reduce the amount of error variance in a study in a number of ways, such as by carefully controlling extraneous variables. Another way to reduce the error variance is by using the same subjects in all of the experimental conditions. For example, if a researcher were interested in the effect of color on mood, subjects might be asked to complete a mood-rating task after sitting in a blue room for 15 minutes. On another day the same subjects might sit in a red room for 15 minutes, after which they would again complete the mood-rating task. Now the researcher can look for changes in the dependent variable that are attributable to the independent variable by looking for changes *within* the subjects' data. An investigation in which each subject receives each level of the independent variable at least once is called a **within-subjects design**.

TYPES OF WITHIN-SUBJECTS DESIGNS

Within-subjects designs also go by a number of other names, including **repeated-measures designs** and **pretest-posttest designs**. In addition, other designs, such as a yoked design or a matched-pairs design, involve different subjects in different experimental conditions, but the data they produce are treated in the same manner as data from within-subjects designs.

In investigations based on what are described as repeated-measures or pretest-posttest designs, one group of subjects is tested two or more times with the same measurement tool. For example, a researcher may wish to investigate the effect of exercise on mood by having subjects rate their moods before and after a moderate workout. The subjects' mood ratings involve a pretest (the rating prior to the exercise) and a posttest (the rating after the exercise).

The term *within-subjects designs* also refers to studies in which a researcher measures an effect by using two or more types of stimuli or materials. For instance, a researcher might be looking at recall of concrete and abstract words. Subjects could be asked to study a list of 20 words (10 concrete nouns and 10 abstract nouns) for 3 minutes, followed by a recall test. Here the researcher would want to compare the number of concrete words recalled with the number of abstract words recalled. This investigation would be considered a type of within-subjects design.

Two types of within-subjects designs actually involve looking for differences between two (or more) different groups of subjects: a yoked design, and a matched-pairs design. In a **yoked design**, each subject is linked with another subject in the other experimental group (or groups).

Bower & Clark (1969) conducted a study that is a good example of a yoked design. The subjects in the experimental condition were given 10 words to study and were told to combine the words into a story; they had as much time as they wanted. The control subjects in the control condition were told to simply study and learn the list of words. The important point, for our purposes, is that each subject in the control group was linked or yoked with a subject in the experimental group on number of minutes to study. This means that, if a subject in the experimental group used 2 minutes and 45 seconds to form a story with the words, the yoked subject in the control group was allowed 2 minutes and 45 seconds to study the words. If another subject in the experimental group used 3 minutes and 15 seconds, his or her yoked subject received 3 minutes and 15 seconds in the control condition.

Even though two separate groups of subjects are involved in the study, the data from a yoked design are analyzed by using procedures appropriate for a within-subjects design, because matching the subjects on a specific variable relates them. [By the way, after studying 12 lists of 10 words each, the control group in the memorization study was able to recall only 13% of the 120 words, while the experimental group was able to recall 93% of the words (Bower & Clark 1969).]

The second type of within-subjects design involving two groups of related subjects is called a **matched-pairs design**. Subjects in a matched-pairs design are matched between conditions on a subject variable (such as IQ score, height or weight) that the researcher believes is relevant to the study. An advantage to matching subjects is that between-group variance is reduced, thus making the study more sensitive. A disadvantage, however, is that, while between-group variance related to the subject variable has been decreased, the researcher may inadvertently have introduced other nuisance variables. The samples may still not constitute equally good representations of their populations; they may be biased in unknown ways. When used cautiously, however, matched-pairs designs can be a useful way to design a sensitive study.

In this chapter I will refer to all of these types of designs as within-subjects designs, for lack of a more general term. It is important that you be aware of the different types of within-subjects designs and be familiar with the different names used to describe them, because they are so interchangeable.

CONCEPT QUESTIONS 8.1	People with facial tics are the subjects of a study intended to assess how treatment of the tic with medication affects the subject's cognitive processes. Each subject is asked to solicit the assistance of a friend or relative who is within three years of the subject's age, is the same gender as the subject, and does not have a facial tic. This second group of volunteers will serve as the control group. What type of within-subjects design is this?

BENEFITS OF THE WITHIN-SUBJECTS DESIGN

Within-subjects designs are very popular among researchers, for some very good reasons. Typically, within-subjects designs require the involvement of fewer subjects than do between-subjects designs; they often require less time to be conducted; subject variables remain constant across the experimental conditions; and relatedly, error variance is reduced, yielding a more powerful test of the effect being investigated.

Within-subjects designs typically require fewer subjects than do between-subjects designs (except in the cases of matched-pairs or yoked designs) because the subjects participate in each of the experimental conditions. If a study uses two levels of the independent variable, and the researcher wishes to have 12 subjects in each condition, then 24 subjects will be required for a between-subjects design. If a within-subjects design can be used instead, only 12 subjects will be needed, because they will participate in both experimental conditions.

In some types of research, such as perceptual research, the subjects' task may require so little time that each subject not only can participate in each experimental condition but can participate in each condition several times. Not only does this reduce the number of subjects needed for the investigation, but each subject's data can be analyzed and considered a "mini-experiment." Thus, you can look for differences among the experimental conditions, *and* you can determine whether significant differences in performance exist among the subjects.

Studies using within-subjects designs tend to require less time to conduct than do those based on a between-subjects design. Because subjects participate in all conditions, less time is spent waiting for subjects to arrive for the next phase of the study. It is not unusual in between-subjects studies to spend more time waiting for subjects than collecting the data. Often the subjects' task takes very little time, such as when it consists of judging the length of two lines or reading a sentence off of a computer screen. In these cases, having the subjects repeat the task a number of times in each of the experimental conditions is much more efficient than is using a between-subjects design.

An important advantage of the within-subjects design over the between-subjects design is the decrease in error variance, which results in a more powerful test of the effect of the independent variable. A researcher using a powerful design has a relatively low likelihood of making a Type II error (failing to find a significant difference when one actually exists). A within-subjects design is more powerful than a between-subjects design because, typically, the same subjects participate in all of the experimental conditions. In other words, the subjects serve as their own control group.

Consider the following two experiments. Two experimenters wish to investigate the effects of sleep deprivation on cognitive abilities. One experimenter chooses to use a between-subjects design. The members of one sample of subjects sleep for 8 hours in a sleep lab; and upon awakening, they perform the digit-span test. (The digit-span is a memory test in which subjects must repeat increasingly long lists of numbers, half the time in the order presented and half the time in the reverse order). The members of a second sample of subjects sleep for only 4 hours in the sleep lab; then, and like the previous group, they perform the digit-span test upon awakening. What statistical test would you recommend that the researcher use? I would suggest an independent-samples t-test (You should review Chapter 6 if this is unfamiliar to you.)

Let's suppose that the 4-hour group has a mean score on the digit-span that is lower than the 8-hour group's mean; but when the researcher conducts the t-test, the null hypothesis cannot be rejected. Why might this be? It's possible that there really is no appreciable difference in digit-span performance between those sleeping 8 hours and those sleeping 4, but it is also possible that the researcher has made a Type II error: a difference exists between the populations, but it was not detected by using this design. An important reason why a Type II error might be made is if a substantial amount of error variance exists among the scores. Recall from our discussion of the F-ratio in Chapter 7 that the number on top of the ratio describes the amount of variance, attributable to the treatment plus error variance, and the number on the bottom represents error variance. This logic also holds for the fraction created when a t-test is calculated. It's possible that our researcher could not reject the null hypothesis because there is too much error variance among the scores.

Although the two experimental conditions vary in number of hours slept, the participants in each group also vary in other ways. Some of the subjects may be able to perform well with relatively little sleep; others may not function well without at least 9 hours of sleep. Some of the subjects may be morning people, while others may be more alert in the evenings. Some may have slept well in the lab, while others may have found the lab distracting and slept poorly. All of these factors and more would contribute to the error variance both within each group of subjects and between the groups; and the greater the error variance is, the more difficult it will be to detect a significant difference between the means.

Our second researcher chooses to test the same hypothesis by using a within-subjects design. In this study, each subject will sleep in the lab twice—once for 8 hours, and once for 4 hours. As in the previous study, they will take the digit-span test each morning upon awaking. Perhaps you are thinking, "the subjects will do better the second night in the lab because they are more familiar with it; there's a confound in the study." Good thinking. To avoid this confound, the researcher counterbalances the experimental conditions such that half of the subjects sleep 8 hours the first night and half of the subjects sleep 4 hours the first night. Although the subjects may perform better after their second night in the lab, this effect is now divided equally between the 8-hour and the 4-hour conditions.

This second researcher has designed a more powerful experiment than the first researcher devised, and thus is less likely to make a Type II error. Although the subjects still vary on how much sleep they need, whether they slept well or poorly, and whether they perform better in the morning or in the evening, these subject variables affect only the variance within each condition. Because the same subjects are in both conditions, the subject variables are held constant; thus error variance between conditions is minimal.

The power and efficiency of within-subject designs make these designs very popular and useful to researchers. But they are not without their flaws and are not suitable for all research problems.

CONCEPT QUESTIONS 8.2	A researcher wants to conduct a study that has three conditions. The researcher wants 20 scores in each condition. If each subject receives each condition once, how many subjects would be needed for a within-subjects design? How many would be needed for a between-subjects design?

DISADVANTAGES OF THE WITHIN-SUBJECTS DESIGN

If within-subjects designs were flawless, no one would use a between-subjects design. But a number of problems detract from the worth of the within-subjects design. For example, within-subjects designs are susceptible to confounds caused by demand characteristics, practice or fatigue from doing the same task a number of times, and side effects of events that occur during the course of the study.

When a subject participates in a study, the subject tries to determine what is expected of her or him, and typically the subject tries to cooperate. The information a subject infers about what the researcher wants is called **demand characteristics**. In a between-subjects design, the subject experiences only one of the experimental conditions and thus is less likely to guess what the researcher's hypotheses are (although this is still possible and must be watched for). In a within-subjects design, however, the subject participates in all of the experimental conditions. The added information may enable the subject to determine the purpose of the investigation, and this can lead to a change in performance. Therefore, demand characteristics can confound the results of a within-subjects design, making it impossible to interpret the data correctly.

Other problems may arise in a within-subjects design if the subjects are required to perform the same task repeatedly. When a subject performs a task numerous times, two things may occur. If the task is difficult enough, the subject's performance may improve, evidencing in a **practice effect**. On the other hand, if required to do the task often enough, the subject may become tired or merely bored.

When performance declines with repetition, this is referred to as a **fatigue effect**. In either case, the changes caused by practice or by fatigue can confound a study unless special care is taken to distribute potential practice or fatigue effects among the experimental conditions by counterbalancing the order of those conditions. We will discuss the importance of the order of the conditions more thoroughly in the next section on counterbalancing to avoid order effects.

Some tasks, when used in a within-subjects design, cannot be presented in a different order; this is because, once the subjects participate in one condition, it afffects their performance in the other condition. When one experimental condition affects performance in another condition, the persisting influence is termed a **carry-over effect**.

Consider a memory researcher who wishes to test the effectiveness of a mnemonic technique involving imagery. The subjects can participate in the control condition (simple memorization without instruction) followed by instruction in the use of the mnemonic and participation in the mnemonic condition. However, the researcher cannot expect to get the same results if the subjects participate first in the mnemonic condition and then in the control condition. The subjects cannot unlearn the imagery mnemonic; and once they have learned something that works, they might very well use it in the control condition. Of course, the researcher could instruct the subjects *not* to use the mnemonic; but besides the obvious demand characteristic problems, telling someone not to make an image is much like telling the person not to think of a pink elephant. (I bet you thought of one.)

Carryover effects, practice and fatigue effects, and effects of demand characteristics that covary with the effect of the independent variable can confound the results and render a study uninterpretable. Yet these potential confounds usually can be foreseen and the researcher can take measures to eliminate their effects. Sometimes, however, an unexpected problem occurs during the study that confounds the results. In some within-subjects designs, subjects are asked to participate in a study that takes a considerable amount of time—such as days, weeks, or even years. If an event occurs during the course of the investigation that might affect the subjects' performance on the dependent measure, a **history effect** may be present.

Imagine a study addressing the effects of caffeine on anxiety levels; subjects may be asked to monitor their coffee intake and their anxiety levels for a month. Each week they are given a supply of ground coffee. The coffee may be decaffeinated, partially decaffeinated, or not decaffeinated at all; but (to avoid demand characteristics) the coffee is supplied in an unmarked canister. During the week that the subjects are provided with caffeinated coffee, several thunderstorms occur. As the researchers expected, the anxiety scores for the week when caffeinated coffee was consumed are higher than those during the other weeks; but the researchers cannot be sure whether the elevation in the scores was caused by the coffee, by the thunderstorms, or by a combination of both.

Most of the flaws and potential pitfalls of within-subjects designs mentioned thus far can be avoided with a certain amount of forethought in adjusting the contours of the deisgn. The last flaw I will discuss, however, is a direct and unavoidable result of a poor design. Occasionally you may encounter a description of a study in which people who scored very high (or very low) on a test participated in some type of treatment and were then retested. Lo and behold, the subjects' scores

FIGURE 8.1   *Regression toward the mean: those with the most extreme scores (X_1)*
tend to have less extreme scores (X_2) upon retesting.

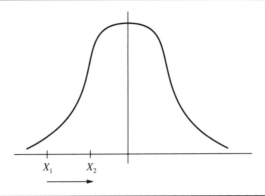

changed, and the mean for the sample drew closer to the population mean. Studies
of this type look impressive to a layperson who is inexperienced in research design;
but in fact their results are in part due to a natural phenomenon called **regression
toward the mean**.

Regression toward the mean occurs when people who initially produced extreme scores subsequently (upon retesting) record less extreme scores. This effect
occurs without any treatment whatsoever. It is related to our old friend, error
variance. Each score reflects both the true score—what one would get in the purest
of situations—and some error variance. If someone scores extremely high on an IQ
test, it is most likely in part because the person is very intelligent (the reflection of
his or her true score) and in part because the person was feeling alert, wasn't hungry,
wasn't distracted, and was able to give his or her full attention to the test. In other
words, all of the other little things that affect performance on a test fell out in this
person's favor. Now, if the same person retakes the test (or a different form of the
test) a few weeks later, the chances are good that the extraneous variables won't all
be quite so favorable. The person is no less intelligent, but his or her score is likely
to decrease. This decrease constitutes natural regression toward the mean. Figure 8.1
presents a graphic representation of this phenomenon.

Unfortunately, research confounded by natural regression toward the mean is
occasionally published. For instance, members of a group of volunteers are given a
test of some type—perhaps a body image distortion test—and those who score the
highest are asked to participate in a research project. The project involves a new
treatment to decrease body image distortion by presenting the subjects with pictures
of models who are of normal size—that is, not especially slim. After looking at
these pictures, the subjects are retested; sure enough, their body image distortion
scores are now lower. With this design, however, there is no way to determine
whether the scores decreased because of the treatment or because of natural regression toward the mean. In Chapter 10, we will discuss research designs that avoid
natural regression toward the mean, enabling studies of this type (with some modifications) to provide useful data.

Although within-subjects designs are not foolproof, most of their flaws can be avoided or minimized with some forethought. The result can be a very powerful and efficient approach to a research question.

CONCEPT EXERCISE	Provide a group of ten friends with ten pennies each, and have them flip each coin. Most of the subjects will produce between four and six heads and between four and six tails. Some, however, will have more extreme scores, such as eight heads and two tails, or vice versa. Select the subjects who produced the most extreme differences between heads and tails, and have them experience your "treatment." Clap your hands over the heads of these people; that's the treatment. Now have the treated individuals flip their coins once more. This time, the differences between the number of heads and the number of tails should be smaller than before. Your treatment has clearly been successful.

Be sure you understand why this "treatment" worked.*

COUNTERBALANCING TO AVOID ORDER EFFECTS

Confounds created by presenting experimental conditions to all subjects in the same order can make research results based on a within-subjects design worthless. There are ways to avoid these confounds, however, through **counterbalancing**. Counterbalancing is the process of presenting experimental conditions to subjects in different orders so that practice effects can be controlled. This can be accomplished by developing either a complete within-subjects design or an incomplete within-subjects design.

THE COMPLETE WITHIN-SUBJECTS DESIGN

In a **complete within-subjects design**, not only does each subject participate in each experimental condition, the subjects do so several times until they have received all possible orders of the conditions. This renders the data from any one subject interpretable as a miniature research project. Together, data from several subjects demonstrate the reliability and the generalizability of any effect noted.

Because all possible orders are experienced by each subject, any effect that might result from presenting conditions in a specific order—including practice effects—is counterbalanced by an instance in which those conditions were presented in the opposite order to the same subject.

ABBA Design The simplest complete within-subjects design involves only two experimental conditions, which we will refer to as conditions A and B. For a complete within-subjects design, each subject experiences condition A followed by

---

* Special thanks to Dr. Eric Corty for this example of natural regression toward the mean.

FIGURE **8.2**   *Graphs of linear and nonlinear practice effects: (a) linear practice effect;*
(b) nonlinear practice effect.

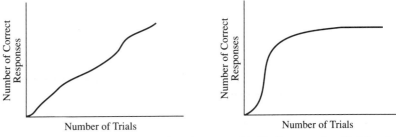

(a)   Linear practice effect: as the number of
trials increases, the number of correct
responses per trial steadily increases.

(b)   Nonlinear practice effect: learning
initially proceeds rapidly; then the
number of correct responses per
trial levels off.

condition B and B followed by A. In fact, this technique is called **ABBA design**
conterbalancing. The ABBA sequence can be repeated as many times as necessary
for the research. For example, if it were repeated three times, the subject would
experience the conditions in the following order: ABBAABBAABBA. By presenting condition A both first and last, this technique controls for practice effects; thus,
any advantage or disadvantage the condition may have conferred to the subject
by being first in the order is counterbalanced by its also occurring last. Similarly,
condition A precedes and follows condition B an equal number of times; thus, any
carryover effects from A to B or from B to A are counterbalanced.

After conducting an ABBA design, the researcher is most likely to group the
data from condition A together and then to group the data from condition B
together. One possibility is to calculate a mean A score and a mean B score for each
subject and then to compare these average A and B scores across subjects, using a
statistical test such as the *t*-test described later in this chapter.

There are a few potential problems with ABBA counterbalancing. One is
related to controlling practice effects. The ABBA technique is very useful if practice
affects performance linearly—that is, if performance gradually improves or gradually deteriorates. If performance increases sharply and then remains steady, however,
the ABBA technique is a poor choice for counterbalancing, since the condition
occurring first in the order is at such a distinct disadvantage that arranging for it to
occur again in the last position will not correct for it. In these situations, researchers
often conduct a number of practice trials until the subject reaches a steady state of
performance; then the ABBA technique can be used. Figure 8.2 presents graphs of a
linear practice effect and of a practice effect that increases at a nonlinear rate.

A second potential problem with the ABBA technique occurs because the
conditions are presented in a standard order. As a result, the subjects may realize that
an ABBA order is being used and may anticipate which condition is next. This can
be a problem if the subject's behavior is affected by this knowledge. For example, if
subjects know that the next task involves responding as quickly as possible to a word
on the screen, they may respond more rapidly than they would if they weren't

anticipating the task. This is analogous to a false start in a race, in which a runner anticipates the gunshot after hearing "get ready, get set, . . . " The runner is responding to internal anticipation and not to the gunshot, and because of this he or she actually starts running before the gun goes off. If the subject is likely to know what condition is occurring next and if this information can affect performance, the ABBA technique should not be used.

Block Randomization An alternative to the ABBA technique, called **block randomization**, involves presenting blocks of conditions in random orders. Blocks of conditions are composed of a single presentation of each of the conditions in the study. Each block is a unique ordering of the conditions. Thus, if a study involves three conditions—A, B, and C—the possible blocks are ABC, CBA, BAC, CAB, ACB, and BCA. These blocks are then presented to each subject numerous times in a random order. The blocks are presented often enough that each condition occurs approximately equally often in each ordinal position; in other words, A occurs first, second, and third approximately equally often within each block; B occurs first, second, and third approximately equally often within each block; and C occurs first, second, and third approximately equally often within each block. If there were three conditions and block randomization were used, each subject might receive the conditions in the following order: ABC BCA BCA CBA CAB BAC ACB. Enough blocks must be presented to let randomization do its job of counterbalancing for practice effects. Using only a few blocks won't suffice.

To make block randomization a bit clearer, let's consider an example. Suppose that a researcher conducts an experiment to study the effect of background color on reading speed. The subjects participate in three conditions: in the first condition, they read white letters off a black background (B); in the second condition, they read white letters off a blue background (Bl); and in the third condition, they read white letters off a green background (G). Each subject will participate in each condition numerous times, and the presentation of these conditions will be organized in blocks. The blocks are a presentation of each of the three conditions, such as first presenting letters on the black background, then presenting letters on the green background, and then presenting letters on the blue background. Because there are three conditions, there are six possible combinations of the three conditions. Each subject will receive a block of the three conditions followed by more randomly chosen blocks of conditions. Table 8.1 presents a possible order for the subjects in this study. The different blocks are numbered, 1–6. By choosing numbers 1–6 from the random numbers table, the researcher can establish a random order for the blocks so that each condition is presented 12 times and all possible orderings of the conditions are used at least once.

TABLE 8.1 *Possible random order of blocks for a three-condition study, using block randomization.*

Blocks: (1)B Bl G   (2)B G Bl   (3)Bl G B   (4)Bl B G   (5)G Bl B   (6)G B Bl

Random order of blocks: 1 2 5 3 6 2 3 1 5 5 4 3

The block randomization technique is useful for creating a complete within-subjects design when more than two conditions are involved and when participation in each condition is not especially time-consuming. With three conditions, there are 6 possible ways to order these conditions; and it is quite reasonable to expect that subjects could participate in a study involving 6 orders of three conditions if the testing procedure is not time-consuming. But if the experiment involves four conditions, the number of possible orders increases to 24; and with five conditions, the number of possible orders is 120. It is still conceivable to ask subjects to judge five stimuli presented in 120 different orders if the task takes no more than a few seconds. But as the time commitment required of a subject increases per condition, it becomes increasingly worthwhile to consider an incomplete within-subjects design.

THE INCOMPLETE WITHIN-SUBJECTS DESIGN

Often the subject cannot be expected to participate long enough to permit use of the block randomization technique, and the ABBA technique may not be appropriate either. In these situations, an **incomplete within-subjects design** may be used. In such a design, each subject receives a unique order of the conditions, and may receive each condition more than once, but a subject does not receive all possible orderings of the conditions. With an incomplete within-subjects design, enough subjects must participate to counterbalance potential order, fatigue, and practice effects.

One incomplete within-subjects technique is called **random order with rotation**. When this technique is used, the experimental conditions are ordered randomly and then presented to the first subject as ordered. The next subject receives a different order of the conditions—one created simply by moving the first condition to the last place and shifting all of the other conditions one place forward. The next subject receives yet another different order—this one created by moving the conditions one place forward again, and shifting the previously first condition to last place. In this manner, all of the conditions are encountered first, second, third, and so on. For example, if four conditions (ABCD) existed in an experiment, the first subject would receive the initial random ordering of these conditions, such as BCAD. The second subject would receive CADB, the third subject would receive ADBC, and the fourth subject would receive DBCA. The next rotation of the conditions restores the original random ordering of BCAD.

Because there are four possible conditions in our example, there are four possible orderings of the conditions, once the initial random ordering has been established. The number of subjects needed for this study, then, should be a multiple of four so that each condition appears in each ordinal position (first, second, third, and fourth) an equal number of times. Thus, a researcher designing a study with four conditions should arrange to have a number of participants drawn from the set 4, 8, 12, 16, 20, . . . , such that the total is evenly divisible by 4.

The number of subjects the researcher chooses to have participate depends on the strength of the effect is being studied, the sensitivity of the dependent measure, and the type of statistical analysis being planned. A study of a strong effect involving a sensitive measure and analyzed with inferential statistics will require fewer subjects than a study of a weak effect involving a relatively insensitive measure and analyzed with nonparametric statistics. In other words, the former study has more power than the latter study and thus is less likely to lead to a Type II error. In the latter study, the probability of making a Type II error can be mitigated by increasing the number of subjects.

The **balanced latin square** (or simply **Latin square**) technique offers another way to counterbalance practice effects in an incomplete within-subjects design. This technique involves presenting each condition once in each ordinal position, and presenting each condition once before and once after each other condition. The number of orderings necessary is equal to the number of conditions in the study; and thus, when written out with one order per line, a square is formed.

Setting up a Latin square can be something of a brain teaser. Some people enjoy the challenge, but others find it frustrating and tiresome. Here is one solution for a Latin square involving four conditions:

ABCD

BDAC

CADB

DCBA

Can you create a solution for a study with six conditions? An answer is given at the end of this chapter. It's not possible to develop a Latin square for experiments involving an uneven number of conditions. Since Latin squares are useful only if an even number of conditions is involved, this constitutes a limitation of the Latin square technique. Otherwise, the Latin square offers a useful means of counterbalancing for practice and fatigue effects.

As with the random order with rotation, the number of subjects chosen to participate in a study that uses a Latin square design should be a multiple of the number of conditions. Again, the precise number of subjects chosen depends on the power of the designed study.

Both the incomplete within-subjects designs and the complete within-subjects designs allow the researcher to conduct an efficient investigation while controlling for potential practice and fatigue effects.

CONCEPT QUESTIONS 8.3

A study is conducted in which subjects are asked to read sentences from a computer screen so that their reading speed can be measured. Some of the sentences contain ambiguous words. In the second half of the study, the sentences are preceded by a short paragraph that provides additional context for the ambiguous words. The researcher finds that subjects read the sentences preceded by context faster than those without context. What might be confounding the results of this study? What problem might occur if the order effects of the context conditions and the no-context conditions were counterbalanced?

TYPICAL ANALYSES OF THE WITHIN-SUBJECTS DESIGN

For between-subjects designs, we have discussed several typical statistical analyses: the independent-samples t-test, the Wilcoxon's rank-sum test, the χ^2 tests of independence and of homogeneity of proportions, and the one-way analysis of variance. For all of these tests except the χ^2, an analogous test can be used when data have been collected using a within-subjects design. In this chapter I will introduce the correlated-samples t-test, the Wilcoxon's matched-pairs signed-ranks test (to be used when exactly two conditions in a study are to be compared), and the one-way repeated measures analysis of variance (to be used when more than two conditions are to be compared).

THE CORRELATED-SAMPLES *t*-TEST

The **correlated-samples *t*-test**—also called the *dependent* or *dependent-samples t-test*, the *matched-pairs t-test*, the *paired-samples t-test*, and the *repeated-measures t-test*—is used to compare the means of two conditions within one study. Typically, each member of a set of subjects has been tested twice on some measure, such as a depression score before and after treatment or a weight measurement before and after a diet program. This analysis might also be used when two types of stimuli are being compared, such as when participants in a study recall concrete and abstract words or when their reading speeds for sentences with and without figurative phrases are compared. Finally, a correlated-samples t-test is also appropriate for use in a matched-pairs or yoked design, where two different sets of subjects participate in the study, but subjects are paired across groups in some manner.

Imagine that a researcher has conducted an experiment in which eight subjects were instructed to roll up a ball of string, either alone or while standing next to another person who was also rolling up a ball of string. Each subject was tested twice—once in each condition. (How would you control for practice or fatigue effects?) The researcher expected to find that, with no instructions to compete, the mere presence of another person performing the same task would induce the subjects to perform the string rolling task faster. The amount of time needed to complete the task in each condition was measured, and the resulting data are provided in Table 8.2. Because each subject provided one pair of scores, a correlated-samples t-test would be an appropriate way to compare the means of each condition. Our null hypothesis for this test is that the means do not differ:

$$H_0: \mu_1 - \mu_2 = 0$$

Our alternative hypothesis is that the condition involving another person has a smaller mean than the alone condition:

$$H_1: \mu_1 - \mu_2 > 0$$

Therefore, we have a one-tailed test of the null hypothesis.

To clarify the purpose of the correlated-samples t-test, let's consider a sampling distribution. This is a **sampling distribution of the differences between pairs of**

TABLE **8.2**   *Amount of time (in seconds) each person spent rolling a ball of*
string in each of two conditions.

Subject	Alone	With Other
1	10.6	8.7
2	15.8	10.2
3	12.5	9.4
4	11.3	11.2
5	10.9	11.1
6	13.6	9.3
7	15.7	13.6
8	14.9	12.8

FIGURE **8.3**   *Sampling distribution, with alpha (= .05) indicated.*

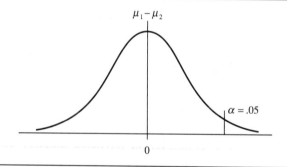

sample means. Imagine the population of people rolling up balls of string alone, and then imagine the population of the same people rolling up balls of string in the presence of another ball roller. Now samples of eight subjects are chosen, and each sample's mean scores in the "alone" and "with other" conditions are subtracted from each other. This is done repeatedly until the entire population has been sampled. If the null hypothesis is true, the difference between the two sample means should be very close to zero. If the presence of another ball roller does decrease rolling time, the mean difference should be significantly larger than zero. To test our null hypothesis, as with the independent-samples t-test, we must assess the likelihood of randomly choosing our obtained difference between the means. As before, we will set α at .05. If the probability of randomly getting our obtained difference from the sampling distribution representing the null hypothesis is less then .05, we reject the null hypothesis and support the alternative. This sampling distribution, with $\alpha = .05$ indicated, is presented in Figure 8.3.

Although we have two sets of scores, our calculations of the correlated-samples t-test actually involve transforming those two sets into one set by creating a set of **difference scores**—the difference between X_1 and X_2 for each pair of scores. This computation is shown in Table 8.3.

TABLE 8.3   *The string-rolling data and the difference scores for each pair of scores.*

Subject	Alone	With Other	d(Difference Scores)
1	10.6	8.7	1.9
2	15.8	10.2	5.6
3	12.5	9.4	3.1
4	11.3	11.2	.1
5	10.9	11.1	− .2
6	13.6	9.3	4.3
7	15.7	13.6	2.1
8	14.9	12.8	2.1
			19

We now have one set of scores (the difference scores) and we can compare the mean of these difference scores with zero (the difference between μ_1 and μ_2, according to the null hypothesis). The calculations from this point on are analogous to those used to calculate the single-sample t-test. The formula for the single-sample t-test is

$$t = \frac{\bar{x} - \mu}{s_{\bar{x}}}$$

The formula for the correlated–samples t-test is

$$t = \frac{\bar{d} - 0}{s_{\bar{d}}}$$

where:

$\bar{d}$ = mean of the difference scores

$d_{\bar{x}}$ = standard error of the difference scores.

There is considerable similarity between these two formulas. The 0 in the correlated-samples formula is directly analogous to the μ in the single-sample formula. In the single-sample formula, μ is the mean of the sampling distribution of scores. In the correlated-samples formula, 0 is the mean of the sampling distribution of difference scores. Difference scores serve as the "data" scores in a correlated-samples t-test, and the standard error of those difference scores is given a new symbol. Thus, just as the standard error is calculated as

$$s_{\bar{x}} = \frac{s}{\sqrt{n}}$$

the standard error of the difference scores is calculated as

$$s_{\bar{d}} = \frac{s_d}{\sqrt{n}}$$

TABLE 8.4   *Study data and d and d² values needed to calculate the correlated-samples t-test.*

Alone	With Other	d	d^2
10.6	8.7	1.9	3.61
15.8	10.2	5.6	31.36
12.5	9.4	3.1	9.61
11.3	11.2	0.1	0.01
10.9	11.1	−0.2	0.04
13.6	9.3	4.3	18.49
15.7	13.6	2.1	4.41
14.9	12.8	2.1	4.41
		19	71.94

where:

s_d = standard deviation of the difference scores

The standard deviation of the difference scores is calculated in the same manner as the standard deviation for any scores:

$$s_d = \sqrt{\frac{\sum d^2 - \frac{(\sum d)^2}{n}}{n-1}}$$

Finally, the degrees of freedom for both the single-sample and the correlated-samples t-tests are equal to $n-1$. For the correlated-samples t-test, n is the number of difference scores. Table 8.4 lists the sample data, together with the d and d^2 values for each sample pair. Using this information, we can perform the calculations for the correlated-samples t-test:

$$s_d = \sqrt{\frac{71.94 - \frac{19^2}{8}}{8-1}}$$

$$= \sqrt{\frac{71.94 - 45.125}{7}}$$

$$= \sqrt{\frac{26.815}{7}}$$

$$= \sqrt{3.8307} = 1.957$$

$$s_{\bar{d}} = \frac{1.957}{\sqrt{n}} = .6920$$

$$\bar{d} = \frac{\sum d}{n} = \frac{19}{8} = 2.375$$

$$t = \frac{\bar{d} - 0}{s_{\bar{d}}} = \frac{2.375}{.6920} = 3.432$$

$$\text{df} = n - 1 = 8 - 1 = 7$$

Our obtained t-value is 3.432. To determine the t_{cv} we consult Table t in Appendix B—the same table we used in performing the single-sample and independent-samples t-tests. Our alternative hypothesis is one-tailed, and $\alpha = .05$, so $t_{cv} = 1.895$. Thus, the obtained t falls within the region of rejection. This suggests that there is a significant difference between the "alone" condition and the "with other" condition. When a person is rolling a ball of string in the presence of another person who is performing the same task, the subject's rate of string rolling increases relative to when the task is performed in solitude.

The correlated-samples t-test is used to compare means between two sets of paired scores. Because it is an inferential statistical procedure, it can only be used when the data are measured on an interval scale or a ratio scale of measurement. This in turn means that the data must satisfy a number of assumptions if the t-test is to be used appropriately. The populations of difference scores should be normally distributed, and the variances of the two sets of scores should be homogeneous. In addition, the sample of subjects should be a random sample from the population it is meant to represent.

The easiest of these assumptions to test is whether the variances are homogeneous. A quick way to test this assumption is to form an F-ratio of the largest variance to the smallest variance:

$$F = \frac{\text{Largest } s^2}{\text{Smallest } s^2}$$

We can then compare this value to an F_{cv} with $n - 1$ degrees of freedom for both the numerator and the denominator. If the obtained F is greater than the F_{cv}, the variances should not be considered homogeneous, but instead should be considered heterogeneous. In our example, the variances for the two conditions are 4.60 and 3.01 for the "alone" and "with other" conditions, respectively (you may want to calculate these variances yourself, for practice). The F-ratio to test for homogeneity of variance would be

$$F = \frac{4.60}{3.01} = 1.528$$

The F_{cv} with 7 and 7 degrees of freedom is 3.79. The obtained value does not fall within the region of rejection, so we can be quite confident that our variances are close enough to equivalent not to violate the t-test's assumption of homogeneous variances.

This test for homogeneity of variance is sensitive to nonnormality; consequently, if the underlying distributions of scores are not known to be normally distributed, another test of homogeneity of variance might be used instead. Tests of homogeneity of variance and normality of distributions can be found in more advanced statistics tests, such as Kirk (1990) and Howell (1987).

When the assumptions for the *t*-test are not met, the results of the *t*-test can be misleading, in which case a nonparametric test may be a better choice.

THE WILCOXON'S MATCHED-PAIRS SIGNED-RANKS TEST

The **Wilcoxon's matched-pairs signed-ranks test**, also called the **Wilcoxon's *T***, is a nonparametric alternative to the correlated-samples *t*-test. To illustrate how the Wilcoxon's *T* is calculated, let's consider a situation in which 11 therapists are asked to judge the effectiveness of a specific therapy for sex abusers when the therapy is used with adult abusers and when it is used with adolescent abusers. The therapists' judgments are made on a 20-point system, where higher scores mean greater effectiveness. The researcher solicits judgments from the membership of a sex-abuser therapist association; therefore, this is not a random sample. In addition, the researcher believes that the judgments are not normally distributed but are skewed, with more therapists judging the therapy to be effective than noneffective. Hypothetical data for this study are provided in Table 8.5.

The null hypothesis for the Wilcoxon's *T* is that the two sets of scores are drawn from the same population—or in other words, that the differences between the pairs of scores sum to approximately 0. In this example, the researcher did not indicate a prediction, so the alternative hypothesis is two-tailed.

To calculate the Wilcoxon's *T*, we must compute difference scores for each pair of scores. If a significant difference exists between the sets of sample judgments, most of the difference scores will be either positive or negative. If no significant difference exists, approximately half of the difference scores will be positive and half will be negative.

The next step involves assigning ranks to the absolute values of the difference scores, and then identifying which ranks are associated with positive differences and which are associated with negative differences. This identification is typically done simply by applying negative signs to the ranks that are based on negative differences.

TABLE 8.5   *Hypothetical judgments of the effectiveness of a treatment for adult and adolescent sex abusers.*

Adults	Adolescents
14	16
12	17
17	18
10	10
8	15
4	10
7	10
9	12
12	16
11	19
18	13

TABLE 8.6 *Data for calculating the Wilcoxon's T, using the hypothetical ratings of therapy effectiveness with adult and adolescent sex abusers.*

Adults	Adolescents	Differences	Ranks	Signed Ranks
14	16	−2	2	−2
12	17	−5	6.5	−6.5
17	18	−1	1	−1
10	10	0		
8	15	−7	9	−9
4	10	−6	8	−8
7	10	−3	3.5	−3.5
12	9	+3	3.5	+3.5
12	16	−4	5	−5
11	19	−8	10	−10
18	13	+5	6.5	+6.5

$\sum + \text{Ranks} = 10$

$\sum - \text{Ranks} = 45$

These negative signs, however, do not indicate negative numbers; rather, they serve to mark the numbers, much like a checkmark.

If there is no difference between the two sets of scores, the sum of the ranks based on the negative differences will be approximately equal to the sum of the ranks based on the positive differences. However, if the two sets of scores do differ then the sums of the ranks based on the positive and negative difference scores will be more disparate. The smaller of these two sums is compared with a T_{cv} to determine if the sets of scores are so different that they are unlikely to have emerged from the same population.

The data for calculating the Wilcoxon's T are illustrated in Table 8.6. Notice that one pair of scores yielded a difference score of zero. When this occurs, that subject's scores are disregarded and n is reduced by one. So although we had 11 participants originally, our analysis will be based on only 10. Notice also that tied difference scores are assigned tied ranks, even when the difference scores have different signs.

The smaller T value is our obtained T; in this case it is 10. To determine whether our sets of scores are significantly different from one another, we compare 10 (our T_{obt}) with the T_{cv} from Table T of Appendix B. For a two-tailed test with $n = 10$, the $T_{cv} = 8$. For the Wilcoxon's T, as for the Wilcoxon's rank-sum test we discussed in Chapter 6, *to allow us to reject the null hypothesis, our obtained value must be equal to or less than the critical value.* Therefore, when $n = 10$, the T_{obt} must be equal to or less than the T_{cv} of 8 to permit rejection of the null hypothesis. Our obtained value is greater than 8; thus, we fail to reject the null hypothesis.

In our data set one pair of scores yielded a difference of 0, and it was removed from the calculations. If a data set yields an even number of 0 differences, then the differences are all assigned the average rank for the set of 0s; therefore, two 0s would be ranked 1.5, four 0s would be ranked 2.5, six 0s would be ranked 3.5, and so on.

Half of the ranks for these 0 differences are then arbitrarily assigned a positive sign, and half are assigned a negative sign. If there is an odd number of 0s, then one 0 difference is randomly selected and removed from the data set, and the others are assigned the average rank of the 0s and positive and negative signs as described above (Kirk 1990).

The Wilcoxon's matched-pairs signed-ranks test is a nonparametric alternative to the correlated-samples t-test. In both cases, the possibility that a significant difference exists between two related sets of scores is tested. When more than two related sets of scores are to be tested, a different type of analysis is necessary—analysis of variance.

WITHIN-SUBJECTS (OR REPEATED-MEASURES) ANALYSIS OF VARIANCE (ANOVA)

When three or more related sets of scores are to be compared, and when the scores meet the assumptions for inferential statistics, a **within-subjects analysis of variance** is an appropriate statistical test (actually, it's also quite appropriate for use with two conditions). This test is also referred to as repeated-measures analysis of variance; and analysis of variance, as mentioned before, is routinely abbreviated as ANOVA. The null and the alternative hypotheses for the repeated-measures ANOVA are the same as for the one-way between-subjects ANOVA. For example, if three test situations are compared, the null and the alternative hypotheses are as follows:

$$H_0: \mu_1 = \mu_2 = \mu_3$$

$$H_1: \mu_1 \neq \mu_2 \neq \mu_3$$

When calculating the ANOVA for a between-groups design, we partitioned the total variance among the scores into between-groups variance and within-groups variance, and then we determined an F-ratio by comparing the between-groups variance with the within-groups variance. In the within-subjects ANOVA, we partition the total variance into three components: the variance among the subjects, the variance among the test situations (such as time of test or materials being tested), and the remaining or residual variance. To determine whether there is any difference among the test situations, we create an F-ratio by comparing the variance among the test situations with the residual variance. An example should help clarify this.

Let's assume that an investigator is interested in studying how ambiguous words (words with two or more meanings, such as "bug" or "fork") are understood. To develop this study, the investigator uses a technique called **cross-modal priming**. In cross-modal priming, subjects listen to a word; then, just after they hear the word, a string of letters appears on a screen. (The technique is called *cross-modal* because two modes of perception are used: audition and vision). The subject must decide as quickly as possible whether the string of letters forms a real word or not. In this study, subjects hear ambiguous words; and after each word, the letter string is presented. The letter string belongs to one of four conditions; it may be a nonword, a word related to the ambiguous word's most common meaning, a word related to

TABLE 8.7   *Hypothetical data (number of errors) for the study of ambiguous words.*

Subjects	Nonwords	Common	Less Common	Unrelated
S_1	7	3	2	5
S_2	8	4	5	7
S_3	6	3	3	5
S_4	8	2	4	8
S_5	5	2	3	4

one of the ambiguous word's less common meanings, or an unrelated word. The researcher has certain expectations. Let's assume that, based on previous research, the investigator expects that the greatest number of errors will be made when the set of letters shown is a nonword, fewer errors will be made when the unrelated word is shown, still fewer when the word related to a less common meaning is shown, and the fewest errors will be made when the word shown is related to the common meaning. Some hypothetical data for this study are presented in Table 8.7. For this example I have created a small set of hypothetical data—much smaller than would be encountered in a typical study—but I believe that it is more important that you expend your energy understanding how and why the ANOVA is calculated than worrying about the arithmetic involved.

A summary table is used to organize the information gained from the repeated-measures ANOVA. It is similar to the summary table developed for a one-way between-subjects ANOVA, but it includes another source of variance. Whereas the one-way between-subjects ANOVA identified three sources of variance (total, between-groups, and within-groups variance), the repeated-measures ANOVA identifies four sources: total variance, variance attributable to the different testing situations (referred to here as *test variance*, but also referred to as *treatment variance* by others), variance attributable to the different subjects, and the residual or error variance.

To calculate the F-ratio, we must first determine the mean squares for the test (MS_{Test}) and the mean squares for the residual (MS_{Res}); in turn, the mean squares are calculated by first determining the sums of squares for these sources of variance (SS_{Test} and SS_{Res}) and the degrees of freedom (df_{Test} and df_{Res}) for each. In the process of determining these, we must calculate the degrees of freedom, the sums of squares, and the mean squares for the subjects component of the variance (df_{Subjs}, SS_{Subjs} and MS_{Subjs}), as well. Although it is not possible to test an F-ratio for the subject factor, the information about the amount of variance attributable to the different subjects can be useful to a researcher engaged in interpreting the results.

To determine the df_{Total}, we subtract one from the total number of scores ($N - 1$) because we have one restraint on the data, and we are estimating the grand mean. Thus, for this example,

$$df_{Total} = N - 1 = 20 - 1 = 19$$

Notice that, in the repeated-measures design, N is the total number of *scores* and not the total number of subjects. In our example, only 5 subjects provide data, but each subject provides data from 4 testing situations, yielding a total of 20 scores.

The df_{Test} is calculated by subtracting one from the number of testing situations, because we have one restraint among the four means of the testing situations. Thus, in the present example,

$$df_{Test} = k - 1 = 4 - 1 = 3$$

where k is the number of test situations.

Similarly, the df_{Subjs} is calculated by subtracting one from the number of subjects tested. Thus, in this example, where there are five subjects, df_{Subjs} is calculated as

$$df_{Subjs} = n - 1 = 5 - 1 = 4$$

where n is the number of subjects.

The df_{Res} is determined by multiplying df_{Test} and df_{Subjs}:

$$df_{Res} = (k - 1)(n - 1) = 3 * 4 = 12$$

Notice that the sum of df_{Test}, df_{Subjs}, and df_{Res} equals df_{Total} ($3 + 4 + 12 = 19$). This can serve as a check to confirm that the degrees of freedom have been calculated correctly.

Our next step is to calculate the sums of squares for each source of variance. We begin with SS_{Total}, which is calculated in the same manner here as it was for the one-way between-subjects ANOVA. Its formula is as follows:

$$SS_{Total} = \sum X^2 - \frac{(\sum X)^2}{N}$$

where X is each score and N is the total number of scores.

To apply this formula, we must first square each score in our data set, and then sum all of the scores and square that sum. These numbers are presented in Table 8.8.

Using the numbers in Table 8.8, we can calculate the SS_{Total}:

$$SS_{Total} = \sum X^2 - \frac{(\sum X)^2}{N}$$

$$= 522 - \frac{94^2}{20}$$

$$= 522 - \frac{8836}{20}$$

$$= 522 - 441.8 = 80.20$$

The SS_{Test} is comparable to the SS_B calculated for the one-way between-subjects ANOVA. The formula for SS_{Test} is as follows:

TABLE 8.8   *Squared and summed data for the repeated-measures example.*

SS	Nonword		Common		Less Common		Unrelated	
	X	X^2	X	X^2	X	X^2	X	X^2
1	7	49	3	9	2	4	5	25
2	8	64	4	16	5	25	7	49
3	6	36	3	9	3	9	5	25
4	8	64	2	4	4	16	8	64
5	5	25	2	4	3	9	4	16
	34	238	14	42	17	63	29	179

$\sum X = 94$ $(\sum X)^2 = 8836$ $\sum X^2 = 522$

$$SS_{Test} = \sum \frac{(\sum X_t)^2}{n_t} - \frac{(\sum X)^2}{N}$$

where X_t are the scores in each test situation and n_t is the number of scores in each test situation.

We can use the numbers in Table 8.8 to calculate SS_{Test} too:

$$SS_{Test} = \sum \frac{(\sum X_t)^2}{n_t} - \frac{(\sum X)^2}{N}$$

$$= \frac{34^2 + 14^2 + 17^2 + 29^2}{5} - \frac{8836}{20}$$

$$= \frac{1156 + 196 + 289 + 841}{5} - 441.80$$

$$= \frac{2482}{5} - 441.80$$

$$= 496.40 - 441.80 = 54.60$$

The formula for calculating the SS_{Subjs} is as follows:

$$SS_{Subjs} = \sum \frac{(\sum X_s)^2}{k} - \frac{(\sum X)^2}{N}$$

where $\sum X_s$ is the total of the scores for each subject and k is the number of test situations.

Thus, to calculate SS_{Subjs}, we must first sum each subject's scores. These data are provided in Table 8.9. The squared sum of each subject's scores is divided by the number of conditions. These scores are then summed. From this number is subtracted the sum of all the scores squared, divided by N. Using the information in Table 8.9, we can calculate the SS_{Subjs} as follows:

TABLE 8.9 *Squared and summed data for the repeated-measures example, including the subjects' totals.*

SS	Nonword		Common		Less Common		Unrelated		SS_{Total}
	X	X²	X	X²	X	X²	X	X²	
1	7	49	3	9	2	4	5	25	17
2	8	64	4	16	5	25	7	49	24
3	6	36	3	9	3	9	5	25	17
4	8	64	2	4	4	16	8	64	22
5	5	25	2	4	3	9	4	16	14
	34	238	14	42	17	63	29	179	94

$$SS_{Subjs} = \sum \frac{(\sum X_s)^2}{k} - \frac{(\sum X)^2}{N}$$

$$= \frac{17^2 + 24^2 + 17^2 + 22^2 + 14^2}{4} - \frac{8836}{20}$$

$$= \frac{289 + 576 + 289 + 484 + 196}{4} - 441.80$$

$$= \frac{1834}{4} - 441.8$$

$$= 458.50 - 441.80 = 16.70$$

The final SS that we need to calculate is SS_{Res} (residual variability). SS_{Total} is a measure of all the variability among the scores, which we are partitioning into the variability attributable to the testing situations, the variability among the subjects, and the remaining residual variability. Therefore, SS_{Res} can most easily be calculated by subtracting SS_{Test} and SS_{Subjs} from SS_{Total}. Thus, for our example,

$$SS_{Res} = SS_{Total} - SS_{Test} - SS_{Subjs}$$

$$= 80.20 - 54.60 - 16.70$$

$$= 8.9$$

Our next step is to calculate MS. Perhaps you remember from Chapter 7 that MS is an estimate of the variance attributable to each source of variability, and that it is calculated by dividing SS by df for each source. Thus, for example, MS_{Test} is calculated by dividing SS_{Test} by df_{Test}:

$$MS_{Test} = \frac{SS_{Test}}{df_{Test}}$$

$$= \frac{54.6}{3}$$

$$= 24.5382$$

Similarly, MS_{Subjs} is calculated as follows:

$$MS_{Subjs} = \frac{SS_{Subjs}}{df_{Subjs}}$$

$$= \frac{16.70}{4}$$

$$= 5.5667$$

And MS_{Res} can be found with the following computations:

$$MS_{Res} = \frac{SS_{Res}}{df_{Res}}$$

$$= \frac{8.90}{12}$$

$$= .7417$$

Before calculating the F-ratio, first consider the MS values we have just calculated. Each MS represents the variance attributable to each source. We can see that the greatest variance is attributed to the test situations, and that relatively little residual or error variance is present. This suggests that our test situations do differ from each other. The variance attributable to the difference among the subjects falls between the amount for the test situations and the amount for the residual variance. It appears that a substantial difference in scores exists among the subjects, although this is not as great as the variance between the test situations. It is possible for the variance among the subjects to be greater than the variance among the tests, too. This information gives the researcher an idea about the sensitivity of the methodology used, as well as about the extent to which subjects tend to differ on the measures being observed.

To determine whether the differences among the test situations is greater than we would expect to encounter by chance, we calculate the F-ratio and compare it with an F_{cv}. The F-ratio for a repeated-measures ANOVA is $\frac{MS_{Test}}{MS_{Res}}$; this ratio compares the variance among the tests (which includes error variance) to the error variance represented by the residual variance. To the extent that this ratio is greater than 1.00, we can be confident that the difference among the tests is not a result of random error. Thus, for our example, it is calculated as such:

$$F = \frac{MS_{Test}}{MS_{Res}}$$

$$= \frac{18.20}{.7417}$$

$$= 24.538$$

To determine whether this F is significantly larger than 1.00 (with $\alpha = .05$), we must compare it with the appropriate F_{cv} listed in Table F of Appendix B. This is the same table we used in Chapter 7 to determine F_{cv} values for the one-way between-groups

"I THINK YOU SHOULD BE MORE EXPLICIT HERE IN STEP TWO."

Courtesy of Sidney Harris

ANOVA. As we did before, we must use two types of df's to find the correct critical value. Across the top of the table, we find the df's for the numerator of the F-ratio—that is, the df_{Test}. Down the left side of the table, we find df's for the denominator of the ratio, df_{Res}. In our example, these numbers are 3 and 12, respectively. The F_{cv} is the number that appears at the point where the row and column associated with these two numbers intersect. Thus, our F_{cv} is 3.49.

Our obtained F is 24.538, which is larger than the critical value of 3.49; thus, we reject the null hypothesis that the test situations do not differ, and we support the alternative hypothesis that a difference exists. Table 8.10 presents the ANOVA

TABLE 8.10 *Summary table with the df, SS, MS, and F-ratio values for the repeated-measures ANOVA example.*

Source	df	SS	MS	F
Test	3	54.6	18.2	24.538
Subjects	4	17.7	5.5667	
Residual	12	8.90	.7417	
Total	19	80.2		

summary table with the df, SS, MS, and *F*-ratio values that we have calculated for this example.

Post Hoc Analyses for Repeated-Measures ANOVA The next question is, which test situations differ from which? We can determine by this using Tukey's HSD or the Newman-Keuls test, as we did in Chapter 7, or by using one of the many other post hoc analyses you might find presented in other statistics books, such as the Scheffé test or Fisher's LSD. Here, we will review the computations for Tukey's HSD. If these computations are not clear to you, refer to Chapter 7, where Tukey's HSD is discussed more thoroughly. You might also calculate the Newman-Keuls test, for additional practice.

The formula for calculating Tukey's HSD, to determine the differences among the means for a repeated-measures ANOVA, is as follows:

$$HSD = Q\sqrt{\frac{MS_e}{n}}$$

where MS_e is MS_{Error} or $MS_{Residual}$ and n is the number of subjects contributing scores to each mean being compared. For our particular example, we can calculate the following HSD values:

$$HSD_{.05} = 4.20\sqrt{\frac{.7417}{5}}$$

$$= 4.20\sqrt{.1483}$$

$$= 4.20(.3851) = 1.6174$$

$$HSD_{.01} = 5.50\sqrt{\frac{.7417}{5}}$$

$$= 5.50(.3851) = 2.1180$$

Table 8.11 lists the differences between the means for the various combinations of test situations in the ambiguity example.

From the results of our HSD analysis, we may conclude that significantly fewer errors were made when the presented word reflected the ambiguous word's common meaning or its less common meaning than when the presented word was a nonword or an unrelated word ($p < .01$ for all significant comparisons).

TABLE 8.11   *Mean differences calculated for the repeated-measure ANOVA example.*

	Nonword	Common Meaning	Less Common Meaning	Unrelated Meaning
	6.80	2.80	3.40	5.80
Nonword 6.80	——	4.00**	3.40**	1.00
Common Meaning 2.80	——	——	.60	3.00**
Less Common Meaning 3.40	——	——	——	2.40**
Unrelated Meaning 5.80	——	——	——	——

NOTE: An asterisk (*) beside a difference value indicates that the value is significant under the standards of Tukey's HSD, with $\alpha = .05$; two asterisks (**) indicate that the difference is significant with $\alpha = .01$.

Assumptions of Repeated-Measures ANOVA To ensure a valid test of the null hypothesis using a repeated-measures ANOVA, we must make sure that the same assumptions necessary for appropriate use of the between-subjects ANOVA are met here, too. In addition, the correlations between pairs of the test situations (in the population) should be equal. For example, the correlation between testing condition 1 and testing condition 2 should be equivalent to the correlation between testing condition 1 and testing condition 3, and to the correlation between testing condition 2 and testing condition 3, in a study with three experimental conditions. The probability of making a Type I error can be affected when this assumption is not met. In these cases, one possible solution is to use a more conservative F_{cv} by using an F-value with 1 and $(n - 1)$ degrees of freedom. This yields a larger F_{cv}, decreasing the probability of making a Type II error. So for the example in this chapter, our F_{cv} (which was 3.49) would be changed to have 1 and 4 degrees of freedom and instead would be 7.71. Advanced statistical textbooks present additional ways to test assumptions and additional techniques to use when certain assumptions are not met.

Repeated-measures analysis of variance is a very useful and flexible statistical technique when used correctly. It allows a researcher to take advantage of the benefits of a within-subjects design, including the possibility of increasing the design's power by reducing error variance. In addition, the within-subjects design is more efficient than the between-groups design, because in most cases fewer subjects are needed to test a hypothesis. It is not surprising, then, that many researchers design their studies so that repeated-measures analysis of variance is the appropriate statistical technique to use to test their hypotheses.

CRITIQUE OF THE WITHIN-SUBJECTS DESIGN

In this chapter we discussed the within-subjects design. In a study utilizing a within-subjects design, subjects typically participate in all of the experimental conditions. In matched-pairs and yoked designs, separate groups of subjects are tested, but each subject is matched with another based on pretest scores or receives the same treatment as another during the investigation. Both in the case of matched or yoked subjects and in the case of subjects who participate in each experimental condition, the advantage of the within-subjects design is that it reduces error variance and thus offers a more powerful statistical test of a hypothesis.

Within-subjects designs are not without their pitfalls, however. The design may be susceptible to confounds caused by demand characteristics. Or because the subject is performing the same task in a number of experimental conditions—often many times in a row—the subject's performance may show a practice effect or a fatigue effect. If the effects of one condition affect the performance in another condition, there are said to be carryover effects in the study design. If carryover effects are present, the data may be totally uninterpretable, and thus a between-subjects design may be superior. Another potential problem, especially when testing is carried out over a relatively long period of time, is that an event occurring outside the experiment may affect the subjects' performance on the dependent measure; this is called a history effect. Finally, a poorly developed study based on a within-subjects design may be susceptible to the effects of regression toward the mean. In these cases, changes in the dependent measure scores attributed to the independent variable are actually the result of a natural tendency for extreme scores to become less extreme with retesting.

A researcher can avoid many potential confounds by designing the study carefully and by counterbalancing the order of the presentations of the experimental conditions. All subjects receive all possible orders of the conditions in a complete within-subjects design. Two possible complete within-subjects designs are the ABBA design and the block randomization design. In an incomplete within-subjects design, each subject receives all of the conditions, but not in every possible order. Such designs include the random order with rotation design and the Latin square design.

Once the design has been established and the researcher has collected the data, the data must be analyzed. There are specific statistical analyses for within-subjects designs. When data are measured on a ratio or an interval scale and meet the assumptions for inferential statistics, the correlated-samples *t*-test and the repeated-measures ANOVA provide the most powerful tests of the null hypothesis. The Wilcoxon's matched-pairs signed-ranks test is appropriate when two groups of scores are being compared and inferential statistics are inappropriate because of a violation of an assumption, such as normality of the distribution of scores or homogeneity of variance, or because the scores are not based on an interval or ratio scale.

Based on the results of the statistical analysis, the researcher draws some conclusions. The reader of the report must determine whether the conclusions are well-founded, whether the statistics actually tested the research question, and whether any uncontrolled confounds may have affected the results.

The within-subjects design can be a powerful and efficient tool, but only when used appropriately. The amount of error variance in the study is reduced relative to a between-groups design, and typically the number of subjects necessary to test a hypothesis is smaller than would be needed in a between-groups design. If one or more of many confounds are allowed to affect the data, however, the data won't be interpretable. Within-subjects designs are only advantageous when they are handled properly.

IMPORTANT TERMS AND CONCEPTS

within-subjects design

repeated-measures design

pretest-posttest design

yoked design

matched-pairs design

demand characteristics

practice effects

fatigue effects

carryover effects

history effects

regression toward the mean

counterbalancing

complete within-subjects design

ABBA design

block randomization

incomplete within-subjects design

random order with rotation

balanced Latin square (Latin square)

correlated-samples t-test

sampling distribution of the differences between pairs of sample means

difference scores

Wilcoxon's matched-pairs signed-ranks test (Wilcoxon's T)

within-subjects (repeated-measures) ANOVA

cross-modal priming

QUESTIONS AND EXERCISES

1. A researcher is developing an idea for a research project in which satisfaction ratings for three types of cars are compared. The subjects will drive a car for 20 minutes and then rate the car on a satisfaction scale. The researcher wishes to have 18 satisfaction ratings for each car.

   a. How many subjects are needed for a between-subjects design? How many subjects are needed for a within-subjects design?

   b. Assuming that the subjects don't wish to participate for much more than an hour, how would you design this investigation to use a within-subjects design and to control for order effects? Would you use a complete or an incomplete within-subjects design?

   c. Determine an order of the vehicles for each of the subjects, assuming that you use an incomplete within-subjects design.

2. A smaller version of the car-rating task described in exercise 1 yielded the following data. Analyze the data, using a repeated measures ANOVA and Tukey's HSD (if necessary), to determine which cars (if any) differ on satisfaction ratings.

Subject	Car 1	Car 2	Car 3
1	8	7	7
2	6	6	4
3	9	6	3
4	5	3	3

3. A German-language teacher wishes to assess the impact of a week-long trip to Germany on students' vocabulary. The teacher believes that a week in Germany will result in a significant increase in vocabulary words. The teacher assesses the vocabulary of a group of students before their trip and after the students return.

   a. What are the teacher's null and alternative hypotheses?

   H_0:

   H_1:

   b. Following is a tabulation of the data collected by the teacher. Assume that these data meet the assumptions necessary for inferential statistics, and conduct an appropriate statistical analysis.

Before	After
98	120
76	85
60	58
47	58
86	94
33	34
94	106
122	146
75	83
65	78

c. Did the week in Germany lead to improved vocabulary scores?

d. What alternative explanations might account for these results?

4. Students at a university have the option to live on a floor in a residence hall that aims to promote wellness—that is, a healthful environment physically, mentally, socially, and spiritually. An investigator is interested in whether living on this floor leads to improved scores on a wellness inventory. People tend to score at the high end of the wellness inventory, so the scores are not normally distributed.

a. What are the investigator's null and alternative hypotheses?

H_0:

H_1:

b. The investigator compares residents' scores on the wellness inventory taken at the beginning of the semester with their scores obtained at the end of the semester. The data are given next. Conduct the appropriate statistical analysis.

Beginning	End
23	24
18	22
14	18
12	9
21	24
23	22
12	15
17	21
18	19
24	24
16	19

c. What conclusions do you draw? What alternative explanations might account for the results?

5. In this chapter, the correlated-samples t-test was calculated to determine whether people rolled a ball significantly faster when with another person who was performing the same task than when alone. The time data (in seconds) are presented in the accompanying table. Use these data to calculate the Wilcoxon's T.

Subject	Alone	With Other
1	10.6	8.7
2	15.8	10.2
3	12.5	9.4
4	11.3	11.2
5	10.9	11.1
6	13.6	9.3
7	15.7	13.6
8	14.9	12.8

a. What are the T_{obt} and the T_{cv}?

b. What conclusions can be drawn from the results of this analysis?

c. How do the results of the Wilcoxon's T and the correlated-samples t-test compare?

6. Subjects in a memory experiment tried to learn words by using rote rehearsal (repeating the information in their heads), while simultaneously identifying the blue slides in a series of colored slides that were flashed on a screen; later, the subjects tried to learn a different list

of words by using an imagery mnemonic (forming mental images of the items to be remembered), again while identifying the blue-colored slides. The purpose of this research was to see whether performing a visual task (identifying the blue slides) interfered with making a mental image. The researcher expected that the subjects would recall fewer words in the imagery condition than in the rote rehearsal condition. The data have equivalent variances, and memory scores are normally distributed.

a. What are the null and the alternative hypotheses?

H_0:

H_1:

b. The data are presented in the accompanying table. Calculate the correlated-samples t-test to determine whether the null hypothesis can be rejected.

Subject	Rote	Imagery
1	13	10
2	12	9
3	8	10
4	9	8
5	10	12
6	11	11
7	10	8

c. What are the t_{cv} and t_{obt} values? According to the statistical analysis, should the null hypothesis be rejected?

d. What confounds may be present in this study?

7. Subjects participate in a study in which their conversations are videotaped. (The subjects are aware of this.) The subjects speak with three people: a good friend, a same-sex same-age stranger, and a same-sex older person. (The order of presentation is varied for each subject.) The conversations are then coded by the researchers for the number of figurative expressions used by the subjects. The researchers believe that the resulting data (listed in the accompanying table) satisfy the assumptions for a repeated-measures ANOVA.

Subject	Friend	Stranger	Old Stranger
1	12	7	4
2	18	12	10
3	9	6	6
4	20	15	18
5	12	10	1
6	7	5	5

a. Calculate the ANOVA to determine whether any significant differences exist among the three conditions.

b. What are the F-ratio and the F_{cv}? Should the null hypothesis be rejected?

c. Calculate the Newman-Keuls test to determine which (if any) means differ significantly. Draw a bar graph of the means. (Don't forget to include error bars.)

d. What conclusions can you draw from the results of your statistical analyses?

A solution for the problem of creating a Latin square with six conditions is

ABCDEF

BDFACE

CFBEAD

DAEBFC

ECAFDB

FEDCBA

9

Factorial Designs

Suppose that a researcher is interested in the effect of positive or negative feedback on a person's confidence in performing certain tasks. In particular, the researcher wants to determine whether receiving positive or negative feedback affects how well women think they would perform on a mathematics test or a reading comprehension test. The researcher predicts that negative feedback has a more deleterious effect on self-confidence when it refers to a mathematics test than when it refers to a reading task. This prediction actually includes two hypotheses: (a) that the negative feedback will have a deleterious effect on self-confidence (as compared with the effect of positive feedback); and (b) that this effect will be stronger for self-confidence measures related to math than for those related to reading. A graph of the predicted results is presented in Figure 9.1.

How will the researcher test these hypotheses? It would be possible, but cumbersome, to carry out a series of experiments that test the effect of negative reinforcement and positive reinforcement as well as the difference between confidence levels in math and in reading. At least four experiments would have to be conducted, each with two conditions. If there were 10 participants in each condition, the researcher would need to solicit the assistance of 80 volunteers. A less cumbersome approach to testing this hypothesis is to develop and conduct one slightly more complex experiment.

In previous chapters, we have discussed the design and analysis of investigations involving one independent variable. In the experiment just described, however, there are two independent variables, each with two levels: the type of reinforcement (positive or negative), and the type of test (mathematics or reading). Researchers can develop investigations that simultaneously test the effects of two (or

FIGURE 9.1 *Predicted effects of type of feedback and type of test on confidence judgments.*

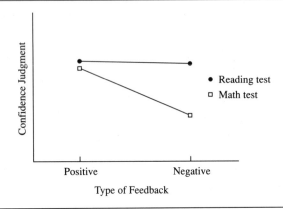

more) independent variables on a dependent measure* *and* determine whether the effect of each independent variable remains the same for each level of the other independent variable. For example, our researcher predicts that the effect of negative feedback is stronger when related to a mathematics tests than when related to a reading test.

This type of design, in which the effects of two or more independent variables on a dependent variable are assessed, is called a **factorial design**. In a factorial design, several hypotheses are tested simultaneously. The effect of each independent variable alone on the dependent measure is determined; these effects are called the **main effects**. In addition—and often of more interest to the researcher—the effect of each independent variable within each level of each other independent variable is determined. This effect is referred to as the **interaction** between the two factors. In this chapter I will explain how to interpret main effects and interactions, as well as how to interpret designs that have only between-subjects variables, only within-subject variables, or a combination of the two. I will also introduce you to designs involving three independent variables.

METHODOLOGY

In previous chapters, we have discussed how to design a research project based on a single independent variable, such as an investigation into the effect of negative and positive feedback on confidence judgments. In this case, the type of feedback is the independent variable and the confidence judgments are the dependent measure. In many cases, however, a researcher is interested in more than just the effect of a single independent variable (or factor) on a dependent variable. Often the effects of two, three, or even more factors are of interest. In our example, the researcher is inter-

---

*Actually, research studies can also involve more than one dependent variable; these types of studies require *multivariate analyses*, which are described in more advanced statistical textbooks.

ested not only in the effect of feedback on confidence judgments, but also in the effect of feedback on confidence judgments about different types of tests.

In our example, the researcher might randomly assign subjects to one of four conditions. In the *positive feedback/math* condition, the subjects will complete a short mathematics exercise and receive positive feedback about their performance. They will then be asked to judge how well they think they would do on a longer test of the same type. In the *positive feedback/reading* condition, the subjects will complete a short reading exercise and receive positive feedback about their performance. These subjects will be asked to judge how well they think they would do on a longer reading test. In the *negative feedback/math* condition, the subjects will receive negative feedback about their performance on the short math exercise before being asked to judge how well they think they would perform on a longer test. The subjects in the *negative feedback/reading* condition will receive negative feedback about the results of a reading exercise before being asked to judge how well they think they would do on a longer reading test.

Of course, the researcher wants to keep the experimental conditions as constant as possible (aside from the independent variables), to avoid introducing extraneous variables that might confound the results. Designing an investigation that involves a factorial design requires the same attention to detail and avoidance of confounds as does designing a study based on a single independent variable. In this particular study, the experimenter might be concerned about demand characteristics. Will the relationship between the type of feedback and the resulting confidence judgments be too obvious, so the subjects guess what the researcher expects to find? The researcher might need to make special efforts to minimize the effect of any demand characteristics. One possibility might be to have the subject complete a number of tasks and to make a number of different types of judgments about them so that the relationship between the confidence judgment and feedback is less obvious. Another possibility is to carry out a small pilot study with just a few subjects and ask these subjects what they think the purpose of the investigation is. It's possible that what seems so obvious to the researcher is invisible to the subjects and that no one will correctly identify the purpose of the study.

Imagine that this study has been carried out and that the researcher finds the following means in each condition:

	Positive Feedback	Negative Feedback
Math Test	80	60
Reading Test	90	85

Using these means, the researcher can identify possible interactions and main effects. For example, the difference in confidence between the positive and negative feedback conditions for the math test is 20 points, while the same difference for the reading test is only 5 points. In addition, the difference between math and reading confidence following positive feedback is 10 points, but the difference between math and reading confidence following negative feedback is 25 points. That these differences are so disparate suggests that the effect of feedback is not consistent across the

FIGURE 9.2   *Graph of the examples means for the effect of feedback and type of test on confidence judgments.*

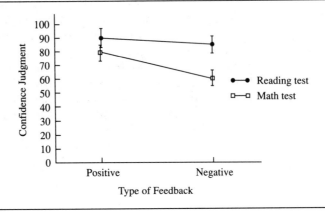

two tests; it appears to have a stronger influence on confidence in mathematics than on confidence in reading. In other words, there is an interaction between type of test and type of feedback; the type of feedback affects the dependent variable differently depending on the type of test to be taken. A graph of these means is presented in Figure 9.2.

The researcher may also wish to identify the potential main effects. This is done by comparing the **marginal means**. The marginal means are computed for each level of an independent variable, disregarding the other independent variable. Let's consider the means again, now with the marginal means also included:

	Positive Feedback	Negative Feedback	Marginal $\bar{x}$'s
Math Test	80	60	70
Reading Test	90	85	87.5
Marginal $\bar{x}$'s	85	72.5	

The $\bar{x}$ for the positive feedback conditions was 85 points, compared with the $\bar{x}$ for the negative feedback conditions of 72.5 points. Perhaps this indicates that the subjects were more confident, in general, after receiving positive feedback. Statistical analysis would be needed to determine whether the difference is statistically meaningful.

The $\bar{x}$ for the mathematics conditions was 70 points, 17.5 points less than the $\bar{x}$ confidence judgments for the reading conditions (87.5 points). This might suggest that subjects were generally more confident in reading than in mathematics; again, statistical analysis would be needed to determine whether these means reflect a statistically significant difference. Graphs of these main effects are presented in Figure 9.3.

FIGURE **9.3**   *Graphs of the main effects for type of feedback (a) and for type of test (b).*

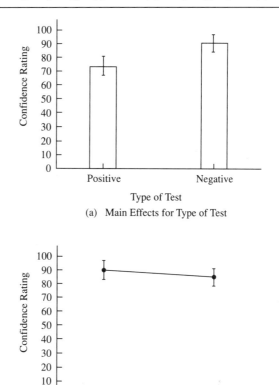

(a) Main Effects for Type of Test

(b) Main Effects for Type of Feedback

CONCEPT QUESTIONS 9.1

Using the example of a study addressing the effects of feedback on confidence judgments, draw a graph that would describe the results if the subjects were more confident after receiving positive feedback than after receiving negative feedback, and if they were more confident in reading than in math, but if there were no interaction between type of test and type of feedback.

The previous example involved two independent variables: type of feedback and type of test. When analysis of variance is used to analyze the data for a project involving two independent variables, the analysis is called a two-way ANOVA. A more informative way to describe the analyses consists of describing the number of levels in each of the independent variables. In this case, there were two levels of feedback and two levels of test; thus, the design of the study could be referred to as a 2 × 2 design. If three types of tests were included, it would be a 2 × 3 design; however, the analysis would remain a two-way ANOVA, because the number of independent variables would still be two.

A researcher could also design a project involving three independent variables. For instance, our example could be expanded to include feedback, test, and gender. Two levels of gender would be involved, along with perhaps three levels of test and perhaps three levels of feedback (positive, negative, and neutral). This project would be described as a 2 × 3 × 3 design, because one independent variable has two levels and the other two independent variables have three levels each. To analyze the data, assuming that they meet the requirements for inferential statistics, the researcher could use a three-way ANOVA.

When a researcher designs a project that involves three independent variables, analysis of variance will supply information about three main effects—one for each variable. In addition, several interactions are analyzed. If we refer to the three independent variables as *A*, *B*, and *C*, the analysis of variance supplies information about the interaction of *A* and *B*, the interaction of *B* and *C*, and the interaction of *A* and *C*. These are called two-way interactions, because they each involve two independent variables. An analysis of variance based on three independent variables also yields information about a three-way interaction, the interaction of *A* and *B* and *C*, which is usually described as the *A* × *B* × *C* interaction. Three-way interactions are somewhat more complicated to graph than two-way interactions, in that they require two graphs. And as you can imagine, a four-way interaction identified through a four-way ANOVA can be very complex to illustrate and often difficult to comprehend.

Factorial designs can be developed with between-subjects variables, as in our example of the effects of feedback and test type on confidence judgments. They can also be developed by using within-subjects designs. For example, a researcher might give the subjects feedback both on a reading exercise and on a math exercise, offering positive feedback on one exercise and negative feedback on the other. Each subject would then be asked for confidence judgments on both types of tests. In this example, both the type of test and the type of feedback would constitute within-subjects variables.

Factorial designs can also be developed on the basis of a combination of within-subjects and between-subjects designs. For instance, if subjects were given feedback on and asked for judgments about both types of tests, test type would be a within-subjects variable. But, if the subjects received only positive feedback or negative feedback, type of feedback would be a between-subjects variable.

HIGHER-ORDER ANALYSIS OF VARIANCE

Analysis of variance is a very flexible analysis that can be used to determine significant differences among means in various research designs. In this section I will discuss and demonstrate the calculations necessary to conduct analysis of variance in several different situations.

TWO-WAY BETWEEN-SUBJECTS ANOVA

Analysis of variance is appropriate in situations in which ratio or interval data are collected on a dependent measure that is normally distributed, and in which the scores within each level of the independent variables have equivalent variances. If you are confident in the normality of the dependent measure, you can calculate an F-ratio of the largest and smallest variances to test for homogeneity of variance. This was discussed in Chapter 8. Tests of normality and other tests for homogeneity of variance can be found in advanced statistics texts such as Kirk (1990) and Howell (1987).

When these assumptions have been met and there are two independent variables and both variables are between-subjects variables (that is, independent samples participate in each level of the independent variable), a **two-way between-subjects ANOVA** is usually an appropriate statistical technique to use.

Suppose that a researcher plans to investigate memory for words. Based on a review of the research literature and on the researcher's own knowledge of memory processes, the researcher hypothesizes that some mnemonic techniques work better with some types of words than with others. In particular, this researcher expects to find that concrete words—that is words that describe real, tangible objects—are recalled better by using either an imagery mnemonic or a verbal elaboration mnemonic than by using rote rehearsal. In rote rehearsal, the subject simply repeats the words over and over again. In verbal elaboration, the subject studies the words by elaborating on their spelling, meaning, relationship to other words, and so on, and does so by engaging in a mental "conversation" about the words. The imagery technique involves creating a mental image of the to-be-remembered words.

The researcher also expects to find that, for abstract words—words that describe concepts, such as honesty or beauty—verbal elaboration mnemonics will be more effective than either rote rehearsal or imagery mnemonics.

The 30 subjects in this study are randomly assigned to one of the two types of words and to one of the three memory techniques. The researcher will use a two-way between-subjects ANOVA (in this case a 2 × 3 ANOVA) to test the null hypothesis that the six different conditions in this study represent the same population:

$$H_0: \mu_1 = \mu_2 = \mu_3 = \mu_4 = \mu_5 = \mu_6$$

The alternative hypothesis, as with the one-way ANOVA, is that the different conditions represent different populations.

$$H_1: \mu_1 \neq \mu_2 \neq \mu_3 \neq \mu_4 \neq \mu_5 \neq \mu_6$$

Some hypothetical data are presented in Table 9.1.

So that a generalizable set of equations can be developed, I will refer to the memory technique factor as the **column factor**, and the word type factor as the **row factor**.

As in a one-way ANOVA, the variability among the scores is partitioned into parts. In a two-way between-subjects ANOVA, there are four parts: the variability between the levels of the column factor, the variability between the levels of the row factor, the variability among the cells (the interaction of the two factors), and the error variance. As with the one-way ANOVA, the variability between the levels of

TABLE **9.1** *Hypothetical example data for the effects of memory technique and word type (numbers represent total words recalled from a set of 20).*

	Memory Technique		
	Rote	Verbal	Imagery
Concrete Word	10	17	18
	10	18	16
	12	16	17
	9	19	20
	16	15	18
Abstract Word	14	18	15
	9	16	12
	11	15	10
	9	15	10
	10	17	9

TABLE **9.2** *Summary table (without any experimental data) for the two-way between-subjects ANOVA example.*

Source	df	SS	MS	F
Column (memory technique)				
Row (word type)				
Row × Column				
Error				
Total				

each factor and the interaction variability contribute to the overall error variance. F-ratios can be calculated to determine how much of the variability is attributable to the independent variables or their interaction, and how much is caused by random error. As before, a summary table is used to summarize the results of the ANOVA calculations. An empty summary table is presented in Table 9.2.

Calculating Degrees of Freedom For no other reason than that the degrees-of-freedom column happens to be the second column in our summary table, let's first determine the degrees of freedom for our various sources of variance. As with the one-way ANOVA, the total degrees of freedom are calculated by subtracting 1 from the total number of observations ($N - 1$); this is done because we are estimating the grand mean, our one restriction. In our example, where there are 30 observations, $df_{Total} = 30 - 1 = 29$.

To determine the degrees of freedom for the between-subjects variable in a one-way ANOVA, we subtracted 1 from the number of levels of the between-subjects variable. In our example, we have two between-subjects variables, but the degrees of freedom are still determined in the same manner: we subtract 1 from the number of levels of each between-subjects variable. Again, we are estimating the grand mean; and for the factor effects, the number of level in each factor is the original number of scores we have to work with. In our example, there are three levels of memory technique (the column factor), so our $df_{Column} = 3 - 1 = 2$. This can be written generally as follows:

$$df_{Column} = c - 1$$

where c is the number of levels of the column factor. Similarly, for word type (the row factor) with 2 levels, $df_{Row} = 2 - 1 = 1$. This can be written more generally as follows:

$$df_{Row} = r - 1$$

where r is the number of levels of the row factor.

The degrees of freedom for the interaction are based on the number of conditions in the design. In our example, one factor has three levels and one factor has two levels, so there are six conditions. To determine the degrees of freedom among the condition means, we multiply the degrees of freedom for the two factors involved in the interaction. Thus, for the interaction of the memory technique and the word type, the degrees of freedom $(df_{r \times c})$ are $(3 - 1)(2 - 1) = 2(1) = 2$. The more general version of this formula is

$$df_{r \times c} = (c - 1)(r - 1)$$

where c is the number of levels of the column factor and r is the number of levels of the row factor.

Finally, the degrees of freedom for the error term are a function of the degrees of freedom within each of the design's conditions. These degrees of freedom are computed by multiplying the number of levels for each factor times each other and then multiplying that product times the number of observations in each cell minus 1:

$$df_{Error} = c(r)(n - 1)$$

where:

c = number of levels of the column factor

r = number of levels of the row factor

n = number of observations within each cell of the design

Thus, for our example,

$$df_{Error} = 3(2)(5 - 1) = 3(2)(4) = 24$$

A double-check of our calculations can be accomplished by summing df_c, df_r, $df_{c \times r}$, and df_{Error}. This sum should equal df_{Total}, and in our example it does. These degrees of freedom have been entered into the summary table shown later as Table 9.4.

Calculating Sums of Squares The next step we must take is to calculate the sums of squares (SS). The SS values represent our calculations of the amount of

TABLE 9.3   *The data from the memory technique and word type study, squared and summed.*

			Memory Technique			
	Rote		Verbal		Imagery	
	X	X^2	X	X^2	X	X^2
Concrete Word	10	100	17	289	18	324
	10	100	18	324	16	256
	12	144	16	256	17	289
	9	81	19	361	20	400
	16	256	15	225	18	324
Total	57	501	85	1455	89	1593
Abstract Word	14	196	18	324	15	225
	9	81	16	256	12	144
	11	121	15	225	10	100
	9	81	15	225	10	100
	10	100	17	289	9	81
Total	53	579	81	1319	56	650

variability among all the scores, as well as the amounts attributable to the different factors, to their interaction, and to error variance. Let's begin with the total sum of squares (SS_{Total}). SS_{Total} is calculated in the same manner here as it was for our one-way ANOVAs: the sum of the scores, squared and then divided by the total number of observations, is subtracted from the sum of the squared scores. The formula is as follows:

$$SS_{Total} = \sum X^2 - \frac{(\sum X)^2}{N}$$

The necessary summing and squaring of scores are presented in Table 9.3. Using the information from Table 9.3, we can calculate SS_{Total} as follows:

$$\sum X = 421$$

$$\sum X^2 = 6097$$

$$SS_{Total} = \sum X^2 - \frac{(\sum X)^2}{N}$$

$$= 6097 - \frac{421^2}{30}$$

$$= 6097 - 5908.0333$$

$$= 188.9667$$

Now let's calculate the sum of squares for the column factor (SS_{Column}). The column factor is a between-subjects factor, since each subject participates on only one level of the independent variable. SS_{Column} is calculated in the same manner as the sums of squares for our independent variable in the one-way between-subjects ANOVA.

To calculate the sum of squares for the column factor, we need to know the total number of scores for each level of the column factor. This can be found by summing the condition scores in Table 9.3 across each level of the row factor. In calculating these sums for SS_{Column}, we proceed as if the row factor did not exist.

Our column sums are as follows:

$$\sum X_{Rote} = 110 \qquad \sum X_{Verbal} = 166 \qquad \sum X_{Imagery} = 145$$

The formula for calculating SS_{Column} looks like this:

$$SS_{Column} = \sum \frac{(\sum X_{Column})^2}{r(n)} - \frac{\sum X^2}{N}$$

where:

$\sum X_{Column}$ = sum of the scores for each level of the column factor

r = number of levels of the column factor

n = number of scores in each cell

$\sum X^2$ = sum of all of the squared scores

N = total number of observations among all the cells

The calculations for SS_{Column} for our example are as follows:

$$SS_{Column} = \sum \frac{(\sum X_{Column})^2}{r(n)} - \frac{\sum X^2}{N}$$

$$= \frac{110^2 + 166^2 + 145^2}{2(5)} - \frac{421^2}{30}$$

$$= 6068.10 - 5908.0333$$

$$= 160.0667$$

We now calculate the sum of squares for the row factor (SS_{Row}) in the same manner. The formula for SS_{Row} looks like this:

$$SS_{Row} = \sum \frac{(\sum X_{Row})^2}{c(n)} - \frac{(\sum X)^2}{N}$$

where:

$\sum X_{Row}$ = sum of the scores for each level of the row factor

c = number of levels of the column factor

n = number of scores within each cell

$\sum X$ = sum of all the scores

N = total number of scores

Now we need to know the sum of each row factor, which can be calculated by summing each row factor in Table 9.3 across each level of the column factor. Our row sums are as follows:

$$\sum X_{\text{Concrete}} = 231 \qquad \sum X_{\text{Abstract}} = 190$$

This permits us to calculate SS_{Row} as follows:

$$SS_{\text{Row}} = \sum \frac{(\sum X_{\text{Row}})^2}{c(n)} - \frac{(\sum X)^2}{N}$$

$$= \frac{231^2 + 190^2}{3(5)} - \frac{421^2}{30}$$

$$= 5964.0666 - 5908.0333$$

$$= 56.0333$$

The next sum of squares to be calculated is that for the interaction of the row and column factors. This calculation involves two steps, the first of which is to calculate something called the sum of squares for the cells. This is a calculation of the variability among the different cells or conditions of the experiment. From this we subtract the variability that we have determined is attributable to the column factor and the row factor separately; this subtraction constitutes the second step of the overall calculation. The remaining variance is attributable to the interaction of the two factors.

The formula for the sum of squares for the cells is as follows:

$$SS_{\text{Cell}} = \sum \frac{(\sum X_{\text{Cell}})^2}{n} - \frac{(\sum X)^2}{N}$$

where:

$\sum X_{\text{Cell}}$ = sum of the scores within each cell of the design

n = number of scores within each cell of the design

The calculations for SS_{Cell} for our example are presented next:

$$SS_{\text{Cell}} = \sum \frac{(\sum X_{\text{Cell}})^2}{n} - \frac{(\sum X)^2}{N}$$

$$= \frac{57^2 + 85^2 + 89^2 + 53^2 + 81^2 + 56^2}{5} - \frac{421^2}{30}$$

$$= \frac{30,901}{5} - 5908.0333$$

$$= 6180.2 - 5908.0333$$

$$= 272.1667$$

From this number, we subtract SS_{Column} and SS_{Row}, and the remainder will be $SS_{c \times r}$. The formula and calculations look like this:

$$SS_{c \times r} = SS_{\text{Cells}} - SS_{\text{Column}} - SS_{\text{Row}}$$

$$= 272.1667 - 160.0667 - 56.0333$$

$$= 56.0667$$

"A WONDERFUL SQUARE ROOT. LET US HOPE IT CAN BE USED FOR THE GOOD OF MANKIND."

Courtesy of Sidney Harris

The remaining sum of squares to calculate is the sum of squares for the error term. The error term is the variability that is not attributable to the column factor, the row factor, or the interaction of the two. It is calculated by subtracting the column, row, and interaction sums of squares from the total sum of squares. The formula and calculations for our example are presented here:

$$SS_{Error} = SS_{Total} - SS_{Column} - SS_{Row} - SS_{c \times r}$$

$$= 188.9667 - 160.0667 - 56.0333 - 56.0667$$

$$= 83.2$$

We have now calculated all of the sums of squares we need in order to conduct our two-way ANOVA with two between-subjects factors. These sums of squares have been added to our summary table and are presented in Table 9.4.

The next set of steps involved in calculating our ANOVA relates to determining the mean squares for each source of variance. The mean squares are calculated in the same manner here as they were for the one-way ANOVAs: each sum of squares is divided by its degrees of freedom. Thus the mean square for the column factor (MS_{Column}) is calculated by dividing SS_{Column} by df_{Column}:

$$MS_{Column} = \frac{SS_{Column}}{df_{Column}}$$

$$= \frac{160.0667}{2} = 80.0334$$

TABLE 9.4   *The summary table for the two-way between-subjects ANOVA example, with df's and SS values included.*

Source	df	SS	MS	F
Column (memory technique)	2	160.0667		
Row (word type)	1	56.0333		
Row × Column	2	56.0667		
Error	24	83.2		
Total	29	188.9667		

TABLE 9.5   *Summary table for the two-way between-subjects ANOVA example, with df's, SS values, and MS values included.*

Source	df	SS	MS	F
Column (memory technique)	2	160.0667	80.0334	
Row (word type)	1	56.0333	56.0333	
Row × Column	2	56.0667	28.0334	
Error	24	83.2	3.4667	
Total	29	188.9667		

The calculations for MS_{Row}, $MS_{c \times r}$, and MS_{Error} are done comparably:

$$MS_{Row} = \frac{SS_{Row}}{df_{Row}}$$

$$= \frac{56.0333}{1} = 56.0333$$

$$MS_{c \times r} = \frac{SS_{c \times r}}{df_{c \times r}}$$

$$= \frac{56.0667}{2} = 28.0334$$

$$MS_{Error} = \frac{SS_{Error}}{df_{Error}}$$

$$= \frac{83.2}{24} = 3.4667$$

The results of these calculatious are presented in the summary table in Table 9.5.

We are now ready to calculate our three F-ratios: one for the column factor, one for the row factor, and one for the interaction of the two. As described in Chapter 7, the F-ratios are a ratio of the variance attributable to a given factor (which includes some error variance) to the variance attributable to random error. To the extent that the ratio is greater than 1.00, it signifies that the variance we have attributed to the factor contains more variance actually related to the factor than variance caused by random error. The F-ratios are calculated by dividing the MS for the given factor by the MS_{Error}. Therefore, the F-ratio for the column factor is

$$F_{Column} = \frac{MS_{Column}}{MS_{Error}}$$

Similarly, the F-ratio for the row factor is

$$F_{Row} = \frac{MS_{Row}}{MS_{Error}}$$

And the F-ratio for the interaction is

$$F_{Interaction} = \frac{MS_{Interaction}}{MS_{Error}}$$

The F-ratios have been calculated for our example and are presented in Table 9.6.

Although our F-ratios are all greater than 1.00, we need to compare each of these numbers to the appropriate F_{cv} to determine whether our probability of making a Type I error is not greater than .05 (or whatever level you, as the researcher, deem appropriate). As with the one-way ANOVA, the degrees of freedom for the F_{cv} are the degrees of freedom for the numerator and the denominator of the F-ratio. Thus, for the column and interaction ratios, the degrees of freedom are 2 and 24; and when we use these to consult Table F in Appendix B, we find an F_{cv} of 3.40 (with $\alpha = .05$). Both of our obtained F's are greater than this critical value. For the row factor, the degrees of freedom are 1 and 24, yielding an F_{cv} (with

TABLE 9.6   *Summary table for the two-way between-subjects ANOVA example, with df's, SS values, MS values, and F-ratios included.*

Source	df	SS	MS	F
Column (memory technique)	2	160.0667	80.0334	23.0863
Row (word type)	1	56.0333	56.0333	16.1633
Row × Column	2	56.0667	28.0334	8.0865
Error	24	83.2	3.4667	
Total	29	188.9667		

$\alpha = .05$) of 4.26. Our obtained *F*-ratio is again larger than this critical value. Therefore, our data have yielded two significant main effects and a significant interaction effect.

What do these results actually mean? Let's revisit our example. Our investigator was comparing three types of memory techniques: rote rehearsal, verbal elaboration, and mental imagery. The predictions made by this researcher were that verbal elaboration and mental imagery would be more effective than rote rehearsal for memorizing concrete words, but that only verbal elaboration would be more effective than rote rehearsal for memorizing abstract words.

The main effect for memory technique (the column factor) is significant, indicating that there is a difference among the three memory technique means. In addition, the main effect for word type is significant, indicating that there is a difference between the two types of words. Finally, the significant interaction suggests that one or more differences exist among the means of the six individual conditions. Posttests will have to be conducted to enable us to determine which means differ from one another and whether our researcher's predictions about the effects of memory technique and word type are supported.

Comparing Means Within a Significant Main Effect   To determine which means differ from which among the three memory techniques, we must conduct post hoc analyses such as Tukey's HSD (introduced in Chapter 6). Calculating Tukey's HSD for the main effect for a two-way ANOVA is identical to calculating it as a posttest for a one-way ANOVA. Our first step is to determine the means we wish to compare. Here we wish to compare the means for each level of memory technique, *ignoring the type of word factor*. From our earlier calculations, we know that a total of 110 words were recalled in the rote rehearsal condition, a total of 166 words were recalled in the verbal elaboration condition, and a total of 145 words were recalled in the mental imagery condition. Ten subjects used each memory technique, so we divide each sum by 10 to determine our means. We then subtract each mean from each other mean to determine the difference between each pair of means. You may recall that a table was made to organize our means and to make certain that no pairs of means were left uncompared. The table of differences between the means looks like this:

		Rote	Verbal	Imagery
		11	16.6	14.5
Rote	11	——	5.6	3.5
Verbal	16.6	——	——	2.1
Imagery	14.5	——	——	——

The following formula can be used to determine the difference between the means needed to maintain $\alpha \leq .05$:

$$\text{HSD} = Q(r, \text{df}_e)\sqrt{\frac{\text{MS}_{\text{Error}}}{n}}$$

where:

Q = studentized range statistic

r = number of means in the independent variable

df_e = degrees of freedom error

n = number of scores used to create each mean

For our example, HSD is calculated as follows:

$$\text{HSD} = Q(r, \text{df}_e)\sqrt{\frac{\text{MS}_{\text{Error}}}{n}}$$

$$= 3.53\sqrt{\frac{3.4667}{10}}$$

$$= 3.53(.5888)$$

$$= 2.078$$

Consulting our table of differences between the means, we see that all three differences are greater than 2.078; thus, all means are significantly different from each other (with $\alpha = .05$). In general, and disregarding the type of word being recalled, verbal elaboration yielded significantly greater recall than did mental imagery and rote rehearsal, and mental imagery yielded greater recall performance than did rote rehearsal.

Our investigator also compared memory for concrete words with memory for abstract words. The main effect for the row factor (type of word) indicates that the means of these two types of words differ significantly from one another. No posttest is needed here because there are only two levels of the word type factor: abstract and concrete. Thus, only one comparison can be made between two means, so we need only look at the means for each level to determine which mean is larger. From our earlier calculations, we learned that a total of 231 concrete words had been recalled by 15 subjects. Therefore, the mean for the concrete words is 15.4 words. For the abstract words, 190 words had been recalled by 15 subjects, yielding a mean of 12.667. Because the main effect for the type of word is significant, we know that the mean of the concrete words recalled (15.4) is significantly greater than the mean of the recalled abstract words (12.667).

Interpreting Main Effects   A significant main effect means that, in general, one or more differences exist among the means of that independent variable. It is important to remember that the main effects *ignore all other factors* included in the study. If no interaction occurs between the significant factor and any other factor, the main effect can be generalized to each level of the independent variable. But, if a significant interaction occurs between the independent variable and some other factor, the main effect *may not* be consistent across all of the levels of the independent variable and, therefore, interpretation of the main effect must be made with care.

Consider our main effect for word type. It indicates that, ignoring type of memory technique, concrete words were recalled with greater frequency than were abstract words. However, we also have a significant interaction between word type and memory technique. This indicates that the difference between concrete and abstract words is not consistent across the three memory techniques. It may be that concrete words are consistently recalled with greater frequency than abstract words, but that for some techniques the difference between recall of concrete words and recall of abstract words is smaller than for other techniques. Or, perhaps the pattern is even reversed for one of the techniques. We must take a closer look at the differences among the means of the interaction before we can determine the relationship between the two factors.

Graphing the Means of an Interaction   An important task in interpreting a significant interaction is to create a graph of the means. The dependent variable (number of words recalled) is always assigned to the *y*-axis. To graph our two-way interaction between word type and memory technique, we will assign one of the

FIGURE 9.4   *Line graph of word type × memory technique interaction.*

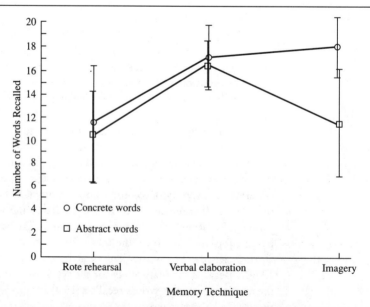

variables to the x-axis. There is no particular rule for determining which independent variable should be presented on the x-axis, although I typically assign the one with the greater number of levels so that there are fewer lines in my graph—one for each level of the second independent variable. The means for each level of the second independent variable are then plotted on the graph and connected with a line. One of the two possible graphs of the interaction for the word type × memory technique interaction is presented in Figure 9.4.

In the graph of the interaction, the lines representing each word type are not parallel. *When an interaction is statistically significant, the lines will not be parallel.* If means are graphed and the lines are nearly parallel, this suggests that no significant interaction occurs between the two variables; that is, the effect of one independent variable is consistent across the levels of the other. Figure 9.5 presents a series of graphs of hypothetical means. Some of these graphs suggest an interaction between the variables, and some do not. Line graphs are often drawn to represent interactions—even when the independent variable is not a continuous variable—because the relationship of the lines to each other (parallel or nonparallel) can be easier to see in a line graph than in a bar graph.

FIGURE 9.5   *Graphs of different patterns of means: interactions [(a), (d), and (f)] and no interactions [(b), (c), and (e)].*

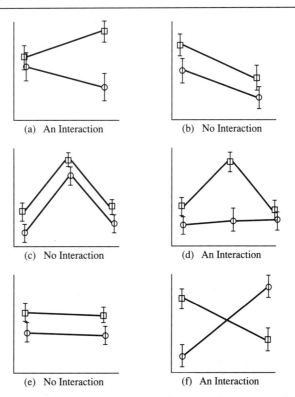

(a) An Interaction

(b) No Interaction

(c) No Interaction

(d) An Interaction

(e) No Interaction

(f) An Interaction

Cicchetti's Modification of Tukey's HSD: A Technique for Comparing Means Within Interactions A graph is an important tool for interpreting an interaction, but additional statistical techniques must be applied to determine which means differ from each other. A common technique for determining differences among means within an interaction involves calculating **simple effects**—in essence, conducting a series of one-way ANOVAs on each level of the independent variables. For simple effects that are significant, a posttest such as Tukey's HSD can be used to compare the means within each level. Many statistical textbooks describe this technique, but I would like to present here a relatively new technique that can be used to solve the same problem in one step.

A technique for comparing means within an interaction was published by Cicchetti in 1973; it is referred to here as **Cicchetti's modification** of Tukey's HSD. As you may recall, Tukey's HSD is used to compare all pairs of means within a one-way ANOVA and is preferred over conducting multiple t-tests because Tukey's maintains α at the desired level (usually .05 and/or .01) for all of the pairwise comparisons. At first blush it might seem appropriate to use Tukey's to compare all of the possible pairs of means with an interaction, but actually we don't wish to make all of the comparisons. We want to make comparisons between means only in instances where only one independent variable changes. For example, we may wish to compare the rote recall of concrete words with the recall of concrete words memorized by using verbal elaboration; here only the type of technique has been changed. Or we might compare concrete words memorized on the basis of imagery with abstract words memorized on the basis of imagery; here only the type of word has changed. We are not interested in comparing means in situations where both independent variables change—for example, where concrete words memorized by using verbal elaboration are contrasted with abstract words memorized by using imagery. We are not interested in this comparison because, if we were to find a significant difference between the two means, we would not know how to interpret it: was it caused by the difference in word type, by the difference in memory technique, or by some combination of both factors? A comparison in which more than one independent variable changes is called a **confounded comparison**. A comparison in which only one independent variable changes is called an **unconfounded comparison**. We wish to make only unconfounded comparisons.

The formula for Tukey's HSD is as follows:

$$HSD = Q(r, df_e) \sqrt{\frac{MS_e}{n}}$$

where:

r = number of means

df_e = degrees-of-freedom error

MS_e = mean squares error

n = number of scores used to calculate each mean

The reason we don't want to use Tukey's HSD to compare the means within our interaction is because, if we used the actual number of means as r in the formula, it would allow us to make *all* the pairwise comparisons among the means, including the confounded comparisons. In other words, Tukey's would be too conservative: α would be set at .05 for all of the possible comparisons, when we only want to make the unconfounded comparisons. We need to find a number for r that is smaller than our actual number of means so that it yields the correct number of comparisons.

Our first step in this task is to determine how many unconfounded comparisons we can make. To do this, I must introduce the notion of combinations. **Combinations** are the ways in which a set of things can be combined into subgroups of a particular size. Thus, if we have three things—A, B and C—we can form one combination of the three things, or three combinations of the three things taken two at a time (A/B, A/C, and B/C). The following formula is used for determining combinations:

$$C_n^x = \frac{X!}{n!(X-n)!}$$

where C_n^x is read as the combination of X things taken n at a time, and ! is a factorial sign.* So, if we have three things and we wish to combine them two at a time, our calculations would proceed as follows:

$$C_2^3 = \frac{3!}{2!(3-2)!}$$

$$= \frac{3!}{2! * 1!}$$

$$= \frac{3 * 2 * 1}{2 * 1(1)}$$

$$= \frac{6}{2} = 3$$

The concept of combinations is necessary for calculating the number of unconfounded contrasts. The formula for determining the number of unconfounded contrasts is as follows:

$$a(C_2^b) + b(C_2^a)$$

where a is the number of levels in the first independent variable, and b is the number of levels in the second independent variable. Using this formula, we can determine how many unconfounded contrasts are possible with our word type and memory technique interaction. We will let a represent the number of levels of word type and let b represent the number of levels of memory techniques

$$a(C_2^b) + b(C_2^a) = 2C_2^3 + 3C_2^2$$

$$= 2\frac{3!}{2!(3-2)!} + 3\frac{2!}{2!(2-2)!}$$

---

* Some of you may not be familiar with factorials. $X!$ is equal to $X * (X-1) * (X-2) * (X-3) * \cdots * (1)$. For example $4! = 4 * 3 * 2 * 1 = 24$.

$$= 2\frac{3*2*1}{2*1(1)} + 3\frac{2*1}{2*1(1)}$$

$$= 2\frac{6}{2} + 3(1)$$

$$= 6 + 3 = 9$$

Therefore, from among our six means, we can make nine unconfounded comparisons.

Now, to modify the Tukey's HSD formula, we need to find a value for r that yields 9 or so pairwise comparisons. To do so first we must make a table that, when read from right to left, will indicate how many combinations can be formed from each value taken two at a time; and when read from left to right, will indicate how many things are needed to yield X number of pairwise comparisons. For example, six things taken two at a time yield the following number of pairwise comparisons:

$$C_2^6 = \frac{6!}{2!(6-2)!}$$

$$= \frac{6*5*4!}{2!(4)!}$$

$$= \frac{6*5}{2*1}$$

$$= \frac{30}{2} = 15$$

Thus, to make 15 pairwise comparisons, we would need six things. Table 9.7 presents the number of pairwise comparisons (in the left-hand column) that one can make based on each r-value (in the right-hand column) between 2 and 10. In the left-hand column, we will look for our number of unconfounded comparisons: the corresponding value in the right-hand column will be our r value for the Tukey's HSD formula.

TABLE 9.7   *Values of r necessary to generate various numbers of unconfounded comparisons.*

Number of Unconfounded Comparisons	Value of r
2	2
3	3
6	4
10	5
15	6
21	7
28	8
36	9
45	10

To return to our example, we wish to make nine unconfounded pairwise comparisons. To use Tukey's HSD, we choose a value for r that yields nine comparisons. By consulting Table 9.7, we find that the closest value to 9 is 10, and that five means are needed to generate ten pairwise comparisons. Therefore, we use 5 as our value of r.

We now continue with our calculations of Tukey's HSD (with $\alpha = .05$). [Notice that $n = 5$ now, because we are comparing the cell means and there were five scores per cell.] The calculations are as follows:

$$\begin{aligned} \text{HSD} &= Q(r, \text{df}_e)\sqrt{\frac{\text{MS}_e}{n}} \\ &= Q(5, 24)\sqrt{\frac{3.4667}{5}} \\ &= 4.17\sqrt{.6933} \\ &= 4.17(.8327) \\ &= 3.4724 \end{aligned}$$

Thus, a minimum difference of 3.4724 is needed between two means in our unconfounded comparisons in order for the difference to be considered significant at the .05 level. Here is a table of the means in our example:

	Rote Rehearsal	Verbal Elaboration	Imagery Elaboration
Concrete Word	11.4	17	17.8
Abstract Word	10.6	16.2	11.2

The nine unconfounded comparisons we can make are the comparisons between means that lie one under or one over the other or between means that lie on the same horizontal plane. In other words, comparisons cannot be made diagonally. These are our nine unconfounded comparisons:

1. Rote/Concrete − Rote/Abstract = 11.4 − 10.6 = .80
2. Verbal/Concrete − Verbal/Abstract = 17 − 16.2 = .80
3. Imagery/Concrete − Imagery/Abstract = 17.8 − 11.2 = 6.60*
4. Verbal/Concrete − Rote/Concrete = 17 − 11.4 = 5.60*
5. Imagery/Concrete − Rote/Concrete = 17.8 − 11.4 = 6.40*
6. Imagery/Concrete − Verbal/Concrete = 17.8 − 17 = .80
7. Verbal/Abstract − Rote/Abstract = 16.2 − 10.6 = 5.60*
8. Imagery/Abstract − Rote/Abstract = 11.2 − 10.6 = .60
9. Verbal/Abstract − Imagery/Abstract = 16.2 − 11.2 = 5.0*

Results marked with an asterisk constitute significant differences between the means. As we make our unconfounded comparisons, we find that five of the nine comparisons are significant. The subjects using rote rehearsal to memorize concrete words recalled significantly fewer words than did those using verbal elabortion or imagery to memorize the same words. Verbal elaboration led to better recall performance for

FIGURE 9.6   *Line graph of the word type × memory technique interaction.*

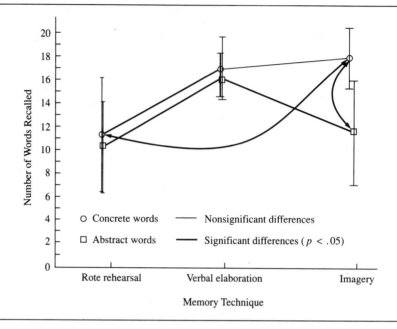

abstract words than did either rote rehearsal or imagery. Finally, imagery recall lead to better recall peformance for concrete words than for abstract words. All of the other differences measured in unconfounded comparisons are not significant. [What conclusions, if any can we make about nonsignificant differences? Review the section on failing to reject the null hypothesis in Chapter 3 if you are unsure.] A graph of the interaction is presented in Figure 9.6, and the significant differences are indicated on this graph.

Our researcher had predicted that verbal elaboration would be more effective than rote rehearsal for both abstract and concrete words, and that imagery would be more effective with concrete words than with abstract words. Both of these predictions are supported by the results of our application of Cicchetti's modification of Tukey's HSD to the data.

CONCEPT QUESTIONS 9.2

A study involves four levels of one independent variable and three of another.

a. How many unconfounded comparisons can be made? List them.
b. What value of r would you use in Cicchetti's modification of Tukey's HSD to compare the means within the interaction?

Cicchetti's modification of Tukey's HSD allows one to compare directly all of the unconfounded means within a significant interaction, without deflating α below .05 (or whatever level you, as the researcher, choose).

OTHER TYPES OF TWO-WAY ANOVAS

Our extended example in this chapter has involved a two-way ANOVA with two between-subject variables. But factorial designs may involve all between-subjects, all within-subjects, or a combination of between- and within-subjects factors. Similarly, two-way ANOVAs are not limited to analyzing factorial designs involving between-subjects factors. Two-way ANOVAs can be used to analyze within-subject designs (where both factors are within-subjects factors) or mixed designs, sometimes called *split-plot design* (where one factor is a between-subjects factor and one is a within-subjects factor).

Let's consider a **within-subjects design** with two factors, *A* and *B*. Like a between-subjects ANOVA, a within-subjects (or repeated-measures) ANOVA provides information about the main effect for *A*, the main effect for *B*, and the interaction of *A* and *B*. Any necessary posttests are calculated in the same manner as for the two-way between-subjects ANOVA. An empty summary table for a two-way ANOVA with two within-subjects variables is presented in Table 9.8.

An example of a study based on a within-subjects design with two factors might involve an investigation of cognitive processes and time of day. In this investigation, the subjects each take two tests: a logic test and a reading test. The subjects take one test in the early morning and one in the late evening. The order of testing and the order of the tests are counterbalanced to correct for any practice effects.

After conducting the study, the researcher has data for four conditions: morning/logic, morning/reading, evening/logic, and evening/reading. There are two levels for each independent variable, and (assuming that the data meet the

TABLE 9.8   *Summary table for a two-way ANOVA with two within-subjects factors.*

Source	df	SS	MS	F
A				$\dfrac{MS_A}{\text{Error}}$
B				$\dfrac{MS_b}{\text{Error}}$
A × *B*				$\dfrac{MS_{A \times B}}{\text{Error}}$
Error				
Total				

necessary assumptions), a 2 × 2 within-ANOVA can be conducted. This analysis would yield information about the main effects for time of test and type of test, as well as about the interaction of time and type of test—just as a between-subjects ANOVA would in a comparable setting.

CONCEPT QUESTIONS 9·3

Following are hypothetical means (and standard deviations in parentheses) generated by a study of the effect of time of test and type of test on performance. Create a graph of the interaction of these variables, as well as of the main effects. Be sure to include the error bars.

		Type of Test	
		Logic	Reading
Time of Test	A.M.	78(6.9)	89(5.3)
	P.M.	64(6.2)	85(5.9)

Another type of factorial design is the **mixed** or **split–plot design**. Split-plot designs gained their name from agricultural research in which plots of land and types of seed were tested simultaneously by planting more than one type of seed in numerous plots. The researcher could then assess whether the seed naturally grew better in some plots than in others, and could also determine whether some seeds were more productive than others. Of course, the researcher was also able to determine whether an interaction occurred between seeds and plots; for example, did one type of seed grow better in a shady plot while another type of seed performed better in a sunny plot?

TABLE 9.9   *Sample summary table for a two-way split-plot design.*

Source	df	SS	MS	F
Between-groups				
B				$\dfrac{MS_B}{\text{Subejcts within } B}$
Subjects within B (error)				
Within-subjects				
W				$\dfrac{MS_W}{\text{Subjects within } B \times W}$
W × B				$\dfrac{MS_{W \times B}}{\text{Subjects within } B \times W}$
Subjects with B × W (error)				
Total				

Now let's consider an example involving one between-subjects variable (B) and one within-subjects variable (W). The ANOVA again yields the same information as is given by a comparable between-subjects ANOVA: main effect for B, main effect for W, and interaction of B and W. The summary table for this type of ANOVA is somewhat more complicated, however (see Table 9.9).

The total variability among the scores in a split-plot design is partitioned among several sources of variability. Initially, it is divided between between-subjects variability and within-subjects variability (the top half and bottom half of the summary table). Then these sources of variability are further partitioned. The between-subjects variability is partitioned into group variability (B; the variability between each group) and variability among the subjects within each group. The latter source of variability constitutes the error term for the between-groups factor; in other words, it is the estimate of the variability attributable to error variance.

The within-subjects variability is also partitioned into additional sources: the variability attributable to the within-subjects variable (W), the interaction of the within-subjects and between-subjects factors ($W \times B$), and the interaction of variability among the subjects within each group and the within-subjects factor (subjects within $B \times W$). This final term is the error term for the within-subjects factor and for the interaction of the between- and within-subjects factors.*

To clarify this, let's consider an example. Imagine that a split-plot design has been used to investigate the effects of time and type of test on test performance. In a split-plot design, one of these factors is a within-subjects factor and one is a between-subjects factor. Perhaps this particular study has been designed so that each subject takes both a logic test and a reading test, but each subject is tested only in the morning or in the evening (not both). Here, type of test is a within-subjects factor, but time of test is a between-subjects factor.

The ANOVA that might be calculated with the data from this study would yield the same type of information as the between- and within-subjects ANOVAs, main effects for test type and time of test, and the interaction of the two.

Although between-subjects, within-subjects, and split-plot designs yield the same information, the decision to use one or another is not arbitrary. The researcher should choose the study design that best fits the situation and allows the researcher to control as many potential confounds as (reasonably) possible. One practical consideration that many investigators weigh when designing their studies is the number of subjects they need to carry out the project. A 2×2 between-subjects design with 10 scores in each condition requires 40 subjects. The same study run as a split-plot design requires 20 subjects. A 2×2 within-subject design with 10 scores per condition requires only 10 subjects.

The number of subjects needed for a study is important from a practical standpoint, but it is not the only consideration. In one situation, a within-subjects design might be best; but in another, the potential for carryover effects on one of the independent variables might call for a split-plot design. In yet another situation, a between-subjects design might be needed to control all of the possible confounds, or

---

*These error terms are appropriate when the researcher has purposely chosen the specific levels of the independent variables. When the levels of the independent variables have been chosen at random, different error terms are appropriate and a more advanced statistical textbook, such as Hinkle, Jiersma & Jurs (1988), should be consulted.

because the independent variables (such as gender) are simply not amenable to a within-subject design.

HIGHER-ORDER DESIGNS AND THEIR INTERACTIONS

Analysis of variance is not limited to one- or two-way analyses. We can, if we wish, conduct three-way or four-way or even higher-order ANOVAs. Practical considerations limit the number of factors that should be added to the analysis, however.

Imagine a situation involving three independent variables: time of test, type of test, and whether the subject considers himself or herself a morning or evening person. A **three-way ANOVA** of this design (2 × 3 × 2 design) would yield three main effects (time of test, type of test, and type of person), three two-way interactions (time × type of test, time × type of person, and type of person × type of test), and one three-way interaction (time × type of test × type of person). We have already discussed two-way interactions in this chapter; but how would one go about graphing and interpreting a three-way interaction?

FIGURE 9.7   *Graph of a three-way interaction: (a) test performance plotted against time of testing for morning people; (b) test performance plotted against time of testing for evening people.*

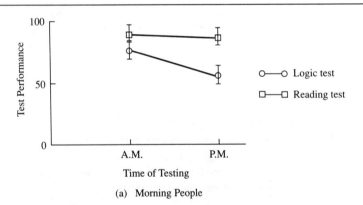

(a) Morning People

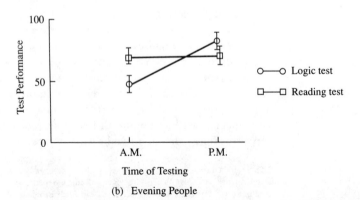

(b) Evening People

Unless one intends to form a three-dimensional model of the interaction, graphing a three-way interaction requires at least two separate graphs. A separate graph must be drawn for each level of one of the independent variables. The decision about which independent variable to divide between the graphs is up to the researcher.

An example is presented in Figure 9.7. In this interaction, the performance of the morning people appears to decrease from morning to evening, and this decrease seems to be greater for the logic test than for the reading test. The evening people, on the other hand, show improvement from morning to evening, and the improvement seems to be greatest for the logic test.

Factorial designs are quite appealing because of their flexibility: so much information can be gained in one investigation. But it is possible to have too much of a good thing, and using too many factors makes interpreting the results very complicated. Four-way ANOVAs, for example, compare four independent variables and yield information about four main effects, six two-way interactions, four three-way interactions and one four-way interaction. Many computer programs allow users to choose which interactions to include in the analyses; thus, a researcher could instruct the computer to disregard some subset of the eleven interactions that a four-way ANOVA yields. However, every factor and interaction that is included and that accounts for some variability reduces the error variance and thus increases the power of the analysis. It can be difficult to decide when adding a factor or including a variable is more trouble to interpret than it is worth.

CRITIQUE OF FACTORIAL DESIGNS

One important consideration in critiquing a factorial design is whether the design and the data meet the assumptions for appropriate use. For analysis of variance, the dependent variable is assumed to be normally distributed within the population, and the variances among the populations being compared are assumed to be relatively homogeneous. Tests of normality and of homogeneity of variance can be conducted when a researcher is unsure whether these assumptions have been met. Serious violations of these assumptions—especially homogeneity of variance when n's are not equal—will affect the probability of making a Type I error.

If homogeneity of variance is a concern, it may be possible to transform the data, perhaps by taking the square root or the logarithm of each data point, so that the variances become homogeneous. The analyses could then be conducted on the basis of these transformed scores. More advanced statistics texts, such as Howell (1987), provide information about transforming data.

As with any experimental design, a reviewer must study the methodology used to uncover the possible presence of confounding variables. For example, might demand characteristics have affected the results? Were there any differences in the manner in which the conditions were treated, other than those called for by the independent variable? Is there evidence that subjects dropped out of the study at different rates related to the experimental conditions? Only if the results are free from confounds can a reviewer have any faith that the results are meaningful.

Because two-way and higher ANOVAs yield both main effects and interactions, interpretations of their results demand special attention. Main effects identify *general* differences between or among levels of a single independent variable. Interactions provide information about how the effect of one variable asserts itself differently at different levels of the other variable. If there is a significant main effect for one variable and if this variable is also involved in an interaction, the main effect results can be misleading. Study the interpretation of the main effect when an interaction is also present. Is the main effect true across all levels of the independent variables, or is the main effect an overgeneralization that does not hold for all levels of the independent variables? When the independent variable is not involved in an interaction, or when the interaction does not contradict the main effect at any point, it is appropriate to emphasize the main effect.

The conclusions one draws from the results of an ANOVA depend not only on the main effects and interactions, but also on the type of independent variables being investigated. Some independent variables are manipulable by the researcher, but others are subject variables and cannot be manipulated. Whenever a subject variable is involved in the results of an analysis, the results imply a relationship or correlation between the subject variable and the dependent measure; causal conclusions are not warranted. If a difference is registered between males and females on body image, this indicates that a relationship exists between gender and body image—not that gender causes one's body image to be different.

In the discussion section, the researcher is likely to draw some conclusions or generate some hypotheses based on the results of the statistical analyses. Everyone's reasoning fails once in a while, and errors in logic or misinterpretations of results have been known to appear in print. Carefully think through the interpretations offered by the authors. Do you agree with these interpretations? Would you have come to the same conclusions? You may be surprised at how often your reasoning differs from that of the authors. There is often more than one way to solve a problem or answer a question. Perhaps you will be motivated to conduct additional research to determine whose answer is better.

Factorial designs provide a useful, flexible, and powerful tool for using a simple study to answer numerous related research questions. Sometimes, in fact, novice researchers get carried away and try to answer too many questions at once, ending up with an unwieldy design and a potential five-way interaction. When used in a well-reasoned, practical manner, however, factorial designs can save time and permit simultaneous comparison of the effects of several variables, thereby answering questions that would be unanswerable with simpler designs.

IMPORTANT TERMS AND CONCEPTS

factorial design	column factor	unconfounded comparisons
main effect	row factor	combinations
interaction	simple effects	within-subjects ANOVA
marginal means	Cicchetti's modification	mixed (split-plot) ANOVA
two-way between-subjects ANOVA	confounded comparisons	three-way ANOVA

QUESTIONS AND EXERCISES

1. For each of the following studies, indicate which variables are dependent, which are independent, what the number of levels is for each independent variable, and whether it is a within-subjects or between-subjects variable.

   a. Male and female children aged 4, 5, and 6 years old were observed playing with other children of the same age. For each child, the duration of time spent in cooperative play with others was measured.

   b. Anorexics and bulimics take a cognitive distortions test twice: upon entering an eating disorders treatment program, and again three weeks later.

   c. Subjects' pulses are measured before a lifting task, directly after the lifting task, and two minutes later. Each subject participates in three lifting tasks on three different days. The task involves lifting 10-, 15-, or 20- pound weights at a rate of once every two seconds for 10 minutes.

2. Smokers and nonsmokers are asked to complete a test of their attitudes toward smoking. Half of the subjects complete the test after waiting in a room where they were seated next to an ashtray full of cigarette butts.

   a. Following are the data from that study. The smoking attitudes test yields a score between 1 and 10, where a higher score indicates a more favorable attitude. Calculate the two-way ANOVA with these data.

Smokers		Nonsmokers	
With Ashtray	Without Ashtray	With Ashtray	Without Ashtray
8	7	2	4
7	6	1	6
8	5	3	5
9	4	2	7
7	5	2	4

   b. Are there any significant main effects or interactions? If so, which (if any) post hoc analyses should be used to further analyze the main effects? The interaction? Do the appropriate analyses.

   c. Interpret the results of your analyses.

3. A researcher tests three different viruses on two types of mice. The viruses are all types of cold viruses: one that typically causes a runny nose, one that typically causes a cough, and one that typically causes congestion and a headache. The two types of mice consist of one group that has received megadoses of vitamins and one group that has received a placebo. The researcher waits several days, and then takes blood samples to determine how sick the animal is from the virus it received. Based on this information, each animal receives a score that indicates how infected it has become (the larger the number, the more infected). The researcher hypothesizes that the vitamin treatment is more effective than the placebo, and that the vitamins are most effective when the virus causes congestion or causes a runny nose. The data are provided next.

		Type of Virus		
		Runny Nose	Cough	Congestion
Mouse's Dietary Supplement	Vitamins	6	7	3
		7	8	5
		5	8	6
		6	9	5
		4	7	3
		4	7	4
	Placebo	8	9	6
		7	8	8
		6	7	7
		8	6	7
		9	8	9
		6	7	6

   a. Calculate the F-ratio to determine whether any significant differences exist among the six conditions.

   b. Are any post hoc analyses necessary? Conduct the necessary analyses to determine which means differ within any significant main effect or interaction.

c. What do the results suggest?

4. A researcher was interested in the effect of weather on mood and had two hypotheses: (1) that overcast days yield more depressed moods than sunny days; and (2) that women are affected more negatively by an overcast day than are men. Subjects were solicited from two sections of a college course (Introduction to Economics). Members of one set of subjects were asked on a sunny day to rate their mood on a 10-point scale (where 1 meant depressed and 10 meant very happy). Members of the other set of subjects were asked on an overcast day to rate their mood. On both days the temperature was 68°F. The test days were three weeks apart. The data are presented next.

		Type of Day	
		Sunny	Cloudy
		7	6
		8	6
	Male	7	4
		6	5
Subject's Gender		5	7
		8	5
		9	5
	Female	7	3
		6	4
		8	2

a. The researcher asks you to help by calculating an F-ratio and conducting any necessary post hoc analyses. If there proved to be any significant main effects in this study, why would it be unnecessary to conduct a post hoc analysis to determine which means differ?

b. How do you interpret the results? Can the researcher claim that good weather helps cause a good mood? What are some alternative explanations for the results?

10

Quasi-Experimental Designs

T hroughout this book, a distinction has been made between true experiments and correlational studies. In true experiments, subjects are randomly chosen or randomly assigned to experimental conditions so that comparison groups are equivalent. The experimental conditions differ only with regard to the levels of one or more independent variables; thus, any difference between the groups' performances on the dependent variables can be attributed to a difference in the independent variable.

A correlational study is characterized by less control by the researcher over the independent variable. In studies with the least amount of researcher control (such as a naturalistic observation), behaviors are observed and recorded, but subgroups within the sample being observed are not necessarily compared. In other studies, groups may be compared, but the independent variable may be a subject variable over which the researcher has no control. For example, males and females may be compared in a study, but clearly the groups do not begin the study as equivalent.

The distinction between a true experiment and a correlational study is not always crystal clear. In many situations, a researcher may be studying a variable that cannot be manipulated—such as age, or gender, or whether a person has arthritis—but the researcher adds considerable control to the testing environment. These cases resemble true experiments in the amount of control that is used, but they do not involve random assignment of the subjects to conditions. Such designs that lie halfway between a true experiment and a correlational study are called *quasi-experimental designs*. In quasi-experimental designs, efforts are made to acknowledge and to limit

303

the effects of threats to the study's internal validity so that the results may be interpreted meaningfully.

The term *quasi-experimental designs* was coined by Campbell & Stanley in a chapter written for the *Handbook of Research on Teaching* (Gage, 1963). This chapter was subsequently presented as a short book, *Experimental and Quasi-experimental Designs for Research* (Campbell & Stanley, 1963). Much of the present chapter is a summary of the Campbell & Stanley book.

CHARACTERISTICS AND TYPES OF QUASI-EXPERIMENTAL DESIGNS

The work by Campbell & Stanley (1963) makes a distinction between true, quasi-, and pre-experimental designs. **True experimental designs** involve randomly choosing or randomly assigning subjects to conditions and conducting the study in such a manner that causal statements can be made about significant differences among the experimental conditions. Much of this book has focused on true experimental designs, and no more needs to be said about them here.

Quasi-experimental designs are conducted when true experiments cannot be carried out, such as in applied settings where, for ethical or practical reasons, subjects cannot be randomly assigned to experimental conditions. These studies provide correlational information and may disconfirm causal statements made in laboratory research. With a quasi-experimental design, causal statements may be made—cautiously—when special efforts have been exerted to account for all the rival hypotheses.

Pre-experimental designs are simple designs for studies that are typically carried out in applied settings. Pre-experimental designs yield investigations in which several alternative explanations for the results are present; they should be conducted when there is no other way to investigate a question. It may be very difficult for an investigator (or for the evaluator of a research project based on a pre-experimental design) to have much faith in the conclusions. Pre-experimental designs can provide evidence of possible relationships among variables, though, and this information may assist researchers in determining whether some area is worth investigating further.

An example will help clarify the distinctions among true, pre-, and quasi-experimental designs. Imagine that a researcher is interested in the effectiveness of a prenatal care program that is aimed at reducing the infant mortality rate within a state. One approach to this problem might be to utilize a pre-experimental design. The researcher might simply compare the infant mortality rate prior to installation of the program with the infant mortality rate after the program had begun. The results of this data collection would be difficult to interpret, however: no matter what the results were, alternative explanations would abound. If the infant mortality rate declined, it could have been the result of increased awareness among the expectant mothers of good health during pregnancy; or it could have been because there was a flu epidemic during the year the pretest data were collected, or perhaps it could be related to an increase in the number of free clinics available to the mothers, and not to the new program specifically. On the other hand, an increase in infant mortality could also be attributed to any number of causes. Perhaps an increased incidence of drug abuse among the mothers counteracted any benefits of the program; or the number of 13- to 16-year-old mothers (whose infants tend to be at higher risk than the average infant) increased markedly during the new program period; or some other factor (such as an unusually harsh winter) resulted in greater infant mortality. Simply comparing the scores of a sample or samples from the "same" population before and after an event does not provide data that can be interpreted in any reasonable manner. For this reason, this type of design is referred to by Campbell & Stanley (1963) as *pre-experimental*.

To try to correct some of the shortcomings of the pre-experimental design, a second population might be included in the design, to be compared during the same time frame with the population participating in the new program. Whether the comparison populations are equivalent or not before the experiment determines whether the design is a true experiment or a quasi-experiment. Designing a true experiment is not feasible in this situation, however. Ethics forbids a researcher from randomly assigning pregnant women to the prenatal care and no prenatal care conditions. Thus, something between a true experimental and a pre-experimental design must be developed.

NONEQUIVALENT CONTROL GROUP DESIGN

One type of quasi-experimental design involves comparing the sample in the experimental group with a sample in a control group drawn from a comparable—but not equivalent—population. In this example, the researcher might attempt to identify a population of pregnant women comparable to the population of pregnant women in the state instituting the prenatal program. For example, if Illinois were the state establishing the program, women in Indiana might serve as a comparable (albeit nonequivalent) population from which a control group sample could be drawn. To constitute truly equivalent sample groups, subjects would need to be randomly assigned to Indiana or Illinois.

A researcher might make the mistake of simply comparing these two samples for the period after the establishment of the prenatal program. This design, comparing two nonequivalent sample groups once, however, is not much better than a design that compares two samples of one population with each other. The alternative explanations for the results prevent the study from providing useful information. Any difference between the infant mortality rates of Indiana and Illinois could be a function of the new program, or it could be because the states started with difference rates in the first place. There is no way to know with this design. Therefore, a one-time comparison of two nonequivalent sample groups is also a pre-experimental design.

A better alternative is to take pretest and posttest measures from both the group of interest and the **nonequivalent control group**. In other words, the infant mortality rate of Illinois and Indiana should be measured prior to the installation of the program and then again after the program has been underway. The pretest measures can be used to assess the equivalency of the two comparison populations, and the posttest measures can be used to assess the relative effect of the prenatal program. For instance, perhaps the Illinois sample begins the study at pretest with a slightly

FIGURE 10.1   *Two possible outcomes of a nonequivalent control group design: (a) evidence that a treatment had an effect; (b) no evidence that the treatment had an effect.*

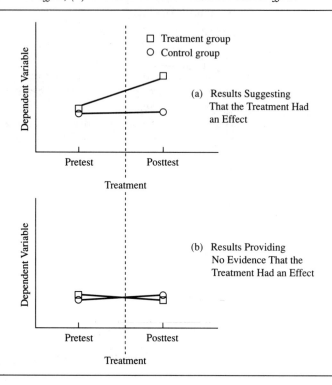

higher infant mortality rate than the Indiana sample, but at posttest the infant mortality rate for Illinois has decreased while Indiana's has stayed constant. That would suggest that the prenatal program did have an effect and that there is a relationship between installation of the program and a decrease in infant mortality. Figure 10.1 presents two possible outcomes of a nonequivalent control group design.

TIME-SERIES DESIGNS

Another type of quasi-experimental design can be used when there is no appropriate nonequivalent population from which to draw a control group. This approach involves making **multiple comparisons of a single group** (population), also called the **time-series design**. Assume that there is no comparable state with which to compare Illinois' infant mortality rates. An alternative approach is to make observations about the infant mortality rate a number of times before and after the installation of the program. This is an expansion of the pre-experimental design described initially, where the researcher chose one time for observation before the program and one time for observation after it had begun. We noted that the number of alternative explanations for the results was rather large. However, we can lessen this problem by making more observations. Then, should a trend emerge where

FIGURE 10.2   *Two possible patterns of results for a study using a time-series design: (a) results suggesting that the program is effective; (b) results not suggesting that the program is effective.*

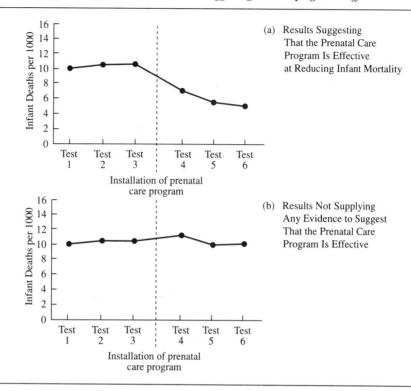

infant mortality decreases over time after the program has begun (assuming that infant mortality hadn't already begun to decrease before the program started) we can have greater confidence that the program is effective. In other words, although for any two observations there may be a number of alternative explanations for the results, the probability is very small that these factors will affect all of the other observations in the long run. Figure 10.2 presents a hypothetical set of outcomes for this research project, as well as another possible outcome.

Another possible quasi-experimental design consists of a combination of the time-series design and the pretest-postest with nonequivalent groups design. It involves making multiple observations of two nonequivalent groups, and it is called the **multiple time-series design**. In our example, the researcher would make multiple observations of the infant mortality rate before and after the installation of the prenatal program in Illinois. Additionally, the researcher would make the same observations in Indiana, where the program was not being initiated. A graph of possible outcomes of a multiple time-series design is presented in Figure 10.3.

In these examples of quasi-experimental designs, different samples were chosen during each test of the experimental and control populations. These same designs can be used, however, to test the same sample or samples multiple times, such as

FIGURE 10.3   *Two possible outcomes of a multiple time-series design: (a) evidence that a treatment had an effect on the dependent variable; (b) no evidence that the treatment had such an effect.*

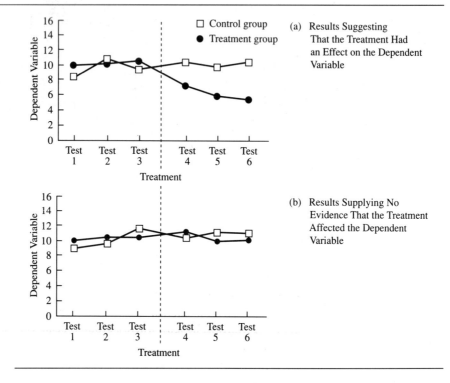

might occur when measuring the effectiveness of a reading program with second-graders. The same second-grade students could be tested multiple times.

Quasi-experimental designs are used to make the best of a less than perfect research environment. In the social sciences, we cannot always use a true experimental design to test our hypotheses; instead, we must patch together designs that decrease the influence of major extraneous variables, yielding results that are interpretable although not ideal. A summary of the three quasi-experimental designs we have just discussed is presented in Table 10.1. In the next section we will consider some of the most important extraneous variables that can affect quasi-experimental designs.

CONCEPT QUESTIONS 10.1   A former high school English teacher of yours asks for your assistance in designing a study to determine whether a teaching system involving a series of weekly quizzes or one with less frequent testing leads to better learning by the students. Describe a possible time-series design, a possible nonequivalent control group with pretest and posttest design, and a possible multiple time-series design that the teacher could use.

TABLE 10.1   *Summary of three quasi-experimental designs.*

Type of Quasi-Experimental Design	Characteristics
Nonequivalent Control Group	Compares two comparable but different groups of subjects before and after treatment of the experimental group.
Time-Series Design	Tests one group several times before and several times after treatment of it.
Multiple Time-Series Design	Tests two nonequivalent groups several times before and several times after treatment of the experimental group.

THREATS TO THE INTERNAL VALIDITY OF QUASI-EXPERIMENTAL DESIGNS

When determining the adequacy of a research design, one needs to foresee criticisms and alternative explanations for results. These alternative explanations and rival hypotheses weaken the internal validity of a study and damage its interpretability. In quasi-experimental designs, where a group is being compared to a nonequivalent control group or where one group is being observed a number of times, it is important to foresee the numerous pitfalls that await the interpretations of the results. Only when these threats to the internal validity of a quasi-experimental design are foreseen and controlled can the researcher cautiously make some causal statements about the results. Here we will discuss eight factors that could weaken the internal validity of a quasi-experimental study.

HISTORY EFFECTS

History effects are results caused not by the independent variable but by an event outside the study that co-occurs with the independent variable. For example, earlier we discussed the possibility that the difference in infant mortality rates before and after the introduction of a prenatal program may have been caused not by the program but by some other co-occurring factor, such as an especially harsh winter. For another example, imagine that a researcher is involved in a program aimed at reducing children's fear of death; unbeknownst to the researcher (who lives in a different location), the night before the final posttest scores are to be measured, a severe thunderstorm strikes the area. Anxiety measures the next day are back at their pretest levels. The researcher may interpret the test results as evidence that the program was a failure, although actually the scores only reflect a short-term reaction to a recent event.

To avoid history effects in research where they are potentially confounding, a researcher might include a number of observations in his or her design. While an unexpected historical event might affect a pair of test scores, such an event (or series of events) is unlikely to affect every test score. Including a control group, even a nonequivalent control group, can also aid in correctly intepreting results affected by historical events. If a control group of children not undergoing a program to lessen anxiety also show a sudden increase in their anxiety levels, the researcher knows that some external source of anxiety may be influencing the test scores and obstructing a fair assessment of the program. Use of a control group to isolate and identify history effects is not always effective, however, as we shall see when we discuss the interaction of selection with other threats to internal validity.

MATURATION EFFECTS

When subjects are tested over time, changes in their scores may be due to the independent variable or they may be caused by maturation. **Maturation effects** are changes in behavior caused by the passage of time, such as growing older, hungrier, or more tired (Campbell & Stanley, 1963). If the children in our hypothetical anxiety study are followed for a significant period of time, their anxieties may decrease simply because, as they grow older, they no longer find the same things scary. Again, a control group can aid in controlling for maturation effects: any changes in behavior noted in both the experimental and control group cannot be a attributed to the independent variable.

TESTING EFFECTS

When subjects are tested repeatedly, the fact that they have been tested before is likely to affect the results of the next test; this is called a **testing effect**. People who repeat standardized tests such as the Graduate Record Exam (GRE) or an intelligence test typically find that their scores are higher the second time. This occurs not because they have gotten significantly smarter between testings, but because they have a better idea of what to expect, what the questions will be like, how to pace themselves, and so on. A change in scores simply as a function of having been tested before also occurs in personality testing and to some degree in tests of prejudice and social attitudes (Campbell & Stanley, 1963). In research, a change in scores from one testing period to another may be a function of this testing effect as well as of any effect of the independent variable. When the testing effect is in the same direction as the expected effect of the independent variable, the researcher runs the risk of mistakenly assuming that the independent variable caused the change in the scores. When the effect of the independent variable and the testing effect are in opposite directions, the net result may be no change in scores even though the independent variable had an effect (albeit hidden). A carefully chosen control group can be used to control for testing effects so that the researcher can more accurately interpret the study's results.

INSTRUMENTATION EFFECTS

Another risk of testing subjects repeatedly is that the accuracy of the instrument being used to measure the subjects may change with continued use. **Instrumentation effects** can occur when actual mechanical equipment is used, such as a scale that

"IT MAY VERY WELL BRING ABOUT IMMORTALITY, BUT IT WILL TAKE FOREVER TO TEST IT."

Courtesy of Sidney Harris

may become less accurate over time, or it can occur when people make the observations. Observers may begin a series of observations with a set of criteria that change somewhat as they become more experienced. Perhaps the criteria become more relaxed, or perhaps they become more stringent. Perhaps the observer becomes fatigued and less accurate over time. When the measuring device fails to measure in the same manner across all observations, an instrumentation effect is likely.

STATISTICAL REGRESSION TOWARD THE MEAN

We discussed **regression toward the mean** in Chapter 8, in the general context of within-subjects designs. It occurs when subjects are chosen because of their extreme scores on a dependent variable or on a variable correlated with the dependent variable. Regardless of the intervention, extreme scores are likely to move toward the mean upon retesting. Regression toward the mean can be prevented simply by not choosing subjects based on extreme scores, or it can be accounted for by choosing a control group whose initial scores were equally extreme. Then, if the experimental group shows a greater change than the control group, this suggests that the change was the result of something more than regression toward the mean.

SUBJECT MORTALITY EFFECTS

Subject mortality (or *subject attrition*), as discussed in earlier chapters, refers to subjects' data not being usable either because the subjects ceased to participate in the study before it could be completed or because a decision was made based on some criterion to drop their data. Subject mortality becomes a threat to the internal validity of a study when the dropout rate is very high (suggesting that there may be something different about the remaining subjects) or when the dropout rate varies between comparison groups. Given that the comparison groups are not equivalent in the first place, but merely as comparable as can reasonably be contrived, having subjects drop from these groups at different rates adds another level of nonequivalency that quasi-experimental designs simply can't tolerate.

SELECTION BIASES

When differences exist between the comparison groups within a study, a **selection bias** has occurred. When a control group is included in a quasi-experimental design, it is nearly always a nonequivalent control group, so a selection bias is practically inevitable. For example, suppose that a researcher is studying the effects of sleep apnea treatment on memory performance. Very likely the researcher will not have access to enough sleep apnea patients to assign some to a no-treatment control group (never mind the ethical concerns). A common technique in these cases is for the experimental group subjects to recruit a friend or family member of approximately the same age to serve as the corresponding control group subject (Hurd, 1989) Clearly there is a selection bias: the control group does not suffer from sleep apnea. But given no better alternative, the researcher must use this design, keeping its shortcomings in mind when interpreting the results of the study.

INTERACTION OF SELECTION WITH OTHER THREATS TO INTERNAL VALIDITY

An interaction of selection with another extraneous variable can occur because the comparison groups are not equivalent and consequently the extraneous variable may affect one group, but not the other. For example, an interaction of selection with history might occur when an event unrelated to the study affects the performance of one group but not the performance of the other (or not to the same extent). Imagine that a researcher is investigating anxiety levels in children and uses a classroom of children in a separate school district as a control group. If a thunderstorm strikes one school district but not the other, there may be different levels of anxiety between the groups because of the storm and not necessarily because of any intervention by the researcher.

Selection can interact with other extraneous variables, too, such as maturation, instrumentation, or regression toward the mean. When these interactions do occur, they can wreak havoc on the interpretations of the results because they cause changes in behavior that are either consistent with or counter to the expected results, and the researcher can never be sure whether the results are exclusively a function of the change in the independent variable or are a function of the interaction of selection with some extraneous variable.

Using a quasi-experimental design is not ideal. But a person doing research on applied topics or in applied settings may often find that a quasi-experimental design is as close to a true experimental design as can be achieved. By carefully considering potential pitfalls and confounds, the researcher can choose a quasi-experimental design that makes the best of a less-then-perfect situation to provide useful and interesting results. Table 10.2 summarizes the various threats to internal validity discussed in this section and the designs that might be used to control for each threat. Of course, choosing a design is only one part of the research procedure; another important part involves the statistical treatment of the collected data.

TABLE 10.2   *Summary of threats to the internal validity of a quasi-experimental study, and designs that may control for them.*

Threat to Internal Validity	Quasi-Experimental Design That May Control It
History effects	time-series nonequivalent control group multiple time-series
Maturation effects	nonequivalent control group multiple time-series
Testing effects	nonequivalent control group multiple time-series
Subject mortality	no control—must watch for
Selection bias	time-series
Interaction of selection with other threats to internal validty	time series
Regression toward the mean	no quasi-experimental control
Instrumentation effects	nonequivalent control group multiple time-series

STATISTICAL TREATMENT OF DATA FROM QUASI-EXPERIMENTAL DESIGNS

The data provided by quasi-experimental designs can be analyzed by using various statistical techniques already discussed in this book. The research question, the type of data collected, and the organization of those data determine which technique or techniques are most appropriate.

Introduced earlier in this chapter was the pretest/posttest with a nonequivalent control group design. This design involves using two independent variables: time (pretest/posttest) and assignment group (experimental/control). A researcher might take a number of approaches in analyzing these scores.

If the dependent measure is measured on an interval or ratio scale and the sample scores on this measure are thought to come from a population of normally distributed scores, analysis of variance would be an appropriate statistical technique to consider. Because the time variable is a within-subjects variable, and group assignment is a between-subjects variable, the appropriate analysis would be a two-way (2 × 2) ANOVA. Do you recall the number of effects this analysis will yield information about? It will yield information about the time effect, the group effect, and the time × group interaction.

Since the subjects in the control group are not truly equivalent to the subjects in the experimental group, the researcher may not be interested in the interaction information. For example, knowing that the pattern of memory improvements among a sample of treated sleep apnea patients from pretest to posttest differs from that for a sample of normal controls may not be especially useful. Sometimes, a researcher will transform the pretest and posttest scores into **change scores**, by subtracting the pretest score from the posttest score. Now, there is only one score (the change score for each subject) and only one independent variable in the study (the assignment group factor). An independent samples *t*-test, or repeated measures ANOVA, can be calculated if the data meet the assumptions for that test. A Wilcoxon's rank-sum test, Mann-Whitney *U*, or Kruskal-Wallis can be done if a nonparametric test is more appropriate. These tests will tell the researcher if the change is significantly greater in one group than in the other.

Sometimes the nonequivalent control group is chosen in such a way that subjects are matched with members of the treatment group. For example, a situation was described earlier in which sleep apnea patients were asked to find a friend or family member of the same age and gender to participate in the control group. Now each member of the sleep apnea group is matched with a member of the control group on age and gender. To compare groups when subjects are matched, a correlated-samples *t*-test, or a Wilcoxon's *T* would be appropriate. If this group effect is part of an ANOVA—such as when comparing the groups with each other at pretest and posttest—then the group factor and the time factor would both be within-subject factors, and a two-way repeated-measures ANOVA might be the appropriate statistical technique to employ.

In other research situations, a χ^2 analysis might be the appropriate test for analyzing data. Imagine a situation in which a researcher asks an equal number of children in two classes whether or not they are afraid of snakes. One class then visits a reptile exhibit. The children once again report whether they fear snakes. Here, the researcher could use a χ^2 test of independence on the data to determine whether visiting the reptile house is likely to have affected the children's fear of snakes.

Another quasi-experimental design discussed earlier was the multiple time-series design, in which an experimental and a nonequivalent control group are compared over a number of pretest and posttest measurements. Again, the researcher has some options. If the number of observations is small enough not to be unwieldy, each measurement might be considered as a separate level of the time variable, and the researcher might be able to conduct a $2 \times k$ analysis of variance with one between-subjects factor and one within-subjects factor, where k is the number of levels within the time factor. Thus, if six measurements were made—three pretests and three posttests—the researcher would conduct a 2×6 ANOVA with time and group as factors. This analysis would yield information about changes across time, changes between groups, and whether any time effect is consistent across the two groups.

One problem with using a two-way ANOVA in which each measurement serves as a level of the time factor is that there may be so much information that the results become difficult to interpret. For instance, the researcher might find a significant difference between the first testing and the third testing (which were both pretests), as well as between the fourth and fifth testings (which were conducted after treatment was introduced). Sorting out all the differences among the testing means can get complicated.

An alternative to comparing all of the testing times with each other is to average across the pretest measures and across the posttest measures for each subject so that, instead of having a score for each measurement, each subject has only two scores: a mean pretest score and a mean posttest score. These mean scores may then be used as the data points in a 2×2 ANOVA with a time factor and a group factor. This data transformation may yield more interpretable results, but at the cost of a loss of information about the specific scores when the data are transformed.

When only one sample of subjects is measured, several times pretest and several times posttest, a time-series design has been used. If the data meet the assumptions for inferential statistics, a one-way repeated measures ANOVA (in which each measurement serves as a level of the time factor) can be conducted. This technique will yield information about differences between and among the testing times. In addition, the data can be transformed as described for the multiple time-series design: finding a mean pretest and a mean posttest score for each subject, and then (in this case) conducting a correlated-samples *t*-test. The results of this analysis will indicate whether there is a general difference between the pretest and posttest scores; but information and sensitivity are lost with the transformation. Thus it may not always be the best analysis to conduct.

This discussion only scratches the surface of appropriate statistical techniques to use with data from a quasi-experimental design. As with any design, the type of data collected and the questions the researcher is trying to answer determine the appropriate statistics to use. Is the question about the degree of relationship between two variables? Then a correlation should be calculated. Does the researcher want to see whether obtained data about the frequency of some event after treatment, such as infant mortality, are consistent with pretest frequencies? Then a χ^2 goodness-of-fit test might be needed. The researcher shouldn't wait until the data have been collected to think about what statistics to use, either; many a set of worthless data has been collected that simply couldn't be analyzed because data analysis hadn't been considered during the planning stage of the project.

CRITIQUING QUASI-EXPERIMENTAL DESIGNS

Quasi-experimental designs are quite common in the research literature because so much of psychological research is applied research, where true experimental designs cannot be conducted. In addition, because the results of applied research are often immediately applicable to everyday situations, the results of quasi-experimental designs are often publicized by the media. Therefore, it is important that the results be interpreted accurately.

Some quasi-experimental designs involve comparing a sample of subjects in one group with a sample of subjects in a nonequivalent control group. Because subjects are not randomly assigned to these conditions, one cannot be very optimistic that the groups are equivalent. Since they are nonequivalent at the outset, any differences between the groups on a dependent measure may be the result either of the independent variable or of some unknown difference between the groups. This difference between the groups must be considered as the conclusions are drawn. What criteria were used to determine that the control group was comparable to the treatment group? Were the subjects matched on any particular variables? In some cases, the control group may be quite comparable, and the threat of selection bias to the studies' internal validity will not be a substantial concern. In others, the bias may be strong and impossible to avoid; consequently, it must be considered in interpreting the results.

Other quasi-experimental designs involve only one sample of subjects tested numerous times. The primary criticism of this design is that we have no evidence that the experimental group is behaving any differently than a control group would, if one had been tested. The greater the number of testing situations, however, and the clearer the change in scores between pre-treatment testing and post-treatment testing, the greater is the likelihood that the treatment did affect the dependent measure.

In all designs—quasi-experimental, pre-experimental, or true experimental—a careful consideration of the design includes identifying possible confounds and constructing alternative explanations for the results. A reader must consider the potential threats to the internal validity of a study and decide for himself or herself whether these threats were adequately controlled. Pre-experimental designs are replete with threats to their internal validity, and the best a reviewer of such studies can do is to try to determine whether the evidence for an effect is strong enough to be worthy of further study. Carefully constructed studies based on quasi-experimental designs can provide information that is as important as the results of well-done experimental studies, and they may be interpreted with nearly as much confidence in the results.

Even in a well-designed research project, the data may be analyzed inappropriately, yielding misleading results. This may be the case when inferential statistics are used in situations where nonparametric statistics are more appropriate. Another possibility involves the misuse of χ^2 tests. Remember, χ^2 analyses require independent observations; thus, they should not be used on data in which each subject has supplied more than one observation.

Because quasi-experimental designs lend themselves to inferential analyses, there is also a risk that a researcher will interpret the results of the inferential statistics as automatically indicating a causal relationship—as the results in a true experiment might. Remember that the type of analysis does not determine whether results may be interpreted causally or as correlations; rather, this determination must be based on the type of design and the quality of controls.

Because efforts are constantly being made to apply knowledge grounded in psychology to the real world, quasi-experimental designs play an important role in research. When such designs are carefully structured and carried out, threats to internal validity can be minimized and important relationships and effects can be revealed. But as with all research designs, caution must be taken so that results are not interpreted inaccurately and so that the results of shoddy research are not given more credence than they deserve.

IMPORTANT TERMS AND CONCEPTS

true experimental designs

quasi-experimental designs

pre-experimental designs

nonequivalent control groups

multiple comparisons of a single group (time-series designs)

multiple time-series design

history effects

maturation effects

testing effects

instrumentation effects

regression toward the mean

subject mortality

selection bias

interaction of selection with other threats to internal validity

change scores

QUESTIONS AND EXERCISES

1. You hear on the news about a research project examining the effectiveness of a children's in-school health program. The researchers compared the number of absences during the school year prior to installation of the program with the number of absences during the school year after the program was installed.

   a. Would you categorize this design as a true experimental, a pre-experimental, or a quasi-experimental design?

   b. Suppose that the researchers found that absences decreased for the year after the health program was established. What conclusions could they come to, if any? What alternative hypotheses may explain the results, if any?

   c. What threats to internal validity are most likely present in this study?

   d. How might you improve this study?

2. In the psychology department of Smarter U., statistics is taught in one of two ways. One course is a standard lecture and discussion course; the other is self-paced/self-taught, involving a series of assignments and tests. You wish to compare these two course formats. Because you have begun this project in the middle of the semester, your only option this term is to present each class with the same exam at the end of the course and compare those scores.

   a. Is this a quasi-experimental, a true experimental, or a pre-experimental design?

   b. What possible statistical analyses are appropriate for testing your hypothesis? (Suggest both parametric and nonparametric types.) What conclusions, if any, would you be able to draw from the results of your analyses? What alternative explanations are there, and what threat(s) to internal validity may be involved?

   c. If you have access to these two courses next semester, too, how might you design your investigation to control for some or all threats to the internal validity of the first approach?

   d. Assuming that the research technique for part c were adopted, what data would be collected, and what analyses (parametric and nonparametric) would be appropriate?

3. One frequent and irritating side-effect of allergies is general fatigue. An allergist asks for your assistance in assessing whether desensitization treatment results in a decrease in fatigue. Desensitization involves injections on (often) a biweekly or monthly schedule over the course of one or more years, and the results are usually cumulative (that is, the patient shows increasing improvement over time).

   a. Describe a one-group-tested-twice pre-experimental design that could be used to test this question, and suggest some alternative explanations for any results it produces.

   b. Describe a one-group time-series design, and explain how it would be superior to the pre-experimental design.

   c. Describe a multiple time-series design, and explain its advantages over the other two designs.

4. A shop owner wants to assess the effectiveness of a shoplifting prevention system that involves using undercover floor-watchers. The shop owner estimates the amount of inventory (in dollars) lost to shoplifters during the month prior to the use of floor-watchers, and compares this with the amount of inventory shoplifted under the new system.

   a. What type of design is being used?

   b. How might the shop owner analyze the data collected for this study?

   c. What potential confounds are there, if any?

   d. What conclusions would you draw from this study?

5. A major corporation moves its headquarters and factory from a small city. Approximately 10% of the city's population worked for this corporation. You wish to assess the effect of this corporation's move on home sales and home prices in the city.

a. You wish to use a multiple time-series design to assess the effect of the move on home prices. You have access to the median home prices calculated for the last two years at six-month intervals for this city and for a city of comparable size and comparable median income. You will have access to this information for future six-month periods, too. How would you design this study? What analysis would you intend to do?

b. You have access to information about the number of home sales for the last two years, calculated every month, in this city (but not in the comparable city). You will continue to have access to this information during the next two years. What kind of study would you design now? What data would you collect, and how would you analyze it?

II

Single-Subject Designs

Until now, our focus has been on research involving groups of subjects. Research on groups is a **nomothetic** approach to research; this approach attempts to identify general laws and principles of behavior. But research on groups is not always the best approach to a problem. Sometimes the answer to a research question deals not with what the average person does in a situation, but with how a particular person acts or reacts. When the focus of research is on the behavior of the individual, the research approach is called **idiographic**. Idiographic approaches generally attempt to identify patterns of behavior within a single individual. Research designed to study an individual's behavior still needs to be planned carefully, with an eye toward objectivity and interpretability. This chapter will focus on the single-subject research design, how it is conducted, its advantages, and its disadvantages.

Single-subject designs are not identical to case studies, although both involve studying the behavior of a single subject. **Case studies** are descriptions of an individual and that person's experiences, but they do not involve any systematic observation of the subject's behavior. Case studies may be very objective or very subjective, and they can utilize a number of methodological techniques: naturalistic observation, surveys, interviews, or archival information (records, letters, private papers, and so on.). Case studies, however, do not typically entail systematic observations of behavior on the basis of experimental designs, as do single-subject designs.

Single-subject designs also focus on a single individual (or at most, a few individuals), but they bring with them the rigors and objectivity of the scientific method in attempting to determine the effect of an independent variable on some dependent variable. The single-subject design has been used in basic research as well as in applied settings, and it is one of the oldest research approaches in the field of psychology.

Wilhelm Wundt, the man most often credited with establishing the first psychological laboratory, studied consciousness through a method known as **introspection**. Introspection involved studying the responses of a single subject to a number of stimuli. In 1860 (actually before Wundt's lab was established), Gustav Fechner published work in psychophysics (the study of our experience of physical stimuli). This research also involved testing one subject (or a very few) repeatedly. Here, for example, a blindfolded subject might be touched on the back with two dull points that are separated by given intervals. The intervals varied randomly, and the subject was asked to report whether he or she felt one or two points. Based on his results with single subjects, Fechner was able to determine the distance at which two distinct points become noticeable to the subject: the **just noticeable difference** or **JND**. Fechner was also one of the first behavioral scientists to use statistics in interpretating his results. He noticed that the same subject's JND would vary from session to session. By applying functions related to the normal curve, he was able to demonstrate that the JNDs varied normally around a mean (Hersen & Barlow, 1976).

Ivan Pavlov's (1928) work, which made a tremendous contribution to the scientific development of classical conditioning, was based primarily on the behavior of one dog, and then established more firmly through replication of the results with other dogs. Another famous researcher, Hermann Ebbinghaus, also utilized the single-subject design. Ebbinghaus (1913) investigated learning and forgetting by having his subject memorize and recall long lists of nonsense syllables. His work yielded the now-famous forgetting curve, which indicates that most forgetting occurs soon after learning. Ebbinghaus's single subject was himself.

With the introduction of statistical methods such as those provided by Karl Pearson, Sir Francis Galton, and Sir Ronald A. Fisher, researchers came into possession of the tools they needed to determine whether it was likely that a particular behavior occurred by chance. In addition, Fisher's advances in conceptualizing induction and inference allowed researchers to generalize their results beyond the limit of their sample. These statistical advances made group research even more meaningful, and this type of research became the standard.

During the first half of the twentieth century, group comparison research took hold in psychology, and by the 1950s, outside of psychophysics, it was virtually impossible to publish research based on a single subject. An important exception to this was provided by B. F. Skinner, whose extensive work on operant conditioning was done by using only one organism at a time and then replicating the results with a few more to demonstrate generalizability. However, to maneuver around psychology's bias against single-subject designs, Skinner and his colleagues established the *Journal of the Experimental Analysis of Behavior*, which specialized in publishing research based on single subjects.

For a number of reasons, the hold that group comparison designs has had on psychology has loosened during the last 40 years. This is especially true in applied research, where group comparison methods present a number of problems.

One problem with group comparison research relates to the ethical concerns of clinicians who wish to assess the effectiveness of a treatment. A group comparison typically involves withholding treatment from a clinical control group. This concern is somewhat paradoxical. Withholding treatment is only unethical if the treatment is known to be effective; but of course, if the treatment is known to be effective, it need not be tested. On the other hand, if the treatment is not known to be effective, withholding it is not unethical. Yet many clinicians and others are very uncomfortable with the idea of withholding any potentially effective treatment from someone who is suffering. So whether or not the argument is rationally sound, it carries considerable emotional weight (Hersen & Barlow, 1976).

Another limitation of group comparisons in applied settings involves the practical problems of identifying and soliciting the cooperation of a large enough sample (Hersen & Barlow, 1976). A researcher who is interested in autism must identify and secure participation of a minimum of 20 autistic subjects to conduct a meaningful group comparison study. Unless the researcher has access to an institution that specially serves autistic individuals, it may take years to collect the relevant data.

Several practitioners of applied research (e.g., Sidman, 1960) have criticized the practice of averaging across subjects, as is done in group comparison data. The argument is that (a) averages hide any nonrandom variance caused by an uncontrolled factor, and (b) they provide a measurement that more often than not fails to represent the actual behavior of any of the participants. An example of an applied research project may make these concerns clearer.

Imagine that a researcher examines two sample groups of phobics; one receives a new treatment, while the other group consists of subjects in the no-treatment control condition. The results suggest that no significant differences exist between the groups, since the average performance of the treatment group, following treatment, is no better than the average performance of the control group. Or to put it another way, the variance between the two groups is not significantly greater than the variance within each group. A closer look at the performance of the individuals involved, however, may provide us with a different picture.

It may be that no significant difference registered, not because the treatment didn't have any effect, but because the effects it had actually canceled each other out; that is, perhaps some of the subjects in the treatment condition improved substantially while others got markedly worse. Why might this happen? Although all of the subjects in the study are phobics, they still differ on innumerable other qualities. Some of the subjects may have been coerced into therapy but did not really want to change; some may have more deeply ingrained phobias than others; some may have additional mental disorders that control the subjects' behaviors moreso than the phobias, etc., etc., etc. In other words, if we limit ourselves to using group comparison, these individual differences will not be addressed, and the effectiveness of the therapy will be based on an average derived from a rather diverse population.

Related to averaging performances is a second consideration. Even if a significant difference is noted between comparison groups, a clinician reading the study cannot determine which patient characteristics were associated with improvement, because the individual differences among the subjects are not addressed. Which subjects showed the greatest improvement? What characteristics did these people have? Group data do not describe the individual subject, rendering it difficult to make use of the results in an applied setting.

An advantage of the single-subject design is that it can determine the effectiveness of a treatment for a specific individual; and replications of that study on similar patients can help determine the generalizability of the treatment. Single-subject designs in applied research are not typically designed to identify general laws and principles of behavior or to identify a treatment that is effective for a broad range of clients. However, single-subject designs used in basic research certainly are capable of revealing general patterns of behavior, as we see in Skinner's work on learning theory and Ebbinghaus's forgetting curve.

TYPES OF SINGLE-SUBJECT DESIGNS

BASELINE MEASURES

The primary purpose behind a single-subject design is to compare post-intervention behavior with a baseline measurement of that behavior. A **baseline** is a measurement of the dependent variable taken when the independent variable has yet to be manipulated. Typically, a baseline measurement is taken before the intervention of the independent variable. In some designs, other baseline measures of the variable of interest are taken during the study; alternatively, baseline measures of several differ-

FIGURE II.I *Graphs representing a stable baseline (a) and a variable baseline (b).*

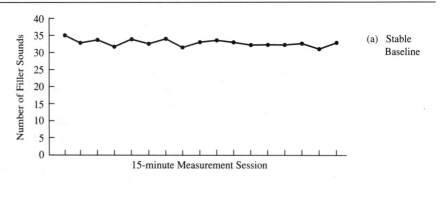

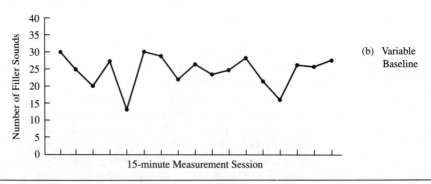

FIGURE II.2   *Beginning of a graph of baseline and treatment scores in which the*
treatment appears to have had a significant effect.

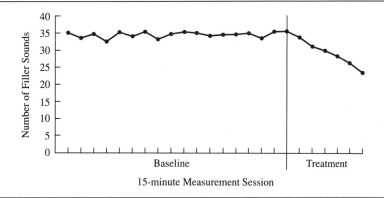

ent behaviors may be taken. When behavior during treatment is compared with
baseline measures taken at times when treatment is not being conducted, the researcher may be able to ascertain whether the treatment is having any effect.

For a difference to be detectable between baseline and intervention measurements, we must establish a stable baseline—that is, a baseline measurement with
relatively little variability. Imagine that a researcher wants to develop a technique to
improve a speaker's verbal presentation. If the researcher were to measure the
number of times a person uses filler phrases and sounds, such as "uh" and "you
know" during a series of 15-minute conversations, several different patterns of
baselines might occur. The baseline presented in Figure 11.1(a) represents a stable
baseline, with little variability across the testing sessions. This is the ideal situation;
if the intervention causes a change in the number of filler sounds, the difference will
be readily apparent, as demonstrated in Figure 11.2. This figure, however, constitutes only a portion of a larger graph; usually, single-subject designs include more
than two phases.

Another possible pattern for a baseline involves considerable variability among
the data (see Figure 11.1(b)). This would occur in our example if the participant
exhibited a widely variable number of filler sounds from one conversation to
another. This is a difficult situation to deal with, because it is much harder to ascertain under these conditions whether a treatment is having an effect. One possible
solution is to continue taking baseline measurements until some stability becomes
evident in the baseline. This sounds easy enough, but it postpones intervention and
extends the duration of the study; and of course, there is no guarantee that the
baseline will ever stabilize.

A second solution involves determining the sources of the variability and controlling these. For example, perhaps the number of times the participant uses filler
sounds varies because the level of anxiety varies from conversation to conversation.
The baseline can be made more stable by holding the anxiety level constant, such as
by making measurements when the person is speaking to a group of 5 to 10 people.
Controlling the variability of the baseline by controlling the sources of the variance,

however, is easier in the laboratory setting of the basic researcher than in applied research.

Still other patterns of baselines are less than ideal and complicate the interpretation of the results. For a fuller description of these problems, consult Barlow & Hersen (1984) or Hersen & Barlow (1976). In addition, statistical techniques exist for comparing a variable baseline to the data from the treatment phases of the study. Again, Barlow & Hersen (1984) and Hersen & Barlow (1976) present possible solutions that are worth considering if a statistical solution is necessary.

SINGLE-SUBJECT TIME-SERIES DESIGNS

You may recall that time-series designs were introduced in relation to quasi-experimental designs. They refer to the class of research designs in which several measurements are made before and after the independent variable is introduced. Many single-subject designs amount to variations on the time-series design.

One of the most common single-subject designs is the **withdrawal design**, which compares a series of baseline measurements to measurements taken after the intervention is introduced. Next, the intervention is withdrawn, and measurements are continued. Intervention is then reintroduced, and further measurements are made. This pattern of intervention and withdrawal may be repeated several times so that the researcher can be certain that the intervention—and not some other, uncontrolled variable—is causing the behavior change. The phases of the study during which no intervention is presented are referred to as **A** phases, and those in which intervention is introduced are called **B** phases. Thus, when a research design consists of baseline (A), followed by the intervention (B), followed by withdrawal (A), followed by renewed intervention (B), the design is referred to as an **ABAB design**.

Perhaps an elementary teacher has a difficult student who talks to and distracts the other students too much in class. The teacher wishes to reduce this disruptive behavior, and the school psychologist suggests an intervention as well as a withdrawal design to test whether the intervention worked or whether the student's behavior changed on its own. The teacher is instructed first to observe and document the child's behavior—in other words, to obtain baseline measures. The teacher notes for one week how often the child distracts the other students each day. This is the A phase. The intervention is then begun. The child is given a sticker for every hour when the child behaves well (for children of the student's age, stickers are inherently reinforcing). The intervention continues for a week; this is the B phase. The teacher is pleased, since the intervention appears to be working; but children also mature quickly, and perhaps this child is simply learning not to distract others. To test whether the effect is caused by maturation or by the sticker intervention, the teacher withdraws the intervention. The teacher does not give the student stickers for good behavior during the next week (the second A phase). As one would expect if the intervention were the cause of the behavior change, the behavior begins to decline and approach baseline levels. The purpose of this whole project was to reduce this child's bad behavior; so the intervention is reintroduced (the second B phase), and again the bad behavior decreases (see Figure 11.3 for a graph of these results).

FIGURE II.3   *Results of an ABAB withdrawal design in which good classroom behavior is reinforced during treatment.*

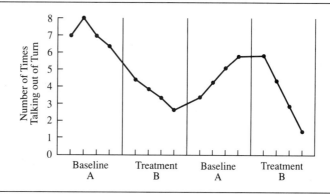

There are many ways to vary the ABAB design. For example, additional withdrawal and intervention phases can be introduced to strengthen the results. Or a second intervention could be introduced, which we will call C. Thus, an ABAC design consists of introducing B after the baseline A is established, then returning to baseline A, and finally introducing C.

A variation of the withdrawal design allows a researcher to test for possible placebo effects. A **placebo effect** occurs when the behavior being studied changes, not because of the particular intervention, but because there was *any* intervention. The presence of a placebo effect can be confirmed when a behavior change is apparent after the introduction of an intervention that is known to be ineffectual. For example, if a patient reports relief from headaches after taking a certain pill and that pill is made of an inert substance, the headache relief is due to a placebo effect. Placebo effects reflect a real, but ususally temporary, change in behavior due to the act of intervention itself.

An ABCB design can be used to assess the effect of a real intervention compared with a placebo condition. After the baseline A is established, the B intervention is introduced, followed by the C placebo condition (a condition involving a non-effectual intervention); this is followed by the B intervention once more. If the effect of the B intervention on the behavior is primarily a function of a placebo effect, there will not be much change between either B phase and the C phase. However, if the B phase behavior is really caused by the intervention and not by a placebo effect, a change to the C phase should trigger a return to behavior that approximates baseline behavior.

REVERSAL DESIGN

The ABAB design is described as a **withdrawal design** because the intervention is withdrawn from the situation. A different approach, called a **reversal design**, involves replacement of the intervention. A reversal design is established by introducing a new and opposite intervention. For example, perhaps two siblings play aggressively with each other, and the parents wish to increase cooperative play between them. A reversal design can be used to assess the effectiveness of an intervention that increases cooperative play. In addition, the reversal design can also be used to assess whether the same intervention might increase the unwanted behavior.

Perhaps a consultant suggests that the children play aggressively because they receive parental attention (albeit negative) when the play is aggressive. The parents are presented with a reversal design that will enable them to test this hypothesis and to assess the effectiveness of an intervention to increase cooperative play between the siblings.

The first phase consists of measuring a baseline of cooperative play; perhaps the number of minutes of cooperative play is recorded during an hour of play each day for four days. During the next phase, the intervention is introduced. Let's assume that the intervention involves ignoring aggressive play and offering adult attention during cooperative play. During the third phase in a withdrawal design, the intervention is withdrawn, and the behavior is observed to see whether it reverts to the baseline level. In the reversal design, however, the intervention is not simply withdrawn; it is replaced by an opposite intervention. Thus, in the third phase of this assessment, the parents would attend to aggressive play and ignore cooperative play. If attention is a mediating factor that can increase either aggressive or cooperative play, then cooperative play should increase during the second phase of the study and should decrease during the third phase. Since the point of the treatment here is to increase cooperative play, a final reversal is needed to leave the children and parents in the condition in which cooperative play receives attention. A graph representing the hypothetical results of this investigation is shown in Figure 11.4.

Reversal designs are not as common as withdrawal designs in areas of applied research such as behavior modification, since situations calling for a true reversal of treatment are rather uncommon (Kratochwill, 1978). However, they can be very

FIGURE II.4 *Results of a reversal design in which the effect of attention on cooperative and aggressive play is assessed.*

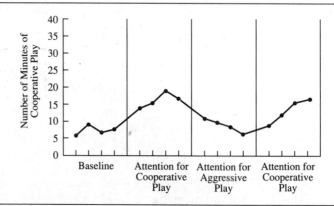

useful in basic laboratory research in assessing the causes and the reversibility of changes in behavior.

ALTERNATING-TREATMENTS DESIGN

A useful technique in both applied research and basic research is a single-subject technique for assessing and comparing the effectiveness of two or more treatments; the **alternating treatments design**, also called the **between–series design**. The alternating treatments design is a variation of the ABAB design that does not require a baseline (although it may be included) and that presents two (or more) treatments to the participant instead of only one. In this design, the first and second treatments may be introduced randomly to the participant, or they may be introduced systematically, with one treatment presented for a given time period followed by the other.

Let's consider an example of an alternating treatments design. Suppose that a researcher wants to assess the relative effectiveness of two techniques for decreasing nail-biting behavior. One technique might involve putting hot pepper on the nails; another might be to have the participant sit on the hands for two minutes whenever the participant realizes he or she has been nail-biting. The researcher observes and records the number of times the fingernails are put up to the mouth. (We wouldn't want to measure duration because the duration of nail-biting when hot pepper has been applied to the nails would be rather short.) Each day the participant opens an envelope that reveals which technique is to be used that day. If the techniques are assigned randomly, there may be many days in a row of one technique or only one day of the technique. The data for the two techniques are graphed together, and a presentation of these hypothetical data is presented in Figure 11.5. According to this graph, although both techniques resulted in decreased nailbiting, the hand-sitting technique appears to have been the more effective.

FIGURE II.5   *Example of results of an alternating-treatments design.*

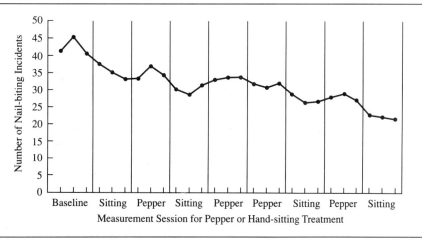

MULTIPLE-BASELINES DESIGN

The single-subject designs described heretofore are all based on the assumption that, at least over the short run of a single phase of an ABAB design, the effects of the treatment are short-lived and that withdrawal of the treatment will result in behaviors' reverting to their baseline levels. This is not true of all treatments, however, nor is it always appropriate to withdraw an effective treatment, even temporarily. In these situations, another technique might be used: the **multiple-baselines design**.

The multiple-baselines single-subject design involves assessing the effect of a treatment on a behavior across two or more situations, or assessing the effect of a treatment on two or more behaviors. Let's first consider affecting a behavior across two or more situations.

Suppose that a person wishes to stop smoking. One approach might be to try to stop smoking in each of several different situations, such as at home in the morning, at work, and at home in the evening. A reinforcement program might be developed in which, for every hour without a cigarette, the person is given 10 points; at the end of the week the points might translate into something desirable to the person, such as a certain amount of money per point or permission to purchase some item, given enough cigarette points.

Initially, baseline measures are taken for the three settings. Intervention is then introduced with respect to one of the settings, such as the "at home in the morning" setting, and baseline measuring is continued for the other settings. After a predetermined number of recording sessions, the intervention is added to the second setting—say, the "at work" setting; baseline measurements continue for the "at home in the evening" setting. Finally, intervention is added to the third setting. Figure 11.6 presents a graph of these hypothetical data.

FIGURE II.6   *Graphs of results of a multiple-baselines design where three settings are compared.*

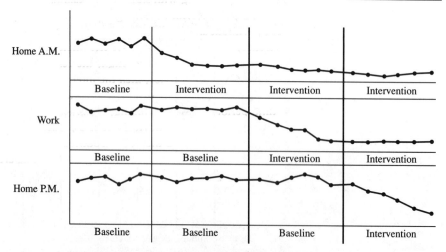

Units of measurement are number of cigarettes (vertical axes).
Six measurements are taken per phase.

FIGURE II.7   *Graphs of sample data for a multiple-baselines design where three behaviors are treated.*

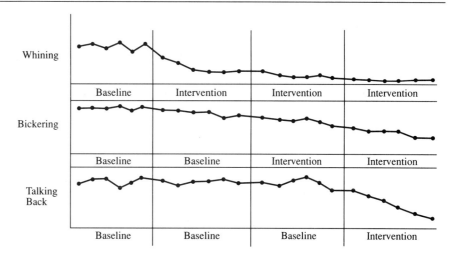

Units of measurement are number of periods without the behavior.
Six measurements are taken per phase.

The multiple-baselines approach offers a more appropriate way to assess the cigarette reduction intervention than would be provided by a withdrawal or reversal design, since one wouldn't want to reinstitute smoking at baseline levels once it had been reduced.

The other way in which the multiple-baselines design might be used is to measure the effect of the intervention on different behaviors. For this example, imagine that a parent wishes to reduce various annoying behaviors a child exhibits, such as whining, bickering with siblings, and talking back to the parent. The parent might install a point system according to which for every day or half-day period that goes by without an incident, a certain number of points are awarded, and these points can subsequently be traded in for television privileges.

To use the multiple-baselines design, the researcher must first make baseline measures of each target behavior; then the intervention is introduced for one of the behaviors. In our example, the parent might treat the whining behavior first, reinforcing time periods without whining; meanwhile baseline measurements would continue for the other two behaviors. After a predetermined number of recording sessions, the treatment would then be introduced to the second behavior—perhaps bickering with siblings. Now both bickering and whining are being treated but the baseline is still being measured for talking back. Finally, talking back is added to the treatment regime. Sample data are presented in Figure 11.7 for this example.

CHANGING CRITERION DESIGN

The last single-subject design that will be introduced here resembles the multiple-baselines design in that it avoids withdrawing treatment. This design is used to assess an intervention when the criterion for that intervention is routinely changed. For

FIGURE II.8   *Graph of results for a changing criterion design.*

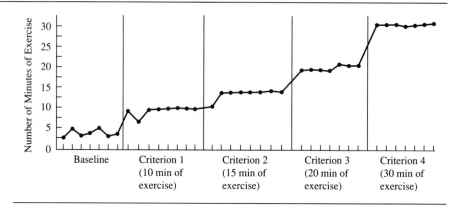

example, imagine that a person wishes to begin a successful exercise program. **A changing criterion design** could be installed to assess the effectiveness of the intervention and, assuming that it is effective, to increase the criterion for the behavior as time progresses. The person might agree to give himself or herself a $2 bonus for every day he or she exercises for 10 minutes. After this criterion has been met for the duration of some preset period of time—say, two weeks—the criterion is increased; now the individual must exercise for 15 minutes per day to earn the $2. Once more, when the criterion has been met for two weeks, it can again be increased, perhaps to 20 minutes per day. This is repeated until the criterion matches the goal for the behavior, which may be to exercise 30 minutes per day. Figure 11.8 presents a graph of data that might be generated by a changing criterion design.

Single-subject designs are useful in both basic research and applied research. But not all research situations are alike, so choosing the appropriate design is important; even then, modifications may be necessary so that the study will yield interpretable results. An important (and often the most challenging) part of a researcher's task is to foresee problems and alternative explanations for the results so that a design that incorporates serious confounds can be avoided. In the following section, some common threats to the internal validity of a single-subject design will be reviewed.

THREATS TO THE INTERNAL VALIDITY OF SINGLE-SUBJECT DESIGNS

In the last chapter, several threats to the internal validity of quasi-experimental designs were discussed. Unfortunately, many of these same factors can also influence the results of single-subject designs.

HISTORY EFFECTS

History effects are a potential problem whenever time elapses between testing times. The probability that some event will covary with treatment decreases as the number of testing times increases and as the number of instances of withdrawal to baseline increases. For example, a behavior change that occurs in an AB design (baseline followed by an intervention) is confounded by history effects because the change may be due to the introduction of the intervention or because of some separate event that co-occurred with the intervention. However, if the intervention is withdrawn and behavior returns to baseline, and then a change is again observed with the reintroduction of the intervention (an ABAB design), the probability that an external event caused all of the behavior changes is rather small.

MATURATION EFFECTS

Another potential threat to the internal validity of a single-subject study is the role of **maturation** on the subject's behavior. A child who shows improvement in classroom behavior after some intervention is introduced may be showing signs of maturation, as opposed to (or in addition to) a response to the intervention. A withdrawal design (reverting to baseline) or multiple-baselines design can be used to test this hypothesis; but, before the experimenter can design a study to test for it, she or he must foresee maturation as a potential confound.

INSTRUMENTATION, TESTING, FATIGUE, AND PRACTICE EFFECTS

Instrumentation effects, as you may recall, occur when a change in measurements is caused by the changing sensitivity and/or accuracy of the measuring tool after repeated use. For example, a scale may become less accurate after extensive use and may need to be recalibrated. **Testing effects** are manifested as improved test scores over the course of repeated testing, primarily because the participant becomes more familiar with the test, understands the tasks involved, and knows what to expect. Consistent increases or decreases across testing situations could be a function of testing effects, instrumentation effects, or (conceivably) both. Similarly, increases or decreases across time could be a function of **fatigue effects** or **practice effects**; this is more likely if testing occurs repeatedly during a short period of time, as more frequently occurs in a laboratory setting. For example, in a situation where a rat's bar-pressing responses are being monitored, the rat's rate of bar pressing it might increase because of practice; or conversely, it might decrease due to fatigue.

SUBJECT BIAS AND DEMAND CHARACTERISTICS

In studies involving human participants, **subject bias** and **demand characteristics** pose a serious threat to result interpretation. Adults, in particular, are likely to be aware that they are involved in the assessment of an intervention; ethical consider-ations probably demand that they be so informed. In an applied setting, the adult may even have instigated that intervention by requesting assistance in changing some behavior. The participant, then, fully expects that his or her behavior will change. The challenge for the researcher is to design the study in such a way as to be able to distinguish behavior changes caused by demand characteristics and subject bias from behavior changes caused specifically by the intervention. An ABCB design that tests for a placebo effect may provide a practicable solution, as might a multiple-baselines design in which intervention is applied systematically to two or more behaviors or in two or more settings. If the baseline measures of the untreated behaviors or settings show a change comparable to the treated situation, subject bias and demand characteristics may be playing a significant role.

EXPERIMENTER BIAS

Finally, the role of the experimenter must be considered when the results of a single-subject design are being interpreted. Experimenters can affect the results of their studies purposely, of course, but more commonly their influence is unintentional. Therefore, it is essential that recording measures be designed to be as objective as possible, ideally to be conducted mechanically or by individuals who are unfamiliar with the design of the study. Only then can the results be relatively free from **experimenter bias**.

All of the preceding threats to the internal validity of a single-subject design are only the beginning. Every design includes some risk from one or more of these threats, but not every situation is equally susceptible to them. The researcher can't use a formula to decide which design to use in which situation; instead he or she must carefully consider the setting, the participant, the behavior being studied, and the time involved, among other factors, in order to anticipate potential confounds. For many researchers, that's half of the fun.

STATISTICAL ANALYSIS OF SINGLE-SUBJECT DESIGNS

First the good news for those of you who are valiantly learning statistical techniques, but have yet to fall in love with them: statistical analyses in single-subject designs are not always necessary. Often the investigator need only "eyeball" the data—that is, graph the results and look for evidence of changes in behavior. If a stable baseline was achieved and behavior clearly changed with each introduction and withdrawal of the intervention, statistical analysis is not needed to demonstrate that the independent variable had an effect. In fact, there is some controversy over using statistical analyses in idiographic research, since the function of statistics is to generalize beyond the given sample of data, whereas the function of idiographic research is to study the individual's behavior.

Statistical analyses do have a legitimate role in single-subject research. When the baseline is not ideal, statistical analyses may reveal a consistent difference between study phases that a simple eyeballing of the data can't reveal. Some researchers have advocated the use of ANOVA and other inferential procedures to analyze the data provided by single-subject designs (e.g., Gentile, Roden & Klein, 1972). Others have argued strongly against the practice (e.g., Levin, Marascuilo & Hubert, 1978).

Inferential statistics such as ANOVA and regression assume not only that the scores are normally distributed and that variances are homogeneous among groups, but also that the error among the data is uncorrelated; that is, the part of the data that is unrelated to the independent variable must also be unrelated to each other from observation to observation. This is a hard row to hoe when all of the data are provided by a single subject.

A technique called **autocorrelation** can be used to determine whether the errors are correlated. Autocorrelation involves correlating each score with the one immediately following it. Thus, if the values in a set of scores were 1, 3, 6, 4, 5, 8, 2, and 9, the scores would be set up as follows to conduct the autocorrelation:

X_1	X_2
1	3
3	6
6	4
4	5
5	8
8	2
2	9

A correlation coefficient is then calculated by using Pearson's r. This correlation coefficient is assessed for its reliability by comparing it with a critical value for r, which can be found in Table r of Appendix B. If the obtained correlation does not exceed the critical value, it is not significant and we may assume that the errors are uncorrelated. If this is the case, inferential statistics such as t-tests and ANOVA may be conducted. However, other commentators have noted that, to avoid increasing the probability of making a Type I error (quick, which one is this?—it is the error of finding a difference when none exists), a researcher should collect 50 to 100 data points per *phase* of the study. This may not be possible in some investigations.

Statistical techniques other than inferential statistics have also been suggested. For instance, a statistic called C has been proposed by Tryon (1982). The C-statistic can be converted into a z-score so that significance can be determined. Levin, Marascuilo & Hubert (1978) have proposed the use of nonparametric techniques to determine the generalizability of the results of single-subject studies.

If the differences between baseline and intervention phases are not readily obvious from a visual inspection of the data, or if it is important to generalize the results beyond the present study, statistical analysis may be useful. If a researcher plans to analyze the results statistically, efforts can be made to increase the likelihood that inferential statistics can be applied. For example, the study can be designed so that 50 to 100 observations are made per phase; and by maximizing the time between observations, the researcher can reduce the likelihood of the errors' being correlated (Levin, Marascuilo & Hubert, 1978).

CRITIQUE OF SINGLE-SUBJECT DESIGNS

Single-subject designs are often used in applied research. In clinically related research, their focus is typically to assess the effectiveness of an intervention. Single-subject designs are also prevalent in basic laboratory research, especially where the task of testing subjects is labor-intensive, or where the focus is idiographic as opposed to nomothetic.

There are several types of single-subject designs, and some of these control particular threats to internal validity better than do others. A critical review of a single-subject investigation should include a determination of whether the design chosen adequately controlled the most likely threats to internal validity. For example, are history effects a possible explanation for the observed results, or could the results be a function of a placebo effect? Ideally, a researcher foresees and mitigates the major threats to internal validity when designing an investigation, but some sneak by or don't appear until too late.

Most single-subject designs involve comparing baseline measures to measures taken during the intervention stage. A reviewer should consider the stability of the baseline measurements. Are the measures fairly stable or are they highly variable? If they were initially quite variable, did baseline measurements continue until they stabilized? Does the baseline tend to increase or decrease over time? If so, how does this compare with the intervention data? Ideally, the baseline is consistent and stable over time so that differences between baseline and intervention measures are readily apparent. Stable baselines don't always happen on their own, unfortunately, especially in applied research.

When the difference between baseline and intervention measures is not readily apparent, or when the researcher wishes to substantiate visual inspection in order to increase the generalizability of the results, statistical analyses might be conducted. ANOVA and *t*-tests are commonly used to analyze single-subject data, but they should only be used when the autocorrelation among the data is nonsignificant and (perhaps) when 50 to 100 data points have been made per phase of the study. Other statistical techniques, such as using the *C*-statistic or nonparametric randomization tests might be also be adopted to assess trends in the data.

Finally, regardless of how the results were obtained, do you agree with the conclusions that were drawn? When reading a research report, whether it is based on single-subject or group designs, you should try to develop your own interpretation of the results prior to reading the author's discussion. If your conclusions differ from the author's, a closer examination is needed of both your logic and the author's logic. If your conclusions agree, you probably have a good grasp of the researcher's project and reasoning. Thinking through the problem for yourself will yield a clearer understanding of the research and its results than you could obtain by passively reading about the study.

Idiographic research takes a different approach from the one we have become familiar with in our discussions of group designs. Idiographic research acknowledges individual differences and does not attempt to average across these differences, as occurs in nomothetic research. The focus of single-subject designs is often on determining the effectiveness of an intervention for a given participant, with less focus on how generalizable those results are to the population. Nonetheless, the results, especially those of basic laboratory research, are often highly generalizeable. The contributions of single-subject designs to knowledge in psychology should not be underestimated; as one of the oldest approaches to data collection, this type of design has provided the foundation for much of our present-day research.

IMPORTANT TERMS AND CONCEPTS

nomothetic research

idiographic research

case studies

single-subject designs

introspection

just noticeable difference (JND)

baseline

ABAB design (withdrawal design)

placebo effect

reversal design

alternating treatments design (between-series design)

multiple baselines design

changing criterion design

history effects

maturation

instrumentation effects

testing effects

fatigue/practice effects

subject bias

demand characteristics

experimenter bias

autocorrelation

QUESTIONS AND EXERCISES

1. A friend of yours wishes to stop smoking. You realize that he wouldn't want to chew gum at the same time as he smoked a cigarette, so you consider proposing a gum-chewing intervention.
   a. Develop the outline for a study that uses a withdrawal design. Determine for how long and in what manner the baseline would be measured, as well as the duration of measurements during each other phase of the study.
   b. Graph hypothetical data to represent the results you would expect.

2. Another person, impressed by your success in helping your friend stop smoking, says that, not only does she wish to stop smoking, but she also wants to stop drinking coffee.
   a. Develop the outline for an assessment study that uses a multiple-baselines design. Determine for how long and in what manner behaviors would be measured during each phase of the study.
   b. Graph hypothetical data representing the results you would expect.

3. A year later your friend asks for your help to kick an annoying gum-chewing habit. You suggest a changing criterion design.

   a. Develop the outline for an assessment study that uses a changing criterion design. Determine the criteria and the intervention for this particular study.
   b. Graph hypothetical data representing the results you would expect.

4. A relative insists that caffeine makes him drowsy.
   a. Use an ABCB design to assess this claim, using coffee in the B phases and decaffinated coffee as the placebo. Determine the manner of measurement and the duration of each phase of the study.
   b. Graph hypothetical data that suggest a placebo effect.
   c. Graph hypothetical data that suggest that caffeine truly does cause this person to become drowsy.

5. When your cat wants a special treat he meows loudly. The meow is annoying, and you suspect that you have unwittingly been reinforcing it by feeding the cat treats when he meows. You wish to try a reversal design to test whether reinforcing another behavior will change the signal for a special treat to something less offensive, such as rubbing against your leg.

a. Design a reversal design to test the effectiveness of the treats as a reinforcer. Determine the duration and the manner of measuring behaviors during each phase of the study.

b. Graph hypothetical results of your study.

6. One article you have read suggests that a hot bath before going to bed will lead to a good night's sleep; another article recommends a glass of warm milk.

a. Design an alternating treatments study to assess the effectiveness of these two approaches. Determine the measurements you will make and the duration of each phase of the study, as well as whether you will alternate treatments randomly or systematically.

b. Graph hypothetical data representing the results you would expect.

12

Physical Traces and Archival Data Collection: Nonreactive Measurement Techniques

A fire inspector walks through what remains of a burned house. By observing whether windows are broken or melted, the inspector can determine where the fire was hottest; by noticing the amount of burning on the floor, the inspector can reconstruct the manner in which the fire spread, and by noting which rooms were more heavily damaged by smoke than by fire, the inspector can determine the room in which the fire originated (Krajick, 1979, as cited in Webb et al., 1981). Fire inspectors, police detectives, and private investigators are often depicted as inferring the behaviors of suspects on the basis of physical evidence left at the scene. Researchers do the same.

Researchers can infer much about people's behavior not only by directly observing that behavior, but also by inspecting the physical evidence left as a result of the behavior. Which animals at the zoo receive the most attention from visitors? Perhaps the wear on the railings around the enclosure can provide the answer. Which automatic teller machines receive the most use in town? A quick count of receipts left behind may provide the answer. When physical evidence is assessed in the absence of the individuals who did the behaving, the researcher is using a **physical trace measure**.

Physical trace measures are **nonreactive measures**: the act of acquiring the measures has no effect on the behavior, because the behavior has already occurred. Physical trace studies are not the only way to acquire nonreactive measures, however. **Archival data** studies involve assessing records (written and otherwise) as a way to make inferences about behaviors, attitudes, beliefs, and so on. In this chapter we will discuss both physical trace and archival data studies, including their advantages and shortcomings, the types of data they provide, some statistical approaches to those data, and various ethical concerns that might arise as a result of using these types of investigations.

PHYSICAL TRACES

Physical trace studies involve studying physical evidence left in the course of the subjects' behavior. This evidence is typically assigned to one of two categories: traces and products. **Traces** are evidence left as a by-product of the behavior, while **products** are items created as end products by the subjects. It's not difficult to imagine anthropologists and sociologists relying on evidence from products to draw inferences about a society. As with any categorical system, however, this one is somewhat arbitrary and contains gray areas where categorization may be difficult. For example, is graffitti a trace or a product? There is no clear distinction. While many psychologists study products, traces are more often the focus of a psychologist's investigation.

TRACES

Traces can be categorized further as accretion measures or erosion measures. **Accretion measures** are based on the accumulation of evidence as a result of some behavior. Examples of accretion measures might included litter as an indication of where people congregate, dirt on doorframes as an indication of the relative age (as related to height) of people entering a room, graffitti on walls as an indication of primary topics of societal concern, and trash in garbage cans as an indication of level of liquor consumption. **Erosion measures** are based on the wearing away of material as a result of some behavior. Examples of erosion measures might include signs of disproportionate wear on carpets or lawns to indicate the usual route of traffic, wear patterns on shoes to determine whether people walk straight or lean to one side or the other, and frequency with which certain light bulbs must be replaced to indicate which rooms are used most often.

Accretion and erosion measures of physical traces can in turn be categorized as either natural or controlled. **Natural trace measures** are based on effects that occur without researcher intervention. For example, the wear on the carpet in a home occurs without the researcher's installing especially cheap carpet in advance. However, should the researcher install carpet that does wear especially easily, the resulting measure would be a **controlled trace measure**. Controlled trace measures involve researcher intervention. For example, if pens were provided to encourage graffiti on a specific wall so that the researcher could assess the content of that graffiti, this would be a controlled trace measure. (Would it be an erosion measure or an accretion measure?)

CONCEPT QUESTIONS 12.1

Categorize each of the following as an accretion measure or an erosion measures.

a. Evidence of explosives on a bombing suspect's hands.

b. Whether or not the binding of a textbook has been broken, indicating whether it had been opened.

c. The amount of litter left after a festival.

d. The number of beer cans in the garbage from selected homes.

e. The amount of newspaper recycled by people participating in a curbside recycling program.

f. Indication of where men carry their wallets, by the wear in the pockets of their jeans.

PRODUCTS

Products differ from traces in physical trace studies in that they are the purposeful creations of individuals. Psychologists and other social science researchers may infer behavior and attitudes from these products as well as from trace information. The number of computer files on a person's computer might provide an estimate of that individual's computer literacy. The number of articles published by college professors might provide an estimate of their scholarly productivity.

Researchers might consider the number of letters submitted to the newspaper editor on a specific topic as an estimate of attitudes toward the issue. Here again is an example of the gray areas between distinct categories. While one person might consider this evidence a physical trace product, another would refer to it as archival data—a written record. We will discuss archival data (and by association, written products) in the second half of this chapter.

The major advantage of physical trace measures is that researchers' monitoring of them has no bearing on the behavior of the subjects. This nonreactivity is very appealing. But a number of drawbacks are associated with using this method, and these prevent it from being the most popular research approach.

DRAWBACKS OF PHYSICAL TRACE STUDIES

Regardless of whether the physical trace measures in a particular case are traces or products, accretions or erosion measures, controlled or natural, an important concern about them involves the validity of the trace as an indicator of the focus behavior. For example, if a researcher was using posters and graffitti as indicators of racial attitudes, it is possible that some of the information presented in these forms was intended not to promote the views expressed but to instigate a dialogue, as occurred at one college (*Chronicle of Higher Education*, 1993), or that a great many posters and letters to the newspaper editor were submitted by one zealot, as has occurred on my own campus. Thus, a researcher could come away with an overestimation of the prevalence of racist attitudes on a campus, based on this particular measurement.

Relatedly, not all traces are equally durable. A good-quality tile floor is likely to show less wear than a poor-quality carpet. To suggest that more people walk on the carpet because it is more worn than the tile would be to risk a Type I error. Similarly, some subgroups of a population may be more or less likely to exhibit a specific behavior and thus may vary in this likelihood of providing a trace. For instance, a researcher might estimate attendance at a glassed-in exhibit by the number of nose prints on the glass; children, however, are probably more likely to leave noseprints than are adults. If the question is whether more children or adults visit the exhibit, the data gathered with this measure may be misleading.

The question of the validity of physical trace measures is directly related to two concepts: the **selective survival** and the **selective deposit** of the physical traces.

Selective survival refers to the notion that some trace or product evidence may not endure over time. Archeologists are faced with the extreme effects of time. Researchers of Mexican cultures have found an abundance of clay sealing stamps used in writing. Since stamps of other materials have not been found, one might be tempted to assume that all stamps were made of clay. However, it could also be that those made of other materials (such as bone or wood) have disintegrated, and that those made of metals have been melted down (Webb et al., 1981).

Selective deposit refers to the unrepresentative occurrence of traces in all situations or by all participants. Again, not all surfaces show wear equally, and not all subjects behave the same. An error in interpretation may occur when trace results are assumed to be more representative then they really are.

Because physical trace evidence is assessed after the behavior has occurred, it is not possible to infer much about the actors. A smudge on the glass indicates that something rubbed against the glass, but whether it was a child's nose or the finger of an adult passerby may not be determinable at this point. These challenges to the validity of physical trace measures are of significant concern. For this reason, physical trace measures are often combined with other research approaches, such as direct observation. If the findings of a physical trace measure are backed by the results of direct observation, the data from each study lends validity to the other.

ETHICAL CONCERNS

Depending on the physical trace being assessed, some ethical considerations may need to be assessed before the researcher undertakes the task. This is primarily an issue when the physical traces might identify the person responsible for the behavior.

A number of research projects have involved sorting through people's garbage to find evidence supporting various hypotheses. Several court decisions have stated that once an item is in the garbage, the original owners can no longer claim it as their property; instead, the items are in the public domain. But while this may legally free the researcher to conduct the research, the potential for ethical dilemmas still exists. The risk to the people producing the garbage is that personal, sensitive information may become available to the researchers, including information implicating the persons in a crime. Researchers should try to hammer out a policy regarding this type of information before they are confronted with an actual instance of the situation (Webb et al., 1981).

There may also be threats to the welfare of researchers who conduct certain types of physical trace studies. One researcher who has conducted extensive garbage studies in Tucson arranges for workers to sign consent forms, receive tetanus shots, and wear lab coats, gloves, and masks to limit the researcher's liability and to protect the workers' health (Webb et al., 1981). Other research may not be as threatening to the researchers' health, but may jeopardize their reputations. Often students suggest checking car locks as an indicator of how safe a neighborhood is perceived to be.

The problem is that researchers checking car locks might find themselves mistaken for individuals with less honorable motives.

The persons who provide physical traces typically are not aware that their traces are being evaluated. The evidence collected may be damaging, embarassing, or incriminating, or the data collection itself may put the researcher and assistants at some risk. The ethical ramifications of the study need to be considered carefully before data collection begins and weighed against the potential value of the research results.

ANALYZING PHYSICAL TRACE DATA

Physical trace studies lend themselves well to the collection of frequency data, as well as to the development of such other types of data as ratings on the degree of some characteristic. The particular manner in which data should be analyzed depends on the type of data collected, its level of measurement, whether it meets the assumptions for parametric tests, and (most important) what question the researcher wants to answer. Let's consider an example of a physical trace study and determine how the data from it might best be analyzed.

Because smoking is banned in classrooms and in administration buildings on my campus, many people stand outside the buildings to smoke cigarettes, resulting in numerous cigarette butts being littered on the ground. This physical trace could serve as a source of information to answer a number of questions.

One such question might be whether an editorial about how shoddy it looks to have cigarette butts littering the ground outside campus buildings has any effect on the number of cigarette butts left there. This question gives us an opportunity to combine physical trace data collection with a time series design. Data might be collected for several consecutive days before the editorial is printed and then for several consecutive days after the editorial.

Assume that we have collected the data in Table 12.1 during the week before and the week after an editorial is published criticizing cigarette butt littering. How might it be analyzed?

A first approach to these data might be to create a graph to illustrate the results. Sketch out a graph for yourself; does there appear to be a decrease in the daily number of cigarette butts littered between the pre-editorial and post-editorial measurements? A graph of these data is presented in Figure 12.1.

TABLE 12.1 *Hypothetical data on number of cigarette butts left on the ground for a week before and a week after a newspaper editorial on the subject.*

Measurement Period	Monday	Tuesday	Wednesday	Thursday	Friday
Pre-editorial	178	134	167	145	162
Post-editorial	102	97	84	83	86

FIGURE I2.I   *Graph of the number of cigarette butts littered daily before and after the publication of an editorial against cigarette butt litter.*

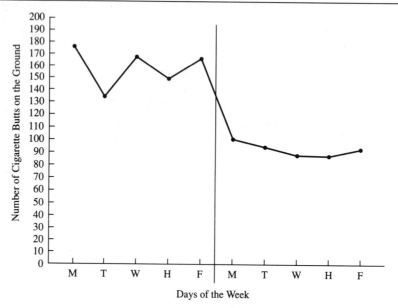

Days of the Week

Editorial appeared in school paper Friday after that day's data had been collected.

A statistical test of our hypothesis would add strength to our conclusions. The question we are trying to answer is whether the editorial affected the number of cigarette butts left on the ground. In other words, did the number of cigarette butts littered daily after the editorial differ from the number of butts littered daily before the editorial? Can you think of one or more statistical techniques that could be used to test this hypothesis?

An inferential test that might be appropriate is the independent samples *t*-test. It tests the difference between the means of two independent samples. To enable us to use this approach, our data should meet the assumptions for an inferential test: the measurements should be made on an interval or ratio scale of measurement; the samples should have a homogeneous variance; the scores of the population should be normally distributed; and the scores should be independent of each other. The data for daily number of cigarette butts have been collected on a ratio scale. The variances, however, are rather different ($s_1^2 = 309.7$; $s_2^2 = 73.3$). The *F*-ratio of these variances with $n_1 - 1$ and $n_2 - 1$ degrees of freedom is not significant, suggesting that we *could* calculate *t* without worrying too much about heterogeneity of variance. However, I'm less confident about the independence of the measures. There are only a finite number of smokers on campus, and the chances are pretty good that any given smoker provided more than one cigarette butt on any given day. Therefore, the number of cigarette butts noted on the first Monday may be related to the number of butts found on that Wednesday, because some of the same people may

TABLE 12.2 *Wilcoxon's rank-sum test calculations for comparing the number of cigarette butts left during the week before the editorial to the number left during the following week.*

Ranks	Pre-editorial Measures	Post-editorial Measures	Ranks
10	178	102	5
6	134	97	4
9	167	84	2
7	145	83	1
8	162	86	3
40			15

$W_{obt} = 15$ $W_{cv}(\text{at } \alpha = .025) = 19$

have left them. To avoid using the *t*-test inappropriately, we should probably resort to a nonparametric alternative.

In Chapter 6 we discussed a nonparametric test that could be used to compare data from two samples: the Wilcoxon's rank-sum test. This test is not restricted by assumptions of independence among the scores or homogeneity of variance. The calculations are provided in Table 12.2, but if you are still unclear about how the test is conducted, you should review the section on the Wilcoxon's rank-sum test in Chapter 6.

According to the results of the Wilcoxon's rank-sum test, we should reject the null hypothesis. (Remember that, with this test, the obtained value must be smaller than the critical value to allow us to reject the H_0.) There is a significant difference in the number of cigarettes left each day before the editorial and each day afterward, with more cigarette butts left before the editorial was printed. Although a significant difference has been found, this does not necessarily mean that the editorial was responsible for the decrease in the number of cigarette butts; however, the evidence we have found is consistent with that hypothesis.

Physical trace studies can be implemented in a number of ways. They can be designed as time-series designs, as comparisons between two or more groups, as single-*n* designs, or in various other ways. The variety of designs is limited only by researchers' imaginations. As we have seen, each design has its advantages and disadvantages, as do physical trace studies themselves. These need to be considered as the study is being designed to ensure that the results are interpretable. Relatedly, how the researcher intends to assess the data should also be determined before data collection so that, if statistical analyses are to be employed, they will be used properly. With a little forethought, physical trace studies can be an important addition to a researcher's toolbox.

ARCHIVAL DATA INVESTIGATIONS

Archival data studies are another versatile type of nonreactive study. Archival data studies are the use of written or otherwise preserved records to investigate behavior. A very rough categorization of archives is to group them as continuous records or discontinuous records. **Continuous** or **running records** are maintained and added to on a routine basis. Income tax reports, the sales records for a shop, the U.S. census, and a diary are just some examples of continuous records. **Discontinuous records** are produced less regularly or only once. Books, newspaper articles, letters to the editor, and letters to friends are all examples of discontinuous records.

Another manner in which archival data soures can be categorized is as either records or documents. Lincoln (1980, as cited in Webb et al., 1981) defines **records** as a written statement presented to provide an account or to attest to an event. Thus, records are produced for the primary consumption of another. In contrast, Lincoln defines **documents** as written or filmed material that (a) are not records, and (b) weren't created in response to some task or request framed by the investigator. Thus, documents are considered to be more personal than records. They were produced primarily for the benefit of the producer, not to provide a more public account of something. Records are created under the assumption that someone, someday, will read the material. My journal is a document; this book is a record. Although the distinction between archives meant for public consumption and those meant for private consumption is an important one to keep in mind, for ease of communication the term *record* will be used in this chapter to refer to both records and documents.

Glance through a newspaper, a magazine, or a library. The wealth of archival sources is awe-inspiring. And the number of questions that can be addressed is infinite. Do women in Peoria marry earlier or later than women in Portland, Maine? How do *Time* and *Newsweek* differ in their presentation of a news event? Does the number of fires in a city increase after a major fire has received extensive news coverage? Do more females than males have their pictures published in the yearbook? Are more babies born in one season than in the others? Is the full moon related to crime and other deviant behavior? Did the institution of a car insurance law affect the cost of insurance premiums? Which professors have the best reputations, and why? Is there a relationship between age or socioeconomic status and vanity license plates? The questions are endless. They can range from the silly to the sophisticated, from the simple to the complicated, but in our information-conscious world—someplace—the information is sitting in an archive waiting to be tapped.

CONCERNS

Because archives are prepared by people other than the researcher, and because the preparers do not know that a particular line of research will ever be conducted, the review and recording of material from archives is nonreactive. The collecting of the data by the researcher thus has no bearing on the information they contain. However, this does not mean that the information collected constitutes a valid representation of the behavior being studied. Archival data suffer from two of the same problems that plague physical trace data: selective deposit and selective survival.

Why do people commit suicide? An archival approach to this question might be to assess the content of suicide notes. An immediate concern, however, is that fewer than 25% of all persons who commit suicide leave notes (Webb et al., 1981). Thus, the notes may not accurately represent the feelings of all suicide victims.

Similarly, an assessment of college professors' lecture notes may not provide an accurate measure of class preparedness, since some professors pride themselves on not working from notes.

Selective deposit of archival data occurs when the records that are maintained do not fairly represent the relevant population. Whether selective deposit is a problem in a particular area of research is not always immediately knowable and may require some additional inquiries. For example, examining letters to the editor of area newspapers may appear to be an excellent way to get a feel for area attitudes toward political questions, community concerns, racism, and so on. However, some editorial boards have different policies than others. Some boards strive for a balance of perspectives, regardless of the proportions of letters received. Others only publish one letter per author per month. Still other papers publish all letters. In addition to a newspaper's publishing policies, its editing policies must be considered. Letters to the editor may or may not be be edited, and whether this occurs is again a function of policy and available space.

Other information in the newspaper is also subject to policies, although these policies may not necessarily be the newspaper's. A local hospital will give the newspaper all of the names of newborns and the babies' parents names, unless the parent is a single mother. In the latter case, the information is made public only upon the request of the mother, who probably has other things on her mind.

Just because information becomes part of an archive, that does not mean that it will remain part of the archive forever. Thus selective survival must also be considered by archival researchers. When data are missing from a running record, the researcher needs to ask why. Was there a fire? Was there a flood? Were documents shredded? Why are these particular data points missing? Do the missing data reflect random destruction or a bias of some type? For example, genealogical or historical research may be hampered because families destroyed the military records of family members who served as mercenaries during the Civil War, a role that some see as less than honorable. Or a study of love letters collected from a sample of individuals may overrepresent present relationships and/or positive relationships. The letters from former lovers with whom the supplier had an argument may have been destroyed in a fit of pique, or letters from earlier loves may have been discarded to protect the feelings of the present attachment.

Archival information, even that presented for public consumption, does not always constitute a wholly accurate representation of information. Biases can occur in the most reputable archival record sources, and documents prepared for private use are sure to reflect the personal beliefs of the creator. Of course, the inherent biases themselves can be food for research.

Etaugh (1980) reviewed the seven most popular women's magazines in America published from 1956 to 1977. From these, she identified nonfiction articles dealing with nonmaternal childcare. Childcare books published during that 20-year period were also reviewed. The contents of these books and articles were coded for their expressed attitude toward nonmaternal childcare. Etaugh found that, in the 1950s and 1960s, the attitudes expressed in the popular press toward nonmaternal childcare were by-and-large negative; but during the 1970s, a shift occurred, and the attitudes became much more favorable. Etaugh postulated that this pattern may have reflected the lag between the emergence of new results of scientific research and the assimilation of these results by popular writers. Further evidence for this hypothesis comes from the finding that the childcare books, which take longer to prepare and publish, expressed more negative attitudes on the subject than did the shorter-production magazine articles.

Interestingly, Etaugh, Carlson & Williams (1992) conducted a sequel to Etaugh's original research, coding articles from women's magazines published in the years from 1977 to 1990 on their attitudes toward nonmaternal childcare. Since 1977 there has been an increase in the number of articles with mixed or negative attitudes. During this same time period, the scientific community has also expressed conflicting opinions regarding nonmaternal childcare, and the researchers suspect that this trend reflects the changing attitude of the scientific community.

The research by Etaugh (1980) and by Etaugh, Carlson & Williams (1992) represents an example of archival research that studies the biases present in those archives. This is not to suggest that the authors of the articles and childcare books held irrational beliefs, but to emphasize that their attitudes are a reflection of the attitudes of their times. As Etaugh points out, those attitudes may be based in part on the scientific information that was available.

As long as archival information is the product of human record-keeping, biases will exist. Biases can be caused by attitudes, of course, or they can be introduced into the archives by error. Errors may be introduced into the archive by the producer of the record or document; the data collector may make errors when recording the information from the original archive; a change in a record-keeping system may make archival information noncomparable; error may be introduced by changing definitions and criteria during the course of record-keeping. A little error here and a little error there can add up to a lot of errors. An archival data researcher must remain conscious of the fact that, just because an archive exists, there is no guarantee that its contents provide an accurate repesentation of reality (Lincoln, 1980, as cited in Webb et al., 1981).

ETHICAL CONSIDERATIONS

A final set of decisions regarding archival research must be made with regard to ethical considerations. When archival research is conducted on the basis of huge sets of anonymous records, issues of privacy and confidentiality are probably of little concern. But working with smaller sets of records, or cross-referencing sets of records, may lead to ethical questions.

In *Academe*, the monthly magazine of the American Association of University Professors, the average salaries of males, females, assistant professors, associate professors, full professors, and so on are provided annually for colleges and universities across the country. A quick perusal of this listing will reveal that some spots are blank. In some cases this is because the information was not available. But in other cases it is to protect the privacy of the one or two people who fall in a particular category at a particular private college. If you are one of two female full professors at a college and you know your salary, it doesn't take too much mathematical finesse to calculate your colleague's salary from a published mean.

Researchers who cross-reference archives may also find themselves in an ethical bind. They may learn information about people that the people would never have given consent for. A cross-reference of those who voted in Republican and Democratic primaries with a mailing list for an adult bookstore, for example, may provide interesting information about the relative numbers of Republicans and Democrats who are on this particular mailing list, but it may also violate the privacy of those on the lists.

Typically, archival research is ethically innocuous, but that does not mean that all instances of archival research are. Each researcher must take into account the particulars of his or her project and consider any anonymity, confidentiality, privacy, and informed consent issues that might be relevant.

Several areas of concern exist for an archival researcher, but archival research can be rewarding nonetheless. Often the sources of information are sound and the researcher can have confidence in its objectivity. But even when the validity of the data cannot be ascertained completely, archival research can be an important addition to a research program that uses a multimethod approach. When archival data supports or is supported by laboratory research, observational studies, surveys, or other research approaches, faith in the veracity of those reports is strengthened.

ARCHIVAL DATA ANALYSIS

The ease of gathering archival data is countered by the frequently cumbersome job of analyzing it. Even when the archives are designed in a well-organized manner, they typically contain more information than the researcher needs. Thus, some procedure for identifying, coding, and recording the necessary information must be devised.

Because the original records are produced for purposes other than the researcher's, archival material often requires content analysis before it can be used to provide answers to the research question. **Content analysis** is a coding system designed and used by the researcher to extract the necessary information from the archives. For example, a student researcher who worked in a college security office conducted a content analysis of parking ticket appeals. By establishing operational definitions for each code, the student was able to code each appeal as apologetic, angry, or neutral. The student researcher also noted from the files whether the appeal had been granted or denied. (What statistical technique would you use to determine whether the type of appeal is associated with the decision on it?) His results suggested that a neutral, facts-only appeal was most often associated with a positive decision. Angry appeals were least likely to be granted. (This is a rather cursory discussion of a study. What other information would you need before you would be willing to accept the results?)

To establish solid interrater reliability, a coding system for content analysis must be clearly stated and easy to use; then raters working on their own will be more likely to supply comparable ratings. The research by Etaugh (1980) and Etaugh, Carlson & Williams (1992) on attitudes toward nonmaternal child-care in the popular press required a content analysis of childcare books and articles. In the 1992 research, two raters independently categorized each article according to the author's statements about the effects of daycare and/or maternal employment on children. There were six categories: entirely negative; mostly negative, but some positive aspects mentioned; evenly balanced between positive and negative; no

Courtesy of Sidney Harris

effects; mostly positive, but some negative aspects mentioned; and entirely positive. The interrater reliability was .90, suggesting that a high level of agreement existed between the two raters even though they did not collaborate on the ratings.

Once data are coded, either via a content analysis or straight from the archives (if one is so lucky), the data must be organized meaningfully. This might involve a graphical representation, tables of descriptive statistics, or statistical analyses of the data.

Coding schemes that involve categorizing information yield nominal frequency data. Hypotheses of this type of data can typically be tested with a χ^2 test. If the coding yields ordinal data, a nonparametric test such as the Wilcoxon's rank-sum test might be appropriate. It's possible, but less likely, for archival research to supply interval or ratio data suitable for inferential statistical analysis. The appropriate statistical technique, if there is one, depends in each instance on the question being asked and the data being collected.

Planning research thoroughly, right down to the manner in which the data will be organized and analyzed, is an important part of the research process. Descriptive questions require only descriptive statistics. Ascertaining the degree of relationship between two variables calls for a correlation. Hypothesis testing demands a different approach. And of course, all depends on the level of measurement of the data and the manner in which it was collected, to determine whether it meets the assumptions of inferential and χ^2 tests.

CRITIQUE OF PHYSICAL TRACE AND ARCHIVAL DATA STUDIES

Physical trace and archival data studies have the major advantage of being nonreactive approaches to the study of behavior. Collecting these types of data has no bearing on the behaviors that they record. For this reason, the information provided by these types of designs can be especially convincing.

Unfortunately, the advantage of nonreactivity is tempered by the disadvantage that the validity of physical trace and archival data is often unknown. Selective deposit (a bias in the production of traces and archival records) and selective survival (a bias in the endurance of traces and records) are two primary sources of concern.

Researchers must also consider the ethical ramifications of their data collection and research. Because the data collection is nonreactive, individuals typically have no opportunity to provide informed consent. Most often, those who produced the physical trace or whose behavior was recorded in the archive are unknown and sometimes unknowable. In other cases, however, it may be possible to identify particular individuals and to make information public that they would not wish known. Researchers should remain conscious of privacy and anonymity concerns as they plan their research.

How the researcher chooses to organize the data will serve to highlight certain aspects of the results. If statistical techniques are implemented, their results can aid in the interpretation of the data. But statistics can also be used inappropriately, yielding misleading results.

The researcher's interpretations of the results of a research project are subject to personal bias and poor reasoning, just as anyone else's interpretations are. Because physical trace and archival data studies are correlational studies, you should be especially watchful for statements of causal relationships.

Physical trace and archival data studies have their weaknesses; and by themselves, they do not provide especially strong evidence. But in combination with other methods, physical trace and archival data studies can strengthen the credibility of research findings and increase the external reliability of those results. They are approaches to research that should not be dismissed lightly.

IMPORTANT TERMS AND CONCEPTS

physical trace measures

nonreactive measures

archival data

physical trace studies

traces

products

accretion measures

erosion measures

natural trace measures

controlled trace measures

selective survival

selective deposit

continuous records (running records)

discontinuous records

documents

records

content analysis

QUESTIONS AND EXERCISES

1. What social science questions might you be able to find answers for from these archival data sources?
   a. Obituaries in your city newspaper.
   b. Science fiction stories from the present and from the 1920s.
   c. Cookbooks.
   d. Junk mail.
   e. Television listings.
   f. Computer software documentation.

2. What physical trace measures might you use to answer questions on these topics?
   a. Political attitudes of college students.
   b. Attitudes toward poetry.
   c. Respect for private property.
   d. Compulsive tendencies among college professors.
   e. Relative importance of punctuality in various cultures.
   f. Nutrition and diet of a given population.

3. Two raters categorized song lyrics for the top 100 songs of one week in 1993 and for the same week in 1983 as having the following themes: sexual, violent, love, or other.
   a. The raters independently rated each song and agree 186 times. What is their inter-rater reliability? (See Chapter 2 for a refresher on interrater reliability.)
   b. The researchers wish to determine whether the number of songs per category differs between these two years. What statistical technique would you suggest they use?
   c. The researchers' data are presented next. Conduct the statistical test you proposed on these figures.

Year	Sexual	Violent	Love	Other
1983	12	5	49	30
1993	18	9	34	39

4. A researcher is interested in what nights different types of television shows are shown during primetime (8 P.M.–10 P.M. Central Time). Television shows were categorized as: sit-coms, drama series, movies, and other (including news shows and documentaries). The following data are the number of shows of each type broadcast each day, tabulated from the television program listings for the three major networks for six weeks.

Day	Sit-com	Drama	Movie	Other
Saturday	7	8	0	6
Sunday	0	6	0	7
Monday	8	6	0	6
Tuesday	7	6	7	6
Wednesday	7	7	6	6
Thursday	6	6	6	6
Friday	7	0	6	7

   a. Draw a graph that depicts the numbers of the different types of shows.
   b. How, statistically, could you answer the question: Are all four types of shows represented equivalently? Conduct the statistical test you proposed.
   c. How, statistically, could you answer the question: Is there an association between type of show and night of the week? Conduct the statistical test you proposed.

5. How would you determine whether photographs of women are as prevalent in your local newspaper as are photographs of men? Relatedly, how would you judge whether the photographs of women make them appear as professional as men? Design your own archival data study to address these questions. Determine the type of data you would collect, any coding schemes you would need, and the operational definitions for the codes. How would you analyze your data? What is your hypothesis about the results? Using your design, collect your data and conduct the statistical tests you proposed. Did your results support your hypothesis?

Probability

We encounter and use probabilities every day, often without noticing them. In the more obvious cases, the weather report states the chance of rain, the political analyst predicts an election winner, Jimmy the Greek provides odds on a football game. But we also encounter probabilities when we take a medication to relieve symptoms, when we buy a new refrigerator, or when we decide to sell our old car to buy a new one. The odds (based on previous research) are that the medication will relieve our symptoms. The results of quality-control work predict that we will buy a functional refrigerator. We are betting that the cost of a new car will be less than the cost of constantly repairing the old car. Probabilities in research are important in hypothesis testing; we reject the null hypothesis if there is a 5% or smaller chance of making a Type I error. In this appendix, I will introduce some basic concepts and rules of probability to serve as a basis for understanding probability in statistics. These rules and concepts, however, are also generalizable beyond research and statistics, and you may enjoy determining the probabilities of various outcomes in your own life.

Probability is the ratio of the number of favorable occurrences to the number of all possible occurrences. So, for example, if there are 35 people in a class, and 17 of them are males, the probability of randomly choosing a male from the class on one draw is 17/35 or .4857. If we referred to choosing a male as A, then $P(A) = .4857$. $P(A)$ is read as "the probability of choosing A." In more general terms, this can be described as:

$$P(A) = \frac{\text{Number of events favorable to } A}{\text{Total number of possible events}}$$

The probability of choosing a female from the class is the same as the probability of *not* choosing a male, and this could be denoted as $P(\overline{A})$—the probability of *not* A. $P(\overline{A}) = 18/35 = .5143$. Notice that the $P(A) + P(\overline{A}) = 1.00$. Probabilities range

FIGURE **A.I**   *Sample space for a single six-sided die.*

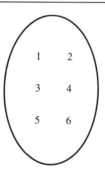

from .00 to 1.00, where .00 means that there is no chance that a particular event will occur, and 1.00 means that the event is certain to occur.

Imagine that you have a single standard die with six sides. If you roll that die, one of six sets of dots will face upward. Each roll of the die is a single event and can be referred to as a **sample point**; the set of all possible sample points is called the **sample space**. The sample space for a single die is presented in Figure A.1. Determining probabilities entails determining the proportion of sample points in the sample space that are favorable to a specific outcome. So, if we wished to determine the probability of rolling an even number, we would begin by identifying the favorable events (2, 4, and 6). The ratio of favorable events to total events is the same as the proportion of sample points in the sample space that are favorable to a specific outcome. In this case, the proportion is .50. Thus, the probability is .50. What is the probability of rolling a number that begins with the letter *t*? [The answer is at the end of this appendix.]

COMPOUND EVENTS

What if we wanted to determine the probability of rolling a number beginning with letter *f or* the letter *t*? We are now combining the probability of two different occurrences into one probability; this is called a **compound event**. In Figure A.2 the sample space is represented with the appropriate sample points for each occurrence circled. The probability of rolling a number beginning with *f* (a four or a five) is

$$P(f) = 2/6 = .3333$$

The probability of rolling number beginning with *t* (a two or a three) is the same: $P(t) = .3333$.

Notice that the two subsets of the sample space do not overlap; in other words, these events are mutually exclusive. **Mutually exclusive** events are entirely independent of each other and belong to only one category. In our example, each of the numbers on the die can belong to only one of three categories: beginning with the

FIGURE A.2   *Sample space for the outcomes of a single die, with the numbers beginning with f and t circled.*

letter *f*, beginning with the letter *t*, or beginning with some other letter. Since a number can only begin with one letter, the events are mutually exclusive.

THE ADDITIVE RULE

To combine the probabilities of mutually exclusive events, we simply add the probabilities for each separate event together. This is known as the **addition rule for mutually exclusive events**. Expressed mathematically, the probability of rolling a number beginning with either the letter *f* or the letter *t* is as follows:

$$P(f \text{ or } t) = P(f) + P(t)$$
$$= .3333 + .3333$$
$$= .6667$$

What if the events are not mutually exclusive? For example, what if we want to determine the probability of rolling an even number *or* a number beginning with the letter *t*? Because the number two belongs to both categories, they are not mutually exclusive. This is represented in Figure A.3, where the two subsets overlap.

If we simply add the probabilities for each event, we will overestimate the probability of the compound event because the probability of rolling a two would be counted twice. To correct this, we simply subtract the probability of rolling a two. We can write this as follows:

$$P(t \text{ or even}) = P(t) + P(\text{even}) - p(t \text{ and even})$$

This will be calculated as:

$$P(t \text{ or even}) = P(2 \text{ or } 3) + P(2, 4, \text{ or } 6) - P(2)$$
$$= .3333 + .50 - .1667$$
$$= .6666$$

FIGURE **A.3**   *Sample space for the rolls of a single die, with the subsets of events for numbers beginning with the letter t and for even numbers identified.*

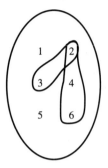

We have just used the **addition rule for nonmutually exclusive events**. This can be written more generally as:

$$P(A \text{ or } B) = P(A) + P(B) - P(A \text{ and } B)$$

Despite its name, the addition rule for nonmutually exclusive events is applicable to mutually exclusive events, too. When events A and B are mutually exclusive, the probability that A and B will occur is 0.

THE MULTIPLICATIVE RULE FOR INDEPENDENT EVENTS

The addition rule is used to determine the probability that A *or* B will occur. A different rule is used to determine the probability that both A *and* B will occur.

To understand the multiplicative rule, we must first understand the concepts of replacement and statistical independence. Let's revisit our class of 35 students (including 17 males and 18 females). Perhaps I want to know the probability of randomly choosing two males in a row. But before I can calculate this probability, I need to know something about the process being used. What I need to know is whether the first person chosen is returned to the class for a chance to be chosen again, or whether the first person chosen is kept from returning to the class. If the first person chosen is returned to the class, the arrangement is called **sampling with replacement**. Here, the sample point is replaced in the sample space, so the class has the same number of students it had for the first random choosing—as if the first choosing had not occurred. When sampling with replacement is used, the events are **statistically independent**; that is, the result of the first event has no effect on the result of the second event.

A person rolling a die twice is sampling with replacement. If a two is rolled the first time, the two nonetheless remains a possible outcome of the second roll.

To determine the probability that two events will occur when these events are statistically independent, we use the **multiplication rule for independent events**, according to which the probability of one event is multiplied by the probability of the other event to yield the probability that both events will occur. This can be written more generally as follows:

$$P(A \text{ and } B) = P(A) * P(B)$$

So, if we want the probability of choosing two males from a class of 35 students that includes 17 males, and the events are statistically independent, we can calculate this probability as:

$$P(\text{male and male}) = P(\text{male}) * P(\text{male})$$

$$= .4857 * 4857$$

$$= .2359$$

Now let's calculate the probability of rolling a single die twice and getting a six both times:

$$P(6 \text{ and } 6) = P(6) * P(6)$$

$$= .1667 * .1667$$

$$= .0228$$

Many people get confused at the distinction between the probability that two independent events will occur and the probability that a single independent event will occur. This confusion often leads to something called the **gambler's fallacy**—the notion that, because an event has not occurred for some time, the probability that it will occur increases. For example, I have three sisters and am myself female. Using the multiplication rule for independent events (because each conception is independent and unaffected by the results of the previous conception), the probability that a person will have four daughters (and no sons) is

$$P(d \text{ and } d \text{ and } d \text{ and } d) = P(d) * P(d) * P(d) * P(d)$$

$$= .50 * .50 * .50 * .50$$

$$= .0625$$

One way to think of this probability is that, in any 100 families of four children, only 6 families' children will consist of four daughters.

The gambler's fallacy rears its ugly head to confuse people when I ask what the probability is that my mother would conceive a fifth daughter. Many people assume that, because a family of four daughters is relatively rare, the probability is pretty small that the next child would be a daughter, too. After all, the probability of conceiving five daughters in a row is .50 * .50 * .50 * .50 * .50, or .03125. However, the probability for any given event is still .50; so, if my mother were to conceive a fifth child, because the events are all independent, the probability of that child's being a daughter is still .50. Still, only 3 in 100 families of five children consist of five daughters.

Should you ever visit a casino, don't fall victim to the gambler's fallacy. If the probability of winning a particular game is .25, it will remain .25 for each game you play. Therefore, even if you have lost 5 games in a row, your probability of winning the next game is unchanged. Each game is an independent event, and its probability remains constant.

THE MULTIPLICATIVE RULE FOR NONINDEPENDENT EVENTS

Sampling with replacement determines whether events are statistically independent. As you may have surmised, if replacement is not conducted, the events are non-independent. Once more, let's visit the class of 35 students (17 males and 18 females). If I choose a person and then do *not* return that person to the class, the size of the class is reduced by 1 student, and the probability of my choosing a particular event changes slightly.

Let's consider the situation where I want to know the probability of choosing a male and a female, when sampling is conducted without replacement.

If I choose twice, there are four possible outcomes: male/female, female/male, male/male, and female/female. Two of these outcomes meet the requirements for choosing a male and a female (male/female and female/male). The multiplication rule for nonindependent events is:

$$P(M \text{ and } F) = P(M) * P(F|M) \quad or \quad P(F) * P(M|F)$$

The symbol, $P(F|M)$ is read as: the probability of choosing a female, given that a male has been chosen. In our example, if a male has already been chosen and *not* been replaced, the probability of choosing a female on the next try is 18/34 or .5294. Therefore, the calculations for determining the probability of choosing a male and a female are as follows:

$$P(M \text{ and } F) = P(M) * P(F|M)$$

$$= .4857 * .5294$$

$$= .2571$$

Equivalently, we may find the probability of a successful outcome (that is, picking a female and a male), given that a female is chosen on the first try:

$$P(M \text{ and } F) = P(F) * P(M|F)$$

$$= .5143 * .50$$

$$= .2571$$

The general formula for the multiplication rule for nonindependent events is as follows:

$$P(X \text{ and } Y) = P(X) * P(Y|X)$$

$$= P(Y) * P(X|Y)$$

Knowing the multiplication rules for independent and nonindependent events and the addition rules for mutually exclusive and nonmutually exclusive events is fundamental to understanding and calculating probabilities.

QUESTIONS AND EXERCISES

1. Suppose that a population consists of 3000 people, of whom 360 are African-Americans 150 are Asian-Americans, and 303 are Hispanic Americans.
    a. What is the probability of randomly selecting an African-American from this population?
    b. What is the probability of randomly selecting an Asian-American?
    c. What is the probability of randomly selecting someone who is *not* a Hispanic American?
    d. What is the probability of randomly selecting an African-American or an Asian-American?
2. Imagine that you have a list of 100 common nouns and you wish to choose some of these words at random to use in an experiment. Of the 100 words, 85 begin with a consonant. Of these 85 words, 75 are one-syllable words and 10 are two-syllable words. Of the 15 words that begin with a vowel, 3 are two-syllable words and 12 are one-syllable words.
    a. What is the probability of your choosing a two-syllable word?
    b. What is the probability of your choosing a two-syllable word or a word that begins with a consonant (for both)?
    c. What is the probability of your choosing either a two-syllable word or a word that begins with a consonant?
    d. Suppose that you choose two words at random and use replacement. What is the probability of your choosing both a one-syllable word and, in addition, a word beginning with a vowel?
    e. Suppose that you choose two words without replacement. What is the probability of your choosing both a two-syllable word and also a word beginning with a vowel?

Answer to the problem in text: The probability of rolling a single die once and getting a number that begins with the letter *t* is 2/6 or .3333.

B

Tables

TABLE A *Random Numbers*

Row Number									
00000	10097	32533	76520	13586	34673	54876	80959	09117	39292	74945
00001	37542	04805	64894	74296	24805	24037	20636	10402	00822	91665
00002	08422	68953	19645	09303	23209	02560	15953	34764	35080	33606
00003	99019	02529	09376	70715	38311	31165	88676	74397	04436	27659
00004	12807	99970	80157	36147	64032	36653	98951	16877	12171	76833
00005	66065	74717	34072	76850	36697	36170	65813	39885	11199	29170
00006	31060	10805	45571	82406	35303	42614	86799	07439	23403	09732
00007	85269	77602	02051	65692	68665	74818	73053	85247	18623	88579
00008	63573	32135	05325	47048	90553	57548	28468	28709	83491	25624
00009	73769	45753	03529	64778	35808	34282	60935	20344	35273	88435
00010	98520	17767	14905	68607	22109	40558	60970	93433	50500	73998
00011	11805	05431	39808	27732	50725	68248	29405	24201	52775	67851
00012	83452	99634	06288	98033	13746	70078	18475	40610	68711	77817
00013	88685	40200	86507	58401	36766	67951	90364	76493	29609	11062
00014	99594	67348	87517	64969	91826	08928	93785	61368	23478	34113
00015	65481	17674	17468	50950	58047	76974	73039	57186	40218	16544
00016	80124	35635	17727	08015	45318	22374	21115	78253	14385	53763
00017	74350	99817	77402	77214	43236	00210	45521	64237	96286	02655
00018	69916	26803	66252	29148	36936	87203	76621	13990	94400	56418
00019	09893	20505	14225	68514	46427	56788	96297	78822	54382	14598
00020	91499	14523	68479	27686	46162	83554	94750	89923	37089	20048
00021	80336	94598	26940	36858	70297	34135	53140	33340	42050	82341
00022	44104	81949	85157	47954	32979	26575	57600	40881	22222	06413
00023	12550	73742	11100	02040	12860	74697	96644	89439	28707	25815
00024	63606	49329	16505	34484	40219	52563	43651	77082	07207	31790
00025	61196	90446	26457	47774	51924	33729	65394	59593	42582	60527
00026	15474	45266	95270	79953	59367	83848	82396	10118	33211	59466
00027	94557	28573	67897	54387	54622	44431	91190	42592	92927	45973
00028	42481	16213	97344	08721	16868	48767	03071	12059	25701	46670
00029	23523	78317	73208	89837	68935	91416	26252	29663	05522	82562
00030	04493	52494	75246	33824	45862	51025	61962	79335	65337	12472
00031	00549	97654	64051	88159	96119	63896	54692	82391	23287	29529
00032	35963	15307	26898	09354	33351	35462	77974	50024	90103	39333
00033	59808	08391	45427	26842	83609	49700	13021	24892	78565	20106
00034	46058	85236	01390	92286	77281	44077	93910	83647	70617	42941
00035	32179	00597	87379	25241	05567	07007	86743	17157	85394	11838
00036	69234	61406	20117	45204	15956	60000	18743	92423	97118	96338
00037	19565	41430	01758	75379	40419	21585	66674	36806	84962	85207
00038	45155	14938	19476	07246	43667	94543	59047	90033	20826	69541
00039	94864	31994	36168	10851	34888	81553	01540	35456	05014	51176
00040	98086	24826	45240	28404	44999	08896	39094	73407	35441	31880
00041	33185	16232	41941	50949	89435	48581	88695	41994	37548	73043
00042	80951	00406	96382	70774	20151	23387	25016	25298	94624	61171
00043	79752	49140	71961	28296	69861	02591	74852	20539	00387	59579
00044	18633	32537	98145	06571	31010	24674	05455	61427	77938	91936
00045	74029	43902	77557	32270	97790	17119	52527	58021	80814	51748

TABLE A *continued*

Row Number										
00046	54178	45611	80993	37143	05335	12969	56127	19255	36040	90324
00047	11664	49883	52079	84827	59381	71539	09973	33440	88461	23356
00048	48324	77928	31249	64710	02295	36870	32307	57546	15020	09994
00049	69074	94138	87637	91976	35584	04401	10518	21615	01848	76938
00050	09188	20097	32825	39527	04220	86304	83389	87374	64278	58044
00051	90045	85497	51981	50654	94938	81997	91870	76150	68476	64659
00052	73189	50207	47677	26269	62290	64464	27124	67018	41361	82760
00053	75768	76490	20971	87749	90429	12272	95375	05871	93823	43178
00054	54016	44056	66281	31003	00682	27398	20714	53295	07706	17813
00055	08358	69910	78542	42785	13661	58873	04618	97553	31223	08420
00056	28306	03264	81333	10591	40510	07893	32604	60475	94119	01840
00057	53840	86233	81594	13628	51215	90290	28466	68795	77762	20791
00058	91757	53741	61613	62669	50263	90212	55781	76514	83483	47055
00059	89415	92694	00397	58391	12607	17646	48949	72306	94541	37408
00060	77513	03820	86864	29901	68414	82774	51908	13980	72893	55507
00061	19502	37174	69979	20288	55210	29773	74287	75251	65344	67415
00062	21818	59313	93278	81757	05686	73156	07082	85046	31853	38452
00063	51474	66499	68107	23621	94049	91345	42836	09191	08007	45449
00064	99559	68331	62535	24170	69777	12830	74819	78142	43860	72834
00065	33713	48007	93584	72869	51926	64721	58303	29822	93174	93972
00066	85274	86893	11303	22970	28834	34137	73515	90400	71148	43643
00067	84133	89640	44035	52166	73852	70091	61222	60561	62327	18423
00068	56732	16234	17395	96131	10123	91622	85496	57560	81604	18880
00069	65138	56806	87648	85261	34313	65861	45875	21069	85644	47277
00070	38001	02176	81719	11711	71602	92937	74219	64049	65584	49698
00071	37402	96397	01304	77586	56271	10086	47324	62605	40030	37438
00072	97125	40348	87083	31417	21815	39250	75237	62047	15501	29578
00073	21826	41134	47143	34072	64638	85902	49139	06441	03856	54552
00074	73135	42742	95719	09035	85794	74296	08789	88156	64691	19202
00075	07638	77929	03061	18072	96207	44156	23821	99538	04713	66994
00076	60528	83441	07954	19814	59175	20695	05533	52139	61212	06455
00077	83596	35655	06958	92983	05128	09719	77433	53783	92301	50498
00078	10850	62746	99599	10507	13499	06319	53075	71839	06410	19362
00079	39820	98952	43622	63147	64421	80814	43800	09351	31024	73167
00080	59580	06478	75569	78800	88835	54486	23768	06156	04111	08408
00081	38508	07341	23793	48763	90822	97022	17719	04207	95954	49953
00082	30692	70668	94688	16127	56196	80091	82067	63400	05462	69200
00083	65443	95659	18238	27437	49632	24041	08337	65676	96299	90836
00084	27267	50264	13192	72294	07477	44606	17985	48911	97341	30358
00085	91307	06991	19072	24210	36699	53728	28825	35793	28976	66252
00086	68434	94688	84473	13622	62126	98408	12843	82590	09815	93146
00087	48908	15877	54745	24591	35700	04754	83824	52692	54130	55160
00088	06913	45197	42672	78601	11883	09528	63011	98901	14974	40344
00089	10455	16019	14210	33712	91342	37821	88325	80851	43667	70883
00090	12883	97343	65027	61184	04285	01392	17974	15077	90712	26769
00091	21778	30976	38807	36961	31649	42096	63281	02023	08816	47449

TABLE A *continued*

Row Number									
00092	19523	59515	65122	59659	86283	68258	69572	13798	16435	91529
00093	67245	52670	35583	16563	79246	86686	76463	34222	26655	90802
00094	60584	47377	07500	37992	45134	26529	26760	83637	41326	44344
00095	53853	41377	36066	94850	58838	73859	49364	73331	96240	43642
00096	24637	38736	74384	89342	52623	07992	12369	18601	03742	83873
00097	83080	12451	38992	22815	07759	51777	97377	27585	51972	37867
00098	16444	24334	36151	99073	27493	70939	85130	32552	54846	54759
00099	60790	18157	57178	65762	11161	78576	45819	52979	65130	04860
00100	03991	10461	93716	16894	66083	24653	84609	58232	88618	19161
00101	38555	95554	32886	59780	08355	60860	29735	47762	71299	23853
00102	17546	73704	92052	46215	55121	29281	59076	07936	27954	58909
00103	32643	52861	95819	06831	00911	98936	76355	93779	80863	00514
00104	69572	68777	39510	35905	14060	40619	29549	69616	33564	60780
00105	24122	66591	27699	06494	14845	46672	61958	77100	90899	75754
00106	61196	30231	92962	61773	41839	55382	17267	70943	78038	70267
00107	30532	21704	10274	12202	39685	23309	10061	68829	55986	66485
00108	03788	97599	75867	20717	74416	53166	35208	33374	87539	08823
00109	48228	63379	85783	47619	53152	67433	35663	52972	16818	60311
00110	60365	94653	35075	33949	42614	29297	01918	28316	98953	73231
00111	83799	42402	56623	34442	34994	41374	70071	14736	09958	18065
00112	32960	07405	36409	83232	99385	41600	11133	07586	15917	06253
00113	19322	53845	57620	52606	66497	68646	78138	66559	19640	99413
00114	11220	94747	07399	37408	48509	23929	27482	45476	85244	35159
00115	31751	57260	68980	05339	15470	48355	88651	22596	03152	19121
00116	88492	99382	14454	04504	20094	98977	74843	93413	22109	78508
00117	30934	47744	07481	83828	73788	06533	28597	20405	94205	20380
00118	22888	48893	27499	98748	60530	45128	74022	84617	82037	10268
00119	78212	16993	35902	91386	44372	15486	65741	14014	87481	37220
00120	41849	84547	46850	52326	34677	58300	74910	64345	19325	81549
00121	46352	33049	69248	93460	45305	07521	61318	31855	14413	70951
00122	11087	96294	14013	31792	59747	67277	76503	34513	39663	77544
00123	52701	08337	56303	87315	16520	69676	11654	99893	02181	68161
00124	57275	36898	81304	48585	68652	27376	92852	55866	88448	03584
00125	20857	73156	70284	24326	79375	95220	01159	63267	10622	48391
00126	15633	84924	90415	93614	33521	26665	55823	47641	86225	31704
00127	92694	48297	39904	02115	59589	49067	66821	41575	49767	04037
00128	77613	19019	88152	00080	20554	91409	96277	48257	50816	97616
00129	38688	32486	45134	63545	59404	72059	43947	51680	43852	59693
00130	25163	01889	70014	15021	41290	67312	71857	15957	68971	11403
00131	65251	07629	37239	33295	05870	01119	92784	26340	18477	65622
00132	36815	43625	18637	37509	82444	99005	04921	73701	14707	93997
00133	64397	11692	05327	82162	20247	81759	45197	25332	83745	22567
00134	04515	25624	95096	67946	48460	85558	15191	18782	16930	33361
00135	83761	60873	43253	84145	60833	25983	01291	41349	20368	07126
00136	14387	06345	80854	09279	43529	06318	38384	74761	41196	37480
00137	51321	92246	80088	77074	88722	56736	66164	49431	66919	31678

TABLE A *continued*

Row Number										
00138	72472	00008	80890	18002	94813	31900	54155	83436	35352	54131
00139	05466	55306	93128	18464	74457	90561	72848	11834	79982	68416
00140	39528	72484	82474	25593	48545	35247	18619	13674	18611	19241
00141	81616	18711	53342	44276	75122	11724	74627	73707	58319	15997
00142	07586	16120	82641	22820	92904	13141	32392	19763	61199	67940
00143	90767	04235	13574	17200	69902	63742	78464	22501	18627	90872
00144	40188	28193	29593	88627	94972	11598	62095	36787	00441	58997
00145	34414	82157	86887	55087	19152	00023	12302	80783	32624	68691
00146	63439	75363	44989	16822	36024	00867	76378	41605	65961	73488
00147	67049	09070	93399	45547	94458	74284	05041	49807	20288	34060
00148	79495	04146	52162	90286	54158	34243	46978	35482	59362	95938
00149	91704	30552	04737	21031	75051	93029	47665	64382	99782	93478
00150	94015	46874	32444	48277	59820	96163	64654	25843	41145	42820
00151	74108	88222	88570	74015	25704	91035	01755	14750	48968	38603
00152	62880	87873	95160	59221	22304	90314	72877	17334	39283	04149
00153	11748	12102	80580	41867	17710	59621	06554	07850	73950	79552
00154	17944	05600	60478	03343	25852	58905	57216	39618	49856	99326
00155	66067	42792	95043	52680	46780	56487	09971	59481	37006	22186
00156	54244	91030	45547	70818	59849	96169	61459	21647	87417	17198
00157	30945	57589	31732	57260	47670	07654	46376	25366	94746	49580
00158	69170	37403	86995	90307	94304	71803	26825	05511	12459	91314
00159	08345	88975	35841	85771	08105	59987	87112	21476	14713	71181
00160	27767	43584	85301	88977	29490	69714	73035	41207	74699	09310
00161	13025	14338	54066	15243	47724	66733	47431	43905	31048	56699
00162	80217	36292	98525	24335	24432	24896	43277	58874	11466	16082
00163	10875	62004	90391	61105	57411	06368	53856	30743	08670	84741
00164	54127	57326	26629	19087	24472	88779	30540	27886	61732	75454
00165	60311	42824	37301	42678	45990	43242	17374	52003	70707	70214
00166	49739	71484	92003	98086	76668	73209	59202	11973	02902	33250
00167	78626	51594	16453	94614	39014	97066	83012	09832	25571	77628
00168	66692	13986	99837	00582	81232	44987	09504	96412	90193	79568
00169	44071	28091	07362	97703	76447	42537	98524	97831	65704	09514
00170	41468	85149	49554	17994	14924	39650	95294	00556	70481	06905
00171	94559	37559	49678	53119	70312	05682	66986	34099	74474	20740
00172	41615	70360	64114	58660	90850	64618	80620	51790	11436	38072
00173	50273	93113	41794	86861	24781	89683	55411	85667	77535	99892
00174	41396	80504	90670	08289	40902	05069	95083	06783	28102	57816
00175	25807	24260	71520	78920	72682	07385	90726	57166	98884	08583
00176	06170	97965	88302	98041	21443	41808	68984	83620	89747	98882
00177	60808	54444	74412	81105	01176	28838	36421	16489	18059	51061
00178	80940	44893	10408	36222	80582	71944	92638	40333	67054	16067
00179	19516	90120	46759	71643	13177	55292	21036	82808	77501	97427
00180	49386	54480	23604	23554	21785	41101	91178	10174	29420	90438
00181	06312	88940	15995	69321	47458	64809	98189	81851	29651	84215
00182	60942	00307	11897	92674	40405	68032	96717	54244	10701	41393
00183	92329	98932	78284	46347	71209	92061	39448	93136	25722	08564

TABLE A *continued*

Row Number										
00184	77936	63574	31384	51924	85561	29671	58137	17820	22751	36518
00185	38101	77756	11657	13897	95889	57067	47648	13885	70669	93406
00186	39641	69457	91339	22502	92613	89719	11947	56203	19324	20504
00187	84054	40455	99396	63680	67667	60631	69181	96845	38525	11600
00188	47468	03577	57649	63266	24700	71594	14004	23153	69249	05747
00189	43321	31370	28977	23896	76479	68562	62342	07589	08899	05985
00190	64281	61826	18555	64937	13173	33365	78851	16499	87064	13075
00191	66847	70495	32350	02985	86716	38746	26313	77463	55387	72681
00192	72461	33230	21529	53424	92581	02262	78438	66276	18396	73538
00193	21032	91050	13058	16218	12470	56500	15292	76139	59526	52113
00194	95362	67011	06651	16136	01016	00857	55018	56374	35824	71708
00195	49712	97380	10404	55452	34030	60726	75211	10271	36633	68424
00196	58275	61764	97586	54716	50259	46345	87195	46092	26787	60939
00197	89514	11788	68224	23417	73959	76145	30342	40277	11049	72049
00198	15472	50669	48139	36732	46874	37088	63465	09819	58869	35220
00199	12120	86124	51247	44302	60883	52109	21437	36786	49226	77837

SOURCE: RAND Corporation, *A Million Random Digits*, Glencoe, Ill.: Free Press of Glencoe, 1955.

TABLE C χ^2 *Critical Values*

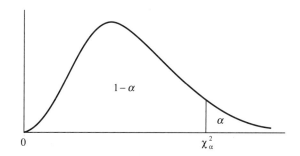

df	.99	.98	.95	.90	.80	.70	.50	.30	.20	.10	.05	.02	.01	.001
1	$.0^3157$	$.0^3628$	.00393	.0158	.0642	.148	.455	1.074	1.642	2.706	3.841	5.412	6.635	10.827
2	.0201	.0404	.103	.211	.446	.713	1.386	2.408	3.219	4.605	5.991	7.824	9.210	13.815
3	.115	.185	.352	.584	1.005	1.424	2.366	3.665	4.642	6.251	7.815	9.837	11.345	16.266
4	.297	.429	.711	1.064	1.649	2.195	3.357	4.878	5.989	7.779	9.488	11.668	13.277	18.467
5	.554	.752	1.145	1.610	2.343	3.000	4.351	6.064	7.289	9.236	11.070	13.388	15.086	20.515
6	.872	1.134	1.635	2.204	3.070	3.828	5.348	7.231	8.558	10.645	12.592	15.033	16.812	22.457
7	1.239	1.564	2.167	2.833	3.822	4.671	6.346	8.383	9.803	12.017	14.067	16.622	18.475	24.322
8	1.646	2.032	2.733	3.490	4.594	5.527	7.344	9.524	11.030	13.362	15.507	18.168	20.090	26.125
9	2.088	2.532	3.325	4.168	5.380	6.393	8.343	10.656	12.242	14.684	16.919	19.679	21.666	27.877
10	2.558	3.059	3.940	4.865	6.179	7.267	9.342	11.781	13.442	15.987	18.307	21.161	23.209	29.588
11	3.053	3.609	4.575	5.578	6.989	8.148	10.341	12.899	14.631	17.275	19.675	22.618	24.725	31.264
12	3.571	4.178	5.226	6.304	7.807	9.034	11.340	14.011	15.812	18.549	21.026	24.054	26.217	32.909
13	4.107	4.765	5.892	7.042	8.634	9.926	12.340	15.119	16.985	19.812	22.362	25.472	27.688	34.528
14	4.660	5.368	6.571	7.790	9.467	10.821	13.339	16.222	18.151	21.064	23.685	26.873	29.141	36.123
15	5.229	5.985	7.261	8.547	10.307	11.721	14.339	17.322	19.311	22.307	24.996	28.259	30.578	37.697
16	5.812	6.614	7.962	9.312	11.152	12.624	15.338	18.418	20.465	23.542	26.296	29.633	32.000	39.252
17	6.408	7.255	8.672	10.085	12.002	13.531	16.338	19.511	21.615	24.769	27.587	30.995	33.409	40.790
18	7.015	7.906	9.390	10.865	12.857	14.440	17.338	20.601	22.760	25.989	28.869	32.346	34.805	42.312
19	7.633	8.567	10.117	11.651	13.716	15.352	18.338	21.689	23.900	27.204	30.144	33.687	36.191	43.820
20	8.260	9.237	10.851	12.443	14.578	16.266	19.337	22.775	25.038	28.412	31.410	35.020	37.566	45.315
21	8.897	9.915	11.591	13.240	15.445	17.182	20.337	23.858	26.171	29.615	32.671	36.343	38.932	46.797
22	9.542	10.600	12.338	14.041	16.314	18.101	21.337	24.939	27.301	30.813	33.924	37.659	40.289	48.268
23	10.196	11.293	13.091	14.848	17.187	19.021	22.337	26.018	28.429	32.007	35.172	38.968	41.638	49.728
24	10.856	11.992	13.848	15.659	18.062	19.943	23.337	27.096	29.553	33.196	36.415	40.270	42.980	51.179
25	11.524	12.697	14.611	16.473	18.940	20.867	24.337	28.172	30.675	34.382	37.652	41.566	44.314	52.620
26	12.198	13.409	15.379	17.292	19.820	21.792	25.336	29.246	31.795	35.563	38.885	42.856	45.642	54.052
27	12.879	14.125	16.151	18.114	20.703	22.719	26.336	30.319	32.912	36.741	40.113	44.140	46.963	55.476
28	13.565	14.847	16.928	18.939	21.588	23.647	27.336	31.391	34.027	37.916	41.337	45.419	43.278	56.893
29	14.256	15.574	17.708	19.768	22.475	24.577	28.336	32.461	35.139	39.087	42.557	46.693	49.588	55.302
30	14.953	16.306	18.493	20.599	23.364	25.508	29.336	33.530	36.250	40.256	43.773	47.962	50.892	59.703

SOURCE: Taken from Table IV, p. 47 of Fisher and Yates: *Statistical Tables for Biological, Agricultural and Medical Research*, published by Longman Group Ltd., London (previously published by Oliver and Boyd, Edinburgh), and by permission of the authors and publishers.

For df > 30, the expression $\sqrt{2\chi^2} - \sqrt{2\,df - 1}$ may be used as a normal deviation with unit variance.

TABLE F   *F-Ratio Critical Values*

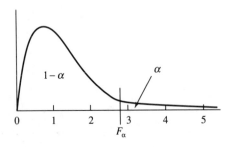

		df for Numerator											
df for Denominator	**α**	**1**	**2**	**3**	**4**	**5**	**6**	**7**	**8**	**9**	**10**	**11**	**12**
	.25	5.83	7.50	8.20	8.58	8.82	8.98	9.10	9.19	9.26	9.32	9.36	9.41
1	.10	39.9	49.5	53.6	55.8	57.2	58.2	58.9	59.4	59.9	60.2	60.5	60.7
	.05	161	200	216	225	230	234	237	239	241	242	243	244
	.25	2.57	3.00	3.15	3.23	3.28	3.31	3.34	3.35	3.37	3.38	3.39	3.39
2	.10	8.53	9.00	9.16	9.24	9.29	9.33	9.35	9.37	9.38	9.39	9.40	9.41
	.05	18.5	19.0	19.2	19.2	19.3	19.3	19.4	19.4	19.4	19.4	19.4	19.4
	.01	98.5	99.0	99.2	99.2	99.3	99.3	99.4	99.4	99.4	99.4	99.4	99.4
	.25	2.02	2.28	2.36	2.39	2.41	2.42	2.43	2.44	2.44	2.44	2.45	2.45
3	.10	5.54	5.46	5.39	5.34	5.31	5.28	5.27	5.25	5.24	5.23	5.22	5.22
	.05	10.1	9.55	9.28	9.12	9.01	8.94	8.89	8.85	8.81	8.79	8.76	8.74
	.01	34.1	30.8	29.5	28.7	28.2	27.9	27.7	27.5	27.3	27.2	27.1	27.1
	.25	1.81	2.00	2.05	2.06	2.07	2.08	2.08	2.08	2.08	2.08	2.08	2.08
4	.10	4.54	4.32	4.19	4.11	4.05	4.01	3.98	3.95	3.94	3.92	3.91	3.90
	.05	7.71	6.94	6.59	6.39	6.26	6.16	6.09	6.04	6.00	5.96	5.94	5.91
	.01	21.2	18.0	16.7	16.0	15.5	15.2	15.0	14.8	14.7	14.5	14.4	14.4
	.25	1.69	1.85	1.88	1.89	1.89	1.89	1.89	1.89	1.89	1.89	1.89	1.89
5	.10	4.06	3.78	3.62	3.52	3.45	3.40	3.37	3.34	3.32	3.30	3.28	3.27
	.05	6.61	5.79	5.41	5.19	5.05	4.95	4.88	4.82	4.77	4.74	4.71	4.68
	.01	16.3	13.3	12.1	11.4	11.0	10.7	10.5	10.3	10.2	10.1	9.96	9.89
	.25	1.62	1.76	1.78	1.79	1.79	1.78	1.78	1.78	1.77	1.77	1.77	1.77
6	.10	3.78	3.46	3.29	3.18	3.11	3.05	3.01	2.98	2.96	2.94	2.92	2.90
	.05	5.99	5.14	4.76	4.53	4.39	4.28	4.21	4.15	4.10	4.06	4.03	4.00
	.01	13.7	10.9	9.78	9.15	8.75	8.47	8.26	8.10	7.98	7.87	7.79	7.72
	.25	1.57	1.70	1.72	1.72	1.71	1.71	1.70	1.70	1.69	1.69	1.69	1.68
7	.10	3.59	3.26	3.07	2.96	2.88	2.83	2.78	2.75	2.72	2.70	2.68	2.67
	.05	5.59	4.74	4.35	4.12	3.97	3.87	3.79	3.73	3.68	3.64	3.60	3.57
	.01	12.2	9.55	8.45	7.85	7.46	7.19	6.99	6.84	6.72	6.62	6.54	6.47
	.25	1.54	1.66	1.67	1.66	1.66	1.65	1.64	1.64	1.63	1.63	1.63	1.62
8	.10	3.46	3.11	2.92	2.81	2.73	2.67	2.62	2.59	2.56	2.54	2.52	2.50
	.05	5.32	4.46	4.07	3.84	3.69	3.58	3.50	3.44	3.39	3.35	3.31	3.28
	.01	11.3	8.65	7.59	7.01	6.63	6.37	6.18	6.03	5.91	5.81	5.73	5.67

TABLE F *continued*

				df *for Numerator*										df *for*
15	**20**	**24**	**30**	**40**	**50**	**60**	**100**	**120**	**200**	**500**	**∞**	**α**	**Denominator**
9.49	9.58	9.63	9.67	9.71	9.74	9.76	9.78	9.80	9.82	9.84	9.85	.25	
61.2	61.7	62.0	62.3	62.5	62.7	62.8	63.0	63.1	63.2	63.3	63.3	.10	**1**
246	248	249	250	251	252	252	253	253	254	254	254	.05	
3.41	3.43	3.43	3.44	3.45	3.45	3.46	3.47	3.47	3.48	3.48	3.48	.25	
9.42	9.44	9.45	9.46	9.47	9.47	9.47	9.48	9.48	9.49	9.49	9.49	.10	**2**
19.4	19.4	19.5	19.5	19.5	19.5	19.5	19.5	19.5	19.5	19.5	19.5	.05	
99.4	99.4	99.5	99.5	99.5	99.5	99.5	99.5	99.5	99.5	99.5	99.5	.01	
2.46	2.46	2.46	2.47	2.47	2.47	2.47	2.47	2.47	2.47	2.47	2.47	.25	
5.20	5.18	5.18	5.17	5.16	5.15	5.15	5.14	5.14	5.14	5.14	5.13	.10	**3**
8.70	8.66	8.64	8.62	8.59	8.58	8.57	8.55	8.55	8.54	8.53	8.53	.05	
26.9	26.7	26.6	26.5	26.4	26.4	26.3	26.2	26.2	26.2	26.1	26.1	.01	
2.08	2.08	2.08	2.08	2.08	2.08	2.08	2.08	2.08	2.08	2.08	2.08	.25	
3.87	3.84	3.83	3.82	3.80	3.80	3.79	3.78	3.78	3.77	3.76	3.76	.10	**4**
5.86	5.80	5.77	5.75	5.72	5.70	5.69	5.66	5.66	5.65	5.64	5.63	.05	
14.2	14.0	13.9	13.8	13.7	13.7	13.7	13.6	13.6	13.5	13.5	13.5	.01	
1.89	1.88	1.88	1.88	1.88	1.88	1.87	1.87	1.87	1.87	1.87	1.87	.25	
3.24	3.21	3.19	3.17	3.16	3.15	3.14	3.13	3.12	3.12	3.11	3.10	.10	**5**
4.62	4.56	4.53	4.50	4.46	4.44	4.43	4.41	4.40	4.39	4.37	4.36	.05	
9.72	9.55	9.47	9.38	9.29	9.24	9.20	9.13	9.11	9.08	9.04	9.02	.01	
1.76	1.76	1.75	1.75	1.75	1.75	1.74	1.74	1.74	1.74	1.74	1.74	.25	
2.87	2.84	2.82	2.80	2.78	2.77	2.76	2.75	2.74	2.73	2.73	2.72	.10	**6**
3.94	3.87	3.84	3.81	3.77	3.75	3.74	3.71	3.70	3.69	3.68	3.67	.05	
7.56	7.40	7.31	7.23	7.14	7.09	7.06	6.99	6.97	6.93	6.90	6.88	.01	
1.68	1.67	1.67	1.66	1.66	1.66	1.65	1.65	1.65	1.65	1.65	1.65	.25	
2.63	2.59	2.58	2.56	2.54	2.52	2.51	2.50	2.49	2.48	2.48	2.47	.10	**7**
3.51	3.44	3.41	3.38	3.34	3.32	3.30	3.27	3.27	3.25	3.24	3.23	.05	
6.31	6.16	6.07	5.99	5.91	5.86	5.82	5.75	5.74	5.70	5.67	5.65	.01	
1.62	1.61	1.60	1.60	1.59	1.59	1.59	1.58	1.58	1.58	1.58	1.58	.25	
2.46	2.42	2.40	2.38	2.36	2.35	2.34	2.32	2.32	2.31	2.30	2.29	.10	**8**
3.22	3.15	3.12	3.08	3.04	3.02	3.01	2.97	2.97	2.95	2.94	2.93	.05	
5.52	5.36	5.28	5.20	5.12	5.07	5.03	4.96	4.95	4.91	4.88	4.86	.01	

TABLE F *continued*

df for Denominator	α	\multicolumn{12}{c}{df for Numerator}

df for Denominator	α	1	2	3	4	5	6	7	8	9	10	11	12
9	.25	1.51	1.62	1.63	1.63	1.62	1.61	1.60	1.60	1.59	1.59	1.58	1.58
	.10	3.36	3.01	2.81	2.69	2.61	2.55	2.51	2.47	2.44	2.42	2.40	2.38
	.05	5.12	4.26	3.86	3.63	3.48	3.37	3.29	3.23	3.18	3.14	3.10	3.07
	.01	10.6	8.02	6.99	6.42	6.06	5.80	5.61	5.47	5.35	5.26	5.18	5.11
10	.25	1.49	1.60	1.60	1.59	1.59	1.58	1.57	1.56	1.56	1.55	1.55	1.54
	.10	3.29	2.92	2.73	2.61	2.52	2.46	2.41	2.38	2.35	2.32	2.30	2.28
	.05	4.96	4.10	3.71	3.48	3.33	3.22	3.14	3.07	3.02	2.98	2.94	2.91
	.01	10.0	7.56	6.55	5.99	5.64	5.39	5.20	5.06	4.94	4.85	4.77	4.71
11	.25	1.47	1.58	1.58	1.57	1.56	1.55	1.54	1.53	1.53	1.52	1.52	1.51
	.10	3.23	2.86	2.66	2.54	2.45	2.39	2.34	2.30	2.27	2.25	2.23	2.21
	.05	4.84	3.98	3.59	3.36	3.20	3.09	3.01	2.95	2.90	2.85	2.82	2.79
	.01	9.65	7.21	6.22	5.67	5.32	5.07	4.89	4.74	4.63	4.54	4.46	4.40
12	.25	1.46	1.56	1.56	1.55	1.54	1.53	1.52	1.51	1.51	1.50	1.50	1.49
	.10	3.18	2.81	2.61	2.48	2.39	2.33	2.28	2.24	2.21	2.19	2.17	2.15
	.05	4.75	3.89	3.49	3.26	3.11	3.00	2.91	2.85	2.80	2.75	2.72	2.69
	.01	9.33	6.93	5.95	5.41	5.06	4.82	4.64	4.50	4.39	4.30	4.22	4.16
13	.25	1.45	1.55	1.55	1.53	1.52	1.51	1.50	1.49	1.49	1.48	1.47	1.47
	.10	3.14	2.76	2.56	2.43	2.35	2.28	2.23	2.20	2.16	2.14	2.12	2.10
	.05	4.67	3.81	3.41	3.18	3.03	2.92	2.83	2.77	2.71	2.67	2.63	2.60
	.01	9.07	6.70	5.74	5.21	4.86	4.62	4.44	4.30	4.19	4.10	4.02	3.96
14	.25	1.44	1.53	1.53	1.52	1.51	1.50	1.49	1.48	1.47	1.46	1.46	1.45
	.10	3.10	2.73	2.52	2.39	2.31	2.24	2.19	2.15	2.12	2.10	2.08	2.05
	.05	4.60	3.74	3.34	3.11	2.96	2.85	2.76	2.70	2.65	2.60	2.57	2.53
	.01	8.86	6.51	5.56	5.04	4.69	4.46	4.28	4.14	4.03	3.94	3.86	3.80
15	.25	1.43	1.52	1.52	1.51	1.49	1.48	1.47	1.46	1.46	1.45	1.44	1.44
	.10	3.07	2.70	2.49	2.36	2.27	2.21	2.16	2.12	2.09	2.06	2.04	2.02
	.05	4.54	3.68	3.29	3.06	2.90	2.79	2.71	2.64	2.59	2.54	2.51	2.48
	.01	8.68	6.36	5.42	4.89	4.56	4.32	4.14	4.00	3.89	3.80	3.73	3.67
16	.25	1.42	1.51	1.51	1.50	1.48	1.47	1.46	1.45	1.44	1.44	1.44	1.43
	.10	3.05	2.67	2.46	2.33	2.24	2.18	2.13	2.09	2.06	2.03	2.01	1.99
	.05	4.49	3.63	3.24	3.01	2.85	2.74	2.66	2.59	2.54	2.49	2.46	2.42
	.01	8.53	6.23	5.29	4.77	4.44	4.20	4.03	3.89	3.78	3.69	3.62	3.55
17	.25	1.42	1.51	1.50	1.49	1.47	1.46	1.45	1.44	1.43	1.43	1.42	1.41
	.10	3.03	2.64	2.44	2.31	2.22	2.15	2.10	2.06	2.03	2.00	1.98	1.96
	.05	4.45	3.59	3.20	2.96	2.81	2.70	2.61	2.55	2.49	2.45	2.41	2.38
	.01	8.40	6.11	5.18	4.67	4.34	4.10	3.93	3.79	3.68	3.59	3.52	3.46
18	.25	1.41	1.50	1.49	1.48	1.46	1.45	1.44	1.43	1.42	1.42	1.41	1.40
	.10	3.01	2.62	2.42	2.29	2.20	2.13	2.08	2.04	2.00	1.98	1.96	1.93
	.05	4.41	3.55	3.16	2.93	2.77	2.66	2.58	2.51	2.46	2.41	2.37	2.34
	.01	8.29	6.01	5.09	4.58	4.25	4.01	3.84	3.71	3.60	3.51	3.43	3.37
19	.25	1.41	1.49	1.49	1.47	1.46	1.44	1.43	1.42	1.41	1.41	1.40	1.40
	.10	2.99	2.61	2.40	2.27	2.18	2.11	2.06	2.02	1.98	1.96	1.94	1.91
	.05	4.38	3.52	3.13	2.90	2.74	2.63	2.54	2.48	2.42	2.38	2.34	2.31
	.01	8.18	5.93	5.01	4.50	4.17	3.94	3.77	3.63	3.52	3.43	3.36	3.30

TABLE F *continued*

					df for Numerator								
15	**20**	**24**	**30**	**40**	**50**	**60**	**100**	**120**	**200**	**500**	**∞**	**α**	**df for Denominator**
1.57	1.56	1.56	1.55	1.55	1.54	1.54	1.53	1.53	1.53	1.53	1.53	.25	
2.34	2.30	2.28	2.25	2.23	2.22	2.21	2.19	2.18	2.17	2.17	2.16	.10	9
3.01	2.94	2.90	2.86	2.83	2.80	2.79	2.76	2.75	2.73	2.72	2.71	.05	
4.96	4.81	4.73	4.65	4.57	4.52	4.48	4.42	4.40	4.36	4.33	4.31	.01	
1.53	1.52	1.52	1.51	1.51	1.50	1.50	1.49	1.49	1.49	1.48	1.48	.25	
2.24	2.20	2.18	2.16	2.13	2.12	2.11	2.09	2.08	2.07	2.06	2.06	.10	10
2.85	2.77	2.74	2.70	2.66	2.64	2.62	2.59	2.58	2.56	2.55	2.54	.05	
4.56	4.41	4.33	4.25	4.17	4.12	4.08	4.01	4.00	3.96	3.93	3.91	.01	
1.50	1.49	1.49	1.48	1.47	1.47	1.47	1.46	1.46	1.46	1.45	1.45	.25	
2.17	2.12	2.10	2.08	2.05	2.04	2.03	2.00	2.00	1.99	1.98	1.97	.10	11
2.72	2.65	2.61	2.57	2.53	2.51	2.49	2.46	2.45	2.43	2.42	2.40	.05	
4.25	4.10	4.02	3.94	3.86	3.81	3.78	3.71	3.69	3.66	3.62	3.60	.01	
1.48	1.47	1.46	1.45	1.45	1.44	1.44	1.43	1.43	1.43	1.42	1.42	.25	
2.10	2.06	2.04	2.01	1.99	1.97	1.96	1.94	1.93	1.92	1.91	1.90	.10	12
2.62	2.54	2.51	2.47	2.43	2.40	2.38	2.35	2.34	2.32	2.31	2.30	.05	
4.01	3.86	3.78	3.70	3.62	3.57	3.54	3.47	3.45	3.41	3.38	3.36	.01	
1.46	1.45	1.44	1.43	1.42	1.42	1.42	1.41	1.41	1.40	1.40	1.40	.25	
2.05	2.01	1.98	1.96	1.93	1.92	1.90	1.88	1.88	1.86	1.85	1.85	.10	13
2.53	2.46	2.42	2.38	2.34	2.31	2.30	2.26	2.25	2.23	2.22	2.21	.05	
3.82	3.66	3.59	3.51	3.43	3.38	3.34	3.27	3.25	3.22	3.19	3.17	.01	
1.44	1.43	1.42	1.41	1.41	1.40	1.40	1.39	1.39	1.39	1.38	1.38	.25	
2.01	1.96	1.94	1.91	1.89	1.87	1.86	1.83	1.83	1.82	1.80	1.80	.10	14
2.46	2.39	2.35	2.31	2.27	2.24	2.22	2.19	2.18	2.16	2.14	2.13	.05	
3.66	3.51	3.43	3.35	3.27	3.22	3.18	3.11	3.09	3.06	3.03	3.00	.01	
1.43	1.41	1.41	1.40	1.39	1.39	1.38	1.38	1.37	1.37	1.36	1.36	.25	
1.97	1.92	1.90	1.87	1.85	1.83	1.82	1.79	1.79	1.77	1.76	1.76	.10	15
2.40	2.33	2.29	2.25	2.20	2.18	2.16	2.12	2.11	2.10	2.08	2.07	.05	
3.52	3.37	3.29	3.21	3.13	3.08	3.05	2.98	2.96	2.92	2.89	2.87	.01	
1.41	1.40	1.39	1.38	1.37	1.37	1.36	1.36	1.35	1.35	1.34	1.34	.25	
1.94	1.89	1.87	1.84	1.81	1.79	1.78	1.76	1.75	1.74	1.73	1.72	.10	16
2.35	2.28	2.24	2.19	2.15	2.12	2.11	2.07	2.06	2.04	2.02	2.01	.05	
3.41	3.26	3.18	3.10	3.02	2.97	2.93	2.86	2.84	2.81	2.78	2.75	.01	
1.40	1.39	1.38	1.37	1.36	1.35	1.35	1.34	1.34	1.34	1.33	1.33	.25	
1.91	1.86	1.84	1.81	1.78	1.76	1.75	1.73	1.72	1.71	1.69	1.69	.10	17
2.31	2.23	2.19	2.15	2.10	2.08	2.06	2.02	2.01	1.99	1.97	1.96	.05	
3.31	3.16	3.08	3.00	2.92	2.87	2.83	2.76	2.75	2.71	2.68	2.65	.01	
1.39	1.38	1.37	1.36	1.35	1.34	1.34	1.33	1.33	1.32	1.32	1.32	.25	
1.89	1.84	1.81	1.78	1.75	1.74	1.72	1.70	1.69	1.68	1.67	1.66	.10	18
2.27	2.19	2.15	2.11	2.06	2.04	2.02	1.98	1.97	1.95	1.93	1.92	.05	
3.23	3.08	3.00	2.92	2.84	2.78	2.75	2.68	2.66	2.62	2.59	2.57	.01	
1.38	1.37	1.36	1.35	1.34	1.33	1.33	1.32	1.32	1.31	1.31	1.30	.25	
1.86	1.81	1.79	1.76	1.73	1.71	1.70	1.67	1.67	1.65	1.64	1.63	.10	19
2.23	2.16	2.11	2.07	2.03	2.00	1.98	1.94	1.93	1.91	1.89	1.88	.05	
3.15	3.00	2.92	2.84	2.76	2.71	2.67	2.60	2.58	2.55	2.51	2.49	.01	

df for Denominator	α	\multicolumn{12}{c}{df for Numerator}

df for Denominator	α	1	2	3	4	5	6	7	8	9	10	11	12
20	.25	1.40	1.49	1.48	1.46	1.45	1.44	1.43	1.42	1.41	1.40	1.39	1.39
	.10	2.97	2.59	2.38	2.25	2.16	2.09	2.04	2.00	1.96	1.94	1.92	1.89
	.05	4.35	3.49	3.10	2.87	2.71	2.60	2.51	2.45	2.39	2.35	2.31	2.28
	.01	8.10	5.85	4.94	4.43	4.10	3.87	3.70	3.56	3.46	3.37	3.29	3.23
22	.25	1.40	1.48	1.47	1.45	1.44	1.42	1.41	1.40	1.39	1.39	1.38	1.37
	.10	2.95	2.56	2.35	2.22	2.13	2.06	2.01	1.97	1.93	1.90	1.88	1.86
	.05	4.30	3.44	3.05	2.82	2.66	2.55	2.46	2.40	2.34	2.30	2.26	2.23
	.01	7.95	5.72	4.82	4.31	3.99	3.76	3.59	3.45	3.35	3.26	3.18	3.12
24	.25	1.39	1.47	1.46	1.44	1.43	1.41	1.40	1.39	1.38	1.38	1.37	1.36
	.10	2.93	2.54	2.33	2.19	2.10	2.04	1.98	1.94	1.91	1.88	1.85	1.83
	.05	4.26	3.40	3.01	2.78	2.62	2.51	2.42	2.36	2.30	2.25	2.21	2.18
	.01	7.82	5.61	4.72	4.22	3.90	3.67	3.50	3.36	3.26	3.17	3.09	3.03
26	.25	1.38	1.46	1.45	1.44	1.42	1.41	1.39	1.38	1.37	1.37	1.36	1.35
	.10	2.91	2.52	2.31	2.17	2.08	2.01	1.96	1.92	1.88	1.86	1.84	1.81
	.05	4.23	3.37	2.98	2.74	2.59	2.47	2.39	2.32	2.27	2.22	2.18	2.15
	.01	7.72	5.53	4.64	4.14	3.82	3.59	3.42	3.29	3.18	3.09	3.02	2.96
28	.25	1.38	1.46	1.45	1.43	1.41	1.40	1.39	1.38	1.37	1.36	1.35	1.34
	.10	2.89	2.50	2.29	2.16	2.06	2.00	1.94	1.90	1.87	1.84	1.81	1.79
	.05	4.20	3.34	2.95	2.71	2.56	2.45	2.36	2.29	2.24	2.19	2.15	2.12
	.01	7.64	5.45	4.57	4.07	3.75	3.53	3.36	3.23	3.12	3.03	2.96	2.90
30	.25	1.38	1.45	1.44	1.42	1.41	1.39	1.38	1.37	1.36	1.35	1.35	1.34
	.10	2.88	2.49	2.28	2.14	2.05	1.98	1.93	1.88	1.85	1.82	1.79	1.77
	.05	4.17	3.32	2.92	2.69	2.53	2.42	2.33	2.27	2.21	2.16	2.13	2.09
	.01	7.56	5.39	4.51	4.02	3.70	3.47	3.30	3.17	3.07	2.98	2.91	2.84
40	.25	1.36	1.44	1.42	1.40	1.39	1.37	1.36	1.35	1.34	1.33	1.32	1.31
	.10	2.84	2.44	2.23	2.09	2.00	1:93	1.87	1.83	1.79	1.76	1.73	1.71
	.05	4.08	3.23	2.84	2.61	2.45	2.34	2.25	2.18	2.12	2.08	2.04	2.00
	.01	7.31	5.18	4.31	3.83	3.51	3.29	3.12	2.99	2.89	2.80	2.73	2.66
60	.25	1.35	1.42	1.41	1.38	1.37	1.35	1.33	1.32	1.31	1.30	1.29	1.29
	.10	2.79	2.39	2.18	2.04	1.95	1.87	1.82	1.77	1.74	1.71	1.68	1.66
	.05	4.00	3.15	2.76	2.53	2.37	2.25	2.17	2.10	2.04	1.99	1.95	1.92
	.01	7.08	4.98	4.13	3.65	3.34	3.12	2.95	2.82	2.72	2.63	2.56	2.50
120	.25	1.34	1.40	1.39	1.37	1.35	1.33	1.31	1.30	1.29	1.28	1.27	1.26
	.10	2.75	2.35	2.13	1.99	1.90	1.82	1.77	1.72	1.68	1.65	1.62	1.60
	.05	3.92	3.07	2.68	2.45	2.29	2.17	2.09	2.02	1.96	1.91	1.87	1.83
	.01	6.85	4.79	3.95	3.48	3.17	2.96	2.79	2.66	2.56	2.47	2.40	2.34
200	.25	1.33	1.39	1.38	1.36	1.34	1.32	1.31	1.29	1.28	1.27	1.26	1.25
	.10	2.73	2.33	2.11	1.97	1.88	1.80	1.75	1.70	1.66	1.63	1.60	1.57
	.05	3.89	3.04	2.65	2.42	2.26	2.14	2.06	1.98	1.93	1.88	1.84	1.80
	.01	6.76	4.71	3.88	3.41	3.11	2.89	2.73	2.60	2.50	2.41	2.34	2.27
∞	.25	1.32	1.39	1.37	1.35	1.33	1.31	1.29	1.28	1.27	1.25	1.24	1.24
	.10	2.71	2.30	2.08	1.94	1.85	1.77	1.72	1.67	1.63	1.60	1.57	1.55
	.05	3.84	3.00	2.60	2.37	2.21	2.10	2.01	1.94	1.88	1.83	1.79	1.75
	.01	6.63	4.61	3.78	3.32	3.02	2.80	2.64	2.51	2.41	2.32	2.25	2.18

					df for Numerator									**df for Denominator**
15	**20**	**24**	**30**	**40**	**50**	**60**	**100**	**120**	**200**	**500**	**∞**	**α**	
1.37	1.36	1.35	1.34	1.33	1.33	1.32	1.31	1.31	1.30	1.30	1.29	.25	
1.84	1.79	1.77	1.74	1.71	1.69	1.68	1.65	1.64	1.63	1.62	1.61	.10	**20**
2.20	2.12	2.08	2.04	1.99	1.97	1.95	1.9l	1.90	1.88	1.86	1.84	.05	
3.09	2.94	2.86	2.78	2.69	2.64	2.61	2.54	2.52	2.48	2.44	2.42	.01	
1.36	1.34	1.33	1.32	1.31	1.31	1.30	1.30	1.30	1.29	1.29	1.28	.25	
1.81	1.76	1.73	1.70	1.67	1.65	1.64	1.61	1.60	1.59	1.58	1.57	.10	**22**
2.15	2.07	2.03	1.98	1.94	1.91	1.89	1.85	1.84	1.82	1.80	1.78	.05	
2.98	2.83	2.75	2.67	2.58	2.53	2.50	2.42	2.40	2.36	2.33	2.31	.01	
1.35	1.33	1.32	1.31	1.30	1.29	1.29	1.28	1.28	1.27	1.27	1.26	.25	
1.78	1.73	1.70	1.67	1.64	1.62	1.61	1.58	1.57	1.56	1.54	1.53	.10	**24**
2.11	2.03	1.98	1.94	1.89	1.86	1.84	1.80	1.79	1.77	1.75	1.73	.05	
2.89	2.74	2.66	2.58	2.49	2.44	2.40	2.33	2.31	2.27	2.24	2.21	.01	
1.34	1.32	1.31	1.30	1.29	1.28	1.28	1.26	1.26	1.26	1.25	1.25	.25	
1.76	1.71	1.68	1.65	1.61	1.59	1.58	1.55	1.54	1.53	1.51	1.50	.10	**26**
2.07	1.99	1.95	1.90	1.85	1.82	1.80	1.76	1.75	1.73	1.71	1.69	.05	
2.81	2.66	2.58	2.50	2.42	2.36	2.33	2.25	2.23	2.19	2.16	2.13	.01	
1.33	1.31	1.30	1.29	1.28	1.27	1.27	1.26	1.25	1.25	1.24	1.24	.25	
1.74	1.69	1.66	1.63	1.59	1.57	1.56	1.53	1.52	1.50	1.49	1.48	.10	**28**
2.04	1.96	1.91	1.87	1.82	1.79	1.77	1.73	1.71	1.69	1.67	1.65	.05	
2.75	2.60	2.52	2.44	2.35	2.30	2.26	2.19	2.17	2.13	2.09	2.06	.01	
1.32	1.30	1.29	1.28	1.27	1.26	1.26	1.25	1.24	1.24	1.23	1.23	.25	
1.72	1.67	1.64	1.61	1.57	1.55	1.54	1.51	1.50	1.48	1.47	1.46	.10	**30**
2.01	1.93	1.89	1.84	1.79	1.76	1.74	1.70	1.68	1.66	1.64	1.62	.05	
2.70	2.55	2.47	2.39	2.30	2.25	2.21	2.13	2.11	2.07	2.03	2.01	.01	
1.30	1.28	1.26	1.25	1.24	1.23	1.22	1.21	1.21	1.20	1.19	1.19	.25	
1.66	1.61	1.57	1.54	1.51	1.48	1.47	1.43	1.42	1.41	1.39	1.38	.10	**40**
1.92	1.84	1.79	1.74	1.69	1.66	1.64	1.59	1.58	1.55	1.53	1.51	.05	
2.52	2.37	2.29	2.20	2.11	2.06	2.02	1.94	1.92	1.87	1.83	1.80	.01	
1.27	1.25	1.24	1.22	1.21	1.20	1.19	1.17	1.17	1.16	1.15	1.15	.25	
1.60	1.54	1.51	1.48	1.44	1.41	1.40	1.36	1.35	1.33	1.31	1.29	.10	**60**
1.84	1.75	1.70	1.65	1.59	1.56	1.53	1.48	1.47	1.44	1.41	1.39	.05	
2.35	2.20	2.12	2.03	1.94	1.88	1.84	1.75	1.73	1.68	1.63	1.60	.01	
1.24	1.22	1.21	1.19	1.18	1.17	1.16	1.14	1.13'	1.12	1.11	1.10	.25	
1.55	1.48	1.45	1.41	1.37	1.34	1.32	1.27	1.26	1.24	1.21	1.19	.10	**120**
1.75	1.66	1.61	1.55	1.50	1.46	1.43	1.37	1.35	1.32	1.28	1.25	.05	
2.19	2.03	1.95	1.86	1.76	1.70	1.66	1.56	1.53	1.48	1.42	1.38	.01	
1.23	1.21	1.20	1.18	1.16	1.14	1.12	1.11	1.10	1.09	1.08	1.06	.25	
1.52	1.46	1.42	1.38	1.34	1.31	1.28	1.24	1.22	1.20	1.17	1.14	.10	**200**
1.72	1.62	1.57	1.52	1.46	1.41	1.39	1.32	1.29	1.26	1.22	1.19	.05	
2.13	1.97	1.89	1.79	1.69	1.63	1.58	1.48	1.44	1.39	1.33	1.28	.01	
1.22	1.19	1.18	1.16	1.14	1.13	1.12	1.09	1.08	1.07	1.04	1.00	.25	
1.49	1.42	1.38	1.34	1.30	1.26	1.24	1.18	1.17	1.13	1.08	1.00	.10	**∞**
1.67	1.57	1.52	1.46	1.39	1.35	1.32	1.24	1.22	1.17	1.11	1.00	.05	
2.04	1.88	1.79	1.70	1.59	1.52	1.47	1.36	1.32	1.25	1.15	1.00	.01	

SOURCE: Abridged from Table 18 in *Biometrika Tables for Statisticians*, Vol. 1, 3rd ed., E. S. Pearson and H. O. Hartley, eds. (New York: Cambridge, 1966). Used with permission of the editors and the Biometrika Trustees.

Error df	α	r = Number of Means or Number of Steps Between Ordered Means									
		2	3	4	5	6	7	8	9	10	11
5	.05	3.64	4.60	5.22	5.67	6.03	6.33	6.58	6.80	6.99	7.17
	.01	5.70	6.98	7.80	8.42	8.91	9.32	9.67	9.97	10.24	10.48
6	.05	3.46	4.34	4.90	5.30	5.63	5.90	6.12	6.32	6.49	6.65
	.01	5.24	6.33	7.03	7.56	7.97	8.32	8.61	8.87	9.10	9.30
7	.05	3.34	4.16	4.68	5.06	5.36	5.61	5.82	6.00	6.16	6.30
	.01	4.95	5.92	6.54	7.01	7.37	7.68	7.94	8.17	8.37	8.55
8	.05	3.26	4.04	4.53	4.89	5.17	5.40	5.60	5.77	5.92	6.05
	.01	4.75	5.64	6.20	6.62	6.96	7.24	7.47	7.68	7.86	8.03
9	.05	3.20	3.95	4.41	4.76	5.02	5.24	5.43	5.59	5.74	5.87
	.01	4.60	5.43	5.96	6.35	6.66	6.91	7.13	7.33	7.49	7.65
10	.05	3.15	3.88	4.33	4.65	4.91	5.12	5.30	5.46	5.60	5.72
	.01	4.48	5.27	5.77	6.14	6.43	6.67	6.87	7.05	7.21	7.36
11	.05	3.11	3.82	4.26	4.57	4.82	5.03	5.20	5.35	5.49	5.61
	.01	4.39	5.15	5.62	5.97	6.25	6.48	6.67	6.84	6.99	7.13
12	.05	3.08	3.77	4.20	4.51	4.75	4.95	5.12	5.27	5.39	5.51
	.01	4.32	5.05	5.50	5.84	6.10	6.32	6.51	6.67	6.81	6.94
13	.05	3.06	3.73	4.15	4.45	4.69	4.88	5.05	5.19	5.32	5.43
	.01	4.26	4.96	5.40	5.73	5.98	6.19	6.37	6.53	6.67	6.79
14	.05	3.03	3.70	4.11	4.41	4.64	4.83	4.99	5.13	5.25	5.36
	.01	4.21	4.89	5.32	5.63	5.88	6.08	6.26	6.41	6.54	6.66
15	.05	3.01	3.67	4.08	4.37	4.59	4.78	4.94	5.08	5.20	5.31
	.01	4.17	4.84	5.25	5.56	5.80	5.99	6.16	6.31	6.44	6.55
16	.05	3.00	3.65	4.05	4.33	4.56	4.74	4.90	5.03	5.15	5.26
	.01	4.13	4.79	5.19	5.49	5.72	5.92	6.08	6.22	6.35	6.46
17	.05	2.98	3.63	4.02	4.30	4.52	4.70	4.86	4.99	5.11	5.21
	.01	4.10	4.74	5.14	5.43	5.66	5.85	6.01	6.15	6.27	6.38
18	.05	2.97	3.61	4.00	4.28	4.49	4.67	4.82	4.96	5.07	5.17
	.01	4.07	4.70	5.09	5.38	5.60	5.79	5.94	6.08	6.20	6.31
19	.05	2.96	3.59	3.98	4.25	4.47	4.65	4.79	4.92	5.04	5.14
	.01	4.05	4.67	5.05	5.33	5.55	5.73	5.89	6.02	6.14	6.25
20	.05	2.95	3.58	3.96	4.23	4.45	4.62	4.77	4.90	5.01	5.11
	.01	4.02	4.64	5.02	5.29	5.51	5.69	5.84	5.97	6.09	6.19
24	.05	2.92	3.53	3.90	4.17	4.37	4.54	4.68	4.81	4.92	5.01
	.01	3.96	4.55	4.91	5.17	5.37	5.54	5.69	5.81	5.92	6.02
30	.05	2.89	3.49	3.85	4.10	4.30	4.46	4.60	4.72	4.82	4.92
	.01	3.89	4.45	4.80	5.05	5.24	5.40	5.54	5.65	5.76	5.85
40	.05	2.86	3.44	3.79	4.04	4.23	4.39	4.52	4.63	4.73	4.82
	.01	3.82	4.37	4.70	4.93	5.11	5.26	5.39	5.50	5.60	5.69
60	.05	2.83	3.40	3.74	3.98	4.16	4.31	4.44	4.55	4.65	4.73
	.01	3.76	4.28	4.59	4.82	4.99	5.13	5.25	5.36	5.45	5.53
120	.05	2.80	3.36	3.68	3.92	4.10	4.24	4.36	4.47	4.56	4.64
	.01	3.70	4.20	4.50	4.71	4.87	5.01	5.12	5.21	5.30	5.37
∞	.05	2.77	3.31	3.63	3.86	4.03	4.17	4.29	4.39	4.47	4.55
	.01	3.64	4.12	4.40	4.60	4.76	4.88	4.99	5.08	5.16	5.23

\multicolumn{9}{c}{r = **Number of Means or Number of Steps Between Ordered Means**}		α	Error df
12	**13**	**14**	**15**	**16**	**17**	**18**	**19**	**20**		
7.32	7.47	7.60	7.72	7.83	7.93	8.03	8.12	8.21	.05	5
10.70	10.89	11.08	11.24	11.40	11.55	11.68	11.81	11.93	.01	
6.79	6.92	7.03	7.14	7.24	7.34	7.43	7.51	7.59	.05	6
9.48	9.65	9.81	9.95	10.08	10.21	10.32	10.43	10.54	.01	
6.43	6.55	6.66	6.76	6.85	6.94	7.02	7.10	7.17	.05	7
8.71	8.86	9.00	9.12	9.24	9.35	9.46	9.55	9.65	.01	
6.18	6.29	6.39	6.48	6.57	6.65	6.73	6.80	6.87	.05	8
8.18	8.31	8.44	8.55	8.66	8.76	8.85	8.94	9.03	.01	
5.98	6.09	6.19	6.28	6.36	6.44	6.51	6.58	6.64	.05	9
7.78	7.91	8.03	8.13	8.23	8.33	8.41	8.49	8.57	.01	
5.83	5.93	6.03	6.11	6.19	6.27	6.34	6.40	6.47	.05	10
7.49	7.60	7.71	7.81	7.91	7.99	8.08	8.15	8.23	.01	
5.71	5.81	5.90	5.98	6.06	6.13	6.20	6.27	6.33	.05	11
7.25	7.36	7.46	7.56	7.65	7.73	7.81	7.88	7.95	.01	
5.61	5.71	5.80	5.88	5.95	6.02	6.09	6.15	6.21	.05	12
7.06	7.17	7.26	7.36	7.44	7.52	7.59	7.66	7.73	.01	
5.53	5.63	5.71	5.79	5.86	5.93	5.99	6.05	6.11	.05	13
6.90	7.01	7.10	7.19	7.27	7.35	7.42	7.48	7.55	.01	
5.46	5.55	5.64	5.71	5.79	5.85	5.91	5.97	6.03	.05	14
6.77	6.87	6.96	7.05	7.13	7.20	7.27	7.33	7.39	.01	
5.40	5.49	5.57	5.65	5.72	5.78	5.85	5.90	5.96	.05	15
6.66	6.76	6.84	6.93	7.00	7.07	7.14	7.20	7.26	.01	
5.35	5.44	5.52	5.59	5.66	5.73	5.79	5.84	5.90	.05	16
6.56	6.66	6.74	6.82	6.90	6.97	7.03	7.09	7.15	.01	
5.31	5.39	5.47	5.54	5.61	5.67	5.73	5.79	5.84	.05	17
6.48	6.57	6.66	6.73	6.81	6.87	6.94	7.00	7.05	.01	
5.27	5.35	5.43	5.50	5.57	5.63	5.69	5.74	5.79	.05	18
6.41	6.50	6.58	6.65	6.73	6.79	6.85	6.91	6.97	.01	
5.23	5.31	5.39	5.46	5.53	5.59	5.65	5.70	5.75	.05	19
6.34	6.43	6.51	6.58	6.65	6.72	6.78	6.84	6.89	.01	
5.20	5.28	5.36	5.43	5.49	5.55	5.61	5.66	5.71	.05	20
6.28	6.37	6.45	6.52	6.59	6.65	6.71	6.77	6.82	.01	
5.10	5.18	5.25	5.32	5.38	5.44	5.49	5.55	5.59	.05	24
6.11	6.19	6.26	6.33	6.39	6.45	6.51	6.56	6.61	.01	
5.00	5.08	5.15	5.21	5.27	5.33	5.38	5.43	5.47	.05	30
5.93	6.01	6.08	6.14	6.20	6.26	6.31	6.36	6.41	.01	
4.90	4.98	5.04	5.11	5.16	5.22	5.27	5.31	5.36	.05	40
5.76	5.83	5.90	5.96	6.02	6.07	6.12	6.16	6.21	.01	
4.81	4.88	4.94	5.00	5.06	5.11	5.15	5.20	5.24	.05	60
5.60	5.67	5.73	5.78	5.84	5.89	5.93	5.97	6.01	.01	
4.71	4.78	4.84	4.90	4.95	5.00	5.04	5.09	5.13	.05	120
5.44	5.50	5.56	5.61	5.66	5.71	5.75	5.79	5.83	.01	
4.62	4.68	4.74	4.80	4.85	4.89	4.93	4.97	5.01	.05	∞
5.29	5.35	5.40	5.45	5.49	5.54	5.57	5.61	5.65	.01	

Source: Abridged from Table 29 in *Biometrika Tables for Statisticians*, Vol 1, 3rd ed., E. S. Pearson and H. O. Hartley, eds. (New York: Cambridge, 1966). Used with permission of the editors and the Biometrika Trustees.

	Level of Significance for One-tailed Test			
	.05	.025	.01	.005
	Level of Significance for Two-tailed Test			
df	.10	.05	.02	.01
1	.988	.997	.9995	.9999
2	.900	.950	.980	.990
3	.805	.878	.934	.959
4	.729	.811	.882	.917
5	.669	.754	.833	.874
6	.622	.707	.789	.834
7	.582	.666	.750	.798
8	.549	.632	.716	.765
9	.521	.602	.685	.735
10	.497	.576	.658	.708
11	.476	.553	.634	.684
12	.458	.532	.612	.661
13	.441	.514	.592	.641
14	.426	.497	.574	.623
15	.412	.482	.558	.606
16	.400	.468	.542	.590
17	.389	.456	.528	.575
18	.378	.444	.516	.561
19	.369	.433	.503	.549
20	.360	.423	.492	.537
21	.352	.413	.482	.526
22	.344	.404	.472	.515
23	.337	.396	.462	.505
24	.330	.388	.453	.496
25	.323	.381	.445	.487
26	.317	.374	.437	.479
27	.311	.367	.430	.471
28	.306	.361	.423	.463
29	.301	.355	.416	.456
30	.296	.349	.409	.449
35	.275	.325	.381	.418
40	.257	.304	.358	.393
45	.243	.288	.338	.372
50	.231	.273	.322	.354
60	.211	.250	.295	.325
70	.195	.232	.274	.303
80	.183	.217	.256	.283
90	.173	.205	.242	.267
100	.164	.195	.230	.254

SOURCE: Abridged from Table VII, p. 63 of Fisher and Yates: *Statistical Tables for Biological, Agricultural and Medical Research*, 6th ed., 1974. Published by Longman Group Ltd., London. (previously published by Oliver and Boyd, Edinburgh), and by permission of the authors and publishers.

TABLE T   *Critical Values for Wilcoxon's Matched-Pairs Signed-Ranks Test*

	Level of Significance for One-tailed Test		
	.025	.01	.005
N	Level of Significance for Two-tailed Test		
	.05	.02	.01
6	0	—	—
7	2	0	—
8	4	2	0
9	6	3	2
10	8	5	3
11	11	7	5
12	14	10	7
13	17	13	10
14	21	16	13
15	25	20	16
16	30	24	20
17	35	28	23
18	40	33	28
19	46	38	32
20	52	43	38
21	59	49	43
22	66	56	49
23	73	62	55
24	81	69	61
25	89	77	68

SOURCE: Adapted from Table I of F. Wilcoxon, *Some Rapid Approximate Statistical Procedures* (New York: American Cyanamid Company, 1949), p. 13.

TABLE t *t Critical Values*

df	Level of Significance for One–Tailed Test					
	.10	.05	.025	.01	.005	.0005
	Level of Significance for Two–tailed Test					
	.20	.10	.05	.02	.01	.001
1	3.078	6.314	12.706	31.821	63.657	636.619
2	1.886	2.920	4.303	6.965	9.925	31.598
3	1.638	2.353	3.182	4.541	5.841	12.941
4	1.533	2.132	2.776	3.747	4.604	8.610
5	1.476	2.015	2.571	3.365	4.032	6.859
6	1.440	1.943	2.447	3.143	3.707	5.959
7	1.415	1.895	2.365	2.998	3.499	5.405
8	1.397	1.860	2.306	2.896	3.355	5.041
9	1.383	1.833	2.262	2.821	3.250	4.781
10	1.372	1.812	2.228	2.764	3.169	4.587
11	1.363	1.796	2.201	2.718	3.106	4.437
12	1.356	1.782	2.179	2.681	3.055	4.318
13	1.350	1.771	2.160	2.650	3.012	4.221
14	1.345	1.761	2.145	2.624	2.977	4.140
15	1.341	1.753	2.131	2.602	2.947	4.073
16	1.337	1.746	2.120	2.583	2.921	4.015
17	1.333	1.740	2.110	2.567	2.898	3.965
18	1.330	1.734	2.101	2.552	2.878	3.922
19	1.328	1.729	2.093	2.539	2.861	3.883
20	1.325	1.725	2.086	2.528	2.845	3.850
21	1.323	1.721	2.080	2.518	2.831	3.819
22	1.321	1.717	2.074	2.508	2.819	3.792
23	1.319	1.714	2.069	2.500	2.807	3.767
24	1.318	1.711	2.064	2.492	2.797	3.745
25	1.316	1.708	2.060	2.485	2.787	3.725
26	1.315	1.706	2.056	2.479	2.779	3.707
27	1.314	1.703	2.052	2.473	2.771	3.690
28	1.313	1.701	2.048	2.467	2.763	3.674
29	1.311	1.699	2.045	2.462	2.756	3.659
30	1.310	1.697	2.042	2.457	2.750	3.646
40	1.303	1.684	2.021	2.423	2.704	3.551
60	1.296	1.671	2.000	2.390	2.660	3.460
120	1.289	1.658	1.980	2.358	2.617	3.373
∞	1.282	1.645	1.960	2.326	2.576	3.291

SOURCE: Taken from Table III, p. 46 of Fisher and Yates: *Statistical Tables for Biological, Agricultural and Medical Research*, 6th ed., 1974. Published by Longman Group Ltd., London. (previously published by Oliver and Boyd, Edinburgh), and by permission of the authors and publishers.

TABLE W   *Critical Values for Wilcoxon's Rank-Sum Test*

$N_1 = 1$

N_2	0.001	0.005	0.010	0.025	0.05	0.10	$2\overline{W}$
2							4
3							5
4							6
5							7
6							8
7							9
8						—	10
9						1	11
10						1	12
11						1	13
12						1	14
13						1	15
14						1	16
15						1	17
16						1	18
17						1	19
18					—	1	20
19					1	2	21
20					1	2	22
21					1	2	23
22					1	2	24
23					1	2	25
24					1	2	26
25	—	—	—	—	1	2	27

$N_1 = 2$

0.001	0.005	0.010	0.025	0.05	0.10	$2\overline{W}$	N_2
					—	10	2
					3	12	3
				—	3	14	4
				3	4	16	5
				3	4	18	6
			—	3	4	20	7
			3	4	5	22	8
			3	4	5	24	9
			3	4	6	26	10
			3	4	6	28	11
		—	4	5	7	30	12
		3	4	5	7	32	13
		3	4	6	8	34	14
		3	4	6	8	36	15
		3	4	6	8	38	16
		3	5	6	9	40	17
	—	3	5	7	9	42	18
	3	4	5	7	10	44	19
	3	4	5	7	10	46	20
	3	4	6	8	11	48	21
	3	4	6	8	11	50	22
	3	4	6	8	12	52	23
	3	4	6	9	12	54	24
—	3	4	6	9	12	56	25

$N_1 = 3$

N_2	0.001	0.005	0.010	0.025	0.05	0.10	$2\overline{W}$
3					6	7	21
4				—	6	7	24
5				6	7	8	27
6			—	7	8	9	30
7			6	7	8	10	33
8		—	6	8	9	11	36
9		6	7	8	10	11	39
10		6	7	9	10	12	42
11		6	7	9	11	13	45
12		7	8	10	11	14	48
13		7	8	10	12	15	51
14		7	8	11	13	16	54
15		8	9	11	13	16	57
16	—	8	9	12	14	17	60
17	6	8	10	12	15	18	63
18	6	8	10	13	15	19	66
19	6	9	10	13	16	20	69
20	6	9	11	14	17	21	72
21	7	9	11	14	17	21	75

$N_1 = 4$

0.001	0.005	0.010	0.025	0.05	0.10	$2\overline{W}$	N_2
		—	10	11	13	36	4
	—	10	11	12	14	40	5
	10	11	12	13	15	44	6
	10	11	13	14	16	48	7
	11	12	14	15	17	52	8
—	11	13	14	16	19	56	9
10	12	13	15	17	20	60	10
10	12	14	16	18	21	64	11
10	13	15	17	19	22	68	12
11	13	15	18	20	23	72	13
11	14	16	19	21	25	76	14
11	15	17	20	22	26	80	15
12	15	17	21	24	27	84	16
12	16	18	21	25	28	88	17
13	16	19	22	26	30	92	18
13	17	19	23	27	31	96	19
13	18	20	24	28	32	100	20
14	18	21	25	29	33	104	21

TABLE W *continued*

			$N_1 = 3$								$N_1 = 4$				
N_2	0.001	0.005	0.010	0.025	0.05	0.10	$2\overline{W}$	0.001	0.005	0.010	0.025	0.05	0.10	$2\overline{W}$	N_2
22	7	10	12	15	18	22	78	14	19	21	26	30	35	108	22
23	7	10	12	15	19	23	81	14	19	22	27	31	36	112	23
24	7	10	12	16	19	24	84	15	20	23	27	32	38	116	24
25	7	11	13	16	20	25	87	15	20	23	28	33	38	120	25

			$N_1 = 5$								$N_1 = 6$				
N_2	0.001	0.005	0.010	0.025	0.05	0.10	$2\overline{W}$	0.001	0.005	0.010	0.025	0.05	0.10	$2\overline{W}$	N_2
5		15	16	17	19	20	55								
6		16	17	18	20	22	60	—	23	24	26	28	30	78	6
7	—	16	18	20	21	23	65	21	24	25	27	29	32	84	7
8	15	17	19	21	23	25	70	22	25	27	29	31	34	90	8
9	16	18	20	22	24	27	75	23	26	28	31	33	36	96	9
10	16	19	21	23	26	28	80	24	27	29	32	35	38	102	10
11	17	20	22	24	27	30	85	25	28	30	34	37	40	108	11
12	17	21	23	26	28	32	90	25	30	32	35	38	42	114	12
13	18	22	24	27	30	33	95	26	31	33	37	40	44	120	13
14	18	22	25	28	31	35	100	27	32	34	38	42	46	126	14
15	19	23	26	29	33	37	105	28	33	36	40	44	48	132	15
16	20	24	27	30	34	38	110	29	34	37	42	46	50	138	16
17	20	25	28	32	35	40	115	30	36	39	43	47	52	144	17
18	21	26	29	33	37	42	120	31	37	40	45	49	55	150	18
19	22	27	30	34	38	43	125	32	38	41	46	51	57	156	19
20	22	28	31	35	40	45	130	33	39	43	48	53	59	162	20
21	23	29	32	37	41	47	135	33	40	44	50	55	61	168	21
22	23	29	33	38	43	48	140	34	42	45	51	57	63	174	22
23	24	30	34	39	44	50	145	35	43	47	53	58	65	180	23
24	25	31	35	40	45	51	150	36	44	48	54	60	67	186	24
25	25	32	36	42	47	53	155	37	45	50	56	62	69	192	25

			$N_1 = 7$								$N_1 = 8$				
N_2	0.001	0.005	0.010	0.025	0.05	0.10	$2\overline{W}$	0.001	0.005	0.010	0.025	0.05	0.10	$2\overline{W}$	N_2
7	29	32	34	36	39	41	105								
8	30	34	35	38	41	44	112	40	43	45	49	51	55	136	8
9	31	35	37	40	43	46	119	41	45	47	51	54	58	144	9
10	33	37	39	42	45	49	126	42	47	49	53	56	60	152	10
11	34	38	40	44	47	51	133	44	49	51	55	59	63	160	11
12	35	40	42	46	49	54	140	45	51	53	58	62	66	168	12
13	36	41	44	48	52	56	147	47	53	56	60	64	69	176	13
14	37	43	45	50	54	59	154	48	54	58	62	67	72	184	14
15	38	44	47	52	56	61	161	50	56	60	65	69	75	192	15
16	39	46	49	54	58	64	168	51	58	62	67	72	78	200	16
17	41	47	51	56	61	66	175	53	60	64	70	75	81	208	17

TABLE W *continued*

N_2	$N_1 = 7$ 0.001	0.005	0.010	0.025	0.05	0.10	$2\overline{W}$	$N_1 = 8$ 0.001	0.005	0.010	0.025	0.05	0.10	$2\overline{W}$	N_2
18	42	49	52	58	63	69	182	54	62	66	72	77	84	216	18
19	43	50	54	60	65	71	189	56	64	68	74	80	87	224	19
20	44	52	56	62	67	74	196	57	66	70	77	83	90	232	20
21	46	53	58	64	69	76	203	59	68	72	79	85	92	240	21
22	47	55	59	66	72	79	210	60	70	74	81	88	95	248	22
23	48	57	61	68	74	81	217	62	71	76	84	90	98	256	23
24	49	58	63	70	76	84	224	64	73	78	86	93	101	264	24
25	50	60	64	72	78	86	231	65	75	81	89	96	104	272	25

N_2	$N_1 = 9$ 0.001	0.005	0.010	0.025	0.05	0.10	$2\overline{W}$	$N_1 = 10$ 0.001	0.005	0.010	0.025	0.05	0.10	$2\overline{W}$	N_2
9	52	56	59	62	66	70	171								
10	53	58	61	65	69	73	180	65	71	74	78	82	87	210	10
11	55	61	63	68	72	76	189	67	73	77	81	86	91	220	11
12	57	63	66	71	75	80	198	69	76	79	84	89	94	230	12
13	59	65	68	73	78	83	207	72	79	82	88	92	98	240	13
14	60	67	71	76	81	86	216	74	81	85	91	96	102	250	14
15	62	69	73	79	84	90	225	76	84	88	94	99	106	260	15
16	64	72	76	82	87	93	234	78	86	91	97	103	109	270	16
17	66	74	78	84	90	97	243	80	89	93	100	106	113	280	17
18	68	76	81	87	93	100	252	82	92	96	103	110	117	290	18
19	70	78	83	90	96	103	261	84	94	99	107	113	121	300	19
20	71	81	85	93	99	107	270	87	97	102	110	117	125	310	20
21	73	83	88	95	102	110	279	89	99	105	113	120	128	320	21
22	75	85	90	98	105	113	288	91	102	108	116	123	132	330	22
23	77	88	93	101	108	117	297	93	105	110	119	127	136	340	23
24	79	90	95	104	111	120	306	95	107	113	122	130	140	350	24
25	81	92	98	107	114	123	315	98	110	116	126	134	144	360	25

N_2	$N_1 = 11$ 0.001	0.005	0.010	0.025	0.05	0.10	$2\overline{W}$	$N_1 = 12$ 0.001	0.005	0.010	0.025	0.05	0.10	$2\overline{W}$	N_2
11	81	87	91	96	100	106	253								
12	83	90	94	99	104	110	264	98	105	109	115	120	127	300	12
13	86	93	97	103	108	114	275	101	109	113	119	125	131	312	13
14	88	96	100	106	112	118	286	103	112	116	123	129	136	324	14
15	90	99	103	110	116	123	297	106	115	120	127	133	141	336	15
16	93	102	107	113	120	127	308	109	119	124	131	138	145	348	16
17	95	105	110	117	123	131	319	112	122	127	135	142	150	360	17
18	98	108	113	121	127	135	330	115	125	131	139	146	155	372	18
19	100	111	116	124	131	139	341	118	129	134	143	150	159	384	19
20	103	114	119	128	135	144	352	120	132	138	147	155	164	396	20
21	106	117	123	131	139	148	363	123	136	142	151	159	169	408	21

TABLE W *continued*

N_2	$N_1 = 11$							$N_1 = 12$							N_2
	0.001	0.005	0.010	0.025	0.05	0.10	$2\overline{W}$	0.001	0.005	0.010	0.025	0.05	0.10	$2\overline{W}$	
22	108	120	126	135	143	152	374	126	139	145	155	163	173	420	22
23	111	123	129	139	147	156	385	129	142	149	159	168	178	432	23
24	113	126	132	142	151	161	396	132	146	153	163	172	183	444	24
25	116	129	136	146	155	165	407	135	149	156	167	176	187	456	25

N_2	$N_1 = 13$							$N_1 = 14$							N_2
	0.001	0.005	0.010	0.025	0.05	0.10	$2\overline{W}$	0.001	0.005	0.010	0.025	0.05	0.10	$2\overline{W}$	
13	117	125	130	136	142	149	351								
14	120	129	134	141	147	154	364	137	147	152	160	166	174	406	14
15	123	133	138	145	152	159	377	141	151	156	164	171	179	420	15
16	126	136	142	150	156	165	390	144	155	161	169	176	185	434	16
17	129	140	146	154	161	170	403	148	159	165	174	182	190	448	17
18	133	144	150	158	166	175	416	151	163	170	179	187	196	462	18
19	136	148	154	163	171	180	429	155	168	174	183	192	202	476	19
20	139	151	158	167	175	185	442	159	172	178	188	197	207	490	20
21	142	155	162	171	180	190	455	162	176	183	193	202	213	504	21
22	145	159	166	176	185	195	468	166	180	187	198	207	218	518	22
23	149	163	170	180	189	200	481	169	184	192	203	212	224	532	23
24	152	166	174	185	194	205	494	173	188	196	207	218	229	546	24
25	155	170	178	189	199	211	507	177	192	200	212	223	235	560	25

N_2	$N_1 = 15$							$N_1 = 16$							N_2
	0.001	0.005	0.010	0.025	0.05	0.10	$2\overline{W}$	0.001	0.005	0.010	0.025	0.05	0.10	$2\overline{W}$	
15	160	171	176	184	192	200	465								
16	163	175	181	190	197	206	480	184	196	202	211	219	229	528	16
17	167	180	186	195	203	212	495	188	201	207	217	225	235	544	17
18	171	184	190	200	208	218	510	192	206	212	222	231	242	560	18
19	175	189	195	205	214	224	525	196	210	218	228	237	248	576	19
20	179	193	200	210	220	230	540	201	215	223	234	243	255	592	20
21	183	198	205	216	225	236	555	205	220	228	239	249	261	608	21
22	187	202	210	221	231	242	570	209	225	233	245	255	267	624	22
23	191	207	214	226	236	248	585	214	230	238	251	261	274	640	23
24	195	211	219	231	242	254	600	218	235	244	256	267	280	656	24
25	199	216	224	237	248	260	615	222	240	249	262	273	287	672	25

N_2	$N_1 = 17$							$N_1 = 18$							N_2
	0.001	0.005	0.010	0.025	0.05	0.10	$2\overline{W}$	0.001	0.005	0.010	0.025	0.05	0.10	$2\overline{W}$	
17	210	223	230	240	249	259	595								
18	214	228	235	246	255	266	612	237	252	259	270	280	291	666	18
19	219	234	241	252	262	273	629	242	258	265	277	287	299	684	19

TABLE W *continued*

N_2	$N_1 = 17$ 0.001	0.005	0.010	0.025	0.05	0.10	$2\overline{W}$	$N_1 = 18$ 0.001	0.005	0.010	0.025	0.05	0.10	$2\overline{W}$	N_2
20	223	239	246	258	268	280	646	247	263	271	283	294	306	702	20
21	228	244	252	264	274	287	663	252	269	277	290	301	313	720	21
22	233	249	258	270	281	294	680	257	275	283	296	307	321	738	22
23	238	255	263	276	287	300	697	262	280	289	303	314	328	756	23
24	242	260	269	282	294	307	714	267	286	295	309	321	335	774	24
25	247	265	275	288	300	314	731	273	292	301	316	328	343	792	25

N_2	$N_1 = 19$ 0.001	0.005	0.010	0.025	0.05	0.10	$2\overline{W}$	$N_1 = 20$ 0.001	0.005	0.010	0.025	0.05	0.10	$2\overline{W}$	N_2
19	267	283	291	303	313	325	741								
20	272	289	297	309	320	333	760	298	315	324	337	348	361	820	20
21	277	295	303	316	328	341	779	304	322	331	344	356	370	840	21
22	283	301	310	323	335	349	798	309	328	337	351	364	378	860	22
23	288	307	316	330	342	357	817	315	335	344	359	371	386	880	23
24	294	313	323	337	350	364	836	321	341	351	366	379	394	900	24
25	299	319	329	344	357	372	855	327	348	358	373	387	403	920	25

N_2	$N_1 = 21$ 0.001	0.005	0.010	0.025	0.05	0.10	$2\overline{W}$	$N_1 = 22$ 0.001	0.005	0.010	0.025	0.05	0.10	$2\overline{W}$	N_2
21	331	349	359	373	385	399	903								
22	337	356	366	381	393	408	924	365	386	396	411	424	439	990	22
23	343	363	373	388	401	417	945	372	393	403	419	432	448	1012	23
24	349	370	381	396	410	425	966	379	400	411	427	441	457	1034	24
25	356	377	388	404	418	434	987	385	408	419	435	450	467	1056	25

N_2	$N_1 = 23$ 0.001	0.005	0.010	0.025	0.05	0.10	$2\overline{W}$	$N_1 = 24$ 0.001	0.005	0.010	0.025	0.05	0.10	$2\overline{W}$	N_2
23	402	424	434	451	465	481	1081								
24	409	431	443	459	474	491	1104	440	464	475	492	507	525	1176	24
25	416	439	451	468	483	500	1127	448	472	484	501	517	535	1200	25

N_2	$N_1 = 25$ 0.001	0.005	0.010	0.025	0.05	0.10	$2\overline{W}$
25	480	505	517	536	552	570	1275

SOURCE: Table 1 in L. R. Verdooren, Extended tables of critical values for Wilcoxon's test statistic, *Biometrika*, 1963, **50**, 177–186, with permission of the author and editor.

TABLE Z *Areas under the Normal Curve*

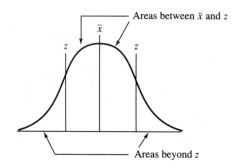

Areas between $\bar{x}$ and z

Areas beyond z

z	Area Between $\bar{x}$ and z	Area Beyond z	Ordinate	z	Area Between $\bar{x}$ and z	Area Beyond z	Ordinate	z	Area Between $\bar{x}$ and z	Area Beyond z	Ordinate
0.00	.0000	.5000	.3989	0.32	.1255	.3745	.3790	0.64	.2389	.2611	.3251
0.01	.0040	.4960	.3989	0.33	.1293	.3707	.3778	0.65	.2422	.2578	.3230
0.02	.0080	.4920	.3989	0.34	.1331	.3669	.3765	0.66	.2454	.2546	.3209
0.03	.0120	.4880	.3988	0.35	.1368	.3632	.3752	0.67	.2486	.2514	.3187
0.04	.0160	.4840	.3986	0.36	.1406	.3594	.3739	0.68	.2517	.2483	.3166
0.05	.0199	.4801	.3984	0.37	.1443	.3557	.3725	0.69	.2549	.2451	.3144
0.06	.0239	.4761	.3982	0.38	.1480	.3520	.3712	0.70	.2580	.2420	.3123
0.07	.0279	.4721	.3980	0.39	.1517	.3483	.3697	0.71	.2611	.2389	.3101
0.08	.0319	.4681	.3977	0.40	.1554	.3446	.3683	0.72	.2642	,2358	.3079
0.09	.0359	.4641	.3973	0.41	.1591	.3409	.3668	0.73	.2673	.2327	.3056
0.10	.0398	.4602	.3970	0.42	.1628	.3372	.3653	0.74	.2704	.2296	.3034
0.11	.0438	.4562	.3965	0.43	.1664	.3336	.3637	0.75	.2734	.2266	.3011
0.12	.0478	.4522	.3961	0.44	.1700	.3300	.3621	0.76	.2764	.2236	.2989
0.13	.0517	.4483	.3956	0.45	.1736	.3264	.3605	0.77	.2794	.2206	.2966
0.14	.0557	.4443	.3951	0.46	.1772	.3228	.3589	0.78	.2823	.2177	.2943
0.15	.0596	.4404	.3945	0.47	.1808	.3192	.3572	0.79	.2852	.2148	.2920
0.16	.0636	.4364	.3939	0.48	.1844	.3156	.3555	0.80	.2881	.2119	.2897
0.17	.0675	.4325	.3932	0.49	.1879	.3121	.3538	0.81	.2910	.2090	.2874
0.18	.0714	.4286	.3925	0.50	.1915	.3085	.3521	0.82	.2939	.2061	.2850
0.19	.0753	.4247	.3918	0.51	.1950	.3050	.3503	0.83	.2967	.2033	.2827
0.20	.0793	.4207	.3910	0.52	.1985	.3015	.3485	0.84	.2995	.2005	.2803
0.21	.0832	.4168	.3902	0.53	.2019	.2981	.3467	0.85	.3023	.1977	.2780
0.22	.0871	.4129	.3894	0.54	.2054	.2946	.3448	0.86	.3051	.1949	.2756
0.23	.0910	.4090	.3885	0.55	.2088	.2912	.3429	0.87	.3078	.1922	.2732
0.24	.0948	.4052	.3876	0.56	.2123	.2877	.3410	0.88	.3106	.1894	.2709
0.25	.0987	.4013	.3867	0.57	.2157	.2843	.3391	0.89	.3133	.1867	.2685
0.26	.1026	.3974	.3857	0.58	.2190	.2810	.3372	0.90	.3159	.1841	.2661
0.27	.1064	.3936	.3847	0.59	.2224	.2776	.3352	0.91	.3186	.1814	.2637
0.28	.1103	.3897	.3836	0.60	.2257	.2743	.3352	0.92	.3212	.1788	.2613
0.29	.1141	.3859	.3825	0.61	.2291	.2709	.3312	0.93	.3238	.1762	.2589
0.30	.1179	.3821	.3814	0.62	.2324	.2676	.3292	0.94	.3264	.1736	.2565
0.31	.1217	.3783	.3802	0.63	.2357	.2643	.3271	0.95	.3289	.1711	.2541

TABLE Z *continued*

z	Area Between $\bar{x}$ and z	Area Beyond z	Ordinate	z	Area Between $\bar{x}$ and z	Area Beyond z	Ordinate	z	Area Between $\bar{x}$ and z	Area Beyond z	Ordinate
0.96	.3315	.1685	.2516	1.41	.4207	.0793	.1476	1.86	.4686	.0314	.0707
0.97	.3340	.1660	.2492	1.42	.4222	.0778	.1456	1.87	.4693•	.0307	.0694
0.98	.3365	.1635	.2468	1.43	.4236	.0764	.1435	1.88	.4699	.0301	.0681
0.99	.3389	.1611	.2444	1.44	.4251	.0749	.1415	1.89	.4706	.0294	.0669
1.00	.3413	.1587	.2420	1.45	.4265	.0735	.1394	1.90	.4713	.0287	.0656
1.01	.3438	.1562	.2396	1.46	.4279	.0721	.1374	1.91	.4719	.0281	.0644
1.02	.3461	.1539	.2371	1.47	.4292	.0708	.1354	1.92	.4726	.0274	.0632
1.03	.3485	.1515	.2347	1.48	.4306	.0694	.1334	1.93	.4732	.0268	.0620
1.04	.3508	.1492	.2323	1.49	.4319	.0681	.1315	1.94	.4738	.0262	.0608
1.05	.3531	.1469	.2299	1.50	.4332	.0668	.1295	1.95	.4744	.0256	.0596
1.06	.3554	.1446	.2275	1.51	.4345	.0655	.1276	1.96	.4750	.0250	.0584
1.07	.3577	.1423	.2251	1.52	.4357	.0643	.1257	1.97	.4756	.0244	.0573
1.08	.3599	.1401	.2227	1.53	.4370	.0630	.1238	1.98	.4761	.0239	.0562
1.09	.3621	.1379	.2203	1.54	.4382	.0618	.1219	1.99	.4767	.0233	.0551
1.10	.3643	.1357	.2179	1.55	.4394	.0606	.1200	2.00	.4772	.0228	.0540
1.11	.3665	.1335	.2155	1.56	.4406	.0594	.1182	2.01	.4778	.0222	.0529
1.12	.3686	.1314	.2131	1.57	.4418	.0582	.1163	2.02	.4783	.0217	.0519
1.13	.3708	.1292	.2107	1.58	.4429	.0571	.1145	2.03	.4788	.0212	.0508
1.14	.3729	.1271	.2083	1.59	.4441	.0559	.1127	2.04	.4793	.0207	.0498
1.15	.3749	.1251	.2059	1.60	.4452	.0548	.1109	2.05	.4798	.0202	.0488
1.16	.3770	.1230	.2036	1.61	.4463	.0537	.1092	2.06	.4803	.0197	.0478
1.17	.3790	.1210	.2012	1.62	.4474	.0526	.1074	2.07	.4808	.0192	.0468
1.18	.3810	.1190	.1989	1.63	.4484	.0516	.1057	2.08	.4812	.0188	.0459
1.19	.3830	.1170	.1965	1.64	.4495	.0505	.1040	2.09	.4817	.0183	.0449
1.20	.3849	.1151	.1942	1.65	.4505	.0495	.1023	2.10	.4821	.0179	.0440
1.21	.3869	.1131	.1919	1.66	.4515	.0485	.1006	2.11	.4826	.0174	.0431
1.22	.3888	.1112	.1895	1.67	.4525	.0475	.0989	2.12	.4830	.0170	.0422
1.23	.3907	.1093	.1872	1.68	.4535	.0465	.0973	2.13	.4834	.0166	.0413
1.24	.3925	.1075	.1849	1.69	.4545	.0455	.0957	2.14	.4838	.0162	.0404
1.25	.3944	.1056	.1826	1.70	.4554	.0446	.0940	2.15	.4842	.0158	.0395
1.26	.3962	.1038	.1804	1.71	.4564	.0436	.0925	2.16	.4846	.0154	.0387
1.27	.3980	.1020	.1781	1.72	.4573	.0427	.0909	2.17	.4850	.0150	.0379
1.28	.3997	.1003	.1758	1.73	.4582	.0418	.0893	2.18	.4854	.0146	.0371
1.29	.4015	.0985	.1736	1.74	.4591	.0409	.0878	2.19	.4857	.0143	.0363
1.30	.4032	.0968	.1714	1.75	.4599	.0401	.0863	2.20	.4861	.0139	.0355
1.31	.4049	.0951	.1691	1.76	.4608	.0392	.0848	2.21	.4864	.0136	.0347
1.32	.4066	.0934	.1669	1.77	.4616	.0384	.0833	2.22	.4868	.0132	.0339
1.33	.4082	.0918	.1647	1.78	.4625	.0375	.0818	2.23	.4871	.0129	.0332
1.34	.4099	.0901	.1626	1.79	.4633	.0367	.0804	2.24	.4875	.0125	.0325
1.35	.4115	.0885	.1604	1.80	.4641	.0359	.0790	2.25	.4878	.0122	.0317
1.36	.4131	.0869	.1582	1.81	.4649	.0351	.0775	2.26	.4881	.0119	.0310
1.37	.4147	.0853	.1561	1.82	.4656	.0344	.0761	2.27	.4884	.0116	.0303
1.38	.4162	.0838	.1539	1.83	.4664	.0336	.0748	2.28	.4887	.0113	.0297
1.39	.4177	.0823	.1518	1.84	.4671	.0329	.0734	2.29	.4890	.0110	.0290
1.40	.4192	.0808	.1497	1.85	.4678	.0322	.0721	2.30	.4893	.0107	.0283

TABLE Z *continued*

z	Area Between $\bar{x}$ and z	Area Beyond z	Ordinate	z	Area Between $\bar{x}$ and z	Area Beyond z	Ordinate	z	Area Between $\bar{x}$ and z	Area Beyond z	Ordinate
2.31	.4896	.0104	.0277	2.66	.4961	.0039	.0116	3.01	.4987	.0013	.0033
2.32	.4898	.0102	.0270	2.67	.4962	.0038	.0113	3.02	.4987	.0013	.0024
2.33	.4901	.0099	.0264	2.68	.4963	.0037	.0110	3.03	.4988	.0012	.0017
2.34	.4904	.0096	.0258	2.69	.4964	.0036	.0107	3.04	.4988	.0012	.0012
2.35	.4906	.0094	.0252	2.70	.4965	.0035	.0104	3.05	.4989	.0011	.0009
2.36	.4909	.0091	.0246	2.71	.4966	.0034	.0101	3.06	.4989	.0011	.0006
2.37	.4911	.0089	.0241	2.72	.4967	.0033	.0099	3.07	.4989	.0011	.0004
2.38	.4913	.0087	.0235	2.73	.4968	.0032	.0096	3.08	.4990	.0010	.0003
2.39	.4916	.0084	.0229	2.74	.4969	.0031	.0093	3.09	.4990	.0010	.0002*
2.40	.4918	.0082	.0224	2.75	.4970	.0030	.0091	3.10	.4990	.0010	
2.41	.4920	.0080	.0219	2.76	.4971	.0029	.0088	3.11	.4991	.0009	
2.42	.4922	.0078	.0213	2.77	.4972	.0028	.0086	3.12	.4991	.0009	
2.43	.4925	.0075	.0208	2.78	.4973	.0027	.0084	3.13	.4991	.0009	
2.44	.4927	.0073	.0203	2.79	.4974	.0026	.0081	3.14	.4992	.0008	
2.45	.4929	.0071	.0198	2.80	.4974	.0026	.0079	3.15	.4992	.0008	
2.46	.4931	.0069	.0194	2.81	.4975	.0025	.0077	3.16	.4992	.0008	
2.47	.4932	.0068	.0189	2.82	.4976	.0024	.0075	3.17	.4992	.0008	
2.48	.4934	.0066	.0184	2.83	.4977	.0023	.0073	3.18	.4993	.0007	
2.49	.4936	.0064	.0180	2.84	.4977	.0023	.0071	3.19	.4993	.0007	
2.50	.4938	.0062	.0175	2.85	.4978	.0022	.0069	3.20	.4993	.0007	
2.51	.4940	.0060	.0171	2.86	.4979	.0021	.0067	3.21	.4993	.0007	
2.52	.4941	.0059	.0167	2.87	.4979	.0021	.0065	3.22	.4994	.0006	
2.53	.4943	.0057	.0163	2.88	.4980	.0020	.0063	3.23	.4994	.0006	
2.54	.4945	.0055	.0158	2.89	.4981	.0019	.0061	3.24	.4994	.0006	
2.55	.4946	.0054	.0154	2.90	.4981	.0019	.0060	3.25	.4994	.0006	
2.56	.4948	.0052	.0151	2.91	.4982	.0018	.0058	3.30	.4995	.0005	
2.57	.4949	.0051	.0147	2.92	.4982	.0018	.0056	3.35	.4996	.0004	
2.58	.4951	.0049	.0143	2.93	.4983	.0017	.0055	3.40	.4997	.0003	
2.59	.4952	.0048	.0139	2.94	.4984	.0016	.0053	3.45	.4997	.0003	
2.60	.4953	.0047	.0136	2.95	.4984	.0016	.0051	3.50	.4998	.0002	
2.61	.4955	.0045	.0132	2.96	.4985	.0015	.0050	3.60	.4998	.0002	
2.62	.4856	.0044	.0129	2.97	.4985	.0015	.0048	3.70	.4999	.0001	
2.63	.4957	.0043	.0126	2.98	.4986	.0014	.0047	3.80	.4999	.0001	
2.64	.4959	.0041	.0122	2.99	.4986	.0014	.0046	3.90	.49995	.00005	
2.65	.4960	.0040	.0119	3.00	.4987	.0013	.0044	4.00	.49997	.00003	

SOURCE: Taken from Table IIi of R. A. Fisher and F. Yates, *Statistical Tables for Biological, Agricultural and Medical Research*, 6th ed., 1974. Published by Longman Group Ltd., London (previously published by Oliver and Boyd, Edinburgh), and by permission of the authors and publishers.

*For values of z greater than 3.09, the height of the curve is negligible and the value of the ordinate is close to zero.

Empirical Research Reports in Psychology: What They Are, What They Say, Where to Find Them, and How to Write Them

One of the responsibilities of a researcher is to make the results of his or her research project known to other interested individuals. In psychology, this is usually done by presenting the research at a conference and/or by publishing a research report in a scholarly journal. The research report is a written description of the research project. It is presented in a standard form used by all the subdisciplines in psychology as well as by many other disciplines. In this appendix, I will discuss the review process that is used to choose reports for publication in journals. I will also show how you can find reports on particular topics. The last section of this appendix will focus on how to write your own research report.

RESEARCH REPORTS: WHAT THEY ARE

Journals are thin paperback books that contain numerous short reports; they are published monthly, bimonthly, or quarterly. Libraries usually have a year's worth of journals (or more) bound together in a single volume, to prevent individual issues from getting lost and to protect the material.

Many scholarly journals do not sell advertising space; consequently, they earn most of their money through annual individual and institutional subscriptions. These subscription rates are not trivial; individual rates might be $25, $75, or more per year, while institutional rates (the rates that libraries are charged) are typically in the hundreds of dollars. For this reason, many smaller libraries may have only the most standard journals in a discipline; they simply cannot afford the annual institutional subscription rates for very many journals. For subscribers to get their money's worth from the journal, the journal must present the highest-quality material available. This is done by carefully selecting research reports for publication, using a thorough review process.

THE REVIEW PROCESS

A manuscript of a research report that is sent to a journal editor is assessed by the editor for appropriateness for that journal. Obviously, if a manuscript on adult memory processes were submitted to *Child Development*, it would be returned to the author with the suggestion that it be submitted to a different journal. If the editor believes that the topic is appropriate, the manuscript is then sent to three reviewers.

The review process used by many scholarly journals is called **blind review**. In a blind review, three reviewers read and critique a manuscript without having any knowledge of its author or authors. By this means, manuscripts written by major researchers in a discipline and manuscripts written by first-time researchers are given equal attention. The reviewers—experts in the topic addressed by the manuscript—evaluate the quality of the research procedure, the logic of the hypotheses, the appropriateness of the statistical analyses, and the thoroughness of the discussion. The reviewers might suggest further research topics or findings that need to be addressed, other statistical tests that need to be performed, or improvements that should be made to the research method itself.

Reviewers make one of three recommendations to the editor: that the manuscript be accepted for publication as is; that certain revisions be made and that the author(s) then resubmit the manuscript for reconsideration; or that the article be rejected and not published in the journal. The editor takes the reviewers' comments into consideration and makes a final decision about the manuscript.

The entire process, from initial submission of the manuscript for review to publication in the journal, can take as little as three months or as long as a year (or more). This is not counting the time required to research an area, design a study, collect the data, perform the statistical analyses, and write the report. The articles that you encounter in a psychology journal represent the product of a great deal of effort and time expended by authors, editors, and reviewers. Ideally, this effort results in a high-quality publication.

A temptation for some researchers is to submit the manuscript to two or more journals simultaneously. This is typically considered inappropriate. A great deal of time and effort put in by the editor and reviewers would be wasted if the author of a report submitted it to multiple journals at the same time. In the long run, this practice would serve only to increase the lag-time from submission to publication.

EMPIRICAL RESEARCH REPORTS: WHAT THEY SAY

Research reports are the most common type of article published in psychology journals and constitute the preferred manner of publicizing the results of research in psychology. The research reports published in psychology journals, like those published in journals for many other disciplines, are written and organized according to the organizational, referencing, and writing style described in the *Publication Manual of the American Psychological Association* (also called the *APA Manual*). The particular format described in the *APA Manual* is referred to as **APA style**. Research reports written in APA style have six important parts: an abstract, an introduction, a methods section, a results section, a discussion, and references.

THE ABSTRACT

The abstract is a very brief, 100- to 150-word summary of the topic and contents of the article. In journal articles it appears at the top of the first page of the article, just after the title. The abstract is also published in a volume of reference texts called *Psychological Abstracts*, and it is also used in computer literature search systems.

INTRODUCTION

The next section of the report is the introduction. In this section, the author or authors describe the specific problem under investigation, the relevant previous research conducted on the problem, and the specific strategy used to address the problem in the present study. Usually, a research article does not contain an exhaustive review of the existing literature, but it discusses any studies that are particularly relevant and develops the background for the study being described. Often, in the last paragraph of the introduction, the author(s) describe the particular hypothesis to be tested (American Psychological Association, 1983).

THE METHODS SECTION

Following the introduction is the methods section of the paper. The methods section provides a precise description of what the researchers did and how they did it; in this sense, it resembles a recipe—detailing the ingredients (the subjects, materials, and equipment) and explaining exactly how the ingredients should be combined (the exact procedure for using the equipment or the materials with the subjects). The methods section must be written in sufficient detail that another person can read it and carry out the research project with little difficulty.

To organize the details of the methods section, the author(s) divide it into several subsections: subjects, materials and/or apparatus, and procedure. The subjects subsection describes the sample of participants in the study. This description includes the subjects' major demographic characteristics: their general geographic location, their type of institutional affiliation (for instance, students at a large midwestern university, or undergraduate students from Yale University), their age or age range, and their gender. Also noted in this subsection is information about the number of participants in the study and about the number assigned to each experimental condition. Just as important is the number of participants who did not complete the study and why these people did not complete it.

A second subsection—the apparatus subsection—describes any special equipment used in the study. Here, the author(s) describe any custom-made equipment and provide the manufacturer's name and the model number of commercially constructed equipment. Typically, one would not describe the type of pencils supplied, or the size of the paper used in a study, unless there was something very special about the pencils and paper that was essential to conducting the study properly. Not all research reports require an apparatus subsection, since not all research requires apparatuses.

Another part of the methods section is the materials subsection, in which the author(s) describe the materials (other than equipment) used in the research project. For example, if psychological tests were administered to the subjects, they would be described in the materials subsection. The author(s) also supply information about the tests' reliability and validity so that a reader has some basis for assessing the appropriateness of these materials.

Researchers often develop their own materials to use in their research. In the materials subsection, they describe how these materials were developed and what they consist of. If the materials are short, such as short vignettes, they may be provided within the text of the subsection. Alternatively, examples of the materials might be provided in a table; or all of the materials might be presented in an appendix.

The final subsection of the methods section is the procedure subsection. Here the author(s) describe the precise procedure used to carry out the study and collect the data. The author(s) provide information about what the subjects were told and whether they were tested individually or in groups. This subsection is especially important to a reader evaluating the research. A researcher cannot simply say that subjects were presented with 20 words and the number of words accurately remembered was recorded; too many important questions are left unanswered by this summary. For how long were the words presented? How were the words presented? Were the subjects alone or with others? Could the subjects speak aloud or were they instructed to study silently? Was the experimenter in the room as they studied, or was each subject alone? The thoroughness of the procedure subsection (in particular) and the methods section (in general) determines whether a reader can or cannot evaluate the study.

THE RESULTS SECTION

The next section of a research report describes the statistical tests performed on the data and the results of those tests. Some knowledge of statistical analyses is necessary to evaluate whether the appropriate statistical techniques were used. Even a novice reader of scientific articles, however, should be able to comprehend the gist of the results, especially if tables and graphs are provided.

THE DISCUSSION SECTION

The results section is typically a rather dry description of statistical results. The interpretation of the results is done in the discussion section. Here the hypotheses of the researchers are revisited, and the results of the data analysis are discussed in light of these hypotheses. The results of previous research are also integrated with the present results. In the discussion, the author(s) tell the reader what the research has contributed, how it has helped resolve the original problem, and what conclusions and implications can be drawn from the results (American Psychological Association, 1983).

A very important part of a research article follows the discussion section: the reference list. In psychology, although each new study makes a contribution, the body of literature as a whole gives the more complete picture. The reference list provides a citation for every source of information mentioned in the body of the text; but unlike a bibliography, it does not include sources not explicitly referred to. Readers can gain a great deal of information about which articles are the most important in an area simply by referring to the reference lists of a number of articles and looking for the most frequently cited articles.

LITERATURE REVIEW FOR PSYCHOLOGICAL RESEARCH: HOW TO FIND RESEARCH REPORTS

Conducting a search for literature relevant to a particular topic can be a challenging endeavor, especially when you consider the hundreds of journals and thousands of articles published every year. Luckily, reference sources and computer programs are available to aid you in your literature search.

A very important printed reference source for psychological research articles is *Psychological Abstracts*, which provides a listing of abstracts of articles printed in a multitude of psychological journals. A new edition of *Psychological Abstracts* is published every month; and every year, a subject index and an author index are published. These indexes (which are also published for each monthly issue) list the abstracts by an abstract number under the appropriate author or authors and under the relevant subject headings or key terms.

Another printed source of references is the *Social Science Index* (*SSI*). This is a quarterly subject and author index of publications in the social sciences. The subject headings in the *SSI* can be useful for suggesting other headings you may not have thought of, because they make use of "see also" and "see reference" commands. The "see also" command leads the user to related or more specific subject headings. The "see reference" command supplies a more appropriate subject heading than the one used. The front part of each issue of the *SSI* contains a list of the periodicals that are indexed.

In addition to printed reference sources, computer systems can be used for literature searches. Among the computer systems relevant to psychology are the Educational Resources Information Center (ERIC) system, the Wilson Index for the Social Sciences (created by the publishers of the *SSI*), and PsycLit—a computer search system for the *Psychological Abstracts*. Not all libraries have these systems, and some may have others. In general, to use these systems, the user conducts a search by author, by title of the reference (if it's known), or by keywords or subject headings. Because the computer system can generate a healthy list of references, it is easy to forget that these systems have their limitations. Not all journals are listed on the computer system, just as not all journals are listed in the published indexes, nor can the computer system span the full length of time that research has been conducted in most areas. Very early references and very new references are likely to be left off or not yet on the system.

To begin a literature search, you need to consider your topic and have an initial idea of how to find information on that topic. Most of your search in the *SSI*, in *Psychological Abstracts*, or on the computer systems will be conducted by searching under appropriate subject headings, using keywords. In *Psychological Abstracts* and the *SSI*, the abstract numbers of information about the abstract is listed in the subject index under keywords. In a computer search, the computer searches for all referenced articles in which those keywords were identified as important by the author. Spend some time thinking about the appropriate keywords to use in your search. If it is available to you, you might skim through the *Thesaurus of Psychological Index Terms* for ideas and appropriate subject headings. *Psychological Abstracts* uses subject headings from this particular source.

Some keywords generate more information than others; the trick is to use a keyword that is general enough to supply a list of relevant articles, but not so general that the list becomes excessively long. To find an example for this appendix, I went to the library to search for information on the stigma attached to being diagnosed with AIDS. Just to see how it was organized, I looked in the March 1993 issue of the *SSI* under AIDS and found 95 references. Luckily, the editors suggested that I "see also – attitudes toward AIDS (Disease)". This subject heading yielded 7 references.

I next tried *Psychological Abstracts* for the same month (March 1993). Here, under AIDS, I was instructed to "see Acquired Immune Deficiency Syndrome." Under this heading I found 29 references for articles and 6 references for chapters. However, there were no subject headings for "attitudes toward AIDS" or "stigma toward AIDS." I was about to broaden my search to the previous year when I found that the subject index for the first part of 1992 was missing. The librarian who saw my puzzled look (and appreciated the irony of my writing this appendix and discovering that the index was missing) immediately and correctly suggested that I use PsycLit—the computer listing of *Psychological Abstracts*.

The edition of PsycLit I examined contained abstracts from January 1987 to December 1992. In response to my entering the keyword "AIDS," the computer informed me that there were 3064 relevant abstracts; under "stigma" there were 330; and under "stigma AIDS" there were 7. My increasingly specific use of keywords yielded fewer and fewer documents. I then continued my search, using the various computer search systems at my library. Table C.1 provides a summary of the keywords I used and the number of references each keyword elicited. The particular keywords that were successful with each system or printed reference varied slightly, so don't be afraid to experiment a little to find the best combination for the sources you have available.

These reference sources, printed lists of abstracts, and computer systems for literature searches provide the user with the article and/or the reference for it. But books, edited books of research projects, and textbooks are all excellent sources for some of the mainstay references on a topic. How else can you find these sources? Consult the card catalog or on-line list of holdings for you library, and seek advice from the reference librarian. Reference librarians have graduate degrees in library science; they possess an incredible wealth of information about how to access the works you need in the library.

TABLE C.I *Summary of computer search system, printed indexes, and keywords used to search for references related to the stigma associated with being diagnosed with AIDS.*

Source	Keywords	Number of References
SSI (4/93)	AIDS	95
	attitudes toward AIDS	7
Psychological Abstracts (4/93)	Acquired Immune Deficiency Syndrome	29 articles; 6 chapters
PsycLit (1/87–12/92)	AIDS	3064
	stigma	330
	stigma AIDS	7
ERIC (1/66–4/93)	AIDS	18,596
	attitude	100,300
	attitude AND AIDS	1362
	attitude AIDS	225
	attitude toward AIDS	14
	stigma AND AIDS	7
ERIX (5/93)	attitude	347
	AIDS	36
	attitude AND AIDS	4
Wilson Index for the Social Sciences (1983–present)	AIDS	1969
	attitude	5173
	attitude toward AIDS	6
	stigma	112
	stigma toward AIDS	0
	stigma AIDS	6

Perhaps the best reference sources of all when you are conducting a literature search in psychology are the reference lists of other relevant articles. Once you have found a few related articles, a quick perusal of their reference lists will identify the important papers in the area and will supply you with the necessary references. One type of article published in psychology journals is a review article, which summarizes research in an area. If you are lucky enough to find a relevant review article, its reference list can be an invaluable source for your literature search.

Unless you have access to a large university library, the chances are good that your library will not house all of the journals that publish articles you need. Do not be shy about using interlibrary loan. Interlibrary loan is a cooperative system among libraries across the country that allows borrowers to receive books and articles from libraries other than their own. Photocopies of articles can be sent to you via your library (often for no charge), and books are lent for a predetermined period of time. The catch with interlibrary loan is the need to plan ahead. It can take from several days to several weeks (and unfortunately, when books are not on the shelf, several months) for the items you requested to get to you. Be kind, be patient, and be early.

Finally, for a complete and up-to-date literature review, be sure to read the most recently published work, which may not be listed in any of the indexing systems yet. To find these works, you must browse through the most important journals in the field you are researching.

Literature searches are time-consuming and at times frustrating, but they are rewarding in the long run. Using a single strategy, such as the reference lists found in books or a computer search system, will not provide you with a complete listing of all the relevant articles on a topic. A complete literature search requires the use of multiple strategies to yield the maximum number of relevant sources.

RESEARCH PROPOSALS AND REPORTS: HOW TO WRITE THEM

The greater your investment in psychology becomes, the greater is the likelihood that you will have to write a research proposal or a research report for a research project. In this section, I will discuss the appropriate type of writing and the desirable format for research reports and proposals.

If you have read articles from psychology journals, you have probably noticed that some are relatively straightforward and easily understood, while others are much more difficult to decipher. My first thought when reading a difficult article used to be that I must not be smart enough to understand it. Later, however, I came to realize that, if I could not understand an article, the fault was not mine, but the article's. Usually, the writing style was too complicated. The author had used big words and confusing sentence structures to say things that could have been expressed much more simply.

Good writing—in English, psychology, biology, or business—follows the same principle: clear thoughts and precise word choice yield high-quality writing.

Clear thinking is probably the more difficult aspect of writing. The writer needs to know exactly what it is that she or he wants to say before writing it down. This is where an outline can be useful. I know many people who balk at the use of an outline; and to be honest, I don't use them in the way my English teachers taught me. Usually, I begin writing, then inspiration strikes, and I suddenly understand what I want to say. Then I jot down a provisional outline—often just a list of topics in an order that I think might be appropriate but that remains open to change. I then usually start writing all over again, because now I have the clarity of thought to write well, and what I'd written before just doesn't come up to the same standard.

Outlines are not mandatory, and there are other ways to reach the same objective of producing an organized paper. Organization is important, not only because it helps the writer think clearly about the topic, but because it allows the reader to understand the material more easily. Organized material is always easier to understand than disorganized material. Organization of a paper can be discussed with respect to the paper as a whole, the subsections of the paper, the paragraphs, or the sentences. Lack of organization at any of these points decreases the coherence and comprehensibility of the work.

We have already discussed the basic organization of a research report in psychology. It has an abstract, an introduction, a methods section, a results section, a discussion section, and references. The organization of a research *proposal* is quite similar. A proposal is a description of a study that *could* be conducted but hasn't been yet. It contains an introduction, a methods section, and expected results section, and references. The methods section in a research report is written in the past tense, since the project has already been conducted. In a research proposal, the methods section is written in the future tense. Likewise, the (forward-looking) expected results section of a proposal replaces the (backward-looking) results and discussion sections of an article. In the expected results section, the author describes what results he or she would expect to find if the study were conducted and explains why these results should be expected.

Each subsection has its own organization, as will be described more thoroughly within the sample paper a bit later in this appendix.

Paragraphs and sentences need to be organized, too. A paragraph typically has a topic sentence, a body that builds or expands on the topic sentence, and a conclusion. Sometimes the conclusion serves as a summary and other times as a transition to the next topic.

Whatever the next topic is, some type of transition must be supplied between paragraphs; otherwise, the paper reads like an arbitrarily arranged list of topics. Your goal is to enable the reader to read through your paper without struggling to see how your paragraphs are related. The statements you begin with and end with—in your paper and in your paragraphs—are specially important, because the reader remembers what was said there and uses that information to understand the paper better.

The beginnings and endings of sentences are also important. These, too, receive more emphasis and are better remembered than the words in the middle of sentences. Consider these sentences:

However, the difference between the two groups was relatively small.

The difference between the two groups, however, was relatively small.

In the first sentence, the word *however* emphasizes the contrast between this statement and some previous statement. In the second sentence, the difference between the groups within the statement is emphasized, which secondarily contrasts with the description of them in some previous statement. The author would use the first sentence if the contrast between statements is most important; she or he would use the second sentence if the difference between the groups within the statement is most important. Choose carefully the words you place at these points of emphasis.

Choosing the words for your sentences is an important task and one not to be taken lightly. If you do not already own a dictionary and a thesaurus, you will find that they are well worth the investment. Every word has a specific meaning, slightly different from any other word. Choosing the best words to describe your thoughts has two benefits. First, it is easier for the reader to understand you; and second, you need fewer words.

Scientific writing should be clear, concise, and to the point. The standard organization of a research report aids the reader in understanding the content of the paper by presenting the different types of information in predictable locations. The literature review appears at the beginning, the description of the methods is placed in the middle, and the discussion of the results goes at the end. In the next section of this appendix, I describe a standard research summary format. In addition, I present the section in a manner intended to illustrate the correct spacing, proper use of heading, appropriate width of margins, and so on, that are expected of papers written in APA style.*

A DESCRIPTION LAID OUT AS A SAMPLE PAPER

---

*In the following sample paper, several sample references have been provided as illustrations, in addition to real references to the *APA Publication Manual*. Only the APA (1983) citations refer to an actual source.

A Short Title

1

The Article's Title:

It Is Centered About Here

The Author's Name or Authors' Names

The Author's or Authors' Institutional Affiliation(s)

Running head: A SHORT VERSION OF THE TITLE IS TYPED HERE

A Short Title

2

Abstract

An abstract is a brief summary of the contents of the article. This is the section of the article that will appear in Psychological Abstracts, in the PsycLit system, and in other indexes and computer search systems. The abstract should tell the reader, in 100 to 150 words, what problem was studied, what the specific characteristics of subjects (such as gender, age, and number) were, what the experimental method entailed (briefly), what the conclusions were, and what the results implied (APA, 1983). Writing a good, clear, short abstract requires practice and editing.

A Short Title

3

The Title of the Article

This next section is the introduction. In this section, the author should introduce the problem. Do not leave the reader wondering about the topic of your research project.

To supply the reader with enough knowledge to understand the importance and relevance of your research, you must provide some background on the topic. This is where you review the most relevant previous research. Typically, a research article does not contain a comprehensive review of the literature (APA, 1983). A research proposal for a dissertation or thesis, however, might very well require a more thorough description of the previous research.

When reviewing the literature, be sure to organize your review so that the discussion of the previous research flows logically. For example, the review might be organized around important concepts or similar methodologies. Try to begin each paragraph with a clear and relevant transition from the previous paragraph. Make the introduction more than a list of project descriptions.

When describing the previous research, you must cite your sources properly. When describing a study, even when using only your own words, you <u>must</u> cite the author(s) of that research. Similarly, if you paraphrase someone's ideas about a theory or concept, you must give the original thinker the credit that is due. Failure to cite sources properly (and that often means at least one citation per paragraph in an introduction) is plagiarism. Accusations of plagiarism can stop a career before it starts.

A Short Title

4

In APA style, references are cited by the last names of the author(s) and the date of the publication. For instance, if this sentence were a restatement of something said or suggested by Smith and Jones in 1993, one way to cite them would be to put the citation information in parentheses at the end of the sentence (Smith & Jones, 1993). Alternatively, I could be more direct: Smith and Jones, in their 1993 discussion of plagiarism, argued that failure to cite sources should be penalized by death. If the entire paragraph describes a particular study, the author(s) and date can be presented in parentheses at the end of the paragraph (Smith & Jones, 1993).

Sometimes more than two authors collaborated on a given study. If three to five authors are involved, all of the authors should be listed the first time the reference is cited (Smith, Jones, Young, & Green, 1978). The next time this reference is used in the paper, only the first author is listed; the rest are referred to by *et al.,* which means "and others" (Smith et al., 1978). If six or more authors are involved—say, Jones, Smith, Sullivan, Sullivan, Green, and Young—you need list only the first author's surname, followed by *et al.* and the date of publication, the very first time you refer to this source (Jones et al., 1990). In the reference list, however, all of the names must be listed.

Occasionally, you might want to quote someone directly. If the quote consists of fewer than 40 words, "put the quote within quotation marks, and follow the quote with the source and page number" (Meyer, 1987, p. 123). Similarly, the author might be mentioned earlier in the

A Short Title

5

sentence: As Meyer (1987) noted in her earlier work on quotations, "Quotations should be used sparingly, and only when they add to the content of the paper" (p. 123). [Notice, by the way, that, when the author is mentioned in the main text of a sentence, the date of the publication appears in parentheses immediately after the author's name.]

Quotes containing more than 40 words require that the wording appear in a block quotation such as this:

> For a block quotation, the left margin is set in five spaces, and the first word of each paragraph within the quote is set in an additional five spaces. Notice, however, that the right margin remains at the same place and that the quote is typed double-space, just as the rest of the paper is. When the quote is complete, citation information that did not appear immediately prior to the quotation is provided in parentheses at the end. This includes the author(s), the publication date, and the page number (Sullivan & Sullivan, 1991, p. 78).

Finally, after the relevant literature has been reviewed, you are ready to tell your readers about the present study. In the final paragraphs of the introduction you should briefly describe your project in general terms (you will be supplying the nitty-gritty details in the methods section). This is also where your hypotheses are introduced and the rationale for your expectations is made clear.

A Short Title

6

Methods

<u>Subjects</u>

The first subsection of the methods section is typically the subjects subsection. In this subsection, you describe the participants of your study. How many subjects participated? How were they selected? How were they assigned to the experimental conditions, and how many were in each condition? Were the subjects volunteers from a course, or were they selected on the basis of some criterion? How many subjects did not complete the study, and why? For surveys, what was the response rate? (APA, 1983).

You should also describe your subjects in terms of their characteristics, such as the type of institution the subjects are affiliated with, their age, and their gender. Finally, you should state that the subjects were treated in accordance with the ethical principles of the American Psychological Association (see Chapter 2; APA, 1983).

<u>Materials</u>

In this next subsection, the materials used in the study are described. When the research involves the use of equipment, such as a tachistoscope, calipers, or scales, the subsection may be referred to as the apparatus subsection. If the research involves use of paper-and-pencil tests or specially designed computer software, the subsection is usually referred to as the materials subsection.

Standard equipment such as tables, chairs, pens, pencils, and paper need not be described in detail. But custom-made equipment should

A Short Title

7

be described thoroughly, perhaps including a drawing or picture of the
item (APA, 1983). The make and model number of manufactured
equipment should also be provided. Any psychological tests used in the
project should be described in this section; and included with the
description should be information about the instruments' validity and
reliability.

Procedure

In the procedure subsection, the author(s) explain, clearly and
completely, all the steps taken in conducting the research. The authors
should describe how people were assigned to groups, or how they
determined whether potential subjects met the criterion or criteria for
admittance to the study. Any counterbalancing or other measures used to
control or balance the effects of extraneous variables should be described
here. The instructions to the subjects should be paraphrased or
summarized. For instance: The subjects were asked to study the list of 20
words for 5 minutes. However, if the instructions included the
experimental manipulation—that is, if the different instructions are
themselves being compared—the instructions should be presented
verbatim (APA, 1983).

Results

In this section, the type of data collected and the statistical
techniques used to analyze them are described. The results of the analyses
are also presented, and general conclusions are made. For example, an

author might say: The results of the independent-samples t-test were

significant, t (12) = 7.62, p < .05; the subjects in the mnemonic condition

recalled significantly more words (M = 15.73) than those in the control

condition (M = 9.36). The author should not expound here on why these

results occurred. The implications of the results are presented in the

discussion section.

When presenting the results of statistical analyses, you should

assume that the reader has a basic understanding of statistics. You do not

need to explain the concept of rejecting the null hypothesis or what a t-test

is used for. You should, however, supply the reader with information

about the value of the test statistics, the degrees of freedom, the

probability level, and the direction of the effect, as was done in the

preceding example (APA, 1983). Do not tell the reader what the critical

value was; given the degrees of freedom, the reader can look it up if he or

she has any questions.

Sometimes, it will be more efficient and easier to understand data

represented in a table or a figure (a graph, picture, or drawing) than listed

as a series of means and standard deviations in the text. Unfortunately,

figures and tables cost the publishers money to produce, so you should

use as few as possible. Any tables or figures that are included should be

referred to in the text, and the reader should be told what to look for.

When typing a table, you should prepare the table on a separate

piece of paper and put it at the back of the manuscript (see Table 1). In the

A Short Title

9

text, following the paragraph in which the table is mentioned, the author

should indicate to the copy editor where the table belongs in the main text,

as follows:

----

insert Table 1 about here

A table is presented at the end of this sample paper so that you can see

how tables are prepared. Notice that the table is double-spaced

throughout.

Discussion

In the introduction, the background for the study was provided

and the hypotheses were described. The methods section detailed how the

study was carried out, and the results section characterized the data that

had been collected. In the discussion section, you interpret those data,

relating them to the previous research. For many researchers, this is the

most interesting part of the paper to write, because it allows them to

express what they see as the most important implications and

contributions of the research—even when the research did not come out as

expected.

Typically, the discussion begins with a general statement of the

data's support or nonsupport of the author's hypotheses. Next, the author

might wish to discuss why some results may not have come out as

expected, or what the implications of the present results are in relation to

previous work and to the underlying theory of the project. What has this

A Short Title

10

project contributed? What questions has it answered? What possible alternative explanations are there for the results? What paths might future researchers follow? Answering these questions should provide a basis for discussing your project.

Conducting research in psychology is a rewarding process, and an important part of that process consists of communicating the results clearly to other colleagues. The organization presented here is standard in psychology. It allows researchers to read a report quickly and understand at once what was done, why it was done, and what it means. The information is presented succinctly, but with enough detail that a reader can evaluate the quality of the project or attempt to replicate the results. I hope that this information will aid you not only in writing your own research reports, but also in reading and evaluating the reports of others. Research is the means by which we gain knowledge in psychology, and to read the reports of the original researchers is to be handed knowledge from the discoverer.

A Short Title

11

References

American Psychological Association. (1983). <u>Publication Manual of the American Psychological Association</u>. Washington, DC: Author.

Jones, R. L., Smith, J. K., Sullivan, J. D., Sullivan, W. S., Green, G. G., & Young, T. W. (1990). Something remarkably prolix, sententious, and orotund. <u>In Digest, 15</u>, 212–298.

Meyer, R. C. (1987). The title of an article is typed like this. <u>The Journal Is Underlined, 23</u>, 34–37.

[NOTE: the 23 is the volume number; it is underlined. The numbers 34–37 are the page numbers; they are not underlined.]

Smith, J. K., & Jones, R. L. (1993). The title. <u>The Journal, 12</u>, 44–78.

Smith, J. K., Jones, R. L., Young, T. W., & Green, G. G. (1978). The article title. <u>The Journal, 17</u>, 48–56.

Sullivan, J. D., & Sullivan, W. S. (1991). <u>The title of a book</u>. Pacific Grove, CA.: Brooks/Cole.

A Short Title

12

Table 1

Mean Body Dissatisfaction Scores for Males and Females Who Had and
Had Not Eaten

	Eating Condition			

	Had		Had Not	
Gender	M	SD	M	SD
Males	6.67	2.45	4.74	2.21
Females	9.13	3.49	6.49	1.96

NOTE: n = 12 per condition.

D

Summation Notation

Throughout this text, we used a shorthand system to describe statistical formulas. This shorthand is known as summation notation. The version of summation notation used in this book is simpler than that used in some other statistical texts. Given the introductory nature of this text, I don't want the shorthand to be more complicated than the concepts that are being presented. An understanding of the summation notation used in this text, however, will give you a strong foundation for comprehending the notation used elsewhere.

The symbol of most importance in this notation system is the uppercase sigma ($\sum$), which is used to indicate summation. Another important symbol is X, which refers to the individual scores. If we are presented with a set of five scores, we might label them X_1, X_2, X_3, X_4, and X_5. To add those scores, we could write out the procedure as follows:

$$X_1 + X_2 + X_3 + X_4 + X_5$$

Alternatively, the same procedure—adding all of the scores—could be written with the $\sum$ as follows:

$$\sum X$$

This is read as "the sum of the X's."

Following is a set of five scores representing the number of correctly recalled words from a list of 10:

$$\begin{array}{c} X \\ \hline 7 \\ 6 \\ 5 \\ 9 \\ 8 \end{array}$$

$\sum X$ for this set of scores is 35; it was calculated by adding all five scores together.

Sometimes we need to square each score before we sum them. This procedure would be written in summation notation as follows:

$$\sum X^2$$

The rules of calculation that you may have learned in algebra class still hold: multiplication and division are carried out before addition and subtraction. Thus, the multiplication of each score by itself (squaring) occurs before the addition of all of the squared scores:

X	X²
7	49
6	36
5	25
9	81
8	64
	$255 = \sum X^2$

If we wanted to sum the scores and then square that sum, we would use parentheses to indicate that the summation should be carried out first. Procedures within parentheses are always carried out before procedures outside the parentheses. This procedure would be written in summation notation as follows:

$$(\sum X)^2$$

The answer would be the one given here:

$$(\sum X)^2 = (7 + 6 + 5 + 9 + 8)^2 = 35^2 = 1225$$

The only way to become comfortable with summation notation is to practice using it. Some problems are provided next to help you become familiar with this statistical shorthand.

EXERCISE

1. Use these data to perform each calculation.

X
2
1
2
3
0
0
1
1

a. $\sum X^2$
b. $\sum X$

c. $(\sum X)^2$
d. $\sum X + 1$
e. $\sum (X + 1)$
f. $\sum X^2 + 2$
g. $\sum (X^2 + 2)$

For additional practice, repeat each procedure requested above, using the previous data set (7, 6, 5, 9, 8), or make up your own data set and practice using summation notation with it.

answers: a. 20 b. 10 c. 100 d. 11 e. 18
f. 22 g. 36

Glossary

ABAB design. A single-subject research design in which the baseline (A) is followed by the intervention (B), followed by withdrawal (A), and then reintroduction of the intervention (B).

ABBA counterbalancing. A technique in which each subject experiences condition A followed by B and condition B followed by A.

accretion measures. Traces or products that occur as a result of some behavior.

action checklist. A recording system used to note the presence or absence of specific behaviors and characteristics.

alpha (α). The probability of making a Type I error.

alternating treatments design. A single-subject design in which two or more treatments are introduced to the subject randomly or systematically such that the effectiveness of each treatment may be compared.

alternative hypothesis or **research hypothesis** (H_1 or H_A). The prediction that the researcher makes about the results of the research; it represents the prediction that a significant difference exists between the groups being compared.

analysis of variance (ANOVA). An inferential statistical test for comparing the means of three or more groups.

applied research. Research whose results are immediately relevant in a practical setting or situation.

auto-correlation. A statistical technique used to determine wheter the errors that are recorded are correlated. Autocorrelation involves correlating each score with the one following it. Thus, if a set of scores is: 1, 3, 6, 4, 5, 8, 2, 9, the scores can be set up as follows to conduct the autocorrelation:

X_1	X_2
1	3
3	6
6	4
4	5
5	8
8	2
2	9

A correlation coefficient is then calculated by using Pearson's r. If the correlation is not significant, the errors are assumed to be uncorrelated.

average deviation (A.D.). The mean distance of each datum in a distribution from the mean of that distribution. The formula for average deviation is

$$\text{A.D.} = \frac{\sum |X - \mu|}{N}$$

basic research. Research whose results may have no immediate practical use.

behavior sampling. A research technique that involves observing subsets of a participant's behavior by observing the behavior at different times and/or in different situations.

beliefs. Statements that are based on personal feelings and subjective knowledge about things that cannot be tested scientifically.

beta (β). The probability of making a Type II error.

between-groups variance. An estimate of the effect of the independent variable plus error variance.

biased sample. A subset of a population that over-represents or underrepresents population subgroups.

carryover effects. Effects that occur when one experimental condition influences performance in another condition in a within-subjects design.

case studies. Descriptions of an individual and that person's experiences that typically do not involve a systematic observation of the subject's behavior.

categorical variable. A discontinuous variable in which each value belongs to one of a set of mutually exclusive groups of values.

ceiling effect. An effect that may occur when the dependent variable yields high scores at or near the top limit of the measurement tool for one or all conditions.

Central Limit Theorem. A mathematical theorem stating that the sampling distribution of the mean will have a mean equal to μ and a variance equal to $\dfrac{\sigma^2}{N}$, and that the distribution will approach the normal distribution as N increases.

change scores. Scores created by subtracting pretest scores from posttest scores.

changing criterion design. A single-subject design used to assess an intervention when the criterion for that intervention is routinely changed.

Cicchetti's modification of Tukey's HSD. An a posteriori technique for comparing means within interactions after a significant F-value has been calculated by using an ANOVA.

chi-square (χ^2) goodness-of-fit test. A nonparametric test that compares obtained categorical observations to the values expected based on previous knowledge, hypothesis, or chance.

chi-square (χ^2) test of homogeneity of proportions. A nonparametric test used when two random samples are chosen and each subject's response is classified as belonging to one of two or more categories. This test determines whether the proportions of responses in each category are equivalent for both samples.

chi-square (χ^2) test of independence. A nonparametric test used when frequency data for two (or more) samples (or one sample divided into two or more groups) have been collected on a categorical variable. This test determines whether the two independent variables are associated or independent.

class intervals. The categories of scores used in grouped frequency distributions to combine individual scores into a more manageable number of groups.

closed questions. Survey, interview, or test questions that ask the respondent to choose from a series of fixed alternative potential answers.

cluster sampling. A research technique in which clusters of elements that represent the population are identified, and then all of the elements in those clusters are included in the sample.

combinations. The ways in which a set of things can be combined into subgroups of a particular size. The formula for determining the number of possible combinations is

$$C_n^x = \frac{X!}{n!(X-n)!}$$

complete within-subjects design. A research design in which each subject participates in each experimental condition several times, until each has received all possible orders of the conditions.

concurrent validity. The extent to which a new measure and an established measure are correlated.

confound. An uncontrolled extraneous variable or other flaw in a research design that permits alternative explanations for the results and thus limits a study's internal validity.

confounded comparison. A comparison between means in which more than one independent variable changes at a time.

confounded results. Results of an investigation that can be accounted for by more than one explanation because one or more extraneous variables are present.

construct validity. The extent to which the results of research based on a new test fit existing findings.

continuous data. Data that fall along a continuum of possible scores. In the case of continuous data, fractional units are possible.

continuous (running) records. Archival records that are maintained and supplemented on a routine basis.

control group. The group or condition in an investigation that does not receive the treatment being tested. The control group is used to demonstrate that any difference between the performance of the control group and the performance of the experimental group resulted from the independent variable and not from some other aspect of the experiment.

controlled trace measure. Traces or products that require the involvement of the researcher in order to occur.

correlated-samples t-test. A parametric test used to compare the means of two related samples or to compare the means provided by one set of subjects tested twice. The formula for the correlated-samples *t*-test is

$$t = \frac{\bar{d} - 0}{d_{\bar{x}}}$$

where:

$\bar{d}$ = Mean of the difference scores

$d_{\bar{x}}$ = Standard error of the difference scores

correlation. A measure of the degree of relationship between two variables. The *strength* of the relationship is represented by the absolute value of the correlation coefficient. The *direction* of the relationship is represented by the sign of the correlation coefficient.

correlational studies. Investigations in which relationships between or among variables can be identified but causal inferences cannot be made, because of the possible effects of uncontrolled variables.

counterbalancing. A procedure for distributing the effect of an extraneous variable across the experimental conditions in a within-subjects design.

critical value. The value of a test statistic at which the probability of randomly choosing a sample that yields an equal-size or larger test statistic is equal to or less than some prespecified probability—typically, .05.

data. Recorded observations.

debriefing. A full explanation of the purpose of an experiment, usually provided after the subjects have participated.

degrees of freedom (df). The number of observations that may freely vary; computed as the number of observations minus the number of restrictions placed on those observations.

demand characteristics. Cues inadvertently provided by the researcher, the research materials, or the research setting that inform the research subject about the purpose of the investigation.

dependent variable. The variable in an investigation that the experimenter *measures* in *both* the experimental and control groups.

descriptive statistics. Procedures that organize, summarize, and describe a set of data.

desensitization. A process by which a researcher slowly moves closer and closer to the subjects until the researcher can sit near or even among the subjects without disturbing them.

discontinuous records. Archival records that are produced less continuously than running records or only once.

disguised participant observation studies. Studies in which the researcher is an active participant in the situation in which the subjects are involved, but the other participants do not know that the researcher is observing their behavior.

documents. Written or filmed material that is not a record and that wasn't created in response to some task or request by the investigator. Documents are produced for one's own purposes.

double-barreled questions. Survey, interview, or test questions worded in such a manner as to ask more than one question at the same time. For example: Do find your job interesting or exciting? It is unclear whether the researcher wants to know whether the respondent's job is more interesting than exciting (or vice versa) or whether the researcher wants to know whether the job is interesting or exciting (on the one hand) or neither (on the other).

double-blind procedure. A research procedure in which neither the experimenter nor the subjects know the condition to which each subject has been assigned.

elements. Members of the sample.

equivalent forms reliability. The degree of consistency between scores when the same person takes two versions of the same test.

erosion measures. Traces or products that occur as a result of the wearing away of material.

error variance. The variation among scores caused not by the independent variable but by randomly occurring factors or by extraneous variables.

event sampling. The random or systematic selection of events to observe that include the behavior of interest.

exact limits. The extended limits of the class intervals used in grouped frequency distributions. The limits are extended by one-half unit above and below the intervals of the scores such that there is no gap between the class intervals of continuous data.

experimental design. A standard arrangement for an experiment; however, experimental designs can also be used to design correlational studies.

experimental group (experimental condition). The group or condition in an investigation that receives a treatment.

experimenter bias. The effect of the experimenter's expectations on the outcome of a study.

experiments. Investigations in which two (or more) equivalent groups of subjects are treated exactly the same in all ways except with respect to the independent variable. Differences in measurements of the dependent variable can then be attributed to the difference in the independent variable. In experiments, one can make causal inferences.

external validity. The extent to which the results of an investigation can be generalized beyond the original study.

extraneous variable. A variable (other than the independent variable) that can affect the dependent variable.

face validity. The extent to which a test appears to be measuring what it is purported to measure.

factorial design. A research design in which the effects of two or more independent variables on a dependent variable are assessed.

familywise (experimentwise) error rate. The probability of making *at least one* Type I error when calculating a set of related comparisons, such as among the group means within an experiment. When multiple comparisons are made, the Type I error rate for the whole set of comparisons can be calculated as

$$1 - (1 - \alpha)^c$$

where:

α = level of significance for each test

c = number of comparisons.

fatigue effect. An effect that occurs when subjects' performance on a task declines because they have done the task repeatedly.

field studies. Highly controlled observational studies that occur in a natural setting where the researcher manipulates an independent variable to assess its effect on a dependent variable.

filter question. A survey or interview question that instructs the respondent or interviewer as to what the next question should be, depending on the answer to the initial question.

floor effect. An effect that may occur when the dependent variable yields scores at or near the lower limit of the measurement tool for one or all conditions.

F-ratio. The statistic produced by an ANOVA; the ratio of between-groups variance to within-groups variance. It is used to determine the effect of the independent variable on the dependent variable.

frequency polygon. A line graph of the frequencies of individual scores, or (for a grouped frequency distribution) the frequencies of the midpoints of each class interval.

funnel questions. A set of survey or interview questions ordered from the most general question to the most specific question.

habituation. A process by which the researcher appears in a setting numerous times until the researcher's presence no longer appears to affect the subjects' behavior.

histogram. A graphical representation of a frequency distribution, in which contiguous bars represent each frequency.

history effect. An effect that arises if an event occurs during the course of the investigation that influences the subjects' performance on the dependent measure.

hypothesis. A possible answer to a research question. Scientific investigations are often designed to test a hypothesis.

hypothesis testing. The process of determining whether the hypothesis is significantly supported by the results of a research project.

idiographic. Related to the study of individuals in an attempt to identify patterns of behavior within the individual.

incomplete within-subjects design. A research design in which each subject receives a unique order of the conditions, and may receive each condition more than once, but does not receive all possible orderings of the conditions.

independent-samples *t*-test. A parametric test for comparing sample means of two independent groups of scores. The general formula for the independent *t*-test is

$$t = \frac{(\overline{x}_1 - \overline{x}_2) - (\mu_1 - \mu_2)}{s_{\overline{x}_1, \overline{x}_2}}$$

independent variable. The variable in an investigation that the researcher changes or *manipulates*; the grouping variable in an investigation.

informed consent form. A form given to each subject prior to participation in a project, describing the purpose of the study and what the subject will be asked to do and including a description of any known risks or benefits related to the study.

Institutional Review Boards (IRBs). Committees of individuals with diverse backgrounds who review proposals for research with human subjects.

instrumentation effects. Effects that occur when a measuring device fails to measure in the same manner across observations.

interaction effect. In a factorial design, the effect of a dependent measure on an independent variable within each level of each other independent variable.

interaction of selection with other threats to internal validity. An effect that occurs when comparison groups are not equivalent and an extraneous variable affects one group but not the other.

internal validity. The extent to which a study actually answers the research questions it was designed to answer. A study with good internal validity has no confounds and offers only one explanation for the results.

interobserver reliability. The degree to which a measurement procedure yields consistent results when different observers use the procedure. One general formula for interobserver reliability is

$$\frac{\text{Number of agreements}}{\text{Number of opportunities for agreement}} \times 100$$

interval measurement scale. A scale of measurement characterized by equal units of measurement throughout the scale. Thus, measurements made with an interval scale provide information about both the order and the relative quantity of the characteristic being measured. Interval scales of measurement, however, do not have a true 0 value; thus, negative values are meaningful.

interviewer bias. An inaccurate record of a subject's behavior that occurs when an interviewer's behaviors, questions, or recording procedures elicit data that are consistent with the interviewer's personal beliefs.

Kruskal-Wallis analysis of variance (Kruskal-Wallis *H*-test). A nonparametric test that compares two or more independent groups of scores. The null hypothesis for the Kruskal-Wallis is that there are no differences among the scores of the different groups.

kurtosis. The relative peakedness or flatness of a distribution.

Latin square. A technique for formulating an incomplete within-subjects design that involves presenting each condition in each ordinal position, and presenting each condition before and after each other condition. The number of orderings necessary is equal to the number of conditions in the study; thus, when written out with one order per line, a square is formed. An example of a Latin square for four conditions is

ABCD
BDAC
CADB
DCBA

laws. Specific statements that are generally expressed in the form of a mathematical equation involving only a few variables. Laws have so much empirical support that their accuracy is beyond reasonable doubt.

leading questions. Survey, interview, or test questions that bias the presentation of information to encourage the respondent to answer in a desired manner.

leptokurtic distribution. A distribution of scores characterized by a frequency polygon with a tall thin peak.

levels of the independent variable. The groups or categories within the independent variable. For instance, depression and elation may be levels of an independent variable called *mood*.

loaded questions. Survey, interview, or test questions that include nonneutral or emotionally laden terms.

mail surveys. Written, self-administered questionnaires.

main effects. The effects of a dependent measure on an independent variable within a factorial design.

matched-pairs design. A research design in which subjects are matched between conditions on a subject variable—IQ score, height, weight, or any other variable that the researcher believes is relevant to the study.

maturation. Changes in behavior caused by the passage of time.

mean. The arithmetic average of the scores in a distribution of scores. The mean is calculated by adding the scores in the distribution and dividing this sum by the number of scores. The formulas for the population mean μ and for the sample mean $\bar{x}$, respectively, are

$$\mu = \frac{\sum X}{N} \quad \text{and} \quad \bar{x} = \frac{\sum X}{N}$$

mean squares. Variance estimates—a shortened name for *mean squared deviation scores*.

measurement. The assignment of names or numbers to objects or their characteristics according to some rule.

median. The middle score, or 50th percentile, in a set of scores.

mesokurtic distribution. A distribution of scores characterized by a frequency polygon whose peak is of medium height and breadth.

midpoint. The center of each class interval in a grouped frequency distribution.

minimal risk. A level of risk to the participants of a research project that is no greater than the level of risk encountered in daily life.

mode. The score in a set of discrete data that occurs most frequently.

multiple baselines design. A single-subject design in which the effectivness of a treatment on two or more behaviors or across two or more situations is assessed.

multiple time-series design. A quasi-experimental design that combines the time-series design and the nonequivalent control groups design by making multiple observations of an experimental group and its nonequivalent control group.

narrative records. A running record of behavior that occurs in a given situation. Narrative records can be created by audiotaping or videotaping a situation, or by writing notes by hand.

naturalistic observation. Unobtrusively observing behaviors in their natural setting. The investigator does nothing to interfere with the subjects' behavior.

natural trace measures. Traces or products that occur without researcher intervention.

negative correlation. A relationship between two variables such that, as one variable increases, the other variable decreases.

nominal measurement scale. A scale of measurement that categorizes objects or individuals. The order of the categories is arbitrary and unimportant.

nomothetic. Related to the study of groups for the purpose of identifying general laws and principles of behavior.

nonequivalent control group design. A type of quasi-experimental design in which the experimental group is compared with a comparable (but not equivalent) control group.

nonparametric tests. Statistical tests that do not require as many assumptions about the population that the sample represents as do parametric tests.

nonreactive. Not affected by the act of acquiring the measures.

nonsystematic subject mortality. The loss of data when subjects terminate their participation in a study or when their data cannot be used for reasons unrelated to the experiment itself.

normal distribution. A family of symmetric, uni-modal, bell-shaped frequency distributions.

null hypothesis (H_0). The prediction that *no significant difference* exists between the groups being compared. It is the result one expects to confirm if the population that the sample is from is the same as the population with which it is being compared.

one-tailed hypothesis. A type of alternative hypothesis in which the researcher predicts the direction of the difference between the groups being compared.

open-ended questions. Survey, interview, or test questions that do not provide specific options for answers, but instead provide room or time for the respondent to formulate his or her own response.

operational definitions. Language in a report that defines the exact procedures used to produce a phenomenon or to measure some variable.

ordinal measurement scale. A scale of measurement in which objects or individuals are categorized, and the order of the categories is important because it reflects an increase in the amount of the characteristic being measured. The categories need not be of equal size.

outliers. Scores in a distribution that, when compared to the others, are inordinately large or small.

parametric tests. Statistical tests in which the sample statistics are assumed to be estimates of population parameters.

parsimony. The assumption that, of two equally accurate explanations, the one based upon the simpler assumptions is preferable.

participant observation studies. Studies in which the researcher actively participates in the situation in which the subjects are involved.

Pearson's product-moment correlation coefficient. A statistic used to determine the correlation between two variables measured on either a ratio or an interval scale. The raw score formula is

$$r_{xy} = \frac{n\sum XY - \sum X\sum Y}{\sqrt{[n\sum X^2 - (\sum X)^2][n\sum Y^2 - (\sum Y)^2]}}$$

personal interview. A type of survey involving a person-to-person meeting between the interviewer and the respondent.

phi coefficient. A statistic used to determine the correlation between two variables when both variables are measured on true dichotomies.

physical trace measure. Data generated from physical evidence that is assessed in the absence of the individuals who created or caused the evidence.

physical trace studies. Investigations involving the study of physical evidence left in the course of the subjects' behaving.

pilot study. A smaller version of a study conducted to answer questions about procedures prior to undertaking the full-scale version of the investigation.

placebo. An inert substance or treatment that has no effect.

placebo effect. An effect that occurs when a behavior change is apparent after the introduction of an intervention that is known to be ineffectual.

platykurtic distribution. A distribution of scores characterized by a frequency polygon that has a short wide peak.

point-biserial correlation. A statistic used to determine the correlation between two variables when one variable is measured on a ratio or interval scale and the other variable is measured on a true dichotomy. The same formula that is used for the Pearson's r can be used to calculate the point-biserial correlation, but the symbol used in the lattr case is r_{pb}.

pooled variance. The average variance of two samples weighted by the degrees of freedom for each sample. The formula for the pooled variance is

$$s_p^2 = \frac{(n_1 - 1)s_1^2 + (n_2 - 1)s_2^2}{n_1 + n_2}$$

population. All of the individuals about whom a research project is meant to generalize.

positive correlation. A relationship between two variables such that, as one variable increases, the other variable also increases.

power. The probability of detecting a difference between the groups being compared if the null hypothesis is false. The formula for power is

$$\text{Power} = 1 - \beta$$

practice effect. An effect that occurs when subjects' performance on a task improves because they have done the task before.

predictive validity. The extent to which a test score is able to predict some outcome.

pre-experimental designs. A type of research in which simple designs are carried out in applied settings yielding results for which there are several alternative explanations.

pretest and posttest measures in the nonequivalent control group design. Measurements made before and after the introduction of a treatment to the experimental group in a nonequivalent control group design.

pretest-posttest design. A research design in which one or more groups of subjects are tested before and after some treatment is administered to the experimental group.

principles. Statements that predict a phenomenon with a specified level of probability.

products. Physical evidence created by subjects.

quasi-experimental design. A type of research design in which nonequivalent groups are compared, a single group is observed a number of times, or both of these techniques are combined.

random assignment. Allocation of subjects to experimental conditions within an investigation in such a way that each subject is equally likely to be assigned to each condition.

random order with rotation. A technique for presenting conditions to subjects in an incompete within-subjects design in which the experimental conditions are ordered randomly, and the first subject receives this order; then the next subject receives another order of the conditions, by moving the first condition to the last place and shifting all of the other conditions up one; then the next subject receives another different order, by moving the conditions one place forward again and shifting the previously first condition to last place; and so on. In this manner, all of the conditions are tested first, second, third, . . . , one time each.

random sample. A sample in which the elements have been selected randomly from a sampling frame.

random selection. A manner of sample selection in which all members of the population are equally likely to be chosen as part of the sample. This should not be confused with haphazardly choosing or arbitrarily choosing elements for a sample.

range. The number of possible values for scores in a discrete data set, or the interval of scores covered by a data set taken from a continuous distribution.

ratio measurement scale. A scale of measurement that provides information about order; all units are of equal size throughout the scale, and there is a true 0 value. The true 0 permits ratios of values to be formed.

reactivity. A change in behavior caused by the subject's knowledge that he or she is being observed.

records. A written statement presented to provide an account or to attest to an event. Records are produced for someone else's consumption.

region of rejection. The area of a sampling distribution that lies beyond the test statistic's critical value. If a score falls within the region of rejection, then H_0 is rejected.

regression toward the mean. The phenomenon that extreme scores, upon retesting, tend to be less extreme, moving instead toward the mean.

reliability. The consistency with which one gets the same results from the same test, instrument, or procedure.

repeated measures design. A research design in which one group of subjects is tested two or more times with the same measurement tool.

response rate. The extent to which people who receive a survey or who are approached to complete an interview respond and complete the survey or interview. A formula for response rate is

Response rate =

$$\frac{\text{Number of responses}}{\text{Number in sample} - (\text{Ineligible and undeliverable requests})} \times 100$$

reversal design. A single-subject design in which the effectiveness of an intervention is tested by withdrawing the intervention and introducing a new and opposite intervention.

sample. A subset of a population.

sampling distribution of means. A frequency distribution of sample means.

sampling frame. A list of all of the members of a population. The sampling frame serves as the operational definition of the population.

scattergram. A graphical representation of a correlation between two variables.

scientific method. The set of procedures used to gain information in the sciences, involving *systematic* observations obtained in an *objective* manner designed to avoid biases by the observer or by the subject of the observations.

score limits. The scores used to mark the unextended limits of class intervals in a grouped frequency distribution.

selection bias. The result when differences exist between the comparison groups within a study.

selective deposit. The unrepresentative occurrence of traces in all situations or by all participants.

selective survival. The result when some subset of trace or product evidence does not endure over time.

significant difference. A difference between two descriptive statistics (such as means) that is of such a magnitude that it is unlikely to have occurred by chance alone.

single-blind procedure. A research procedure in which either the subjects or the experimenter does not know the condition to which each subject has been assigned.

single-group design. A research design in which a statistic describing a single sample of scores is compared with a known population parameter; typically, a sample mean is compared to a population mean, where the null hypothesis is that no difference exists between the sample's mean score and the population's mean score.

single-subject designs. Research designs in which only one subject need be observed. Single-subject designs are done with the goal of eliminating as many alternative hypotheses for the results as possible.

situation sampling. Making observations in different settings and circumstances in order to obtain a representative sample of behavior.

socially desirable responses. Responses that reflect what the respondent believes is deemed appropriate by society, but that do not necessarily reflect the respondent's true beliefs, attitudes, or behaviors.

Spearman's rho (ρ). A statistic used to determine the correlation between two variables that have been ranked. The formula is

$$\rho = 1 - \frac{6\sum d^2}{n(n^2 - 1)}$$

split-half reliability. The degree of consistency within a test, calculated by comparing scores on one half of a test with the scores on the other half of the test.

standard deviation. The square root of the population variance σ or of the sample variance s; the formulas for these two statistics, respectively, are

$$\sigma = \sqrt{\sigma^2} \quad \text{and} \quad s = \sqrt{s}$$

standard error of differences between means. The standard deviation for the sampling distribution composed of differences between sample means.

standard error of the mean. The standard deviation for the sampling distribution. The formula for this statistic is

$$\sigma_{\bar{x}} = \frac{\sigma}{\sqrt{N}}$$

standard normal distribution. A normal distribution with a mean of 0 and a standard deviation of 1.

static checklist. A recording system used to note characteristics that will not change during the course of the observation.

statistical analysis. The summarization and analysis of data.

stratified sampling. A sampling technique performed to guarantee that the sample fairly represents specific subgroups of the population called *strata*; elements of the sample are chosen from the identified strata.

structured observation studies. Studies in which the researcher intervenes in a way other than (or in addition to) participating in the situation, but in which control over the situation is less than that in field studies.

Student's *t* distributions. A family of distributions that, like the normal distribution, are symmetric and bell-shaped but, unlike the normal distribution, have a different distribution for each sample size.

subject mortality (subject attrition). The loss of data that occurs when subjects terminate their participation in a study or when their data cannot be used.

subjects. The participants in a scientific research project from whom data are gathered.

subject variable. A measurable characteristic of the subject (such as height, cranium size, or gender) that cannot be manipulated by a researcher. When used as an independent variable, subject variables provide correlational information but not causal information.

sums of squares. The top of the variance formula, where the deviation scores are squared and then summed.

systematic sampling. A technique in which elements of a sample are not chosen randomly, but instead are chosen according to some specific plan or strategy.

systematic subject mortality. The loss of data that occurs when subjects belonging to one experimental condition terminate their participation in a study at a higher rate than do subjects in another experimental condition.

telephone surveys. Surveys conducted over the telephone.

testing effects. The phenomenon in which repeated testing leads to better scores.

test-retest reliability. The degree to which a test yields the same score when the same person takes it twice.

theory. A set of related statements that explain and predict phenomena. The statements used in a theory can be laws, principles, or beliefs.

time sampling. A technique that involves determining the times at which observations will be made in an effort to obtain a representative sample of behaviors. Time sampling may be done **randomly** or **systematically**.

time-series designs. A type of quasi-experimental design in which multiple observations are made of a single group.

traces. Evidence left as a by-product of behavior.

true zero. A value representing the absence of the characteristic being measured.

truly dichotomous variable. A discrete, nominal variable that has only two alternative values and no underlying continuum between the two values.

Tukey's Honestly Significant Difference (HSD). An a posteriori test designed to allow the researcher to make all pairwise comparisons among the sample means after finding a significant F-value with an ANOVA. The formula for HSD is

$$\text{HSD} = Q\sqrt{\frac{\text{MS}_W}{n}}$$

where Q is the studentized range statistic.

two-tailed hypothesis. A type of alternative hypothesis in which the researcher simply predicts that the two groups being compared differ, but does not predict the direction of that difference.

two-way between-subjects ANOVA. An analysis of variance conducted when a research situation involves two independent variables and both variables are between-subject variables.

Type I error. Rejecting the null hypothesis when it is true.

Type II error. Failing to reject the null hypothesis when it is false.

unconfounded comparison. A comparison between means in which only one independent variable changes at a time.

undisguised participant studies. Studies in which the researcher actively participates in the situation in which the subjects are involved, and the other participants are aware that the researcher is observing their behavior.

validity. The extent to which the dependent variable measures what it is purported to measure.

variance. A measure of dispersion in which the average squared deviation from the mean is determined for a distribution of scores. The formulas for population variance σ^2 and for sample variance s^2, respectively, are

$$\sigma^2 = \frac{\sum(X - \mu)^2}{N} \quad \text{and} \quad s^2 = \frac{\sum(X - \mu)^2}{N - 1}$$

The corresponding raw score formulas are

$$\sigma^2 = \frac{\sum X^2 - \frac{(\sum X)^2}{N}}{N} \quad \text{and} \quad s^2 = \frac{\sum X^2 - \frac{(\sum X)^2}{N}}{N - 1}$$

Wilcoxon's matched-pairs signed-ranks test (Wilcoxon's T). A nonparametric alternative to the correlated-samples t-test that compares pairs of scores that were created by testing subjects twice.

Wilcoxon's rank-sum test. A nonparametric test in which the null hypothesis proposes that the scores of two groups were drawn from the same population.

withdrawal design. A single-subject design in which an intervention is introduced after the baseline and is then withdrawn, to determine whether the intervention affects performance.

within-groups variance. An estimate of the population error variance.

within-subjects design. A research design in which each subject receives each level of the independent variable at least once.

within-subjects (repeated-measures) analysis of variance. An analysis of variance conducted when three or more related sets of scores are to be compared, and when the scores meet the assumptions for inferential statistics.

yoked design. A research design in which each subject is linked with another subject in the other experimental group (or groups).

z-scores. Standard scores that indicate the number of standard deviations a raw score lies above or below the mean. The formula for a z-score is

$$z = \frac{X - \bar{x}}{s}$$

Bibliography

Agresti, A., & Finlay, B. (1986). *Statistical methods for the social sciences* (2nd ed.). San Francisco: Dellen.

American Heritage Dictionary. (1978). Boston: Houghton Mifflin.

American Psychological Association. (1982). *Ethical principles in the conduct of research with human participants*. Washington, DC: Author.

American Psychological Association. (1983). *Publication manual of the American Psychological Association* (3rd ed.). Washington, DC: Author.

Bakeman, R., & Gottman, J. M. (1989). *Observing interaction: An introduction to sequential analysis*. Cambridge: Cambridge University Press.

Bales, J. (1988, November). Breuning pleads guilty in scientific fraud case. *APA Monitor*, 12.

Barber, T. X., & Silver, M. J. (1968). Fact, fiction, and the experimenter bias effect. *Psychological Bulletin Monograph Supplement, 70* (6, pt. 2), 1–29.

Barlow, D. H., & Hersen, M. (1984). *Single-case experimental designs*. New York: Pergamon Press.

Black student posted racist notes. (1993, February 24). *Chronicle of Higher Education* p. 5.

Bower, G. H., & Clark, M. C. (1969). Narrative stories as mediators for serial learning. *Psychonomic Science, 14*, 181–182.

Camilli, G., & Hopkins, K. D. (1978). Applicability of chi-square to 2 × 2 contingency tables with small expected frequencies. *Psychological Bulletin, 85*, 163–167.

Campbell, D. T., & Stanley, J. C. (1963). *Experimental and quasi-experimental designs for research*. Chicago: Rand McNally.

Christensen, L. B. (1988). *Experimental methodology* (4th ed.). Boston: Allyn & Bacon.

Cicchetti, D. U. (1972). Extension of multiple-range tests to interaction tables in analysis of variance: A rapid approximate solution. *Psychological Bulletin, 77*, 405–408.

Department of Health and Human Services. (1981, January 26). Final regulations amending basic HHS policy for the protection of human subjects. *Federal Register, 46* 16.

Dillman, D. A. (1978). *Mail and telephone surveys: The total design method*. New York: John Wiley & Sons.

Ebbinghaus, H. (1913). *Memory* (Trans. by H. A. Ruger & C. E. Bussenius). New York: Teachers College Press, Columbia University.

Elmes, D. G., Kantowitz, B. H., & Roediger, H. L., III. (1989). *Research methods in psychology* (2nd ed.). St. Paul: West.

Erdos, P. L. (1983). *Professional mail surveys*. Malabar, FL: Robert E. Krieger.

Erikson, D. (1990, June). Blood feud: Researchers begin fighting back against animal-rights activists. *Scientific American*, 17–18.

Etaugh, C. (1980). Effects of nonmaternal care on children: Research evidence and popular views. *American Psychologist, 35*, 309–319.

Etaugh, C., Carlson, P., & Williams, B. (1992, July). *Changing attitudes toward day care and maternal employment as portrayed in women's magazines: 1977–1990.* Presented at the meeting of the 25th International Congress of Psychology, Brussels, Belgium.

Finley, C., & Corty, E. (1993). Rape on the campus: The prevalence of sexual assault while enrolled in college. *Journal of College Student Development, 34,* 113–117.

Funk & Wagnalls standard dictionary. (1983). New York: Lippincott & Crowell.

Gage, N. L. (Ed.) (1963). *Handbook of research on teaching.* Chicago: Rand McNally.

Gentile, J. R., Roden, R. H., & Klein, R. D. (1972). An analysis of variance model for the intrasubject replication design. *Journal of Applied Behavior Analysis, 5,* 193–198.

Gravetter, F. J., & Wallnau, L. B. (1985). *Statistics for the behavioral sciences: A first course for students of psychology and education.* St. Paul: West.

Gregson, R. A. M. (1983). *Time series in psychology.* Hillsdale, NJ: Lawrence Erlbaum.

Grisso, T., Baldwin, E., Blanck, P. D., Rotheram-Borus, M. J., Schooler, N. R., & Thompson, T. (1991). Standards in research: APA's mechanism for monitoring the challenges. *American Psychologist, 46,* 758–766.

Groves, R. M., & Kahn, R. L. (1979). *Surveys by telephone: A national comparison with personal interviews.* New York: Academic Press.

Hays, W. L. (1988). *Statistics* (4th ed.). New York: Holt, Rinehart & Winston.

Hersen, M., & Barlow, D. H. (1976). *Single-case experimental designs: Strategies for studying behavior change.* New York: Pergamon Press.

Hinkle, D. E., Wiersma, W., & Jurs, S. G. (1982). *Basic behavioral statistics.* Boston: Houghton Mifflin.

Hinkle, D. E., Wiersma, W., & Jurs, S. G. (1988). *Applied statistics for the behavioral sciences* (2nd ed.). Boston: Houghton Mifflin.

Hochstim, J. R. (1967). A critical comparison of three strategies of collecting data from households. *Journal of American Statistical Association, 62,* 154–159.

Holden, C. (1991). GAO and DOD get into a cat fight. *Science* (January 18, 1991), 265.

Howell, D. C. (1987). *Statistical methods for psychology* (2nd ed.). Boston: Duxbury.

Howell, D. C. (1992). *Statistical methods for psychology* (3rd ed.). Boston: PWS-Kent.

Hurd, M. W. (1989). Short-term memory before and during treatment of sleep apnea. Unpublished masters thesis. Bradley University.

Information please almanac, atlas and yearbook: 1993 (46th ed.) (1993). Boston: Houghton Mifflin.

Jones, S. R. G. (1992). Was there a Hawthorne effect? *American Journal of Sociology, 98,* 451–468.

Kahn, R. L., & Cannell, C. F. (1957). *The dynamics of interviewing: Theory, technique, and cases.* New York: John Wiley & Sons.

Kalat, J. W. (1990). *Introduction to psychology* (2nd ed.). Belmont, CA: Wadsworth.

Kantowitz, B. H., Roediger, H. L. III, & Elmes, D. G. (1991). *Experimental psychology: Understanding psychological research.* St. Paul: West.

Kazdin, A. E. (1982). *Single-case research designs.* New York: Oxford.

Kirk, R. E. (1990). *Statistics: An introduction* (3rd ed.). Fort Worth: Holt, Rinehart and Winston.

Kirkham, G. L. (1975). Doc cop. *Human Behavior, 4,* 16–23.

Krajick, K. (1979, July). Seattle: Sifting through the ashes. *Police Magazine,* 10–11.

Kratochwill, T. R. (Ed.), (1978). *Single subject research: Strategies for evaluating change.* New York: Academic Press.

Leavitt, F. (1991). *Research methods for behavioral scientists.* Dubuque, IA: Wm. C. Brown.

Levin, J. R., Marascuilo, L. A., & Hubert, L. J. (1978). N = nonparametric randomization tests. In T. R. Kratochwill (Ed.), *Single subject research: Strategies for evaluating change,* pp. 167–196. New York: Academic Press.

Lincoln, Y. S. (1980). *Documentary analysis and record utilization: New uses for old methods.* Paper prepared for presentation at the Annual Meeting, American Educational Research Association, Boston (April 1980).

Marascuilo, L. A., & McSweeney, M. (1977). *Nonparametric and distribution-free methods for the social sciences.* Monterey, CA: Brooks/Cole.

McBurney, D. H. (1990). *Experimental psychology* (2nd ed.). Belmont, CA: Wadsworth.

Middlemist, R. D., Knowles, E. S., & Matter, C. F. (1976). Personal space invasions in the lavatory: Suggestive evidence for arousal. *Journal of Personality and Social Psychology, 33,* 541–546.

Milgram, S. (1963). Behavioral study of obedience. *Journal of Abnormal and Social Psychology, 67,* 371–378.

Milgram, S. (1977). Ethical issues in the study of obedience. In S. Milgram (Ed.), *The individual in a social world,* pp. 188–199. Reading, MA: Addison-Wesley.

Miller, N. E. (1985). The value of behavioral research on animals. *American Psychologist, 40,* 423–440.

Pavlov, I. P. (1928). *Lectures on conditioned reflexes.* New York: International Publishers.

Pihl., R. D., Zacchia, C., & Zeichner, A. (1981). Follow-up analysis of the use of deception and aversive contingencies in psychological experiments. *Psychological Reports, 48,* 927–930.

Raymond, C. (1991). Study of patient histories suggests Freud suppressed or distorted facts that contradicted his theories. *Chronicle of Higher Education, 37* (37), 4–6.

Ring, K., Wallston, K., & Corey, M. (1970). Mode of debriefing as a factor affecting reaction to a Milgram-type obedience experiment: An ethical inquiry. *Representative Research in Social Psychology, 1*, 67–88.

Roman, M. (1988, April). When good scientists turn bad. *Discover*, 50–58.

Rosenhan, D. L. (1973). On being sane in insane places. *Science, 179*, 250–258.

Rosenthal, R. (1978). How often are our numbers wrong? *American Psychologist, 33*, 1005–1007.

Shaughnessy, J. J., & Zechmeister, E. G. (1990). *Research methods in psychology* (2nd ed.). New York: McGraw-Hill.

Sidman, M. (1960). *Tactics of scientific research: Evaluating experimental data in psychology*. New York: Basic Books.

Sieber, J. E., & Stanley, B. (1988). Ethical and professional dimensions of socially sensitive research. *American Psychologist, 43*, 49–55.

Smith, S. S., & Richardson, D. (1983). Amelioration of deception and harm in psychological research: The important role of debriefing. *Journal of Personality and Social Psychology, 44*, 1075–1082.

Spatz, C. (1993). *Basic statistics: Tales of distributions* (5th ed.). Pacific Grove, CA: Brooks/Cole.

Stevens, S. S. (1951). Mathematics, measurement, and psychophysics. In S. S. Stevens (Ed.), *Handbook of experimental psychology*, pp. 1–49. New York: John Wiley & Sons.

Sudman, S., & Bradburn, N. M. (1982). *Asking questions: A practical guide to questionnaire design*. San Francisco: Jossey-Bass.

Tryon, W. W. (1982). A simplified time series analysis for evaluating treatment interventions. *Journal of Applied Behavior Analysis, 15*, 423–429.

van Lawick-Goodall, J. (1971). *In the shadow of man*. Boston: Houghton Mifflin.

Webb, E. J., Campbell, D. T., Schwartz, R. D., Sechrest, L., & Grove, J. B. (1981). *Nonreactive measures in the social sciences*. Boston: Houghton Mifflin.

Wright, H. (1960). Observational child study. In P. Mussen (Ed.), *Handbook of research methods in child development*, pp. 71–139. New York: John Wiley & Sons.

Index